UNDERSTANDING RESEARCH METHODS ~

UNDERSTANDING RESEARCH METHODS ~

SECOND EDITION

GERALD R. ADAMS
University of Guelph

JAY D. SCHVANEVELDT
Utah State University

Longman
New York & London

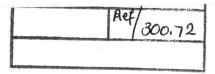
Understanding Research Methods, Second Edition

Longman, 95 Church Street, White Plains, N.Y. 10601

Associated companies:
Longman Group Ltd., London
Longman Cheshire Pty., Melbourne
Longman Paul Pty., Auckland
Copp Clark Pitman, Toronto

Senior editor: David J. Estrin
Production editor: Ann P. Kearns
Cover design: Anthony R. Morabito
Production supervisor: Anne P. Armeny

Library of Congress Cataloging-in-Publication Data

Adams, Gerald R., 1946–
    Understanding research methods / Gerald R. Adams, Jay D.
Schvaneveldt. —2nd ed.
        p.   cm.   Includes index.
    ISBN 0-8013-0415-6
    1. Social sciences—Research—Methodology.   I. Schvaneveldt, Jay
D.   II. Title.
H62.A418   1991
300′.72—dc20   90-6535
                                                                   CIP

2 3 4 5 6 7 8 9 10-HA-9594939291

Contents

PREFACE *vii*

INTRODUCTION: HOW TO USE THIS BOOK *1*

SECTION I: FOUNDATIONS OF SOCIAL SCIENCE RESEARCH   5

    1: Thinking about Research and Science *7*
    2: Philosophical Issues in Social Science Research *25*
    3: Reviewing the Literature *48*
    4: Validity and Reliability *75*

SECTION II: BASIC RESEARCH DESIGNS   99

    5: Research Designs: Exploratory and Descriptive *101*
    6: Research Designs: Field Studies and Field Experiments *119*
    7: Research Designs: Experimental–Causal *134*

SECTION III: ELEMENTS OF MEASUREMENT AND SAMPLING   147

    8: Levels of Measurement and Scaling *149*
    9: Samples and Uses of Sampling *171*

SECTION IV: DATA COLLECTION STRATEGIES   195

    10: Obtaining Data: Questionnaire and Interview   *197* ✳

    11: Obtaining Data: Observational Techniques   *228* ✳

    12: Obtaining Data: In the Laboratory   *252*

    13: Obtaining Data: Projective and Indirect Methods   *266*

    14: Obtaining Data: Documents of the Past   *285*

    15: Obtaining Data: Evaluation Research   *309* ✳

SECTION V: DATA ANALYSIS AND REPORT WRITING   325

    16: Conceptualizing the Process of Data Analysis   *327*

    17: Understanding Research Results   *338*

    18: The Research Proposal and Scientific Report   *366*

EPILOGUE   *381*

APPENDIX   *389*

INDEX   *395*

Preface

Basic and applied research serves as the foundation on which all social science training rests. Indeed, to train effective professionals some fundamental knowledge must be conveyed about how to generate and properly use research.

This text (Second Edition) has been written for students in social science training programs such as social work, home economics, child and family studies, sociology, psychology, communications, nursing, and related areas. This book has emerged from the authors' extensive experience in teaching research methods and is designed to help students to (1) understand and execute the basic research process and (2) judge the worth and utility of research as a knowledgeable consumer. *Understanding Research Methods* is an innovative text developed for undergraduate or introductory graduate education in basic and applied social science programs. The text focuses upon helping the student to understand as well as conduct research. But most important, the text emphasizes how the individual can become a more knowledgeable *consumer* of social science research.

We invite would-be researchers and consumers of research (preventionists, interventionists, educators, counselors, therapists, applied paraprofessionals, etc.) to learn about how research data are generated and interpreted in order to increase their competence in understanding the research process. We are fully aware that few students who enroll in a class on research methods will become active researchers or that they necessarily should do so. Our contention, however, is that while this text has vital content for those who will do research, it is also a highly appropriate text for students who are interested in improving their capacity and skills at reading and using research to solve problems, engage in effective prevention or intervention activities, or become a knowledgeable consumer of facts. It is no longer a matter of wanting or not wanting to know about research methodology; we believe it is a matter of necessity in a society that literally bombards one with multiple and often conflicting ideas, claims, reports and counter reports. Increasingly, to be a competent and fully functioning member of society, one must come to understand basic scientific processes, learn how to discern false assertions from questionable data, and develop the ability to conclude when something is truly significant and meaningful as opposed to merely having the pretense of importance. But research and social science are not void of a humanistic quality; to be an informed researcher or an informed consumer, understanding and caring are required.

But caring without understanding can lead to a number of errors, miscalculations, and disappointments. Further, understanding without care or concern for utility, application, or purposefulness is also costly and frequently nonproductive. Recognizing that social science needs both qualities, this is a text for students who are concerned with both the *generation and application* of social science. It is designed for those who aspire to be researchers, consumers of research, or a combination of researcher and consumer.

To gain an understanding of the research process, we hope that our comments about the generation and consumption of research provide a foundation for a continuing dialogue between students and their instructor. We believe an active professional in our society must play both roles (consumer and researcher) many times in the course of his or her career. All researchers are consumers, while many consumers are required in their professional roles to also engage in occasional research activities. Recognizing the dual role behind training in research methodology, this text begins each chapter with a brief statement on the general importance of the chapter to the role of a researcher and consumer. Further, throughout the 18 chapters we have prepared boxed inserts with *tips for consumers*. These tips include practical conceptual information about evaluating research.

Like many research method books, chapters have been prepared on such basic elements of research as sampling, measurement, and research design. Unlike most traditional texts, however, this work includes several unusual features. In Chapter 2, we provide an extensive review of the relationship between ethical and philosophical issues and the scientific process. In Chapter 3, we conceptualize and summarize the essential elements of reviewing the literature and provide some very practical information on review sources. In Chapter 4, we provide an extensive review on issues of validity and reliability. In several remaining chapters on obtaining data we refer back to specific validity and reliability issues surrounding each data collection strategy. To facilitate the student's understanding of distinctions between research design and data collection procedures, several chapters are presented on the more conceptual nature of design. These design chapters are followed by highly illustrated chapters on how data are obtained. We believe this distinction enhances a student's understanding of the design and data collection process. While most texts on the subject of research include chapters on measurement and sampling, we have attempted to present these two elements in a concrete, easy-to-read format.

In the final section we have prepared two chapters on data analyses and preparation of a research report. Data analyses are presented in the context of decision-making activities with both conceptual and practical illustrations provided for each. The report writing chapter is designed to assist consumers of research in reading reports while providing the foundation for understanding how a research report is written and the basic information needed therein.

To facilitate students' understanding of the material several special features have been included in the text. *Key words* (or concepts) are listed at the beginning of each chapter. *Study guide questions* are listed to direct the student to essential elements of each chapter. *Comprehensive summaries* at the end of each chapter highlight the most essential principles and facts. Further, all principles and ideas are illustrated by examples in a broad-based approach to basic and applied social science. Each chapter then contains basic, classical, and contemporary examples to illustrate the formulation, execution, and conclusions that come from doing research. To learn about research, how to do it and to use it, one must have more than abstractions, exhortations, descriptions, or procedural steps; one must have some dynamic and interesting examples to read, to become involved with, and on which to reflect. Therefore, we have provided numerous illustrations throughout the text that should have high appeal and interest to students. Finally, at the end of each chapter we have prepared several basic problems or applications for students to complete. These applications provide a hands-on exercise that will allow the student to have a personal experience with many of the concepts summarized in the chapter. We believe having students complete these exercises (or similar ones devised by the instructor) will enhance the learning process and provide greater meaning and clarity to the research process.

Finally, this text was written with the student in mind. The pedagogical elements of the text were prepared to enhance understanding and facilitate learning. Its format, structure, and contents are derived from several years of teaching both undergraduate and graduate students in research methodology courses. We hope all students who read this text come to enjoy a growing ability to understand and evaluate research. Further, we thank the many past generations of undergraduate and graduate students who helped to shape our experiences and structure the contents of this book.

Introduction: How to Use This Book

From the outset the major goal of this text was to write for students. Too many texts are written to impress colleagues or to establish one's identity by forwarding some "new" philosophy in the field. We believed that students (in the social sciences) were in dire need of a solid text that was addressed to student interests, had broad coverage, illustrated research principles with useful and entertaining examples, and incorporated a teaching approach for research methodology for both future researchers and consumers of research.

In this section, we speak to the reader about using this book. For optimal utility, both students and instructors should know the basic rationale for the structure, pedagogical layout, and goals of the text. The text layout has proven to be a very effective method of reaching students and we believe it helps to correct many of the deficiencies found in standard texts. Further, our market assessment shows that a *great variety* of students enroll in a social science research methods course and that a multi-faceted approach is needed to serve more adequately this diverse audience. We attempt to meet the training needs of this wide array of students through the chapter make-up, student helps (boxed inserts and tips), and especially research examples that come from a broad range of disciplines. Furthermore, some of these examples fall into the classical studies category and others are from the more recent published research. We believe that students should be familiar with both the foundation provided by "classic" research and the more current rationale for research if they are to be both competent doers of, as well as consumers of, social science research.

Each chapter contains the following components:

- outline of the chapter's contents
- key terms contained in each chapter
- study guide questions at the beginning of each chapter

- points of view
- multiple research examples (pointed out by the symbol ◄ in the margin)
- tips for consumers
- summary of major points
- problems and exercises at the conclusion of each chapter
- list of references for the chapter, including those identified as being useful for additional study

Now a word about using each of these features:

1. *Outline of each chapter.* In contrast to most other social science method texts, in fact almost any kind of text, the detailed outline for each chapter appears at the beginning of each chapter rather than in the Contents. In this text it is provided as the beginning of each chapter to give you a detailed overview and to prepare you to grasp the general message of the chapter in outline form. A careful review of the chapter outline increases your ability to acquaint yourself with the chapter's intent.

2. *Key terms.* Major concepts for each chapter have been identified and appear in a section preceding each chapter. The purpose of this section is to alert you to key terms that are associated with the topical coverage that follows. This section serves as a guide to main terms and ideas, including the definitions, discussions, and illustrations that give more complete meaning to specific terms. We have found that this approach is more helpful to you than merely giving a brief definition with the key words. The reader can ponder the terms in the context of full chapter treatment. The terms are italicized when they first appear and are defined in context.

3. *Study guide questions.* As a companion learning device for the key terms section, each chapter also contains six central study guide questions following the key terms. A careful reading of these questions will orient you to major ideas covered in the chapter. We believe reading becomes more functional if it is, in part, directed by goals or questions. Once a chapter has been read, we recommend that you reread the study guide questions to determine how thoroughly each can be answered. This process can be repeated as necessary, including using the study guide questions as important elements in preparation for various examinations while using the text.

4. *Points of view.* On critical issues we compare contrasting points of view. Then, we provide our own viewpoint on the issue. By doing so, you can read about how researchers and educators arrive at conclusions about controversial issues.

5. *Research examples.* As noted in the Preface, examples are a main feature of this text. Examples are not simply an additional element; they are central to the learning process and are identified by symbols in the margin. By reading the examples you will be aided in defining, illustrating, and implementing the research process.

6. *Tips for consumers.* Two sections of each chapter contain vital information for those readers who are particularly interested in application, evaluation, and utility of methodological principles in the conduct of everyday life. As noted in the Preface, a major goal of this text is to teach research methodology to both the potential doer (generator) of research as well as the huge number of you who will primarily consume and apply the findings of research in your prevention and intervention activities. The tips for

consumers are designed to help the process of application and interpretation of research findings and conclusions.

7. *Summary.* The summaries have been prepared to highlight some of the major points of the chapter. By reading the summary at the end of the chapter, your identification and recall of major ideas will be reinforced.

8. *Problems and exercises.* Each chapter concludes with a series of questions, activities, and exercises that are designed as opportunities for "trying out" some of the ideas presented in the chapter. Some items deal with recall and reflection, others with activities to be performed, and some are activities that one would do with other students or complete in a community setting. The main thread that runs through all problems and exercises is the notion of "can you do something or complete some research activity as a result of studying the respective chapter?"

9. *References.* A list of references is located at the end of each chapter. This list contains all citations to examples, documentations, and suggested sources for additional reading on a specific topic. You may find these references helpful in directing you to pursue reading of the examples in their entirety or in doing additional reading on areas that interest you.

SECTION I

Foundations
of Social Science Research

The scientific process is a complex, yet very logical, procedure for generating empirically sound answers to researchable questions. In the four chapters of this section, we review many of the major elements underlying an understanding of research methodology and the scientific process. Even though the scientific process is logical, actual research is often a process of trial and error, exploring hunches, and repeating procedures many, many times. In Chapter 1, we demonstrate in practical ways how and why the scientific process can be useful in understanding social behavior. In Chapter 2, we show how the scientific process has a strong and meaningful connection with philosophical views on the nature of human behavior. Likewise, we explore the interrelationship between philosophy, ethics, and research activities. While in everyday conversation we speak to our own theory of this-or-that issue, few individuals are really sure of what is actually meant by the concept of theory. Therefore, in this chapter we explore what is meant by a researchable theory and become familiar with the workhorse of science—the hypothesis.

Many readers will be familiar with the meaning of what is referred to as the literature review. Prior to reading this text you have likely completed a review of research literature for a term paper in a freshman or sophomore course. However, we believe you will find there is much yet to learn about the utility and purpose of a literature review. In Chapter 3, you will be introduced to many handy hints and resource references that you should find immediately useful in completing a literature review.

Chapter 4 includes an extensive summary on how to evaluate the reliability and validity of research findings and measurement devices. This chapter provides you with the basic knowledge needed to critically assess the usefulness of measurement devices utilized in social science research.

Collectively, the first four chapters provide the foundation for reading and understanding the material in the remaining chapters.

CHAPTER 1

Thinking about Research and Science

OUTLINE

Introduction
Doing Research–Consuming Research
The Practice of Research
Methodology, Data, Theory
Answers to Novel Questions
A Policy–Consumer Illustration
What Are Research Methods?
  A Frame of Reference
Regularity and Predictability
The Research Steps
How Does One Study Human Behavior?
The Empirical Approach
The Language of Research Methods
Thinking about Science
Summary
Problems and Applications
References

KEY TERMS

Data
Research methodology
Theory
Frame of reference

Regularity and patterns
Empirical
Scientific method

STUDY GUIDE QUESTIONS

1. What are the main elements of the empirical approach in conducting research?
2. In thinking about science, what main features apply to both the doing and consuming of research?
3. Identify and logically arrange the major steps in conducting scientific research.
4. How can research in the social sciences provide useful answers to novel questions? What about answers to routine daily questions?
5. What is meant by the "practice of research" and how does this differ from the methodology in doing research?
6. What are the characteristics of questions that researchers would say are "good questions" in relation to the goals of science?

Role of the Scientist

Research deals with the problems of life. These problems are manifest in the school realm, family and personal life, school functioning, crime, travel, leisure, and a host of other areas. The scientist needs to take an objective orientation yet be personally interested as well as motivated to engage in a specific study. Not all problems are solved by research. Perhaps the major outcome of many research projects is a clearer illustration of the complexity of an issue. To engage in empirical thinking, use the scientific approach, and engage competently in rewarding research requires training and commitment. Some problems can be solved without the aid of research tools, but social science is sufficiently complex that thorough understanding of research methodology greatly enhances quality work.

Role of the Consumer

Consumers have greatly benefited from the findings of research. These findings and applications have filtered into almost every facet of life. It has become common merely to dismiss many problems or only to assign them a "problem" status for a short duration because there is a calm belief that scientific research will very soon solve them. Today, the consumer's role must become increasingly active; the conscientious consumer must know how specific research is done, not just that someone has done it. Consumers need to be team members with those who conduct research, and the careful study of research methods assures that this projected team will be a functional reality. The typical citizen in the world today is highly educated and exposed to extensive media. This type of citizen makes demands on the researcher that are more pressing and more complex than in times past.

INTRODUCTION

What can social science research methods accomplish for you? Are the information and way of thinking they provide helpful to a consumer in society? How is research started and completed? What are the essential stages of the research process? These and other important questions will be covered in this text. This chapter seeks to provide a partial overview of the research process. Examples, illustrations, terminology, goals of research, as well as steps in the research scheme are illustrated. It is an orientation chapter and no attempt is made to be exhaustive or systematic, but we do attempt to provide a brief panoramic perspective.

The central purpose of the chapter is to inform you about basic strategies in conducting research and the ways of employing these strategies in applied situations. We speak to both the researcher and the consumer of research, an approach that we feel is unique and is one long overdue. Our approach is straightforward in that we include the standard areas of coverage and unique in that we cover such areas as ethics, literature reviews, projective techniques, evaluation, and observational methodology. Further, the text is prepared in chapter format to aid a wide range of students in various disciplines using social science research methodology. Through the use of abundant instructive examples we seek to inform, illustrate, and integrate the principles of research methods so that both the researcher and the consumer of research achieve a sense of understanding.

Much of what we know about society, the family, individual behavior, and social problems is directly attributable to the scientific method applied to these areas. In an attempt to provide perspective for the text, we shall provide several very different and, we hope, interesting examples of research in social science to illustrate how research helps people, how it can be used to solve problems, and how one does research. Please note that these examples have both broad policy and individual consumer implications.

To begin with, note the research by Gortmaker (1979), who found that poverty is ◄ specifically associated with risk of both neonatal and postnatal death in infants. In fact, the death rate for infants born in poverty is almost 50% higher than that experienced by infants born outside poverty. This relationship was determined by careful analysis of data already accumulated by various agencies over a period of time, and the analysis enables one to see the relationship between income level and infant death rate. Gortmaker asserts that the risk factor to poverty-born infants could be greatly lowered by providing free and comprehensive health care to all pregnant mothers and their newborns.

In a study of maternal employment, Eggebeen (1988) found that the number of preschool children and their ages coupled with the amount of family income were the primary factors that predicted maternal employment. The level of the mother's education was also an important issue in regard to maternal employment.

In another study (Newport, 1979), the question of who switches from one branch of ◄ religion to another was studied. The single biggest switch was the movement of people out of religious systems altogether. The average age of the "switcher" to the "no religion" category was lower than that of members of the person's original religion. Newport found relatively little movement among major groups—Catholics, Jews, and Protestants. Most of the switching was intra-Protestant, and interestingly, 40% of the married switchers moved to the religious affiliation of their nonswitching spouse. Research on religious orientation, interfaith marriage, and religious switching has implications for marital stability and happiness, kin interaction, and childrearing practices. In a related study, Glenn (1987) observed the "no religion" trend over time and found that from the late 1950s to the early 1980s, there was a steady trend toward no religion. This shift has leveled off and even reversed itself in the 1980s.

Another study reports that overcrowding in the home correlates with a high number ◄ of problems for people (Gove, Hughes, & Galle, 1979). Gove and his associates assert that the makeup of their sample permits them to make broad generalizations concerning crowding:

1. Number of persons per room is a useful and objective measure of crowding.
2. Poor mental health is strongly associated with crowding.
3. Child care tends to be poor in crowded homes.
4. Poor physical health in crowded homes seems to stem from obtaining insufficient sleep, catching infectious diseases, lack of adequate rest, too many chores, and inadequate care from others when one is sick.
5. Lack of privacy is a common and significant problem.

▶   The very perplexing question of capital punishment was assessed in 1988 by Peterson and Bailey. From their observations extending from 1975 to 1984, they concluded that capital punishment had no appreciable impact on the rate of homicide.

It is readily apparent that the studies on infant death and poverty, maternal employment, religion-switching, overcrowding in the home, and capital punishment represent very complex problems. The need for survival, worship, and living space are a trio of concerns that are important to an understanding of our society as well as interesting and challenging concerns to a number of past researchers. Through these examples, we wish to emphasize the complexity of researching these kinds of topics and assert that in order to evaluate a study's findings we need an understanding of how research is carried out, how data are generated, and how conclusions are made. This is what understanding research methodology is all about.

DOING RESEARCH—CONSUMING RESEARCH

John F. Kennedy, in his 1962 message to Congress, presented four basic rights that all consumers should enjoy in the United States: (1) the right to safety, (2) the right to be informed, (3) the right to choose, and (4) the right to be heard. Porter (1979) noted that "one of the basic challenges facing the consumer movement in the 1980s was to re-emphasize these original goals and to make clear that their aim is to disperse power and information to you, the individual, not consolidate it within a bureaucracy" (p. 1195). She further asserted that the only real protection for the consumer is to be informed and on guard. Porter's comments reflect our thoughts in inviting students to learn about research procedures and principles of scientific thinking, sampling, and decision making, to mention just a few of the major principles relevant to the consumption of ideas and research. This is not a consumer-advocacy text nor does it focus on decision making. It is a research methods text meant to teach students how research data are generated and interpreted so as to increase their competence as researchers and consumers.

Certainly, not all students in a research methods class will become active researchers. Our specific point is that while this text has a vital content for those who will do research, it is equally appropriate for all students who work and live in a society where increasingly the daily world has to be interpreted in an evaluative context, a decision-making mode, and a frame of reference that comes directly from what is covered in research methodology. It is no longer a matter of wanting or not wanting to know about research methodology; we believe it is a matter of necessity in the Western world, where one is daily bombarded with multiple, often conflicting ideas, claims, reports, and committee investigations. To be a competent, functioning member of society requires that each of us knows about basic scientific processes, how to discern false from valid assertions, and how to ascertain when something is truly significant rather than merely appearing to be important. Both competent and informed researchers and informed and effective consumers of research have to understand and be caring.

Caring without understanding can lead to a number of difficulties, miscalculations, and disappointments. Understanding without caring or concern for utility, application, or purposefulness is also costly and at times nonproductive. It should be noted that all knowledge is potentially useful, and endlessly creative applications can be determined. Figure 1.1 depicts our view on the utility of research methodology for researchers and consumers of research.

Using this conceptual model, researchers and consumers of research can ask a number of critical questions, some more research-focused and others more consumer-related (see Table 1.1). The questions are only suggestive, and readers should create their own questions to extend and supplement these basic guide items. It is obvious that many of the questions in Table 1.1 could be placed in either list; this interrelatedness serves as appropriate documentation for the importance of knowing about research methodology from both a practitioner and consumer orientation.

In addition to developing the ability to describe, predict, test theories, and solve problems, another reason for studying research methods relates to being an informed consumer of research and scientific writing. If you are preparing for a career in home economics, social work, sociology, nursing, political science, family and child studies, psychology, education, or public policy, methods constitute the tools you will use in your

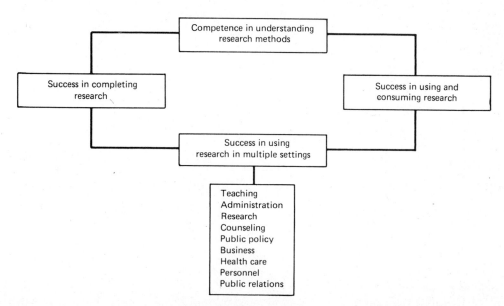

Figure 1.1. Competence in Understanding Research Methods

TABLE 1.1. Questions for Researchers and Consumers of Research

Researchers	Consumers of Research
1. How do I get a good research idea?	1. How can I tell if this research is good?
2. How do I answer this question?	2. How can this idea help me?
3. How do I solve this problem?	3. How can I apply these findings?
4. How should I acquire data?	4. Is this solution a believable one?
5. What constitutes valid data?	5. Will this apply in my situation?
6. How should I avoid bias?	6. How can I interpret the report?
7. How are data analyzed?	7. What part should be emphasized?
8. What should I put in the research report?	8. What do I really need to know?
9. How do I replicate my research?	9. How long will this research finding be useful?

daily work. Research in any of these disciplines necessitates a thorough understanding of the principles of research methods.

THE PRACTICE OF RESEARCH

Research in any field seeks to generate new information of knowledge that, in turn, can be applied to solve problems, improve the quality of life, and provide a better understanding of conditions in a field. The practice of research may be the business of those engaged in the research process, but almost all people in a society can benefit from an increased understanding of such areas as consumerism, mental health, socialization practices, and the impact of the economy of the family. The generation of knowledge is important, but the optimal utility of the new knowledge is somewhat dependent on the ability of the consumer to understand, interpret, and apply these new "facts" to specific problems or situations. The scientist is also a consumer of research, a point seldom pondered. Too often it has been assumed that only the researcher need be informed about how research is completed. Actually, a significant portion of our lives is made up of pursuing questions that ask when, what, why, where, and how.

But what are science and research methodology? Dellow (1970) notes that science is merely a body of knowledge organized in a useful way and that this knowledge has been derived using the scientific method. He goes on to explain that the scientific method is nothing more than thinking according to a set of rules; in fact, it is "organized common sense" (p. 16). This point of view should help us to realize that we use the scientific approach on a regular basis, but that we typically do not practice it systematically enough to claim to be engaging in science.

The methodology of social science has the same goal as do all other types of science, specifically, searching for truth. Myrdal (1969) describes this process as seeking "truer knowledge," permitting us to discard ideas once considered valid, but clearly inferior when compared with more up-to-date knowledge. When this process occurs, the researcher and the consumer of research profit to the degree that they are informed about the research and its potential for leading to a more rational life. Myrdal notes that most people aspire to be more rational and like to think of themselves as rational creatures. Understanding research methodology is an excellent way to foster the rational process in thinking, living, discovery, and everyday application. Myrdal continues:

By increasing true knowledge and purging opportunistic, false beliefs in this way social science lays the groundwork for an ever more effective education: making people's beliefs more rational, forcing valuations out in the open, and making it more difficult to retain valuations on the lower level opposing those on the higher level. (Myrdal, 1969, p. 41)

It is important for both the researcher and consumer of research to have the capacity for rationality, evaluation, and an objective questioning that will lead to replacing less effective ideas with more effective ones. Just as the scientist must be able to communicate effectively with co-workers, the consumer of research must be able to understand and communicate about the processes of science. This interplay of questioning, searching, evaluating, and applying is never ending. We believe that learning about and becoming accustomed to thinking through a research perspective benefits the individual throughout life. Cultivating this lifelong benefit is one of the foremost goals in inviting researchers and consumers of research to join together and learn more about research methodology in the social sciences to achieve more rational and, with luck, more meaningful and purposeful lives in society.

METHODOLOGY, DATA, THEORY

We have contended that an understanding of research methodology leads to the ability to be more effective both as a researcher and a consumer of research. This assertion holds true because *data* (ideas, facts, knowledge) are generated using *research methodology* (tools for obtaining useful information). In other words, information is partially defined by the techniques used to gather it, so understanding those techniques will make the information more meaningful to us. We can evaluate data in a variety of ways to determine validity, utility, and applicability. When a researcher has accumulated sufficiently rigorous observations, it becomes possible to explain and understand events, and this insight accumulates to something referred to as theory. *Theory* is an explanation for events, a rationale for why something occurred; it is the scientific explanation of a condition that has been observed. Figure 1.2 shows the relationship among research methodology, data, and theory.

In everyday life, the researcher works with all three parts of this interchange; in fact, he or she typically does not think of three separate parts as we have shown here. In

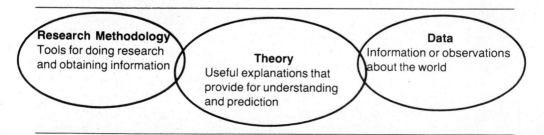

Figure 1.2. Interrelationships of Methodology, Data, and Theory

contrast, the consumer is probably most concerned with information, second with explanations, and probably least of all with the research tools. However, if one is to be an informed and competent consumer of research, it is clear that one has no choice but to be knowledgeable about the methods of acquisition.

ANSWERS TO NOVEL QUESTIONS

Where do good ideas for research topics come from, and how does one know what to pursue in research? Most researchers have the problem of limiting topics, of scaling down their ambitions to work on topics that are manageable. Intellectual curiosity, resources for completing a project, and relevance to consumers of research are three common factors in deciding about a topic. All problems selected for research invariably entail some problems and frustration, and even the simplest question can be perplexing. The following example illustrates topic selection and the processes of opening up an area for research.

▶ In 1977, George De Leon attempted to show that "winos" retained their hair much longer than the typical male in the United States. Observations in his Brooklyn neighborhood and elsewhere had led him to suspect that "bums" do not go bald! "Black, white, old, young, short, tall, all of them had a full mop of hair that wouldn't quit.... Inexplicably, it seemed that boozing burned out the guts but grew hair" (p. 62).

In an attempt to verify his observation, De Leon's students engaged in a series of interviews in the Bowery section of New York City. The students worked in teams, one doing the interviewing and the other observing how much hair was on the head. The teams interviewed over 60 Bowery "bums." The conclusion was that only about 25% fell in the "bald" category, an extremely low proportion for their age. After criticism from students on the bias in the design and the lack of a comparison group, further work was carried out. Eighty more derelicts were interviewed and, in addition, observations and interviews were carried out with "sterling" males, men encountered at Bloomingdale's department store or driving on Fifth Avenue. Also, De Leon and his students studied 49 professors at Wagner College. He found that 71% of the professors were balding, while 53% of his "sterlings," and only 36% of the "bums," were losing hair.

Why do alcoholics on the Bowery seem to retain their head of hair longer than college professors or businessmen? De Leon argues that hair retention of the derelicts is not due to a carefree, nonstressful life, but rather is associated with the biochemical activity of alcohol, and he asserts that some medical literature confirms this association. In total De Leon made a casual observation, formed an opinion, and later carried out a small creative research project to test his hunch. His hunch was verified by data. He concluded, "Seeking the truth is always an adventure; the scientist is in all of us" (p. 66).

We agree with this latter assertion by De Leon and believe that the scientist in all of us can be nurtured, trained, and coached to do many interesting and useful things. De Leon did this particular research not in a laboratory, but in the natural world where people presented different life-styles, and these accumulated years of life-style became the focal point for a question of specific interest.

This drinking and hair retention study helps to illustrate the diversity of research topics and the novel ways in which we may come up with a topic for study. People in social settings and the wide array of people growing, developing, and acting in society constitute the arena in which social science research is conducted. The curious student can think of dozens of interesting observations that can be cast into researchable questions.

A POLICY–CONSUMER ILLUSTRATION

We now present a more serious and profound example, a policy implication study that deals with crime, police strength, and two modes of obtaining security for the population. This research shows how scientific methodology can serve both the scientific community and the masses of consumers in society. Furthermore, it demonstrates the potential complexity of research and why one needs to obtain specific skills in both conducting and consuming research.

Wright, Rossi, Daly, and Weber-Burden (1981) reviewed issues surrounding the debate over crime in America and access to handguns. Questions on guns, alarms, locks, dogs, and other security devices have been disputed in both newspapers and serious studies over the past two decades. The subject is still a hot topic because both opponents and proponents sincerely believe in their arguments.

In an attempt to clarify further this debate on control of crime, McDowall and Loftin (1983) focused on the relationship between the demand for firearms and crime in the streets and general civil disorder. Their research took place in the city of Detroit and covered the years 1951 to 1977. McDowall and Loftin determined the number of handgun licenses that were issued per capita at different times. Detroit was selected because of a large population base coupled with a high rate of crime.

McDowall and Loftin's data show that violent crime rates and police strength have direct impact on the public interest in and purchase of handguns. High crime rates prompted people to buy handguns, while an increase in the police force produced a sharp drop in the purchase of handguns.

Findings like this help to explain the difficulty of implementing city, state, or national regulations regarding control of guns. When a police force expands, manifesting the capacity of controlling crime, and people's confidence in police is high, interest in the ownership of handguns is relatively low. When crime is high (as during a major riot) or when cities cut a police force for economic reasons, confidence in collective security goes down and the citizenry move more toward the individual security of private ownership of guns. These findings illustrate a frustrating aspect of crime control: When crime and disorder manifest themselves with muscle, "both a collective benefit for gun control and an individual interest in the right to own a gun" are visible and justifiable arguments going on simultaneously (McDowall & Loftin, 1983, p. 1157).

In summary, this research by McDowall and Loftin illustrates how research procedures can be applied to describing massive social problems. These data show that the protection people want can come from either collective or individual approaches. An increase in the crime rate, a riot, or any other great disruption in personal security makes the population feel less confident in the collective security and propels them to seek individual security (i.e., purchasing guns).

Another illustration of public policy research is the research done by Fawcett,

Seekins, and Jason (1987) on child passenger safety. Their work influenced legislation aimed at protecting children in at least two states.

What are the policy implications for city governments, police departments, homeowners, schools, and other specific groups? What additional research should be done on this topic? What could consumer groups do to help complete needed research on this topic? In what role do you feel most challenged and motivated with regard to crime and personal security—consumer of research or the scientist engaged in research?

WHAT ARE RESEARCH METHODS?

Research methodology is the application of scientific procedures toward acquiring answers to a wide variety of research questions. The skillful use of research procedures is an art; learning about their use is the business of this text. The language of research methods, the strategies involved, and limitations of certain methods are important for the scientist to know. In order to make intelligent decisions, the consumer of research also should have a basic understanding of how scientific research is conducted.

Is a particular type of housing related to mental well-being? Is the rate of suicide influenced by community size or religiosity? What creates social unrest in certain youth groups? These questions are very complex, but the scientist can obtain relevant information, for example, by interviewing people, assessing public documents, reviewing historical documents, observing people in specific social settings, and having people complete questionnaires.

Research methodology helps us use scientific principles in responding to questions such as the ones just presented. Like other scientist, the social scientist seeks to inform, solve problems, describe situations in an accurate and clear manner, generate new ideas, test hypotheses, and pose new questions for research. We believe that most students have used parts of the scientific method in their everyday life and that it has become a central part of their approach to school and life. Just living and growing up is a special laboratory-type experience in problem solving, and many useful scientific observations have occurred as a result of certain reflections about growing up in human groups.

In contrast to free-flowing everyday experience, research methodology applies a systematic approach to problem solving and data collection to ensure that one has useful data, that the results can be understood by others, and that the procedures can be carried out by someone else at a later time. With data gathered in research, we can explain, predict, describe, and eventually relate current studies with other research.

▶ The homemaker who observes that a certain oven cleaner is more efficient than another is likely to continue purchasing the more efficient brand. This decision is based on observation, application, and evaluation. The farmer who applies fertilizer to one plot of the farm and not to another and then compares the yield is prepared to make a judgment about the future utility of fertilizer application. Once again, observation, application, and evaluation are involved. If each plot of land has 10 acres and the one with no fertilizer yielded 70 bushels of oats per acre while the plot with fertilizer treatment yielded only 75 bushels per acre, the farmer may decide that the extra effort and expenses do not warrant the usage. But is he correct in this decision? Perhaps the fields were not comparable in soil composition, amount of moisture, weed control, insect infestation, and a variety of other variables. In the case of the two oven cleaners, the homemaker might have used the "more efficient" one when the oven was fairly clean. It becomes clear that if we really want to know the relative effectiveness of anything we need systematic approaches.

Training in research methods sensitizes one to the importance of being open and objective. For example, if interviewers in a certain community are interested in assessing the degree to which people are satisfied with their housing, they must be prepared to cope with a variety of issues that might influence the respondent's answers. Apart from subjective matters such as the family's general satisfaction with life, objective measures concerning age of housing, construction material, size of family, location, state of upkeep, and furnishings would be important in considering reactions to the question, "How satisfied are you with your house?"

A Frame of Reference

Just as one may be attracted or offended by brief swim wear, one may seek out a particular type of research question to study. Your attitude toward the swim wear might be, in part, a function of your sex, body build, religiosity, age, and marital status.

For example, one's attitude toward nuclear war is strongly influenced by knowledge of nuclear issues and the consequences of war. Roscoe and Goodwin (1987) showed that young people are very poorly informed about nuclear issues. In this case, the researchers found that knowledge impacts attitude, and attitude in turn heavily influences the frame of reference of belief that one has about nuclear war.

The type of research question you study is equally influenced by your frame of reference. A *frame of reference* is a way of looking at issues—a system of values or a philosophy of life. Research methodology should concern itself with both methods and theory—methods for the reasons just covered and theory because it provides explanation and understanding. Theory serves as a guide and interpretation to research. Method supplies the logic, processes, and procedures for acquisition of data and the processing of information. Social science research is not a battle of methods versus theory; rather, the two are mutual partners (Merton, 1968).

REGULARITY AND PREDICTABILITY

One basic premise of all areas of research is that *regularity* or norms guide the issues being studied. If all phenomena were unique or haphazard, research would be impossible, but in reality there is seldom a unique object, idea, or event. If something is unique, it is one of a kind and no one can say much about it. But, where *patterns* do exist, we are interested in describing them and in ascertaining their causes and consequences. We are also interested in patterns or trends over time, in different settings, and under varied conditions. The motivation to seek for patterns is varied—satisfying curiosity, understanding crises, having fun, assessing social problems, making money, responding to professional demands to "publish or perish" and/or seeking recognition, and feeling scientific commitment (the person is hooked).

THE RESEARCH STEPS

Since research is a detailed process, one must guard against confusion in understanding its various steps, as one breaks down procedures into smaller and smaller components. We hope that our illustrations and examples help you to understand the large research picture. Here is a brief outline of the major steps in the research process:

1. A statement of the problem or issue is given.
2. A reduction or refinement of the problem occurs and the problem is restated with a research orientation.
3. A research design is formulated and mapped out for use.
4. Ways to obtain relevant data are developed, tested, and made ready for use.
5. The data are collected in accordance with research rules.
6. The data are analyzed and results are interpreted.
7. The findings are typically written in a report, publication, or some other medium to communicate to or influence others.

The degree to which each step is emphasized would vary according to purpose, sample size, and whether one was seeking to describe, illustrate, predict, or test. Furthermore, action taken in one stage has a direct bearing on other stages, providing a special need for understanding the whole process. Likewise, this process must be completed in context as discussed in Tips for Consumers 1.1.

Tips for Consumers 1.1

All disciplines, schools of thought, and scientific groups have their "bag of tricks" or "tools of the trade" for completing various activities. In social science research this bag of tricks or tool case is known as research methodology. *Method* refers to all of the steps involved, from thinking about a research question to analyzing collected data. Method in this context refers to the "how" of getting the job completed and the "context" for doing it. Consumers of research need to be aware of "the large picture" as well as the many, many small steps involved in conducting research. Just as scientists err when they project something out of context, so do the consumers of research err when they read, apply, or interpret some point out of context. The scientist has an obligation to inform the consumer, and the consumer has an obligation to be informed about and sensitive to context.

HOW DOES ONE STUDY HUMAN BEHAVIOR?

Most of the tools and techniques used in the study of society are not unknown to college students. In social science, as in all fields, we attempt to ask important questions and use procedures that are ethical in obtaining valid and reliable data. There are really only a few basic ways in which information can be obtained from or about people:

1. We can ask questions in person.
2. We can have respondents write answers to questions.

3. We can ask other people for their opinions about the issue (or person) under study.
4. We can observe the person in action.
5. We can study the physical residue of a person's behavior—diaries, notes, schedules, housing arrangements, trash (e.g., Jack Anderson, reporter, did detailed studies on the habits of the late J. Edgar Hoover by raiding his garbage cans).
6. We can use disguised techniques to obtain some types of information.

We have to ask questions that are answerable and worthy of the time, energy, and expense necessary to complete research. It has been pointed out earlier in this chapter that some questions are not answerable by research and it goes without saying that these should be avoided. Good questions lend themselves to verification—that is, we can "prove" whether ideas are true or false.

We are most often interested in what people do, why they do these activities, where they do them, how often they do them, and the consequences of doing them. This is the core of the study of social behavior; in short, our focus is the study of ourselves, those with whom we associate, and the social forces embedded in society. Since people are both acting and reacting creatures, our task is greatly complicated, but likewise what lies ahead is a fascinating research for answers to questions that may be so routine no one has ever asked them before. Human behavior within a complex social network is the arena in which social research methods are learned and applied. It was within this context that Gordon W. Allport commented, "If we want to know how people feel: what they experience and what they remember, what their emotions and motives are and the reasons for acting as they do—why not ask them?" (Allport quoted in Selltiz, Johoda, Deutsch, & Cook, 1961, p. 236).

THE EMPIRICAL APPROACH

Research methods, as illustrated and defined in this text, focus on empirical data. *Empirical* refers to phenomena or observations that are experienced or assessed by the senses—touch, sight, hearing, smell, or taste. Empiricism contrasts with other approaches that do not rely on experimental-objective methods for the collection and analysis of data. The empirically oriented social scientist "goes into" the social world and makes observations about how people live and behave. The nonempirical approach merely asserts, comments, or editorializes on the questions. The empirical approach can be replicated (repeated) by others, while the latter cannot. The empirical approach was used in the previous examples in this chapter: the homemaker who compared multiple brands of oven cleaner, the farmer who assessed plots with and without fertilizer, and the students who observed the relationship between hair retention and alcoholism. Social science research methods are present and widely used because of the empirical approach.

Empirical data come from experimental-counting procedures of some type. In contrast, ideas produced from speculations, arguments, or just conversation may be most interesting but do not easily lend themselves to objectivity, replication, or counting. Research seeks to answer questions with standardized procedures, to see if the answers hold true in a variety of settings, and then to invite other experimenters to replicate the results. This process is the goal and business of science, and research methodology refers to the tools necessary to accomplish this mission. (See Tips 1.2.)

Tips for Consumers 1.2

In thinking about research and science on a day-to-day basis, it is necessary to employ empirical thinking. Empirical thinking involves the processes of observation, listening, tasting, touching, and smelling—the five major methods for assessing one's world. It is important for consumers to practice systematic thinking and develop the habit of using the empirical approach in reading and evaluating various research reports, in order to be able to

1. have objective criteria for evaluation;
2. have a point of view that continually probes, assesses, and criticizes material that is consumed;
3. make judgments and decisions that would be most helpful on both a short-term and long-term basis.

Developing an empirical perspective helps the consumer of research to be more objective and less arbitrary and increases the probability that one obtains both a sense of understanding and a level of satisfaction.

THE LANGUAGE OF RESEARCH METHODS

Clearly, there is a body of concepts, terms, and ideas that must be learned; we have already discussed some of them. A common language—a common reference point—is necessary if we are to read journal reports skillfully and intelligently, consume research beneficially, and carry out defensible studies of our own. (As mentioned earlier, the main concepts or ideas will appear under the Key Terms section at the beginning of each chapter.

We realize that research methods terminology and the various steps involved in research will probably not make ideal dinner conversation, but we maintain that one can have a good time in the study of these methods and that the determined reader will reap rich benefits. Learning the language of methodology necessitates understanding new terms as well as learning the special meaning of other concepts used in day-to-day natural language. For example, the person on the street may think of theory as being synonymous with untested ideas, makeshift thinking, or crazy, impractical notions. The social scientist, on the other hand, uses this same term as a reference tool to describe how someone or something behaves.

THINKING ABOUT SCIENCE

▶ Archimedes was a Greek philosopher who lived 287 B.C. to 212 B.C. and is credited with a most important scientific approach to experimentation. Hiero, who reigned at this time, had a crown made and became suspicious that the goldsmith might have introduced silver into the crown, making is something less than the pure gold ordered. The question could readily have been answered by assaying the crown—that is, determining the composition of metals in the crown, but this would have required partial destruction of the crown. Archimedes was charged with answering the question of whether the crown was pure gold without damaging it, and it was this question he pondered one day as he soaked in the soothing waters of his bath. He noted that the water rose as he entered and receded when he stepped from the bath and that the water pressed up against his body. This scene was the context for the discovery of displacement, when Archimedes is said to have jumped from his bath and run into the street shouting "Eureka!" which means "I have found it." He had found that when a body or object is placed in water it will displace an amount of water equal to its own volume. Knowing that silver is less dense than gold (that is, has less weight per volume), he realized that a given weight of silver would displace more water than the same weight of gold. He reasoned that if the crown was alloyed with silver, it would have a larger volume than the same weight of pure gold. He compared the volumes of the crown and the pure gold and was able to conclude that indeed the goldsmith had introduced silver or some other bulk metal into the crown. Thus, Archimedes was able to answer a most difficult question without bringing any type of destruction to the king's crown.

The Archimedes illustration is pertinent to us as we think about science and methodology. He was confronted with a problem, asked questions, engaged in experimentation, gathered data, and came through with a successful conclusion. His problem was an important one, his methodology worked, and he made a significant contribution to science. Water has always reacted to immersed bodies, but this phenomenon did not serve as a scientific purpose until Archimedes was able to use it in a systematic manner.

As a resource, methodology allows scientists to complete work according to certain rules and thus deal with a variety of problems. The research steps mentioned earlier of asking a question, defining a problem, conducting research to obtain data, interpreting the data, and coming to a conclusion constitute the major components of the *scientific method*.

The scientific way of thinking as an approach to life has had an interesting struggle ◄ and its use is really quite recent in the history of mankind. Over 300 years ago a group of famous scholars and scientists in England decided to gather together regularly and discuss work and their mutual frustrations. They did this on a weekly basis in the home of John Wilkins at Oxford. After meeting at Oxford for the first years, they started regular meetings at London in 1658. Other men in this gathering included such notables as Robert Boyle, Robert Hooke, Christopher Wren, and William Petty, with King Charles II of England and Isaac Newton later joining the group as members. At first they called themselves the "Invisible College," as a protest against what they perceived as the rule-bound and sterile activities of Oxford and Cambridge. These great thinkers wanted more observation and experimentation in research. They eventually became known as the Royal Society and had a great impact on science as we know it today.

The history of science and the scientific method is rich; it is a history of replication, the accumulation of workable ideas, and the commitment to submit all answers to further evaluation in an attempt to determine if they will hold true. Over time the best ideas and theories tend to be replaced with better ideas and theories—the ultimate goal of science. An idea must be testable; it must be possible to refute. After all, one can build a better mousetrap only when it is possible to test the trap for effectiveness and then incorporate better features based on a series of experiments.

Social science research involves the application of the scientific method to the study of human relations and social conditions. We can use scientific methods to study such diverse problems as crowd behavior, cheating at a university, marital conflict and happiness, coal-mining strikes, and race riots. Previous research has produced a wealth of information about these issues, but unfortunately, policy and decisions are often made with little regard to such data. Also, in many areas there is too little accumulation of useful information to be applied. Both conditions—too little application and too little accumulated information—should increase awareness of the need for knowledge both about conducting and consuming research.

While common sense and logic, and even intuition, have important roles in science, social science aspires to solve problems following high specific techniques. Because of those techniques, social science should be recognized as a sound science (Homans, 1967) and not simply an amusing pastime. Raymond Rosdick clarifies this position in his comments:

> There seems to be a widespread belief that we are all social scientists, all of us economists, and in the egalitarian democracy of ours, any man's ideas on any problem in sociology are as good as any other man's. We need to realize that what is true of physics and biology is true in this area also. The same degree of special knowledge is required. Social issues cannot be clearly defined and understood except on the foundation of hard, painstaking work. (Quoted in Chase, 1948, p. 8)

SUMMARY

In this chapter we have covered a wide spectrum of issues to set the stage for the text that follows. We have indicated that research methodology is a process, a set of tools, or even an art for doing the work of science.

1. Asking important researchable questions enables one to gather useful data. When these data are properly interpreted they can be helpful in answering the original research questions and providing important guides in problem solving. When patterns of data are sufficiently useful in explaining events, we refer to them as theory.
2. The major steps in the scientific process are:
    a. Identify the issue.
    b. Restate the issue in a scientific context.
    c. Formulate a research design.
    d. Collect the data.
    e. Analyze the data.
    f. Report the findings.
3. Empiricism was contrasted to other systems of thought and was defined as obtaining information scientifically, based on factual evaluations of observed events and issues.

4. The scientific method and research methodology are useful to both researchers and consumers. Skillful use of methods permits one to identify the issues of concern as well as evaluate the findings of other scientists.

5. It was stressed that one must be able to understand the interrelationship between research methods, data collection and analysis, and theory if one is to be a competent consumer of research in the modern world.

6. Research methodology in the social sciences can be used in many different areas and disciplines, including home economics, history, sociology, psychology, political science, nursing, and family science.

7. Finally, Chapter 1 provided a variety of examples of research in several areas to help illustrate how one obtains and asks a research question and how data are collected to respond to a research question.

PROBLEMS AND APPLICATIONS

1. What are the main elements of the scientific approach to problem solving?

2. What are the main steps in research?

3. Contrast the major strengths and uses of social science research with some of its major limitations or difficulties in solving societal problems.

4. Does social science research have a direct application in solving social problems in a consumer-oriented world? How?

5. What are the main elements of research from an experimenter's versus a consumer's point of view?

6. How many of the key terms from this chapter can you now define and apply to conducting and/or consuming research?

REFERENCES

Chase, S. (1948). *The proper study of mankind: An inquiry into the human relations.* New York: Harper and Brothers.

De Leon, G. (1977). The baldness experiment. *Psychology Today, 11*(5), 62–63, 66.

Dellow, E.L. (1970). *Methods of science.* New York: Universe Books.

Eggebeen, D.J. (1988). Determinants of maternal employment for white preschool children. *Journal of Marriage and the Family, 50* (1), 149–159.

Fawcett, S. B., Seekins, T., & Jason, L.A. (1987). Policy research and child passenger safety legislation: A case study and experimental evaluation. *Journal of Social Issues, 43* (2), 133–148.

Glenn, N.D. (1987). The trend in "no religion" respondents to U.S. national surveys, late 1950s to early 1980s. *Public Opinion Quarterly, 51* (3), 293–314.

Gortmaker, S. L. (1979). Poverty and infant mortality in the United States. *American Sociological Review, 44,* 280–297.

Gove, W. R., Hughes, M., & Galle, O. R. (1979). Overcrowding in the home: An empirical investigation of its possible pathological consequences. *American Sociological Review, 44,* 59–80.

Homans, G.C. (1967). *The nature of social science*. New York: Harcourt, Brace and World.

McDowall, D., & Loftin, C. (1983). Collective security and the demand for legal handguns. *American Journal of Sociology, 88*, 1146–1161.

Merton, R. K. (1968). *Social theory and social structure*. New York: The Free Press.

Myrdal, G. (1969). *Objectivity in social research*. New York: Pantheon Books.

Newport, F. (1979). The religious switcher in the United States. *American Sociological Review, 44*, 528–552.

Peterson, R. D., & Bailey, W. C. (1988). Murder and capital punishment in the evolving context of the post-Furman era. *Social Forces, 66*(3), 774–807.

Porter, S. (1979). *Sylvia Porter's new money book for the 80's*. New York: Doubleday.

Roscoe, B., & Goodwin, M. P. (1987). Adolescents' knowledge of nuclear issues and the effects of nuclear wars. *Adolescence, 22*(87), 803–812.

Selltiz, C., Johoda, M., Deutsch, M., & Cook, S.W. (1961). *Research methods in social relations*. New York: Holt, Rinehart and Winston.

Wright, J. D., Rossi, P. H., Daly, K., & Weber-Burden, E. (1981). *Weapons, crime, and violence in America: A literature review and research agenda*. Amherst: Social and Demographic Research Institute, University of Massachusetts. (Report)

CHAPTER 2

Philosophical Issues in Social Science Research

OUTLINE

Introduction
Ethics and the Scientific Process
The Ethical Responsibility of Researchers
Two Special Issues in the Ethics of Social Science
Research with Special Populations
Financial Incentives
A Case of Ethical or Unethical Experimentation
Philosophical Frames of Reference and Their Implications for Social Science
Frames of Reference
Psychology: Individual Behavior
The Mechanistic Reference
The Organismic Reference
The Interactional Reference
Conclusion
Sociology: Social Process
The Social Fact Reference
The Social Definition Reference
The Social Behavior Reference
Conclusion
Theories of Social Behavior
On Evaluating the Quality of a Theory
The Hypothesis: On Putting Theory to Work

Summary
  Ethics
  Frames of Reference
Problems and Applications
References

KEY TERMS

Ethical responsibility
Research code of ethics
Frames of reference: psychology and
    sociology

Theories
Hypotheses
Causation
Material versus efficient cause

STUDY GUIDE QUESTIONS

1. What relationship is there between ethics and the scientific process?
2. What role do "right to privacy" and "scientific benefit versus cost" play for an ethical researcher?
3. What is meant by a philosophical frame of reference and where does it play a role in the scientific endeavors of social scientists?
4. Is there more than one way of thinking about causality?
5. What is meant by a theory? How does one evaluate the quality of a theory?
6. Can a hypothesis be developed in various forms? Where does a hypothesis come from?

Role of the Scientist

This chapter is an overview of the association between philosophical belief and ethical decision making in the research process. From the perspective of a future scientist you should note the potential dilemmas associated with determining ethical conduct.

While you may have been told or read that there is no place for *belief* in the research process, we shall demonstrate that the practice of science actually begins with a belief. We urge you, in particular, from the role of a future scientist to attend to the manner in which belief influences theory constructions and hypothesis-generating activities.

Role of the Consumer

As a consumer of science you should turn to research for guidance in intervention or prevention program development. Therefore, you should be aware of the interrelationship between hypothesis testing and the ethical responsibility associated with being a scientist. In actuality, we believe that the scientist's role transcends "hypothesis testing." Certain important questions about human behavior may never fully be answered by the scientist because of ethical constraints.

In learning how to apply research it is useful to recognize how all social science research begins with a "belief" about the actual nature of human behavior and social process. Consumers (e.g., interventionists or policymakers) should understand how a school of thought or a scientist's beliefs influence specific research activities. Understanding the belief system behind the theory will be useful in identifying theories that are consistent with one's views.

INTRODUCTION

All research begins with a foundation in the philosophy of science. Part of the philosophy of science focuses on ethical conduct. In simple terms ethical guidelines provide us with a moral code of conduct. Further, these moral codes indicate what is generally thought to be acceptable and unacceptable behavior in the research process. While science is commonly portrayed as being "value free," we hope you will come to agree with us that it is far from that.

In this chapter we shall examine two major aspects of the philosophy of science. We shall introduce you to the association between ethical guidelines and research activities, and to the implications of philosophical perspectives in theory or hypothesis development.

ETHICS AND THE SCIENTIFIC PROCESS

If ethics are rules of conduct, how are the limits of ethical science defined? For example, is it ethical to study an individual's garbage? Sifting through a person's garbage may provide important information on food patterns, use of consumable products, amount of volume of newspaper and magazine consumption, and the like, but it can also reveal information on alcohol consumption, personal correspondence, use of birth-control techniques, medical problems, and other personal facts that a person may not wish to have others know.

Is it acceptable moral conduct when a scientist provides false information to a research subject in the hope of observing the effects of a lowered level of self-esteem on interpersonal behavior? Or in an experimental laboratory setting, can a scientist be considered ethical if he or she pressures research subjects to continue to shock another person at increasing wattage for failure in a learning task? While an immediate answer may be an emphatic "no," closer examination of these illustrations may leave us less sure of the answer.

What if the study of garbage provided important clues as to how certain viruses are transmitted? Of if garbage research gave us potential solutions to necessary energy conservation in homes? Then too, if studies manipulating self-esteem demonstrated that such manipulations of government authorities might be perceived as threatening to national security and might ultimately lead to war, would we be inclined to stop such research? If research pressuring subjects to comply with the demands of authorities provided answers to why individuals engage in immoral actions when a leader so commands, would we be opposed to such research? One need only think about CIA actions, the Watergate break-in, or the effects of the Nazi party on a whole nation to recognize the potential importance of such research. But questions of research ethics cannot be readily answered with simple "yes" or "no" answers. There are times when the risk to subjects may outweigh a potential research outcome, but there are also cases in which the possible benefit may outweigh potential harm to subjects. One of the most dramatic illustrations of outcome outweighing risk is found in medical research. If a clinical population is dying of AIDS (Acquired Immune Deficiency Syndrome), using an experimental drug with unknown or potentially dangerous side effects may be warranted. The patients are dying or will soon die—according to our current knowledge. The potential for prolonging life may outweigh the possible side effects in that a cure may be found. However, should the drug be ineffective or harmful to the patients, the outcome would be the same—death. Should the drug be effective, the outcome would benefit both the patient and society through the knowledge it would create and the possible uses with other patients.

In remaining accountable to society, scientists have imposed on themselves certain ethical codes of conduct. The scientific community has recognized that there are both moral and immoral ways of gathering facts. Social science, like all branches of scientific inquiry, is limited by ethical constraints or principles of moral scientific conduct. In this chapter we will take a brief look at some of the many issues associated with social science ethics.

The Ethical Responsibility of Researchers

Professional codes of ethics for the conduct of research have been prepared and endorsed by many branches of social and medical science. For example, codes of ethics have been prepared by such professional organizations as The American Sociological Association (1984), American Psychological Association (1981,1987), American Nurses Association (cited in Bower & Gasparis, 1978), Committee on Ethics in Research with Children (1977), American Academy of Pediatrics Committee on Drugs (1977), American Association of Public Opinion Research (cited in Bower & Gasparis, 1978), the Society for Research in Child Development (1990), and the American Anthropological Association (1983).[1] Also federal agencies such as the Department of Health, Education and Welfare's National Institutes of Health and their commissions (National Commission for the Protection of Human Subjects of Biomedical and Behavioral Research [1977]; Privacy Protection Study Commission [1976]) have prepared guidelines on ethical conduct for funded research. Two themes are found in all of these code of ethics statements: (1) the *right to privacy,* and (2) the relationship between individual *cost* and scientific *benefit.*

At first, it may seem an easy task to ensure an individual's right to private and

---

[1]Robert Bower and Priscilla Gasparis' text, *Ethics in Social Research,* provides an extended list of professional societies with ethical codes. Interestingly, the American Home Economics Association does not have a formal ethical code.

confidential treatment. By blanketing a subject's identity, a social scientist can hide the individual behind the data. The Privacy Study Commission has recommended

> As a general rule, any information or record collected or maintained in individually identifiable form for a research or statistical purpose should not be used to make any determination about an individual without the specific authorization of the individual to whom the record pertains. (1976, p. 7)

But can we actually guarantee our research subjects such anonymity? It has been pointed out that a "court of competent jurisdiction" can subpoena research data, leading to legal and other risks for participants (Bond, 1978). Most researchers are probably unaware of this possibility. For example, Carroll and Knerr (1977) reviewed several cases in which research data have been requested for what Bond termed "purposes which would allow a determination about an individual" (Bond, 1978, p. 146). In other words, this is to be a legal or social determination.

Bond summarizes several illustrations. In one, a federal grand jury requested in 1972 that a Harvard professor of political science reveal the identity of research informants in an investigation of the infamous "Pentagon Papers." The noncompliant researcher was imprisoned for more than a week before being released. The professor would not reveal his sources, indicating that a violation of confidentiality would make it impossible to conduct future research on politically sensitive issues. In another case, a team of researchers conducting a federally funded investigation of social welfare were subpoenaed on 14 occasions to provide the names of individuals thought to have committed welfare fraud. It is reported that the General Accounting Office and Senate committee also exerted pressure on the researchers to identify individual subjects. Once again the researchers refused on grounds of the subjects' "rights to privacy." While research codes of ethics demand the protection of privacy and confidentiality, government policy may make adhering to these codes difficult. Nonetheless, by keeping the subjects' responses separate from their identification, addresses, or social security numbers, the researcher has a good chance to maintain confidentiality (see Box 2.1).

Beyond ensuring rights to privacy, research ethics require that a subject's experimental risk, both physical and psychological (see Box 2.2) be kept to a minimum. When risk is involved, the researcher is expected to (1) inform the participant, (2) do everything in his or her power to obviate unnecessary risk, and (3) where potential harm is deemed greater than the potential scientific benefit, refrain from experimentation. Fortunately, much of social science involves minimal risk (Koocher, 1983; Bond, 1978), particularly, minimal physical risk. Psychological injury is more likely, however, notably from investigations that cause embarrassment or other emotional upset. Table 2.1 (p. 32) provides a general guideline for determining research techniques that are least likely and most likely to be perceived as creating discomfort.

In order to uphold privacy and create a reasonable cost–benefit ratio, the primary tool in dealing with risk is the *informed consent form*. Subjects are typically provided with a general written statement on research objectives, potential benefits and risks, rights to confidentiality, and decisions to terminate involvement at will. Federal funding regulations frequently require that subjects sign such a document rather than give a verbal agreement. However, as Bond (1978) points out, a signed informed consent form may

---

BOX 2.1. Guidelines for Maintaining Confidentiality

Fowler (1984) has suggested several techniques for maintaining confidentiality.

1. Data files should be labeled by an identification number only. If names or addresses need to be connected with each file a separate list should be kept under lock-and-key that provides names, addresses, and identification number material.
2. All individuals working with the data and the data collection process need to be committed to maintaining confidentiality for each and all respondents.
3. Completed responses should be available to staff personnel only.
4. Identifiers should be removed from the responses as soon as possible. Should non-staff personnel examine the material, all links to identification should be removed first.
5. Individuals who might be able to make a link between the identification number or system and the individual responding should not be given access to the data.
6. In all cases, researchers should never present data that allow others to identify the individual. Further, upon completion of the project all material should be either stored in a secured location or destroyed.

---

actually place subjects at "social injury" or "legal" risk given that all research documents can be subpoenaed by officials. A signed form is particularly jeopardizing in experiments on such socially sensitive issues as drug abuse, prostitution, gambling, and criminal behavior. Therefore, when subjects are at risk from disclosure, it is sometimes preferable to have merely a verbal agreement.

Social psychologist Brewster Smith (1976) has related the emphases on privacy and the cost–benefit ratio to two contrasting perspectives. Informed consent and the right to privacy, he argues, are espoused by the popular "humanistic" movement, which emphasizes the rights of the individual. In contrast, issues related to the participant's welfare are emphasized by the "utilitarian" tradition. This framework seeks a balance between the cost to a subject and the benefit of research information. Both frameworks, Smith argues, are found in contemporary codes of research ethics. Although both are important, either can fail in guiding the researcher's activities. Therefore, Smith (1976) contends that "when the principle of informed consent fails us we turn to harm/benefit analysis" (p. 447). That is, when informed consent is not reasonably possible, our next concern is for the balance between possible subject harm and scientific benefit. Let us examine a research question that highlights this issue.

The study by Duster, Matza, and Wellman (1979) summarizes the dilemma of the scientist who is required by federal guidelines to obtain the informed consent signatures of subjects who would be at risk should the data be subpoenaed. In an investigation commissioned by the Department of Housing and Urban Development to investigate discrimination against blacks by real estate agents, some 300 blacks and 300 whites answered local newspaper advertisements for housing units. One black and one white research confederate answered each advertisement and compared responses by the agents. Blacks were discriminated against 75% of the time when attempting to rent and 62% of the time when attempting to buy. As Duster et al. (1979) remarked about this particular illustration,

BOX 2.2. Assessing Psychological Discomfort

To maintain a sense of scientific integrity and goodwill toward science, research subjects should not leave an experience feeling they have just escaped, perhaps narrowly, psychological harm at the hands of a "mad" social scientist. There are real and potential dangers in underestimating the potential stress and discomfort to experimental procedures and there are ethical considerations in failing to inform the subjects of possible risk in obtaining their consent.

Farr and Seaver (1975) have suggested two types of errors that an investigator could potentially make in judging the potential harmfulness of an experimental procedure. First, the scientist could administer an experimental procedure that was judged to be harmless when in actuality it is dangerous to the research subject. This error should always be avoided and is surely the issue that has given rise to ethical principles to begin with. The second error is less obvious. That is, an investigator could avoid using an experimental procedure that appears harmful or dangerous to the subject when in reality it is innocuous. Farr and Seaver point to Gergen's (1973) concern on this potential error, noting that ethical principles may keep many scientists from using scientifically worthwhile experimental procedures falsely judged as dangerous, therein keeping the accumulation of important scientific contributions from emerging. Such concerns might be appropriate in research situations using nonreactive measures (such as observations) or experimental conditions under which a slight discomfort might be experienced, but total disclosure of the experimental condition might substantially alter the research situation or findings and perhaps invalidate the experimental effect on the subject's behavior.

Farr and Seaver (1975) have piloted a procedure that might be utilized in empirically determining the subject's perception of both physical and psychological discomfort and perceived invasion of personal privacy. Subjects were asked to read 20 procedures, extracted from the research literature, that might create threats to physical comfort, 15 procedures that were thought to be viewed as varying in their threat to psychological discomfort, and 36 experimental techniques that might be viewed, in varying severity, as an invasion of personal privacy. Subjects then were asked to rate each procedure on a series of 5-point scales to measure perceived discomfort and invasion of privacy. Table 2.1 summarizes several of the least extreme and most extreme procedures. These data, the authors argue, can be used as a "set of anchors" to compare the perceived degree of stress of discomfort of a given investigation.

If the National Committee Against Discrimination in Housing had applied for research funds from HEW, their investigation would clearly have been considered a risk to the financial status of the real estate agents they wanted to study ... [but] in order for the HUD researchers to receive informed consent from the real estate agents under investigation, the staff would have had to tell the realtors something like, "Our hypothesis is that you are engaged in discrimination." (1979, p. 139)

If signed consent forms had been required of subjects they would have been at risk from disclosure and they would have been informed and discrimination would not have occurred. Therefore, given that risk from disclosure was possible and informed consent unfeasible, a harm/benefit ratio analysis directed the researchers' conduct. Assuming that

TABLE 2.1. Examples of Research Procedures Viewed As Least Likely or Most Likely to Have Perceived Effects on Physical or Psychological Discomfort and Invasion of Privacy

	Least Likely	Most Likely
Perceived physical discomfort	Run up and down steps for one minute	Hold a hand in a bucket of ice for one hour
	Eat no food for six hours prior to study	Band tightened around the arm to see how much pain could be tolerated
	Wear earphones over which continuous white noise (from a small fan, etc.) is heard	Receive repeated electric shock of the maximum tolerable intensity
Perceived psychological discomfort	Judge the more attractive person in each of 50 pairs of photographs	The experimenter tells you that a test you took in the experiment indicates that you have homosexual tendencies
	Be the elected leader of a group that has to work together to construct an object out of tinker toy parts	While you are recalling a lost list of words you were to learn, another subject receives a shock for each mistake you make
	Move a handle to keep a pointer aligned with a fast-moving target	Sit in a small room for 10 minutes with the thing you are most afraid of
Perceived invasion of privacy	Questionnaire about hometown family size, and family mobility—name signed	Personality inventory measuring heterosexual/homosexual orientation—name signed
	Occupational interest test—name signed	Wear nonpainful electrodes measuring physiological reactions to pictures of nude men and women
	Questionnaire about size of high school attended, athletic participation, and college major—name signed	Questionnaire about past sexual experiences—name signed

Source: From J. L. Farr and W. B. Seaver (1975). Stress and discomfort in psychological research: Subject perceptions of experimental procedures. *American Psychologist, 30,* 770–773, Tables 1, 2, and 3. Copyright 1975 by the American Psychological Association. Reprinted by permission.

none of the realtors was identified by name or address there was no obvious harm to them. Without consent forms, therefore, the researchers still functioned as ethical scientists, while obtaining important information about housing problems.

Guidelines associated with rights to privacy and cost–benefit ratios are only two of the many concerns found in research codes of ethics, but they appear to be the foundations on which all code statements are built. (See Tips 2.1.)

Tips for Consumers 2.1

The quality of research evidence is likely to be influenced by the ethical conduct of the social scientist. One can speculate that

1. to the extent that anonymity (confidentiality) is threatened on highly sensitive questions, research subjects are likely to respond with guarded or socially desirable responses;
2. physical and psychological risk threatens subjects' willingness in cooperating with researchers and makes social science vulnerable to undesirable perceptions by the public at large.

To assess the degree to which these two factors have (or may have) affected results in reading research reports, look for information about informed consent. Did the researcher review with each subject rights to privacy, the possibility of risk, or ability to withdraw if desired? Failure to do so might have resulted in biased results!

Two Special Issues in the Ethics of Social Science

Social science, as a science of human behavior, obligates researchers to study a wide array of human conditions. To do so, researchers, at times, are required to study special populations and provide incentives for participation. Both activities have their own ethical considerations, which we shall briefly examine.

Research with Special Populations.   Research involving the use of incarcerated, mentally ill, or legally underage subjects provides an added ethical dilemma to social science researchers. Do experimenters need to obtain verbal or written permission from these subjects? Can these subjects rationally and knowingly give informed consent? The answers are frequently ambiguous. An acutely psychotic patient is not likely to be sufficiently in touch with reality to give a rational "yes" or "no." A child, however, can typically agree or not agree to the experience. The debate over the use of children in experimentation has led to a report and recommendation explicitly on this topic.

The National Commission for the Protection of Human Subjects of Biomedical and Behavioral Research (1977) has proposed eight explicit guidelines for research involving children. In essence these guidelines state that both parent (or guardian) and child (when possible) should give informed consent, and where feasible the adult should accompany the child during the research project. All research involving children should be reviewed by an institutional review board, and adequate provisions must be made to ensure privacy and confidentiality of responses for both children and their parents. (The review board generally consists of colleagues from the university, lay persons, and a university lawyer.) When appropriate, experimentation should be conducted first with animals, adults, or older children to ensure minimal risk to infant or very young subjects. Also, children who are "wards of the state" should not be used as research subjects without the appointment of an "advocate" to serve in the best interest of the child and intercede when necessary to protect the rights and welfare of the child. While other specific guidelines are offered in the commission report, this summary represents stipulations suggested for research on a special research population.

Particular care must be taken in using special populations, including the poor, aged, and transient, who maintain few power groups to represent them and uphold their well-being. Further, we contend that any population used for research that might lead to policymaking decisions by state and federal agencies should be considered a "special population."

Financial Incentives.   Paying subjects for their participation in a given research project is a fairly common practice, but the ethical implications of payment have been ignored in the professional literature. Once a subject enters a research setting under verbal agreement to receive financial remuneration for the participation time, is the experimental situation equivalent to an employer–employee relationship in which the boss may simply say there is risk involved with this job, but you agree to work for the designated monetary sum and recognize the risk involved? We are certain this form of thinking frequently prevails. However, one may question its implications for the research participant's welfare. Further, one might wonder if paying the subject obligates the individual as a good employee to give the experimenter/employer what is perceived as being the right or correct behavior.

Since we know that payment for service definitely affects how people feel about participation, there are a number of questions one should consider. Should the researcher and subject view payment for participation as pay for cooperation and time, or is it for risk and possible nuisance? If the pay is sufficiently high, then is all guilt or concern for ethical behavior eliminated? Have researchers routinely viewed the token rewards we give subjects as a "thank-you" or a modified bribe? Finally, the question of being bought off directly emerges: For a fast buck, a subject in need (maybe a college student) and a desperate investigator agree to the risk or unethical practices that seem justified in the situation. Subject desperation or vulnerability must not be exploited. (As a college student, how do you view financial incentives for research participation?)

▶ *A Case of Ethical or Unethical Experimentation.*   It would be beneficial to examine an illustration of an ethical dilemma. We have chosen a Stanford University investigation dealing with prison behavior (Zimbardo, Haney, Banks, & Jaffe, 1973). As a consequence of the Stanford prison experiment, Zimbardo has received a great deal of notoriety and has been much criticized in the professional literature over questions of ethical research behavior (e.g., Savin, 1973).

The mock prison study (Zimbardo, 1973) examined interpersonal dynamics of a prison-like environment through a very realistic simulation of the prison experience. American and Canadian students from a wide variety of backgrounds participated in the project. A variety of manipulations created a real sense of imprisonment with one group of students role-playing guards, another role-playing prisoners. While neither group was instructed formally on how to play their roles, the intent of the simulation study was conveyed to both groups through the behavior of the research staff for the guards and what appeared to be a real arrest by the local police force for the prisoners.

Both guards and prisoners were continuously observed in their interactions. Observations were augmented by video- and audiotaping, self-report measures, and individual interviews. The general results were that the mock prison experience led to undesirable and seemingly pathological behavior from many of the subjects. Guards became verbally and physically violent and used dehumanizing behavior in the treatment of their wards. Prisoners began to show apparently psychotic behavior and signs of chronic dependence or learned helplessness. Indeed, Zimbardo, acting as the superintendent of the prison, was compelled to terminate the investigation prematurely because of the psychological risk to the participants.

Criticism in the professional literature on the ethics of social scientists highlighted the importance of ethical issues. Savin (1973) is among the more critical of Zimbardo's work. Zimbardo (1973) reviews several of the personal attacks from Savin's discussion:

> Some choice instances are: "One cannot make a prison into a more humane institution by appointing Mr. Zimbardo its superintendent"; "professors in pursuit of their own academic interests and professional advancement" are subverting the teacher–student relationship; there are some psychologists who are "as obnoxious as the law allows," who show "a morally obtuse zeal" in the pursuit of their careers, and who can be likened to a used car salesman; finally, "on occasion there is a hell like Zimbardo's" (p. 245). Further, Savin (1973) concludes his criticisms with this statement: "Professors who, in pursuit of their own academic interests and professional advancement, deceive, humiliate, and otherwise mistreat their students are subverting the atmosphere of mutual trust and intellectual honesty without which, as we are fond of telling outsiders who want to meddle in our affairs, neither education nor free inquiry can flourish." (p. 149)

But is such a strong and personal attack warranted? Should we, or should we not, be allowed to complete simulation studies of this type, where research participants are aware of the general nature of the investigation? Can we reasonably expect each investigator to be omniscient and predict well ahead every and all possible consequences of the study? Zimbardo (1973) appears to have followed the essence of the general guidelines found in a research code of ethics, but still the consequences for the subjects were undesirable as measured by most professional standards. The subjects were aware of the nature of the study, they had consented freely, they were paid for their participation, they could terminate involvement of their own volition, and above all, they were never instructed on how to act—they had the freedom to behave as their conscience directed them. Yet immoral behavior became the norm, not the exception. What is your ethical judgment on this experiment? Was it justified? (In Chapter 11 we summarize another controversial study by Humphreys (1970) regarding impersonal sex in public places. What ethical considerations are evident from reading this study?)

PHILOSOPHICAL FRAMES OF REFERENCE AND THEIR IMPLICATIONS FOR SOCIAL SCIENCE

Besides the philosophical debates raised by ethical issues, there is another way in which philosophy and social science interrelate. Each of us has beliefs about the nature of mankind and how and why individuals behave as they do. These beliefs come to be reflected in theory construction and hypothesis testing; that is, our own views of the essence of mankind direct the scientific research process in subtle but important ways.

Further, these differing beliefs define us as belonging to different schools of thought in the varying subdisciplines of social science.

An initial impression of science might suggest it has no room for such beliefs, but nothing could be further from the truth. Scientists, like politicians or theologians, are also influenced by their personal beliefs about the nature of things. In social science, it is individual beliefs about the *fundamental nature of man and his relationships* that are most likely to influence the scientific process. These abstract beliefs or viewpoints are sometimes called *world views, paradigms, frames of reference,* or *models of man.* In this chapter we shall refer to these abstract beliefs about the nature of man as *frames of reference.*

We shall begin with an exploration of what is meant by a frame of reference. After briefly reviewing several illustrations of existing frames of reference, we shall examine their use in theory and hypothesis testing.

Frames of Reference

A researcher's frame of reference helps to *define meaningful research problems* and *establish criteria for truth*. That is, a frame of reference focuses upon a central social process of interest and establishes criteria for how "truth" will be defined. Criteria used in defining truth are in actuality rules for accepting information that supports or falsifies the researcher's questions about behavior.

A frame of reference guides the establishment of criteria for truth through the acceptance of what is judged to be the determinant of causality. Causality refers to cause-and-effect relationships. Most frames of reference which influence social science accept one of two types of causal determinants.One causal determinant is referred to as material causation. *Material causation* implies that the "object is the substance which constitutes the object" (Overton & Reese, 1973, p. 75). That is, the individual's neurology, physiology, or genetic substance is the causal factor for specific behavior. For example, in a social service setting the staff might assume the individual could not help behaving in the manner exhibited because the person has an organic dysfunction causing the client's behavior. Thus, the individual's organic problems triggered the behavioral outcome. In contrast, an *efficient cause* assumes an external agent or variable is the causal factor determining the behavior. (Many contemporary researchers and practitioners use the term *conditional* or *functional relationship* in place of the term *cause.*) It is assumed that external physical or social forces cause the behavior. Once again, returning to a social service setting, an illustration of efficient cause would be when staff members agree behavior (e.g., delinquency) is caused by some external social force (e.g., a broken home). In this illustration the external social effects of a broken home influence the individual's behavior.

Beyond the more abstract dimension, a frame of reference also provides direction for appropriate methods for testing research problems. This points to the very essence of the intent of this text—a review of the varying research methodologies available for scientific discovery. However, a frame of reference also guides the researcher in defining what kind of research information (data) will be gathered and gives direction as to how data can be interpreted (Overton & Reese, 1973). In future chapters we shall review the more common forms of gathering facts (data).

In overview, at the very foundation of the research process, a scientist's frame or reference establishes the basic categories of psychological and sociological behaviors to be considered in theory construction. Therefore, it clarifies or defines the specific features to be carefully outlined in a theory. Once these behavioral categories are established, certain abstract definitions of how truth can be derived are established through the interrelationships of independent and dependent variables. Further, only specific methodologies become acceptable research strategies to establishing truth within a given frame of reference.

Let us provide some further clarification through a brief exploration into some common frames of reference that emerge in contemporary psychology and sociology. We choose the illustrations from these two basic social science disciplines only because of their clarity in formulation in current research. Illustrations from other social science disciplines such as history, political science, or anthropology could likewise be found. Indeed, an excellent classroom activity might be to identify other frames of reference and "dissect" their major philosophical elements.

Psychology: Individual Behavior

Psychological-based research, be it in the fields of home economics, child development, family studies, or other allied social science programs, has three major frames of reference that function as the foundation of research efforts. These differing frames of reference are often labeled *mechanistic, organismic,* and *interactional* perspectives.

The Mechanistic Reference.   The basic assumption of the *mechanistic frame of reference* is the belief that man is a simple reactive being. That is, human behavior is a direct response to physical and social stimulation associated with interpersonal and environmental stimuli. A simple metaphor to this perspective is the machine. The machine is merely reactive; someone must start it, stop it, and maintain it. With individuals, the mechanistic frame of reference assumes that a person parallels the reactive machine with individual behavior dependent on environmental causation (efficient). The individual is seen as being reliant on the environment. As Overton and Reese (1973) contend, "in its ideal form the reactive model characterizes the organism, like other parts of the universal machine, as inherently at rest, and active only as a result of external forces" (p. 69). Thus, behavior is viewed as the direct consequence of stimulation, with the machine (behavior) unable to initiate its own occurrence.

The Organismic Reference.   In comparison to the mechanistic perspective the *organismic frame of reference* to development and behavior views individuals as active beings; that is, individuals selectively synthesize and integrate experiences, progressively changing and transforming themselves with time and experience. In the metaphoric machine analogy, the organismic frame of reference would require a machine with "artificial intelligence," capable of synthesizing and integrating information, selecting relevant from irrelevant facts, and maintaining a sense of self-direction and growth. This allows the organism to be indirectly reliant on the environment.

The Interactional Reference.   Interactionalism assumes a position halfway between the other two psychological frames of reference. This perspective assumes that characteristics of the individual are well suited for some, but not all, situations. Thus, individuals with a certain psychological trait (e.g., anxiety) might do well in one environment and very poorly in another. Using the machine analogy, it might be assumed that we have two machines capable of varying operations—the operations are similar but the machines vary in their speeds in completion of a task. In a setting where time is not crucial, the slow machine is as useful and effective as the fast machine. However, when time is of the essence, only the fast machine (regardless of the fact that both machines provide the same product) is useful.

Conclusion.   Each of these three psychological frames of reference is a viable perspective to the study of human behavior. However, they all have different focuses on the causes of behavior and human development. In the mechanistic framework, one focuses on research problems in which environmental factors are thought to be the primary cause of behavior. In the organismic perspective, the researcher focuses on the study of the inner strengths and weaknesses of the individual. Finally, in the interactional perspective, the researcher focuses on how certain types of individuals perform and cope in varying social environments.

These frames of reference likewise are carried into the many varying forms of psychological intervention. For example, Ritterman (1977) has shown how each perspective influences the emphases of family therapy. (Interested readers should examine his article for further insight into the influences of frames of reference on therapy and intervention practices.)

Sociology: Social Process

Like psychology, sociology has numerous frames of reference that influence research activities. As Eckberg and Hill (1979) have indicated, a frame of reference serves as an exemplar (model) for puzzle solving. Each exemplar provides the mechanism for communication between like-minded scientists on how one should engage in "puzzle-solving" research. When a group of social scientists lock themselves into a "fairly rigid, highly elaborate framework of beliefs" (Eckberg & Hill, 1979, p. 928), a common approach to social problems emerges. Thus, any given frame of reference has its disciples (followers) who adamantly support a uniform way of looking at research problems through acceptable methodology and theoretical perspective.

Ritzer (1975) has, for example, outlined three frames of reference that are established in the field of sociology and social work. Ritzer argues that each frame of reference provides the function of (1) an exemplar (model) for those scientists maintaining such a perspective, (2) offers an image of the acceptable subject matter, while (3) outlining important theoretical constructs and defining appropriate methods and measurements. Based on Ritzer's work, we shall briefly describe three additional frames of reference and illustrate each reference model's major exemplary, image, and methodological assumptions.

The Social Fact Reference.   Built on the early work of Emile Durkheim, this frame of reference maintains that social facts are external to an individual and are coercive on behavior. Therefore, there is a social reality independent of the individual. An exemplar for this perspective is the work of Warriner (Ritzer, 1975). Warriner's work on social groups has led to a position that the group is a phenomenon in and of itself—totally independent of individual psychology. Thus, group process is studied to identify coercive effects on the individual and can never be understood by reference to the individual alone. In this perspective, the images or topics of investigation are roles, values, groups, and the family, to name a few. These very topics compose the social facts of this frame of reference. The best known theoretical orientation that has evolved from the social fact frame of reference is that of structural functionalism. The primary unit of analysis is social institution. An individual's behavior is examined through the social facts of the institution, with the institution viewed as external and coercive to the individual. The interview and questionnaire are primary tools thought to assist in the study of social facts.

The Social Definition Reference.   Frequently attributed to the early work of Max Weber, a social definition frame of reference focuses on social action. Thus, the main function of sociology from this perspective is to study human behavior that has some subjective meaning to the individual actor. Behavior of sociological interest must have meaning and give direction or it is of little interest to a social definitionist. The subject matter images, or topics of interest, focus on mental process, social relations, and interactions. According to Ritzer (1975), the creative process that occurs between a stimulus and a response is of primary interest to a social definitionist. One of the more well known theories based on a social definition frame of reference is symbolic interactionism. Symbolic interactionism focuses on how an individual comes to place meaning on social experience and studies the dynamic and creative mental processes which mediate social experiences and individual behavior. Due to the focus on social action and individual meaning, it should be apparent as to why the methodological tool most frequently used is observational methodology. To understand social meaning and the interpersonal process, the researcher must examine this social process over time in a natural setting.

The Social Behavior Reference.   As we have seen earlier in this chapter, mechanistic perspectives view human beings as relatively simple reactive mechanisms. As in psychology, sociologists who maintain this frame of reference are inclined to believe that the focus of sociology is the study of the functional relationship between behavior and "reinforcement contingencies" in an environmental setting. Thus, the image or topics of study are primarily external stimuli, individual responses, and their functional relationship. Exchange theory as outlined by B. F. Skinner in psychology or George Homans in sociology serves as an ideal theoretical illustration of this frame of reference. An understanding of how reinforcement contingencies used by the social group can lead an individual to conform to group standards and norms ideally requires a method of study that can identify cause-and-effect (functional) relationships. Proponents of this perspective prefer to use the experimental laboratory method in their research endeavors.

Conclusion.   We have seen from both psychology and sociology illustrations that there are a variety of frames of reference in social science. It should be noted that all other scientific disciplines have frames of reference that function in a similar way. Further, it should now be clear that a frame of reference is built around a *belief* system. This belief system deals with certain assumptions about the nature of mankind and social behavior. Once understood and popularized, this belief system or frame of reference accumulates followers who share a common belief and communication system. In the study of the history of social science, this phenomenon has been called a "school of thought." Once a "school" is established, certain research topics based on the belief of mankind and social behavior become the focus of attention. But any given school of thought has its hiatus. Every frame of reference will, within time, come to be challenged by another. Thus, every frame of reference will rise up, reach its peak influence, and fall away to another perspective. Sometimes schools merge, but more often than not they merely become outdated. Thus, every frame of reference that gains a broad-based support in the scientific community will likely have its impact but will be replaced eventually by another perspective. Generally, however, the replacement of any frame of reference with another is a slow process; this accounts for the consistency in theoretical constructs for relatively long periods of historical time.

THEORIES OF SOCIAL BEHAVIOR

While a frame of reference may be a by-product of larger social and/or cultural factors, the varying theories evolving from that perspective are likely to be more closely associated with the individual intellectual activity of the scientist. Theory construction is a complicated and delicate task. No machine or computer is likely to replace the intellectual activity of the individual scholar. Theory development requires experience, observation, and critical thought. But what are the specific properties of a theory? What is specifically meant by theory?

A *theory* is a series of statements (propositions) that collectively explain associations believed to prevail in a comprehensive body of facts. Stated another way, a theory is an explanation for something believed to be true. A useful theory provides a series of logically deduced statements that attempt to explain the relationship between two or more things in such a manner that the proposed relationships are empirically testable. A theory finds its ultimate utility, and scholarly disciples, when it can be shown to predict and explain behavior over repeated tests in a variety of situations (replications).

For example, if one believes frustration is likely to lead to anti-social or aggressive behavior, such a relationship is a proposed cause-and-effect relation (a proposition). However, one could build an argument that due to early socialization experiences one child might learn to become aggressive when frustrated, while another might learn to become constructive (use the energy to try harder). Such a theoretical explanation (as found in this example) helps to preserve a certain degree of formal consistency in the propositions that are tested in theory construction, yet allows for the differentiation of complex human behavior.

There are certain essential ingredients to a useful theory. First, it must specify the elements of social behavior. Second, it must delineate proposed cause-and-effect relationships. Third, the terms (variables) in the theory must be clearly and concisely stated so as to be testable. This is called operationalization. Each of the independent and dependent variables must be defined well enough to allow for a researcher to build representative measures of both. Finally, a useful theory must provide some meaningful *insight* into appropriate research methodology that might be used to gather evidence in support of the proposition(s) outlined in the theory itself.

In other words, theories are tools of explanation. They provide useful statements on proposed causal factors to specific behaviors. Theoretical propositions, as extensions of frames of reference, offer meaningful integration of thought about how behavior manifests itself and what causes these manifestations of behavior.

On Evaluating the Quality of a Theory

Understanding the dimensions or variables commonly found across different theories is an important step toward appreciating the utility of theory in the research process. But what are the criteria for evaluating the practical utility of a specific theory? In a classic statement, Toulmin (1962) has offered three main criteria. The first criterion is the *deployability* of the theory. Deployability refers to the degree to which the terms (variables) in the theory can be used in describing the effects of a new setting or event. The second criterion deals with the *scope* of the theory. What is the range of phenomena to which the theory is applicable? While scope refers to the empirical derivations of a theory generated through its frame of reference, deployability refers to the set of relationships used in formulating the logical propositions of the theory. Finally, a theory can be evaluated in terms of *precision*. Although frames of reference are based on a belief system, which can neither be proven absolutely true or false, theories derived from any frame of reference can be evaluated on the application of the reference rules provided by the reference perspective.

In summary, a theory should give a sense of understanding to human behavior. It should have the capacity to predict behavior and explain why and how it occurs. The more precise, generalizable, and complete the theoretical propositions are, the more utility they offer. However, to make this determination, theory must be put to an empirical test.

The Hypothesis: On Putting Theory to Work

The scientist puts theory to work through individual, testable hypotheses, which are the bases of research. A *hypothesis* is, in actuality, the operational definition of one of the propositions set forth in a theory. Typically, the hypothesis consists of a statement about a cause-and-effect relationship between an independent and dependent variable(s). It is a predictive statement specifying the relationship between two or more variables. In many ways the meaning of hypothesis parallels that of the *hypothetical proposition*. English and English (1958), in their classic dictionary of social science terminology, define hypothetical proposition as "a statement consisting of two parts: an *antecedent* clause introduced by *if* (or some equivalent) which states the condition under which a certain result will occur or under which a certain conclusion will be reached, and a *consequent* which states the occurrence or the conclusion" (p. 246). Therefore, a hypothetical proposition, which is thought to be assessed through a testable hypothesis, is a matter of making a formal cause-and-effect statement. This cause-and-effect relationship is the stated relationship between the independent and dependent variable. The independent variable is that variable which is either manipulated or statistically controlled by the researcher and is believed to be a factor that causes certain changes in the dependent variable. The dependent variable, on the other hand, is left to freely change as a function of the independent variable. It is the measure by which we gauge independent variable effects. As stated in the definition of a hypothetical proposition, it is the operational measure of the "consequence."

While a hypothesis makes a prediction, based on theoretical guidance or a general hunch, it always includes a testable statement of the relationship between two or more variables. The testable relationship can actually come in the form of a predicted association between two or more variables in which there is no assumed causality, or it can be a test of a cause-and-effect relationship. In the former case, the hypothesis includes a statement which implies when one variable occurs so must another, but does not infer which variable causes the other or if there is any causal relationship between the variables at all. For example, a researcher might hypothesize that child abuse and neglect are associated with poor school adjustment. In this example, the researcher is not assuming child abuse causes poor school adjustment nor that poor school adjustment causes child abuse. In contrast, in the latter type of hypothesis, the hypothesis assumes a predicted relationship between two variables. For example, a researcher might assume that high self-esteem is predictive of good school grades. In this case, the hypothesis has provided a testable statement that predicts positive self-esteem is the causal factor of getting good grades. Of course, a counter hypothesis, that is equally testable, might be that good school grades create high self-esteem.

A good hypothesis provides the testable statement of a theory. It should be stated in a manner that allows the researcher to provide both supportive data as well as data that might falsify the statement. Without the opportunity to either support *or* negate the statement, science is not well served.

There are two general types of hypotheses with differing functions. Likewise, these hypotheses can be written in differing formats. First, there is the *idiographic hypothesis,* which is directed at predicting an individual's behavior or action. In this form of a hypothesis there is no intent of predicting beyond the individual. Thus, the prediction is associated solely with the idiosyncratic condition of the individual. For example, we might predict, for a close friend, that "John will get angry and throw the newspaper on the floor each time he reads that his favorite football team has lost a game." In understanding and predicting John's behavior, this is a useful hypothesis. However, it is less useful if we wish to understand the reaction of the average football fan to losing. Therefore, the second type of hypothesis deals with the condition. The *nomothetic hypothesis* focuses on studying or testing the average response to the same condition across many persons. In this case, the researcher might test the hypothesis that "the most frequent response to reading one's favorite football team lost will be reflected in throwing the paper." The idographic hypothesis is useful in studying the individual, while the nomothetic hypothesis is best used when one wishes to understand and estimate the average or most typical response over a larger sample of persons. The first form of a hypothesis provides data useful only to the uniqueness of John; the second form of a hypothesis provides a test of data over a wider and more generalized group of individuals.

Hypotheses are written in two basic styles. The first style is commonly called the *null* hypothesis. In this form the statement is written indicating there is no relationship between the variables. For example, the scientist might predict that "level of intelligence is not associated with school grade success." The scientist then attempts to find facts that either support or negate the null association. The second style is frequently referred to as a *directional* hypothesis. This style is commonly used when previous research has demonstrated the possibility of a directional relationship between two or more variables. For example, we already know a great deal about the important relationship between IQ and school grades. The general trend is for persons with higher IQs to get good, not poor, grades. Therefore, it would be appropriate for us to use a directional hypothesis in place of the null hypothesis. Thus, a directional hypothesis might read that "level of intelligence is positively associated with higher school grades."

Beginning students of research methodology should not be confused by the use of a null versus directional hypothesis writing style. Both styles require a hypothesis statement that allows the researcher to provide data (or facts) which either confirm or negate the prediction. Thus, both styles accomplish the function of hypothesis testing. (See Tips 2.2.)

Tips for Consumers 2.2

The relationship between a theory of social behavior and the hypothesis is an important one. A good hypothesis:

1. clearly emerges from a logical association between two or more variables;
2. specifies whether an association is expected without a statement of cause-and-effect, or indicates which variable causes the other;
3. is unambiguously testable.

To assess the quality of a research report, a consumer should ask whether the hypothesis has met these three conditions. If it does not, the whole research study and its utility are jeopardized.

SUMMARY

This chapter is important both to those who wish to become scientists and to consumers of scientific literature. The research data gathered, the problems addressed, the theories developed, and the hypotheses tested are influenced by the philosophical underpinnings of the scientist and interventionist. The assumptions we share about beliefs in the nature of mankind direct our ethical judgments and research activities. Through published materials, conversations, and local, state, and national conventions, the interventionist and the scientist alike share beliefs through subtle communications, speeches, manuscripts, and conversations. As such, science is not devoid of philosophical issues.

In this chapter we have explored two primary arenas in which science and philosophy merge and intertwine in highly meaningful and complex ways.

Ethics

Ethical dilemmas abound in the world around us. There are ethical dilemmas in teaching, research, intervention, and even in simple everyday exchanges between individuals. In many ways, science begins with ethics. Codes of ethics direct the types of questions asked and the manner in which they are studied (answered). As consumers of research, we must recognize that certain research questions remain unanswered due to ethical dilemmas associated with providing an answer. We have all heard of the horror stories of Nazi Germany and human experimentation in concentration camps. In search of medical answers to hypotheses, unethical physicians mutilated and surgically experimented with human beings. Yet the answers were not worth the barbaric and inhumane treatment of people. We must, therefore, keep in mind that as we search the research literature for direction to our intervention programs, gaps may appear in what we know. Many gaps exist in our understanding of human behavior because the scientist is ethical and refrains from engaging in unethical conduct. From yet another perspective, many an ethical scientist finds herself or himself in ethically compromising situations. As Zimbardo experienced, safeguards were established, yet unforeseen events emerged. There are a great many situations in which guidelines are unclear. In later chapters we shall review the most common types of research methodology with some special issues associated with ethical conduct in social science research.

The major points reviewed in this chapter about ethics include the following:

1. Research codes of ethics have been prepared by several professional organizations and societies. Informed consent and rights to privacy guidelines are found in all of them.
2. Complicated ethical questions emerge in social science. For example, special precautions may be called for in using special research populations such as children, the aged, the poor, or the mentally ill.
3. Frequently, social scientists use financial incentives for participation. However, it is unclear whether this is interpreted as a bribe or payment for services rendered.

Frames of Reference

A future scientist should profit by coming to recognize that individual belief systems do influence the research process. In every undergraduate and graduate training program in home economics, child development, or family studies in North America, one or more frames of reference influence both the course work offered for students and the research activities engaged in by the faculty. In some programs one "school of thought" dominates, with almost no attention given to other perspectives. In other programs a variety of world views compete for attention and student-disciples. To establish a viable community of scholars, a program may even lose sight of its frame of reference and its limitations and strengths. Sometimes students may even feel they are experiencing an indoctrination process rather than a broad educational experience. It is, however, with no ill-intent that faculty proselytize their students into their belief system or frame of reference. Rather, it is with utmost conviction that faculty believe in their own frame of reference and present it to their students.

Students in research training might, however, be cautious about quickly internalizing the dominant, or exclusive, frame of reference of their training program. New frames of reference and modifications of existing world views are most likely to occur when young "disciples" challenge the existing framework. Advancement in science is likely to occur only if beginning students listen to, yet remain skeptical of, existing frames of reference.

Consumers of research should come to recognize that much of social and behavioral science is influenced by existing frames of reference. Sometimes these world views, or frames of reference, are sympathetic to contemporary social problems, sometimes not. While it might be maintained that all research has some implications for intervention or application, it is true that certain frames of reference and their corresponding theories may be more difficult than others to apply to real world application. Nonetheless, it is not uncommon to hear social science students say, "All they talk about around here is theory, but it doesn't fit real world problems." Perhaps professors hear this more frequently than they should because they don't teach our applied students that all of research is based on some belief system. And in social and behavioral science it is the belief about the real nature of mankind that influences our theory construction and hypothesis testing. Should students come to understand the basic elements of a theory's major frame of reference, they would more readily see the potential application of individual research studies for intervention or prevention programs.

In this chapter, we have examined several of the major interrelationships between frames of reference, theories, hypothesis testing, and the research process. Social science does not occur in a vacuum. It is a social activity influenced by society at large. Contrary to frequently observed statements which indicate there is no room for "belief" in the scientific process, social and behavioral science begins with a philosophically based belief system.

To summarize, some of the major points that have been presented about this subject include the following:

1. Frames of reference or world views, as philosophical abstractions based on belief, influence the research process in multiple ways. World views have influences on the types of problems explored, acceptable criteria for truth, theory construction, and hypothesis testing.

2. Frames of reference, more specifically, are world views or belief systems about the nature of man's fundamental characteristics.

3. Scientists' frames of reference do not evolve of their own volition. Rather, they are the product of cultural and socio-historical events (e.g., economic and political influences). Hence, science is not free from the events occurring around it.

4. While frames of reference give birth to theories, hypotheses are the workhorses of theory.

    a. A theory is a set of interrelated propositions about two or more phenomena, variables, events, or objects.

    b. A hypothesis is a testable, operationalized statement about an associative or cause-and-effect relationship.

5. It is proposed that several criteria can be used to evaluate the utility of a specific theory. These criteria include deployability, scope, and precision.

    a. Deployability refers to the pragmatic utility of the theory in describing behaviors across a wide range of settings.

    b. Scope refers to the range of variables to which the theory is applicable.

    c. Precision deals with the accuracy in the application of rules of inferences provided by the frame of reference from which the theory is derived.

PROBLEMS AND APPLICATIONS

1. Put together from the students enrolled in your class several six-member Research Ethics Committees. Pick several articles at random from such journals as *Public Opinion Quarterly, Home Economics Research Journal, Child Development, Journal of Personality and Social Psychology, American Sociological Review, American Educational Research Journal,* or *Journal of Youth and Adolescence.* Have several committees pass judgment on ethical considerations for the same articles. Have each committee state the group opinion and justify its rationale. What philosophical principles guide each committee decision? How do the various committees differ?

2. In your own social science discipline can you identify a frame of reference other than those outlined in the text that guide hypothesis testing? Compare this frame of reference with those outlined in this chapter. How are they similar? How are they different?

3. Pick a theory from your own discipline, specify the main tenets of the theory, and criticize or evaluate the quality of that theory.

4. Select a theory, analyze the process it describes, and delineate the social mechanism that influences this process. As a class practice develop testable hypotheses regarding cause-and-effect associations from the theory.

REFERENCES

American Academy of Pediatrics Committee on Drugs (1977). Guidelines for the ethical conduct of studies to evaluate drugs in pediatric populations. *Pediatrics, 60,* 1–10.

American Anthropological Association (1983). *Professional ethics.* Washington, D.C.: American Anthropological Association.

American Anthropological Association (1973). *Professional ethics: Statements and procedures of the American Anthropological Association.* Washington, D.C.: American Anthropological Association.

American Psychological Association (1987). *Casebook on ethical principles of psychologists.* Washington, D.C.: American Psychological Association.

American Psychological Association (1973). *Ethical principles in the conduct of research with human participants.* Washington, D.C.: American Psychological Association.

American Psychological Association (1981). Ethical principles of psychologists. *American Psychologist, 36*: 633–638.

American Sociological Association. (1984). *Code of ethics.* Washington, D.C.: American Sociological Association.

American Sociological Association. (1968). Toward a code of ethics for sociologists. *American Sociologist, 3,* 316–318.

Bond, K. (1978). Confidentiality and the protection of human subjects in social science research: A report on recent developments. *American Sociologist, 14,* 144–152.

Bower, R. T., & Gasparis, P. (1978). *Ethics in social research.* New York: Praeger.

Carroll, J. D., & Knerr, C. R. (1977). Written statement prepared for submission to the Privacy Protection Study Commission, Public Hearing, January 5th and 6th, 1977, U.S. Senate, Washington, D.C.

Committee on Ethics in Research with Children. (1977). Ethical standards for research with children: Society for research in child development. Cited in DHEW Publication No. (05) 77-004. *Report and recommendations: Research involving children.* Washington, D.C.: U.S. Printing Office.

Department of Health, Education and Welfare, National Institutes of Health. (1973). Protection of human subjects: Policies and procedures. *Federal Register, 38,* 31, 738–749.

Duster, T., Matza, D., & Wellman, D. (1979). Fieldwork and the protection of human subjects. *American Sociologist, 14,* 136–142.

Eckberg, D. L., & Hill, L. (1979). The paradigm concept and sociology: A critical review. *American Sociological Review, 44,* 925–937.

English, H. B., & English, A. C. (1958). *A comprehensive dictionary of psychological and psychoanalytical terms.* New York: David McKay.

Executive Office of the President, Office of Science and Technology. (1967). *Privacy and behavior research.* Summarized in *American Psychologist, 22,* 345–349.

Farr, J., & Seaver, B. (1975). Stress and discomfort in psychological research: Subject perceptions of experimental procedures. *American Psychologist, 30,* 770–773.

Fowler, F. J., Jr. (1984). *Survey research methods.* Beverly Hills: Sage.

Koocher, G. P. (1983). Ethical and professional standards in psychology. In B.D. Sales (Ed.), *The professional psychologist's handbook.* New York: Plenum, pp. 77–109.

Kuhn, T. S. (1962). *The structure of scientific revolutions.* Chicago: University of Chicago Press.

National Commission for the Protection of Human Subjects of Biomedical and Behavior Research. (1977). *Report and recommendations: Research involving children,* DHEW Publication No. (05) 77-004. Washington, D.C.: U.S. Printing Office.

Overton, W. F., & Reese, W. H. (1973). Models of development: Methodological implications. In J. R. Nesselroade & H. W. Reese (Eds.), *Life-span developmental psychology: Methodological issues.* New York: Academic Press.

Pepper, S. C. (1942). *World hypotheses.* Berkeley: University of California Press.

Privacy Protection Study Commission. (1976, December). *Notice of hearings and draft recommendations: Research and statistics.*

Ritterman, M. K. (1977). Paradigmatic classification of family therapy theories. *Family Process, 16,* 29–48.

Ritzer, G. (1975). Sociology: A multiple paradigm science. *American Sociologist, 10,* 156–167.

Savin, H. B. (1973). Professors and psychological researchers: Conflicting values to conflicting roles. *Cognition, 2,* 147–149.

Smith, M. B. (1976). Some perspectives on ethical/political issues in social science research. *Personality and Social Psychology Bulletin, 2,* 445–453.

Society for Research in Child Development. (1990, Winter). SRCD Ethical standards for research with children. *SRCD Newsletter,* 5–7.

Toulmin, S. (1962). *The philosophy of science.* London: Hutchinson University Library.

Zimbardo, P. G. (1973). On the ethics of human intervention in human psychological research: With special reference to the Stanford prison experiment. *Cognition, 2,* 243–256.

Zimbardo, R. G., Haney, C., Banks, W. C., & Jaffe, D. (1973, April 8). The mind is a formidable jailer: A Pirandellian prison. *New York Times Magazine,* pp. 38–60.

CHAPTER 3

Reviewing the Literature

OUTLINE

Introduction
Goals to Achieve
Doing the Review
  Steps in a Literature Search
Review Sources
  Abstracts
  Indexes
  Computer Retrieval Systems
Three Illustrations
Summary
Problems and Applications
References

KEY TERMS

Abstracts
Bibliography
Card catalog
Indexes
Literature
Note taking

Primary sources
Reference sources
Replication
Retrieval systems
Secondary sources

STUDY GUIDE QUESTIONS

1. Why is it necessary to conduct a review of literature in doing quality scientific work?
2. Identify the main ways that one can relate and integrate a specific research project with previous research.
3. What are the main characteristics and functions of indexes in doing research?
4. What are the main characteristics and functions of abstracts in doing research?
5. If notes are to be optimally useful, what are three or four main factors that should guide the researcher in taking notes?
6. If a review of literature indicates that work has already been completed on your proposed research plan should you abandon the project? Why or why not?

Role of the Scientist

It is critical for a scientist to know in what areas other researchers have worked and the nature of their work. The identification of problems, refinement of ideas, specification of research procedures, measurement clarity, and understanding of results can all be facilitated by comprehensive review of previous work. It is not enough to test your own ideas; you must be able to assess your ideas in the context of others and to replicate, extend, or modify them in terms of establishing thinking. The resources for reviewing the literature—indexes, abstracts, reference works, journals, and rapidly changing retrieval systems—are essential to the scientist. Knowing how to use them constitutes a vital phase in completing high quality research.

Role of the Consumer

A consumer can determine whether a given purchase was a "good buy" only if he or she knows the types of goods for sale and the price range on each. Likewise, a competent consumer of research needs to know the range of work on the topic being studied, not just a specific report. The literature review is a key tool in telling the consumer what is new, important, believable, and useful. The scientist must be able to conduct a literature review to complete a project, whereas the literature review is important to the consumer in order to assess, understand, and form conclusions about the work being presented.

INTRODUCTION

Reviewing the literature—Is this a redundant chore or a necessary step? An ordeal to be endured or a fulfilling learning experience? What has been your experience in doing a review of the literature? Most of us have done a variety of literature reviews—the freshman English paper, a book review, or a review in some specialty. A review of the literature should be just that—a review. In the field of scholarly publications, there are over 65 languages, 200 countries represented, and 100,000 journals published and available for a review. Several years of intensive reading are produced every 24 hours. In the United States alone, there are over 2,000 fiction titles published yearly and over 18,000 nonfiction titles published. With such rapid and massive data accumulations, we need literature reviews and skillful ways of extracting key ideas from these masses of literature.

A review of literature for a research project serves essentially the same purpose as a road map and travel plan for a journey. Both provide a base of information on which to carry out the respective endeavors. And just as the unexpected emerges in travel plans, the unanticipated develops in a review of the literature. But what shall we call or designate as the literature? As viewed in this chapter, literature is all information in printed or oral form that is available on your topic of research interest. At once the need for refinement and reduction occurs. One cannot possibly cover all the literature on broad topics; and as we shall illustrate, there is little need to attempt such a feat.

The purpose of research is discovery and explanation, and we shall argue that either purpose is frustrated if the researcher is not sufficiently attuned to observe, evaluate, and make decisions. Boyd (1961) notes that Moses G. Farmer, an inventor, was so upset after reading the first description of Bell's telephone that he was sleepless for a week. He engaged in self-criticism since he believed he should have made the discovery—it had almost emerged in shadowy form a dozen times but he never formulated his findings. We believe that a review of literature can help in organizing thoughts, giving shape to "shadowy ideas," and achieving new insights. Previous literature is important for taking perspective, for documenting the status of an issue, and for justifying or motivating additional investigation. While previous work can be instructive, it should not be seen as the ultimate or final word, as Whitehead (1961) cautions:

> A science which hesitates to forget its founders is lost. It is characteristic of science in its earlier stages...to be both ambitiously profound in its aims and trivial in its handling of details.
>
>   But to come very near to a true theory, and to grasp its precise application, are two very different things, as the history of science teaches us. Everything of importance has been said before by somebody who did not discover it. (p. 3)

GOALS TO ACHIEVE

 The main goal to achieve in the literature review is developing a knowledge and understanding of the previous work or activity in regard to the topic being researched. The literature review also addresses the important need to inform the investigator as to the main findings, trends, areas of debate or controversy, areas of neglect, and suggestions for additional research.

The literature review is also a necessary step in the research process and helps identify important research ideas as well as refine possible hypotheses. Most of us obtain new insights, ideas, and leads by observing human behavior, talking with others, and critically reading what others have written. Literature is perhaps the key domain for identification and refinement because published material has been explicitly prepared for that purpose. It is the one domain whose existence depends on sharing, criticism, expression, and replication. The crucial question looms: How can we test or replicate if we are unfamiliar with what others have done on a host of ideas?

A good review of literature is an investment in economy. Many investigators have scrapped initial ideas by investing in a good review. Why? Because a careful review permits one to determine if the ideas are worth the commitment, the investment, or the trouble. It illuminates the merit of a research problem by showing what others have done, what they have found, and the procedures for carrying out the work. Our new insight turns out to be a rather old idea many times. In other situations the review permits us to channel or refocus our research commitment.

In many cases, perhaps the great majority, the review of literature gives us additional insight and decision tools for doing research. Nominal (a label or name) as well as operational (tells how a variable or verbal concept will be measured) definitions take on additional clarity and sharpness. A literature review enables one to perceive the state of the art regarding a particular problem. We receive exposure to procedures used by others, including sampling designs. One of the critical payoffs in reviewing the literature is the building of hypotheses. We may start off with a hunch in reviewing the literature; we end up with a hypothesis. We sometimes start off with a hypothesis (a proposed tentative statement of relationship) and derive propositions (often used interchangeably with hypothesis, but sometimes a proposition is meant to assert more support for a relationship than a hypothesis). Finally, we enter the area of concern with propositions, and through careful review, reworking, and synthesis we may end with theory.

How can one replicate without review of previous work? Research should be conducted so that others may repeat the same procedure and obtain the same results—*replication*. If we accept the axiom that the scientific method requires careful replication, then we have no choice but to study the work of others carefully. When method, operation, and purpose are carefully spelled out in a well-written research study, we have the necessary information needed for replication. One reason for so little replication in social science research is the lack of carefully integrated literature reviews. Additionally, new instruments are continually developed with little evidence of reliability and validity because researchers do not take advantage of instruments already available and many times carefully described in existing literature. The wheel is continually rediscovered as each investigator plunges out into the lonely desert of empiricism as opposed to marching in formation with those who have already left useful research signposts.

We must mention one other important idea about hypotheses and theory. If hypotheses emerge from the literature review and theoretical reworking, a strong argument can be made for construct validity (validity based on testing a theory, typically a new measure compared to an already existing one) and integration of theory. If the hunches and hypotheses are isolated, fragmented, and lacking in scope, then we have little basis for relating our work with that of others. If this is the case, the subsequent report is likely to be buried in the academic heap even if it is published.

A basic way of relating research with that of others is through a literature review that builds and weaves in with other research. The review of literature helps to assure that the newly generated results will be fitted and cemented into the "wall of knowledge and theory." A thorough review helps to determine the direction of additional research on the topic, provides specifics for measurement considerations, and helps to assure that the research focuses on the main objectives or purposes of the study. Without this integrative feature in research study, the likelihood of the study being an isolated piece of work is high. If this happens, then the new "brick of data" is unlikely to be integrated into the "wall of knowledge."

DOING THE REVIEW

Assuming that one has completed the preliminary reading program that helped identify the problem, we now pursue the critical review of research related to our area of focus. Availability and access to library resources are assumed as we cover the remaining sections of this chapter. Creative and dedicated minds can work out the questions in design or raise critical concerns, but nothing substitutes for appropriate sources when the goal is to pursue and understand what others have written. There are many valuable sources for additional reading on using the library and reviewing the literature such as that by Bart and Frankel (1981).

There are many legitimate places to start in a review of literature, but we believe that perhaps the best strategy is to talk with professors or colleagues who have done work in the area. Obtain the benefit of their knowledge about sources and use this as a base to start the more intensive library research.

It is important to know the library in which you will work. Arrange for a tour and become familiar with services, holdings, and policies. Enrolling in a class in library science may be very useful to the beginning student. We also invite the student to make friends with librarians, tell them about your project and what you hope to achieve. Typically, they will be interested in your project and will enjoy your sharing your work with them.

Once in the library, the *card catalog* (in many libraries it is now a film catalog) is the logical place to start. The card catalog is to a library what an index is to a book—it is an essential tool to inform you about the holdings of the library and where the books are located. With the exception of documents, reference materials, and periodicals, the card catalog is a functional index to the library. Most libraries have the cards set up by both author and subject matter and one can start the literature search with either. These cards are particularly helpful in locating a text on your topic as well as providing some idea of what the library holds relating to the topic.

It is likely that the card catalog and other traditional procedures for workings in a library and completing a literature search will undergo very significant changes in the future. New indexes, abstracts, and better filing systems have been common in the twentieth century, but it will be retrieval systems and other computer aids that will greatly alter the skills needed in functioning as either a researcher or consumer of research in the library setting.

Search for citations according to subject matter, authors, and key words. These help to identify both primary and secondary sources. A *primary source* is an original piece of work on the topic. One is likely to identify published research reports, symposium collections, monographs, and other types of primary sources. These can be extremely useful in the initial stages. A central monograph illustrates someone's review of literature, research design, findings, and a good list of references.

A *secondary source* refers to other work indirectly. Instead of reading a book or article, it is reading an article or a book about the works. Textbooks, handbooks, reviews of literature, encyclopedias, and a variety of other sources would be classified as secondary. Secondary sources are very useful to obtain a broad overview of the topic. A text will typically contain a good review of work on a given topic—say intermarriage. Reading such a chapter gives one the basic ideas, research concerns, and exposure to problems while researching the topic. The secondary source is useful in identifying the key references—it is a simple task to locate the primary sources at this point. While secondary sources are useful, there are some attending problems. One can never be quite sure that the text writer or reviewer was accurately reflecting the material from the original source. A review or synthesis can be slanted, biased, or very abbreviated. To assure coverage as needed, to check out distortion and biases, and to become familiar with firsthand reports, the researcher should generally make it a practice to work out of primary sources.

To summarize, a review of literature helps one select and develop a research topic. A literature review also enables one to build on and add to the work of others—it helps to assure that the project will be integrated with previous work. Sometimes one does a review of literature hoping to prove the originality of the proposed topic (and this may actually be the case on a very few topics), but it is more important to integrate than it is to isolate a topic as the net result of searching the literature.

A carefully completed review of literature is bound to be instructive to the reader in terms of evaluating methods, procedures, and data analyses. Thus, one certainly needs to be aware of what was found, but how it was found may be of equal importance.

After vast reading and extensive note taking, the materials must be organized into a meaningful review of literature. One should avoid the temptation to merely list the author's name and year and then proceed through all of the references ending up with an author-by-author account of what was read. Organize the notes and write the literature review with a goal in mind, typically treating the major topics first and then moving on to second or third order treatment. One should always tell the reader how the review is organized and give instructions on how it should be read.

The ultimate use of the completed review of literature is to arrive at the point where one can say, "I am at the cutting edge of this topic." You have read, reviewed, synthesized, and built into and on all previous relevant work. You have reached the frontier of knowledge on your topic—now you can forge onward into unknown and unexplored questions.

Steps in a Literature Search

With common access to copy machines and computer search hard copy printouts, the process of note taking has greatly changed. On some projects it is common for a researcher to merely make a copy of the key articles, underline key parts, make margin notes, and then write a first draft directly from the copies. Most researchers will still find it productive to take selective notes. We realize that there are many proven methods for note taking and if you or your department have a method that is accepted or required, by all means use it. We have found from our own work and working with students that the following approach is very helpful for most projects and present it as a good system.

Step One.   Step one is to have the topic clearly focused. We also assume that you have talked with professors, friends, and other colleagues who might offer valuable suggestions on the topic refinement.

Step Two.   With a clearly focused problem or topic, it is time to move to Step two in the review process. We see Step two as gaining an understanding of the layout of the library if this is not already known. Essential parts of this step include knowing the location of the card catalog, the reference section, and the various subject matter distribution by floor or area. It is also important to visit with a librarian in this stage and obtain an orientation of the library.

Step Three.   Step three is the reference search. With the background and orientation on the topic it is usually best to start in the card catalog section and search under topical categories. Take the necessary efforts to assure that call numbers are complete and accurate, that titles and author names are sufficient for this stage, and that you are thorough in your search. Step three, reference acquisition, can then move to abstracts, indexes, and other useful reference sources available in the library. The computer-assisted search is also a vital means of locating useful references on the identified topic. As sources are identified, Step three can be extended by assessing the references at the end of each article. Review articles are especially helpful at this stage of the literature search. The literature review continues with literature identification and location until one is reasonably certain that all useful references have been identified and the materials have been located.

Step Four.   Step four involves the reading of the now identified sources and note taking. We recommend a quick reading of the abstract and summary to determine the utility of the article for the review. If these indicate that the article really fits the topic, then a more detailed reading can follow. It is now time for note taking. Since few of us are capable of recalling all that we read, it is important to use a note-taking procedure to help us remember and organize ideas from our reading that we will want to use in writing a final review of literature. We recommend that these be made on note cards of a size that is convenient for you. The advantage of note cards is that they are more durable, can be easily shuffled, and can be bound together or placed in a note file. If you have numbered your reference cards, then you can readily transfer the number to the note card and the complete reference need not be written again.

We have found that it is most efficient to take notes in an abstracted form rather than to attempt to record the complete narrative. Recording the key ideas in your own words avoids the problem of messy or garbled quotes. Furthermore, this procedure forces the note taker to be more selective and to focus on the topic rather than wildly recording material that will not be used later. Additionally, have firmly in mind why you want to remember or use the materials you have read before the note taking begins. This means that the article will have to be carefully read before note taking begins and this leads to better notes as well as to a more accurate understanding of the article. As a general rule, read and take notes on current literature first and then move, if necessary, to the older material.

A full and accurate reference is the first thing of importance to put on your note card. Notes should be written in a style you can use now, and possibly sometime later, in writing the review of literature. Legibility, accuracy, and clarity are all needed in developing good note cards. Spending the time as you go along for documentation and detail is a good investment. Many students and seasoned researchers have spent hours or even days attempting to run down a reference to something they have used or to clarify a garbled quotation.

A good supply of cards and pencils constitutes the essential tools for note taking. Complete and accurate references can be greatly facilitated by using a standard form containing the subject area, complete reference, and a note stating where the references were obtained (abstract, index, card catalog, etc.), as shown in Figure 3.1.

Cards prepared as in Figure 3.1 can be manipulated as necessary according to subject area, title, and author, and the results are well worth the time involved in preparation. This type of card is a permanent statement of what you have, where it can be found, and constitutes the information necessary for making up a reference list when the report is completed. Numbering note cards to correspond to a number on the reference cards may also prove useful.

While taking notes, it is to your advantage to summarize in your own words as this will force you to understand what the author is presenting, will encourage you to be more selective, and will avoid the problem of quoting the author when no quote is needed or intended.

Most of us are in a hurry when we take notes and we offer this advice and caution to the student. First of all, if the article is a key one, is detailed, or especially if it has many charts or tables, make a copy. This will save time and reduce mistakes in taking notes on this type of material. The copy machine has greatly influenced note taking and traditional searching procedures, and there is really no need to take notes on selected materials when for 25¢ one can have the complete copy on which to work. Secondly, do not take notes with the plan of recopying them later; this only takes more time. Take them accurately and legibly the first time around. Keep in mind that notes are not the final product; they are merely a means to an end—to help complete a useful and defensible review of literature.

Step Five.   Step five involves the process of reading, reviewing, and shuffling the note cards until both the order and content are in sufficiently good form to start the first draft of the paper. A double check of reference cards and note cards to assure that the numbers are correct and both piles are arranged the same way should permit you to start writing. Here is where cards or separate sheets of paper really facilitate the writing of the first

```
Subject

        Author. "Title." The periodical, Volume (no.);
        pages, date.

                                    Source of reference
```

Figure 3.1. Card Format for References

draft. One can shuffle, arrange, delete, and lay out materials to see a semi-finished product very quickly and in many possible styles.

Step Six.   Step six includes writing the first draft. Most writers need to go through at least one draft before they go to a final copy, so we encourage reviewers to get a reasonably good draft completed as soon as possible. It is often a foolish temptation to shuffle endlessly, to delay, and unduly avoid the final step of completing a draft. When the first draft is completed it is useful to "get away" from it for awhile before starting to edit and polish the article.

Step Seven.   Step seven involves the final preparation of the manuscript along with an accurate reference list. One should correlate between citations in the body of the paper and the reference list to assure that all references cited in the body are in the list. Use of appropriate headings, citations, and format style are important throughout the whole review process. They *must* be carefully checked at this point. One should prepare the paper for the requirements of the methods class or for the department or the society for which you may be completing the paper. Most of the social sciences now use some variation of the American Psychological Association style (APA).

The review of literature is now complete. If the paper was a review paper the task is completed. If one is doing primary research, one is now prepared to begin the next steps in the research process. (See Tips 3.1.)

Tips for Consumers 3.1

The research scientist needs to review the relevant literature in order to integrate, replicate, and expand scientific knowledge on a specific project. Consumers of research also need to understand and know how to execute a review of literature in order to make competent decisions as well as to have a more complete understanding concerning competing points of view. Consumers should be prepared to execute the following activities in regard to a review of literature:

1. Read and critically evaluate a literature review completed by another reviewer.
2. Complete and prepare a review of literature that would be useful to other researchers and consumers.
3. Be able to use a literature review to inform, persuade, and educate both yourself and others.

While the consumer of research may not ever complete a major research project, it is very likely that consumers of the computer-based, decision-oriented society of the future will have to know how to use the basic resources in a library, including computer search facilities. In short, consumers of research may not have to assume the responsibility of conducting research, but they must be prepared to read, critically evaluate, and synthesize the work of others. *Purposeful reading, assessment,* and *synthesis* constitute the three core elements of dealing with literature review that impact on the consumer in society.

REVIEW SOURCES

A great variety of journals and periodicals contain the best up-to-date treatment of scientific areas. A periodical is a publication issued at regular intervals (e.g., four times per year), covers a specific discipline or sub-area, and will continue to be published for an indefinite time. Most fields have several journals, reviews, yearbooks, or magazines. The social sciences have thousands of these periodicals, and keeping up with knowledge or even finding what you need to find would be next to impossible if it were not for two very valuable helps—*indexes* and *abstracts*.

We devote detailed attention in this chapter to indexes and abstracts because we believe they are the most important and heavily used sources in doing a review of literature. Indexes and abstracts represent for the periodicals what the card catalog does for the library. Most *indexes* list articles alphabetically under subject, title, and author headings, and of course, provide the source of the individual article. Indexes provide direction for use, a list of periodicals indexed, the time period covered, and a guide for any abbreviation used. Both researchers and consumers will find indexes helpful in locating all relevant information according to key words by using selected indexes.

Abstracts represent capsule reports or summaries of articles published in a given journal. Abstracts can quickly provide the reader with three very important helps in completing a review of literature. First of all, abstracts provide a summary of what was found or what is known as a result of a specific published article. Second, the abstract provides the reader with a full reference and other methodological information about a study. Finally, with this summary and reference in hand, the reader can make a judgment as to whether he or she needs to locate and read the full article in its original state. In many studies, the abstract will provide all the basic information needed on the area being covered. In other cases, however, the abstract may dictate that the original article is a very valuable resource for the project and must be carefully read completely. It is a simple matter after having identified the article and reference in the abstract form to go directly to the journal in which it was published and review the study in as much detail as desired.

We recommend that one initially talk with others who are knowledgeable about sources and then do basic work in the card catalog. We will now treat in sequence some of the other major sources for a review of literature. We will cover abstracts, indexes, retrieval systems, and specific volumes on instruments and subject identification.

Our selection of abstracts and indexes is based on the mission of this text, to provide a sense of understanding for both researchers and consumers of research in a variety of social science disciplines. Students in these disciplines will find useful abstracts and indexes in the following section. Become familiar with these sources and use them on a regular basis as you complete assignments for this class as well as other projects. We recommend that you review all of the sources in a general way so as to know the wide range of sources available for reviewing research and finding key sources in the social and behavioral sciences. In addition to this general assessment, we invite you to focus on those abstracts and indexes central to your discipline or area of interest. Finally, this extensive section on abstracts and indexes is included as a resource which you should find useful in your professional career, but we assume that great flexibility will be employed in how students both review and use the sources included.

Abstracts

Abstracts represent summary statements of expanded reports and are typically arranged according to author and subject matter. They provide the reader with a reference and the basic report or findings.

Abstracts in Anthropology.   This abstract is issued quarterly and starts with Volume 1 in 1970. Abstracts are grouped in four sections: Archaeology, Ethnology, Linguistics, and Physical Anthropology. Beginning with Volume 1, Number 4, both author and subject indexes are included. This abstract also provides an annual cumulative author and subject index.

Abstracts on Criminology and Penology.   This abstract is international in scope and covers material related to the causes of crime and juvenile delinquency, the control and treatment of offenders, criminal procedure, and the administration of justice. It started in 1961 and was originally known as *Excerpta Criminologica*. It is published in the Netherlands.

Abstracts of Health Care Management Studies.   This abstract has been published quarterly since 1965. The broad coverage focuses on studies of management, planning, and public policy related to the delivery of health care.

Criminal Justice Abstracts.   This series contains detailed abstracts of current world-wide literature and a comprehensive review of material related to criminal justice. It is published by the National Council on Crime and Delinquency and started in 1968.

Social Work Research and Abstracts.   This series started in 1965 and offers abstracts of both original research papers and articles in social work and related fields. Problems faced by social workers, social work researchers, and analytical reviews of research are presented. It has an annual cumulative index and is arranged according to author and subject heads. This abstract was previously known as *Abstracts for Social Workers*. The *Biological Abstracts* series was started in 1927 and covers the world's biosciences research. It has an author, concept, generic, subject, and biosystematic index and covers topics ranging in scope from aerospace and underwater biological effects to virology. Volume 1 of the *Child Development Abstracts and Bibliography* series was published in June 1927, and it is one of three publications of the Society for Research in Child Development. The topics abstracted are arranged according to main categories, and an author as well as a subject index is printed with each issue. Fifty to sixty journals are reflected in a typical issue. This abstract arranges materials around five areas:

1.   Biology, health
2.   Cognition, learning, perception
3.   Social psychological, cultural, and personality studies
4.   Educational process
5.   Psychiatry, clinical psychology

Crime and Delinquency Abstracts.   This abstract is published by the National Clearing-house for Mental Health Information by the National Institute of Mental Health. It contains coverage on current published scientific and professional literature and ongoing research projects. It was formerly entitled *International Bibliography on Crime and Delinquency,* going back to Volume 1 in 1964.

Developmental Disabilities Abstracts.   This abstract was originally entitled *Mental Retardation Abstracts* and started in 1965. The author and subject index leads to coverage arranged on medical, developmental, treatment and training, programmatic, family, and personnel aspects.

Dissertation Abstracts International.   Previously known as *Dissertation Abstracts,* it changed titles to "reflect the enlargement of University Microfilms International's dissertation publication program to include dissertations from European universities." It is published monthly—gathering data from more than 375 cooperating institutions in the United States, Canada, and Europe. All dissertations published by University Microfilms International are abstracted in *Dissertation Abstracts International, Dissertation Abstracts International* is divided into two sections: (A) Humanities and (B) Sciences. Starting with Volume 27, Number 1, the A and B sections are paginated separately and may be identified by the letters A or B following the page numbers. Beginning with Volume 36, Number 1, Humanities (A) is categorized into five main headings:

  IA.   Communications and the arts
  IIA. Education
  IIIA. Language, literature and linguistics
  IVA. Philosophy, religion and theology
  VA.   Social sciences

The Sciences (B) are also categorized:

  IB.   Biological sciences
  IIB. Earth sciences
  IIIB. Health and environmental sciences
  IVB. Physical sciences (pure and applied)
  VB.   Psychology

Beginning with Volume 30, Number 1, *Dissertation Abstracts International* contains a **Key Word** title index, and bibliographical entries are classified and arranged alphabetically by important key words contained in the title. An author index is also published in each issue of Sections A and B and is cumulated annually. An entire study can be purchased from University Microfilms on either microfilm or xerox. A very significant fact about *Dissertation Abstracts International* is that it makes a statement in printed form about all doctoral research in progress; of course, not all dissertations are eventually published.

Environmental Abstracts.   This abstract started publication in 1971. It has a subject index with accession numbers and covers all aspects of environmental affairs from air pollution to wildlife protection. The series covers both published and nonprinted materials (radio and television programming, films, and filmstrips). Major conference proceedings, newspaper stories, and significant environmental entries from the *Federal Register* are included. A classified main entry section provides a complete citation with abstract. A calendar of conferences is included in each issue. Literature searches from the computerized data base are available on inquiry.

Exceptional Child Education Abstracts.   This series started with Volume 1 in 1969–1970 and is published by the Council for Exceptional Children. It contains an author, title, and subject index. Materials covered are relevant for instruction, teacher education, administration, methods, and curricula in exceptional child education.

Food Science and Technology Abstracts.   This series is divided into 19 sections ranging from basic foods to standards, laws, and regulations. Within each section the abstracts are in random order with a subject index. The series started in 1969.

Gerontological Abstracts.   This reference tool, started in 1976, is published six times a year at Ann Arbor, Michigan. It is world oriented in scope and is useful to all who seek to understand, plan, or deliver services to the elderly.

Historical Abstracts.   From Volume 1, started in 1955, to date, this series represents a bibliography of the world's periodical literature. Part A covers Modern History, 1450–1914, and Part B covers Twentieth Century Abstracts, 1914 to the present. Abstracts focusing on United States and Canadian history are found in the section, American: History and Life. This abstract has an author and subject index in each issue and is published four times per year.

Home Economics Research Abstracts.   This series is published by the American Home Economics Association and is limited to master's theses and doctoral dissertations completed in a calendar year in various schools of Home Economics and related fields. The areas are indexed according to these categories:

1.   Family relations and child development
2.   Family economics and home management
3.   Institutional administration
4.   Textiles and clothing
5.   Art, housing, furnishings, and equipment
6.   Home economics communications and home economics education
7.   Food and nutrition

It contains a fairly detailed summary of the research and the abstracts are collected on a voluntary basis by the National Association Office.

Hospital Abstracts. This monthly issue, started in 1961, provides an overview of the world literature in relationship to hospitals and administration of hospitals. It is published by the Department of Health and Social Security in London.

Human Resources Abstracts. This source is published with the cooperation of the Institute of Labor and Industrial Relations and was formerly entitled *Poverty and Human Resources Abstracts.* It has an international scope and covers the following areas:

1. Unemployment and underemployment
2. Education and training
3. Vocations
4. Careers
5. Working conditions and job satisfaction
6. Affirmative action
7. Income distribution and living standards
8. Economic development
9. Migration and social change
10. Social service delivery
11. Housing

The utility of the index is facilitated by having an author and subject index within these categories.

Nutrition Abstracts and Reviews. This abstract started with Volume 1 in 1931, and is a quarterly with an annual, cumulated, combined table of contents, and author–subject indexes. It is issued under the direction of the Commonwealth Agricultural Bureau Council, the Medical Research Council, and the Rowett Research Institute. Titles are given in the original language with English translations.

Psychological Abstracts. The publishers of this abstract series report that it is a nonevaluative summary of the world's literature in psychology and the related fields. It was first published in 1927 and now abstracts over 850 journals, technical reports, monographs, and other scientific documents. Each abstract is about 30–50 words in length, and the abstract is published monthly. The abstracts are categorized under 16 major classifications and are arranged alphabetically by first author in each section. The entries are numbered consecutively in the two volumes produced each year. Each issue has an author and subject index and a three-year cumulative index is also available. The use of key words in *Psychological Abstracts* began in 1967 on a machine readable tape that provides the basis for automated search and retrieval services known as Psychological Abstracts Information Services (PsyclNF). The sixteen areas that are covered are:

1. General psychology
2. Psychometrics
3. Experimental psychology (human)
4. Experimental psychology (animal)

5. Physiological psychology
6. Physiological intervention
7. Communication systems
8. Developmental psychology
9. Social programs and social issues
10. Experimental social psychology
11. Personality
12. Physical and psychological disorders
13. Treatment and prevention
14. Professional personnel and professional issues
15. Educational psychology
16. Applied psychology

Research Relating to Children.   This abstract comes under one of the twenty clearing-houses of the Education Resources Information Center (ERIC), is published out of Washington, D.C., and was started in 1948. It includes reports of research in progress or recently completed research on the following:

1. Bibliography (The March 1976–August 1976 issue [No. 37] featured an extensive bibliography on child abuse and neglect.)
2. Long-term research
3. Growth and development
4. Special groups of children
5. The child in the family
6. Socioeconomic and cultural factors
7. Educational factors and services
8. Social services
9. Health services

Sage Family Studies Abstracts.   This abstract started in 1979 and contains an excellent cross-index to some 250 abstracts in each issue. It is published four times per year and covers books, articles, pamphlets, government publications, significant speeches, and legislative research reports.

Sage Race Relations Abstracts.   This series is published on the behalf of the Institute of Race Relations and dates from 1975. It covers all aspects of race relations, is scholarly in content, and represents perhaps the best source for materials about race relations. It is intended to be useful for both observers and participants, and the coverage includes materials of European, Scandinavian, American, and Latin American origin.

Sage Urban Studies Abstracts.   Each issue contains about 250 separate abstracts of books, articles, government publications, speeches, and other materials relevant in understanding the broad area of urban studies. This abstract service started in 1973.

Sociological Abstracts.   These abstracts are published by the American Sociological Association, the Eastern Sociological Society, the International Sociological Association, and the Midwest Sociological Society. Five issues per year are published, and each has an author and subject index. A total accumulative index was published in 1978. All abstracts are presented under one of the following 29 categories:

1.   Methodology and research technology
2.   Sociology: History and theory
3.   Social psychology
4.   Group interaction
5.   Culture and social structure
6.   Complex organization
7.   Social change and economic development
8.   Mass phenomena
9.   Political interaction
10.   Social differentiation
11.   Rural sociology and agricultural economics
12.   Urban structures and ecology
13.   Sociology of the arts
14.   Sociology of education
15.   Sociology of religion
16.   Social control
17.   Sociology of science
18.   Demography and human biology
19.   The family and socialization
20.   Sociology of health and medicine
21.   Social problems and social welfare
22.   Sociology of knowledge
23.   Community development
24.   Policy, planning, forecasting, and speculation
25.   Radical sociology
26.   Environmental interactions
27.   Studies in poverty
28.   Studies in violence
29.   Feminist studies

Women's Studies Abstracts.   This quarterly started in 1972 and reflects the range of concerns written about in academic programs and the research focused on the women's movement. Coverage is understandably broad, ranging from women and advertising to femininity, property laws, and women as scientists.

World Agriculture Economics and Rural Sociology Abstracts.   This abstract is prepared by the Commonwealth Bureau of Agricultural Economics and has both an author and subject index. The series covers such topics as agricultural policy, rural life, and the farm family. The abstract started with Volume 1 in 1959.

World Textile Abstracts.   This publication is prepared by the Textile Research Associations and abstracts material published in the technical and scientific literature of the whole world. Areas covered are:

1. Fibers
2. Yarns
3. Fabrics
4. Chemicals and processes
5. Clothing and made-up goods
6. Mill engineering
7. Management, analysis testing, quality control
8. Polymer science

The abstract has subject, author, number, and annual indexes.

Indexes

Indexes constitute a fruitful and comprehensive source for reviewing the literature. Several of the central ones to the study of social processes and human behavior have been included in this section. An index is designed to categorize topics according to major themes and provide information for location. The following selection of indexes is presented to reflect the indexes most helpful to a wide range of research and consumership review in the social sciences.

American Doctoral Dissertations.   This index is a complete listing of all doctoral dissertations accepted by American and Canadian universities. It is compiled from commencement programs issued by the universities; therefore, the completeness of a given issue relies on institutional cooperation. The index includes a number of entries not compiled by *Dissertation Abstracts International.* It is published on a school-year basis and arranged by author, subject, and institution. The index started with Number 1, 1933–1934.

Arts and Humanities Citation Index.   This new index provides an author, source, subject, and citation index to over 900 of the world's leading journals in arts and humanities. The coverage ranges from architecture to theology and started in 1977.

Cumulative Book Index.   This is a record of books published in a given year and contains an author, subject, and title index. It is an international bibliography of books published in English, but excludes government documents, most pamphlets, and specific types of paperback books. It started with Volume 1 in 1902.

Cumulative Index to Nursing and Allied Health Literature.   This index, which started in 1956, is a central source for nursing and health related work. Over 250 journals are indexed including all major nursing periodicals in English as well as selected periodicals in the allied health professions:

1. Cardiopulmonary technology
2. Health education
3. Laboratory technology
4. Medical assistant
5. Medical research
6. Occupational therapy
7. Physical therapy and rehabilitation
8. Radiologic technology
9. Respiratory therapy
10. Social service in health care

Current Contents.   This weekly series provides the reader with titles of papers and all other materials from thousands of journals in the following major sections: Life sciences, agriculture, biology and environmental sciences, and social and behavioral sciences. For example, the Social and Behavioral Sciences Section covers nearly 1,400 journals reporting worldwide research and practice.

Current Index to Journals in Education.   This index covers more than 700 publications—mostly core periodical literature in the field of education. All articles listed are indexed by one of the 20 ERIC clearinghouses. The specific function of this index is to serve the information needs of practicing educators, reference librarians, and educational researchers. It is published monthly.

Education Index.   *Education Index,* first published in 1929, stands as a major cumulative author and subject matter index to educational material in the English language. The focus is on periodicals but also covers proceedings, yearbooks, bulletins, monographs, and materials printed by the United States government. Subject areas indexed include:

1. Administration
2. Preschool education
3. Elementary education
4. Secondary education
5. Higher and adult education
6. Teacher education
7. Counseling and guidance
8. Curriculum and curriculum materials

Materials for these categories come from the following subject areas:

1. Art
2. Applied science and technology
3. Audiovisual education
4. Business education
5. Comparative and international education

6.   Exceptional children and special education
7.   Health and physical education
8.   Languages and linguistics
9.   Mathematics
10.   Psychology and mental health
11.   Religious education
12.   Social studies
13.   Other relevant education research

Over 300 different publication sources are entered under the various categories mentioned.

The Gallup Opinion Index.   Under the direction of George Gallup of the American Institute of Public Opinion at Princeton, New Jersey, this index presents public opinion in the areas of political, social, and economic trends. The first issue, Number 1–7, was published in 1965. The index is now published monthly.

Humanities Index.   This is one of the two indexes superseding the *Social Science and Humanities Index,* which was discontinued in 1974. The main body of the index consists of author and subject entries to periodical articles. Subject areas indexed include:

1.   Archaeology
2.   Classical studies
3.   Area studies
4.   Folklore
5.   History
6.   Languages and literature
7.   Literary and political criticism
8.   Performing arts
9.   Philosophy
10.   Religion and theology
11.   Related subjects

It is published four times per year beginning with Volume 1 (1974–1975).

Index of Economic Articles.   This index cites over 200 different journals—journals believed to be most helpful to researchers and teachers of economics. It has both a subject index and author index and started with Volume 1, which covered the period of 1886–1924.

Index to Literature on the American Indian.   This index started in 1971, is published annually, and seeks to serve readers who wish to know about the first Americans. Over 80 subject areas are covered in a typical volume, and coverage ranges from acculturation and ethnobotany to water rights.

Index Medicus.   This index is prepared and sold by the Superintendent of Documents, United States Government Printing Office. It is the National Library of Medicine's monthly bibliography of the literature of biomedicine and cites the serial journal literature and selected monographs. No abstracts are cited.

The content of each entry is described by terms from Medical Subject Headings (MeSH). An article is logged into this system by drawing on the important concepts contained therein. One can narrow or broaden the word search by using "tree structures" in which MeSH terms are grouped into 14 subject categories and then arranged in a hierarchical manner. Information is presented in author and subject listings, with literature in 20 other languages cited.

Index to Periodical Articles by and about Blacks.   This volume dates from 1941 and has been known by previous titles, the most recent one being *Index to Periodical Articles by and about Negroes.* This is a good index for material in all areas related to African-American studies and includes all Black-American periodicals. As an example of coverage, the 1980 volume indexed over 3,000 articles that had appeared in 23 periodicals.

Index to Religious Periodical Literature.   This index is published by the American Theological Library Association and covers 1949–1952 (Volume 1) to date. It is now published semi-annually (beginning in 1977) and covers the areas of church history, biblical literature, theology, history of religion, sociology and psychology of religion, and other areas in humanities and current events. It contains author and subject matter indexes.

Public Affairs Information Services (PAIS).   This is a selective subject listing of the latest books, pamphlets, government publications, reports of public and private agencies, and periodical articles relating to economic and social conditions, public administration, and international relations. It includes all articles in these areas published in English worldwide. It is issued weekly and cumulated five times a year. PAIS is keyed to central periodical references and focuses on useful library materials in the field of economics and public affairs. Emphasis is placed on factual and statistical information.

Readers' Guide to Periodical Literature.   This is a very general index featuring author and subject matter indexes, as well as an author listing of citations to book reviews following the main body of the index. It is published semi-annually and indexes more than 100 magazines and popular publications. The index began with Volume 1, 1900–1904.

Science Citation Index.   This major index is published quarterly and covers all disciplines: journals, published proceedings, symposia papers, monographs, and multi-authored books. This index readily enables the user to identify the name and publication location of someone being cited in a given research or review article. Also, it identifies whether a piece has been cited, applied, or criticized. One can start with key words or an author's name. *Science Citation Index* is almost exhaustive in word coverage. The first volume was published in 1964.

Social Science Index.   This is the other of the two indexes superseding the *Social Sciences and Humanities Index,* which ceased publication in 1974. The main body of the index consists of author and subject entries to periodicals in the following fields:

1. Anthropology
2. Area studies
3. Economics
4. Environmental science
5. Geography
6. Law and criminology
7. Medical sciences
8. Political services
9. Psychology
10. Public administration
11. Sociology
12. Related subjects

Over 200 sources are indexed in this publication. Prior to publication of *Social Sciences and Humanities Index, International Index to Periodical Literature,* the first volume covering 1907–1915, was the index source to materials in the previously mentioned areas.

Social Sciences Citation Index.   This is similar to *Science Citation Index* and contains an international multidisciplinary listing of the literature of the social, behavioral, and related allied social sciences. It began with Volume 1 in 1973. It has key term, source, and citation indexes.

United States Political Science Documents (USPSD).   This index series is published by the University Center for International Studies at the University of Pittsburgh and started with Volume 1 in 1975. It includes main sources in political science, policy studies, international affairs, and the social sciences.

Computer Retrieval Systems

The decade of the seventies brought about an entirely new and sophisticated approach to bibliographic searching. Probably the greatest innovation of this entire decade was the ability of a library to access by machine many bibliographic sources for the student in a more sophisticated and exact manner. This has increased the ability of the library and its staff to service the diversity of needs in a manner that previously would have been unthinkable.

Early in the decade computer retrieval was used primarily as an adjunct to in-house assembling and publishing purposes. Early in the seventies, the National Library of Medicine data base became accessible for public use and established the efficacy of using computers as storing and retrieving sources. The commercial retrieval services began their expansion shortly thereafter and have multiplied at a phenomenal rate. By 1980, just a few years after the first commercial vendors made these services available, well over 125 data bases on a widely diversified subject span were available. The current number of bases is very extensive.

Tips for Consumers 3.2

In conducting or evaluating a review of literature, the consumer of research should be attentive to date of material cited, type of materials used, and the level of objectivity employed. Generally, new materials, reputable journals of professional societies, and a dispassionate stance by the writer, are indicators that quality work has been completed. Careful attention to these three points will do much to promote competence in both reviewing the literature as well as using it in a variety of ways.

It has been observed that "statistics lie" or that "you can prove anything with facts and figures." Consumers need to be aware of this assertion and cope with it by knowing how to locate and use sources such as indexes, abstracts, monographs, review volumes, and other literature sources helpful in understanding some issue. The ability to be intense without emotional involvement constitutes a major consumer goal. The ability to argue or prove is useful, but the commitment for objective understanding is truly a noteworthy attribute of the informed adult.

These computerized data bases, accessible for searching from computer terminals, are frequently the computerized counterpart of printed indexes and abstracting services. Many of these indexes and abstracting services are prepared for machine use in original format. Other data bases are constructed from the printed copies, and the information is then adapted and loaded onto magnetic tapes which then may be accessed from computer terminals with the aid of a librarian.

Although the actual "page turning," isolating, and sorting is done by the machine, the process of identifying materials is very similar to doing a hand search. The subject of interest must be described by subject terms. Although you may be somewhat familiar with the terminology in the field of study, it is wise to utilize the indexes and thesauruses provided to identify as precisely as possible the materials that you require for the bibliographic search.

The library staff will explain the possibilities of their given situation (i.e., which vendors they may access, which data bases are available, the costs, and whether or not appointments must be made in advance). When you and the librarian have decided which data bases would be advantageous to use, the librarian can assist in preparing a search profile that will isolate the citations of the subjects of choice. (See Tips 3.2 for helpful hints in doing a review.)

THREE ILLUSTRATIONS

Now that we have assessed the function of a literature review, major tools to be used in the review, and some methodological pointers in conducting a review, we will provide three examples of what a review can do for the researcher. The first example outlines formal hypotheses extracted from the literature on economics and revolution. The second example deals with theory development in relationship to early marriage. The third example utilizes meta-analysis to make a decision based on the review.

The reader is invited to read these studies in their entirety to grasp the several steps of a review in extracting hypotheses or propositions from previous work; the major steps are briefly presented here. The researcher should focus on assessing the selected articles for review, as this will help the reader decide which to include or reject according to the importance of the findings. Secondly, the reviewer will obtain a "sense about" themes, issues, main findings, or commonalities within a given study as well as across studies. These themes serve as a mapping outline for the network of concepts and statements that eventually make up hypotheses. Third, the extent of agreement within studies, as well as across studies, becomes apparent. This process is one of counting, weighing, and evaluating the findings presented by the various authors being read. The fourth step is one in which a reviewer sees the major patterns with high support, those with medium support, and perhaps other findings which are isolated, fragmented, or have only minimal support in a single study. A finding receiving support from only one study does not necessarily mean that the finding is not true or useful; we are referring here only to the extent that a finding is supported by multiple studies.

In the fifth step, we attempt to integrate and reduce the range of findings into broader statements of understanding. This step is a specific way of dealing with findings that range broadly, as well as those that are isolated or emergent-type results. Finally, this general review process, implementing in particular the previously mentioned steps, permits the researcher to state in a specific way the hypotheses that may have been dispersed throughout all of the articles reviewed. In sum, five processes occur:

1. Identification of specific statements
2. Grouping of statements
3. Integrating the statements
4. Reducing statements and casting them into a hypothesis language
5. Selecting those that provide a statement of the knowledge on the topic or that will serve as the base for additional research.

Example One

Kelley and Klein (1977) posit that a violent overthrow of traditional elites by a revolution is probably one of the dramatic transformations that a society can experience. Their theory argues that peasants are better off in the short run following a revolution; but relative to those who are better off economically, the peasants do not do as well. Also, those with better education, more resources, or even luck have more than their share of new opportunities. The end result is that the peasants end up with more inequality in regard to economics, education, and status inheritance after the revolution. They formalize eight hypotheses from their literature review:

1. In the short run, a radical revolution produces a more equal distribution of physical capital and, for those coming of age just afterward, less status inheritance.
2. In the short run, a radical revolution causes a shift in the basis of stratification, making human capital (education, knowledge, technical and linguistic skills, etc.) a more valuable source of occupational status and income.
3. A revolution does not immediately benefit the poorest of its supporters as much as it benefits those who possess human capital or have been able to retain physical capital.

4. In the long run, peasants are better off after a radical revolution.
5. By allowing peasants to utilize their resources more fully, radical revolutions set loose forces which tend in the long run to produce steadily increasing economic inequality among them.
6. In the long run, radical revolutions produce increasing educational inequality among peasants.
7. Among peasants, radical revolutions create forces which tend in the long run to produce more status inheritance through both economic advantage and education.
8. In the society as a whole, inequality and status inheritance following a radical revolution will first decrease, then stabilize, and finally either (*a*) remain low if nonpeasants remain well off and there is no economic development in the countryside, or else (*b*) steadily increase and perhaps in time exceed prerevolutionary levels in poor societies in which there is substantial economic development.

From these hypotheses the authors present a formal model that is capable of explaining radical and social changes which reduce exploitation.

In this article we see the statement of a guiding theory, a careful review of the literature in which Kelley and Klein formalize their eight hypotheses, and a formal model emerging from the hypotheses. The studies reviewed focus primarily on South America, Cuba, China, and historical examples from the Old World. Our point in presenting the hypotheses in their completeness is to emphasize that they were gleaned and formulated from the literature. They did not just suddenly come to the authors.

Example Two

The causes and consequences of early marriage were explored in some detail by Bartz and Nye (1970). They engaged in an extensive review of literature on early marriage and eventually restated a broad range of statements in propositional form. Drawing on exchange theory (Homans, 1961) and formal language of theory building (Zetterberg, 1965), Bartz and Nye carefully analyzed some 29 articles and presented a formalized theoretical explanation of the antecedents and consequences of early marriage. Twenty-three propositions are restated from the review; these are refined into three theoretical propositions:

1. Within a social class, the greater the heterosexual involvement at an early age, the more likely early marriage will occur.
2. The greater the positive discrepancy between satisfactions anticipated from marriage and satisfactions received from currently occupied roles, the more likely early marriage will occur.
3. The lower the social class, the more likely early marriage will occur.

Bartz and Nye then formulate derived theoretical propositions, discuss the consequences of early marriage, and relate their propositions to the more general area of exchange theory. Their review also enables them to identify several gaps in the literature on which they invite more research.

Example Three

► A third and final example of a literature review that achieves a specific goal comes from the work of Crain and Mahard (1983) who completed a very detailed meta-analysis of 93 research studies that focused on 323 different samples of black students experiencing desegregation. Both authors carefully read each of the 93 studies, averaging about three hours per study, and coded various themes according to methodologies employed. They focused on control group and type of design and categorized these into seven different types. Their overall conclusion was that desegregation does promote black achievement and that the greatest impact occurs in the primary grades.

The key point in this example is that one can employ a specific strategy such as meta-analysis, review many extant articles in regard to policy issue, and then make a decision based on that review. Meta-analysis is a technique for assessing materials that permits a reviewer to systematically count and evaluate previous findings and then to make generalizations. We predict that literature reviews of this type will become more common. With retrieval systems widely available to researchers and consumers, decisions, policy recommendations, knowledge assessments, and general information on a variety of topics will be increasingly available with relative ease.

Furthermore, these three examples provide good illustrations of the problems under study—early marriage, the impact of revolution on peasants, and school desegregation. These articles illustrate the process of defining the problem, of describing the problem, and clarifying the concepts related to these areas. What has been done and what now needs to be done in relationship to these areas is clarified by their reviews. We now know more about what should be stressed in additional research as well as what to avoid, such as measurement problems of conceptual clarity difficulties. The theory and hypotheses in these studies may be very useful to us in defining where to start, how to organize our review, and how to place our new questions into a proper perspective. A thorough study of related literature places the researcher in a better position to interpret the significance of research questions or findings.

A good review of literature permits one to be informed and knowledgeable about a given topic—a valuable goal in itself. Awareness, sensitivity, and assertiveness all stem from being informed. If we seriously wish to implement Plan A over Plan B, then the materials reviewed should provide information necessary for this type of decision making. In regard to our examples, many points already covered in this chapter are illustrated, including: a review of literature gives one the competitive edge—without this status one cannot function effectively as a researcher or consumer of research in a complex dynamic society. Bartz and Nye (1970), Kelley and Klein (1977), and Crain and Mahard (1983) permit us to join minds with experts on the topics of early marriage, revolutions, and school desegregation in order to know what types of projects are being covered and to profit from their suggestions about what should be done or what direction new research should take.

The three examples of a literature review reported here focus on hypotheses, theory development, and decision making, but a literature review is also useful to determine the current state of thinking on a given topic, to inform the reader about the range of controversy on a topic, and to instruct the reader about various schools of thought in a discipline. A literature review informs the reader about research approaches, instruments for measurement, where certain activities are occurring, gaps in information, and directions for additional research, while cautioning the novice about the prospects of work in selected areas. If one knows about the holdings available in the library, knows how to use basic sources such as indexes and abstracts, and has worked out a useful procedure for note taking and maintaining accurate references, then that person is well on the way to completing a variety of successful literature reviews in the area of focus.

SUMMARY

1. A review of the literature is important in the research process as it provides background, perspective, and technical knowledge useful in the conducting of research.
   a. In addition, a literature review enables the researcher to integrate new research with previous work and structure the review so as to extend science.
   b. Theoretical linkage is also enhanced when one is familiar with and builds onto past research.
2. Knowing the library and resources available helps greatly in doing the review, as does the assistance of a reference librarian.
3. The card catalog, abstracts, indexes, and computer retrieval systems are vitally important, as they provide guidance for locating the many journals, reports, monographs, texts, and related work necessary for your research topic.
4. A review of literature is a necessary and basic step in preparation to assure that the research undertaken is well conceived, integrative, and justifiable.
   a. A carefully completed review facilitates arriving at a comprehensive, analytic understanding of a research area. In specific cases, the review may convince the researcher to abandon an original for a more profitable research focus.
5. Accuracy in citation, completeness in references, and detailed technical information are essential in the preparation of a professional paper.
6. In the cases of theses and dissertations, a good review of literature facilitates completing the project, ensuring a workable as well as acceptable product.
7. Competent researchers and consumers need to have the experience and benefits of exchanging ideas with others. A review of literature provides one with the opportunity to gain knowledge and become informed from the work of others.

PROBLEMS AND APPLICATIONS

1. What are some of the main ways that consumers of research can use reviews of research literature to guide decisions in everyday life?
2. Taking all things into consideration what are the main "do's" and "don'ts" in conducting a review of literature that one must be aware of before beginning a research project?
3. Select three different areas of research (specific topics) and then identify the literature review sources for each that would be most helpful.
4. Discuss various strategies of note taking when reviewing the literature. What strategies do you use? What are the main limitations and strengths of the methods you use?

5. Contrast the strengths and weaknesses of using primary versus secondary sources in conducting a review of literature. When is it justifiable to use one versus the other?

6. Organize class members into groups, have them review their ideas and practices in regard to literature reviews, and then have a chairperson from each group report to the entire class.

REFERENCES

Bart, P., & Frankel, L. (1981). *The student sociologist's handbook.* Glenview, Ill.: Scott, Foresman.

Bartz, K. W., & Nye, F. I. (1970). Early marriages: A propositional formulation. *Journal of Marriage and the Family, 32,* 258–268.

Boyd, T. A. (1961). *Prophet of progress.* New York: E. P. Dutton.

Crain, R. L. & Mahard, R. E. (1983). The effect of research methodology on desegregation—achievement studies: A meta-analysis. *American Journal of Sociology, 88* (5), 839–854.

Homans, G. C. (1961). *Social Behavior: Its elementary forms.* New York: Harcourt, Brace and World.

Kelley, J., & Klein, H. S. (1977). Revolution and the rebirth of inequality: A theory of stratification in postrevolutionary society. *American Journal of Sociology, 83,* 78–99.

Whitehead, A. N. (1961). The organization of thought. In R. K. Merton (Ed.), *Social theory and social structure.* Glencoe, Ill.: The Free Press.

Zetterberg, H. L. (1965). *On theory and verification in sociology.* Totowa, N.J.: Bedminster Press.

CHAPTER 4

Validity and Reliability

OUTLINE

Introduction
Criteria for Believing One's Sources: Measurement
    Validity of Assessment Devices
        Face Validity
        Criterion-related Validity
        Content Validity
        Construct Validity
        Summary
    Reliability of Assessment Devices
        Test–Retest
        Equivalent-Forms
        Split-Half Method
        An Illustration
Some Criteria for Believing One's Sources: Research Findings
    Validity of Findings
        Factors Limiting Internal Validity
        Factors Limiting External Validity
    Reliability of Findings
Summary
Problems and Applications
References

KEY TERMS

Internal validity

External validity

Extraneous variables

Face validity

Criterion-related validity

Content validity

Construct validity

Correlation coefficient

Test–retest

Equivalent-forms method

Split-half method

Coefficient of stability

Coefficient of equivalence

Coefficient of internal consistency

Reliability

Validity

STUDY GUIDE QUESTIONS

1. What is meant by validity? How can one assess whether a research assessment device is a valid measure?
2. How does the concept of reliability differ from that of validity? When is an assessment device considered to be reliable?
3. Are the concepts of internal and external validity interrelated? How are they similar? How are they different?
4. What factors can limit internal validity?
5. What factors limit external validity?
6. What role does replication play in social science?

Role of the Scientist

Assessment and evaluation are primary tools of science. The consistency and trustworthiness of measurement are central to good science. In this chapter we focus on the reliability and validity of assessment. Criteria for assessing reliability and validity are discussed. Students pursuing a scientific career should focus on the criteria used to develop or construct a reliable and valid assessment device.

Role of the Consumer

In the process of application and utilization of science one must understand the criteria underlying the validity and reliability of a research report. A consumer should be assured that data are truthful and useful. A careful consumer should make certain that trustworthy measurement has been used in any research study that is used to make policy, prevention, or intervention decisions. Further, prior to establishing a prevention or intervention program, consumers (therapists, educators, policymakers, etc.) should be informed and knowledgeable, while being guided by empirical documentation in their program activities. Therefore, consumers should study and understand the techniques that scientists use to measure behavior and to establish both validity and reliability about their findings.

INTRODUCTION

In everyday life when we engage in problem solving we seek information that can be used to arrive at efficient solutions. Success in problem solving depends to a large degree on obtaining correct information and using that information to derive logical possibilities and decisions. Decisions in science likewise require getting correct and precise information. Indeed, good science is impossible without reliable and valid information.

But what is actually meant by valid and reliable information (facts)? In simple terms, *validity* refers to the general correctness and appropriate representativeness of facts, while *reliability* refers to the consistency or dependability of the fact itself. In everyday life, validity and reliability of information determine its trustworthiness.

In this chapter we provide the foundation upon which all good science relies—an understanding of reliability and validity. Before we examine some of the fundamental issues underlying the establishment of reliability and validity in measurement, we shall make one central point evident: that is, measurement is the foundation of all scientific effort. The variables (be they objects, events, or behaviors) are ideally derived from theory and are the phenomenon to be measured. In order to successfully measure these variables, it is necessary to define the variables in precise terms and to measure them in an accurate and consistent manner. What then are the criteria for assuring accurate and consistent measurement?

CRITERIA FOR BELIEVING ONE'S SOURCES: MEASUREMENT

Scientists use certain widely accepted criteria to guide research judgments. Foremost, one expects that all data consist of validly measured behavior. Therefore, each research report should indicate the degree to which the investigator has measured what was initially set out to be measured. If the investigator indicates that academic achievement is to be measured, can the consumer be sure that some other related attribute isn't actually being assessed (e.g., high independence, verbal skills, or differences in learning strategies)? The task of assuring validation of research measurement devices may be the hardest task in doing credible social science research. Unlike the physical sciences, in which a great deal of measurement is mechanical, social scientists must continually develop new research tools to supplement direct observation of behavior. For example, it is unlikely that a scientist will actually observe family violence. Therefore, the researcher develops self-report measures of such behavior. To do so requires the development of measures that reflect actual experience of violent family events.

What then are the standards used by researchers to assure reliable and valid measurements? How is evidence reported on the reliability and validity of assessment devices?

The Joint Committee on Testing Procedures, initiated by cooperative effort by the American Equational Research Association, the American Psychological Association, and the National Council on Measurement in Education, and supported by the American Association for Counseling and Development, the Association for Measurement and

Evaluation in Counseling and Development, and the American Speech-Language-Hearing Association, have prepared a *Code of Fair Testing Practices in Education* (1988). This code provides useful information on the development and selection of appropriate tests and the interpretation of scores, addresses issues of fairness, and provides guidelines on informing test takers. Further, *Standards for Educational and Psychological Tests* (1974) and related testing handbooks (e.g., Anastasi, 1988) offer extensive guidelines for the development of reliable and valid research instruments. Many of the essential guidelines are used here to assist you in understanding the criteria on which reliability and validity of research measures are judged.

For consumers of assessment devices we have provided recommendations from the *Code of Fair Testing Practices in Education* (1988) regarding recommendations on what test developers should provide and criteria test users should use in selecting assessment devices. These recommendations are found in Boxes 4.1–4.4 (pp. 79–82).

Validity of Assessment Devices

The validity of research measures deals with *what is actually being measured by the assessment device.* That is, what properties are actually being measured by the assessment process?

Although it seems easy to think in terms of valid or invalid measurement, this is not always a correct perspective. Rather, one should think in terms of a particular usage. Instruments can be used in appropriate or inappropriate ways. Most assessments are specific to the behavior, attitude, or expectation they are designed to validly predict. For example, there is low to poor validity in the use of dogmatism scales for predicting mathematical reasoning or height of an individual, but high validity for predicting prejudicial attitudes.

Table 4.1 (p. 81) summarizes the four general types of validity questions that are answered in building good research instruments. Each type calls for different, yet interrelated, questions. Prior to placing unquestioning "faith" in a given research result, the competent consumer or researcher assures himself or herself that the measurements reported in the research report have at least met certain minimal levels of validity. These specific standards will be discussed in order from most common to least common availability.[1]

Face Validity.   The most common, yet least scientifically sound, form of validation is called face validity. When one reads a test and asks what do the test items appear to be measuring, one is dealing with the issue of face validity. Although it can be argued that face validity of any instrument should be what the test is measuring visually without empirical validation, this can never be assured. It is possible that any given test item can appear to be measuring one thing when in reality it is measuring another. Sometimes these differences can be very subtle; however, it is always important that researchers

---

[1]The following discussion is primarily directed at rating scales as opposed to observational techniques. Nonetheless, the discussion is pertinent to both types of data collection techniques. For a further discussion on complexities not covered in a typical introduction text, interested readers should examine an article by Saal, Downey, and Lahey (1980) and a monograph by Kirk and Miller (1986).

BOX 4.1. A. Developing/Selecting Appropriate Tests*

Test developers should provide the information that test users need to select appropriate tests.

Test users should select tests that meet the purpose for which they are to be used and that are appropriate for the intended test-taking populations.

Test developers should:

1. Define what each test measures and what the test should be used for. Describe the population(s) for which the test is appropriate.

2. Accurately represent the characteristics, usefulness, and limitations of tests for their intended purposes.

3. Explain relevant measurement concepts as necessary for clarity at the level of detail that is appropriate for the intended audience(s).

4. Describe the process of test development. Explain how the content and skills to be tested were selected.

5. Provide evidence that the test meets its intended purpose(s).

6. Provide either representative samples or complete copies of test questions, directions, answer sheets, manuals, and score reports to qualified users.

7. Indicate the nature of the evidence obtained concerning the appropriateness of each test for groups of different racial, ethnic, or linguistic backgrounds who are likely to be tested.

8. Identify and publish any specialized skills needed to administer each test and to interpret scores correctly.

Test users should:

1. First define the purpose for testing and the population to be tested. Then, select a test for that purpose and that population based on a thorough review of the available information.

2. Investigate potentially useful sources of information, in addition to test scores, to corroborate the information provided by tests.

3. Read the materials provided by test developers and avoid using tests for which unclear or incomplete information is provided.

4. Become familiar with how and when the test was developed and tried out.

5. Read independent evaluations of a test and of possible alternative measures. Look for evidence required to support the claims of test developers.

6. Examine specimen sets, disclosed tests or samples of questions, directions, answer sheets, manuals, and score reports before selecting a test.

7. Ascertain whether the test content and norms group(s) or comparison group(s) are appropriate for the intended test takers.

8. Select and use only those tests for which the skills needed to administer the test and interpret scores correctly are available.

---

*Many of the statements in the Code refer to the selection of existing tests. However, in customized testing programs test developers are engaged to construct new tests. In those situations, the test development process should be designed to help ensure that the completed tests will be in compliance with the Code. (Copyright 1988 by the National Council on Measurement in Education. Reprinted by permission of the publisher.)

BOX 4.2.   B. Interpreting Scores

Test developers should help users interpret scores correctly.

Test developers should:

9. Provide timely and easily understood score reports that describe test performance clearly and accurately. Also explain the meaning and limitations of reported scores.

10. Describe the population(s) represented by any norms or comparison group(s), the dates the data were gathered, and the process used to select the samples of test takers.

11. Warn users to avoid specific, reasonably anticipated misuses of test scores.

12. Provide information that will help users follow reasonable procedures for setting passing scores when it is appropriate to use such scores with the test.

13. Provide information that will help users gather evidence to show that the test is meeting its intended purpose(s).

Test users should interpret scores correctly.

Test users should:

9. Obtain information about the scale used for reporting scores, the characteristics of any norms or comparison -group(s), and the limitations of the scores.

10. Interpret scores taking into account any major differences between the norms or comparison groups and the actual test takers. Also take into account any differences in test administration practices or familiarity with the specific questions in the test.

11. Avoid using tests for purposes not specifically recommended by the test developer unless evidence is obtained to support the intended use.

12. Explain how any passing scores were set and gather evidence to support the appropriateness of the scores.

13. Obtain evidence to help show that the test is meeting its intended purpose(s).

BOX 4.3.   C. Striving for Fairness

Test developers should strive to make tests that are as fair as possible for test takers of different races, gender, ethnic backgrounds, or handicapping conditions.

Test developers should:

14. Review and revise test questions and related materials to avoid potentially insensitive content or language.

Test users should select tests that have been developed in ways that attempt to make them as fair as possible for test takers of different races, gender, ethnic backgrounds, or handicapping conditions.

Test users should:

14. Evaluate the procedures used by test developers to avoid potentially insensitive content or language.

15. Investigate the performance of test takers of different races, gender, and ethnic backgrounds when samples of sufficient size are available. Enact procedures that help to ensure that differences in performance are related primarily to the skills under assessment rather than to irrelevant factors.

15. Review the performance of test takers of different races, gender, and ethnic backgrounds when samples of sufficient size are available. Evaluate the extent to which performance differences may have been caused by inappropriate characteristics of the test.

16. When feasible, make appropriately modified forms of tests or administration procedures available for test takers with handicapping conditions. Warn test users of potential problems in using standard norms with modified tests or administration procedures that result in non-comparable scores.

16. When necessary and feasible, use appropriately modified forms of tests or administration procedures for test takers with handicapping conditions. Interpret standard norms with care in the light of the modifications that were made.

TABLE 4.1. Types of Validity

Type	Research Question Addressed
Face validity	Does the assessment device appear to measure the subject matter under consideration?
Criterion-related validity	Does the individual's test score predict the probable behavior on a second variable (criterion-related measure)?
Content validity	Does the assessment device adequately measure the major dimensions of the behavior under consideration?
Construct validity	Does the assessment device appear to measure the general construct (element) it purports to measure?

assure the consumer of research findings that their measurements are validly constructed. The consumer of research, likewise, should ask for no less. However, any consumer of research should expect at a minimum that the investigators have dealt with the issue of face validity.

At times it is necessary, however, to be less obvious in the construction of measurement devices. When a researcher is measuring socially sensitive attitude or behaviors, it may be occasionally necessary to use a research instrument with low face validity.

For example, if we were interested in studying middle-class Caucasians' attitudes toward black Americans, we might not get true responses if one were to ask, "Do you have positive, neutral, or negative feelings toward having your children go to school with black children?" Many people, to make themselves look liberal, might answer this question in the positive. To eliminate this possibility, some researchers develop less

BOX 4.4.   D. Informing Test Takers

Under some circumstances, test developers have direct communication with test takers. Under other circumstances, test users communicate directly with test takers. Whichever group communicates directly with test takers should provide the information described below.

Test developers or test users should:

17. When a test is optional, provide test takers or their parents/guardians with information to help them judge whether the test should be taken, or if an available alternative to the test should be used.
18. Provide test takers the information they need to be familiar with the coverage of the test, the types of question formats, the directions, and appropriate test-taking strategies. Strive to make such information equally available to all test takers.

Under some circumstances, test developers have direct control of tests and test scores. Under other circumstances, test users have such control. Whichever group has direct control of tests and test scores should take the steps described below.

Test developers or test users should:

19. Provide test takers or their parents/guardians with information about rights test takers may have to obtain copies of tests and completed answer sheets, retake tests, have tests rescored, or cancel scores.
20. Tell test takers or their parents/guardians how long scores will be kept and indicate to whom test scores will or will not be released.
21. Describe the procedures that test takers or their parents/guardians may use to register complaints and have problems resolved.

(Copyright 1988 by the National Council on Measurement in Education. Reprinted by permission of the publisher.)

straightforward measurement devices. For example, a researcher might ask, "Do you believe all schools should be racially integrated?" Or another question might read, "Do you believe all neighborhoods should be designed to enhance the integration of black families into white neighborhoods?" In this manner, less direct questions may appear to have low face validity, but due to the sensitive nature of the research, questions may need to be rather subtle.

A cautionary comment should be made here. Face validity problems can be reflected in test biases associated with unrecognized cultural differences, incorrect content, and related problems. For further reading we suggest interested students read Green (1978), Anastasi (1988), and Flaugher (1978) for a more extended discussion of such problems in measurement.

Criterion-related Validity.   There are two specific types of criterion-related validity. *Predictive validity* means the assessment device is associated with some additional variables that offer theoretical predictiveness between the assessment device and some important behavior. Usually these criterion variables are assessed at some point after responses are obtained on the key assessment measure. However, they may occasionally be assessed at the same time with the new assessment treated as a predictor of behavior on some second measure.

For example, in a recent study of our own (Curtis & Adams, in press) we have developed a self-report measure of stress for use with adolescent populations. The measure requires the adolescent to read a series of statements (e.g., I am nervous) and then select the degree to which each represents the subject's current emotional state (e.g., not at all, sometimes, always). To assess predictive validity we utilized stress theory ◄ which suggests that stress is predictive of poor social adjustment and greater degree of psychopathology. So we had high school age adolescents complete the stress scale and respond to measures of adjustment and psychopathology. As expected, students with high self-perceived stress levels also indicated problems with adjustment and, correspondingly, evidence of psychopathology.

Concurrent validity, in comparison to predictive validity, refers to the manner in which the assessment device is associated with either (*a*) a second test measuring the same construct, or (*b*) behaviors thought to be appropriate for so-called *known criterion groups* (i.e., groups known to differ on the behavior under consideration). The main distinction between the two types of criterion-related validities is that predictive validity usually is associated with a later behavior or action that takes some time to arrive at a cumulative product or outcome, while concurrent validity is associated with behavior that occurs simultaneously with the central measure.

Returning to our development of a stress scale (Curtis & Adams, in press), to ◄ establish concurrent validity we first compared adolescents' responses to our stress items and a measure of anxiety. Stress theory suggests that anxiety is one emotional state that is associated with stress. Indeed, we found that higher stress levels were associated with higher levels of anxiety. Likewise, we identified students with low and high test anxiety from a large introductory class at our own university. Treating these research subjects as two known criterion groups who should manifest different levels of stress during testing periods, we administered the stress scale in the middle of a midterm examination. As expected, the low test anxiety subjects reported very little stress, while the high test anxiety subjects reported very high levels of stress during the examination.

Content Validity. Content validity deals with the thoroughness or completeness of the measurement device. That is, does the assessment strategy cover the major dimensions or factors of the subject matter under assessment? Representativeness of items assessing the behavior is of key interest here. Generally a representative sample of items measuring a particular construct is defined on theoretical and logical grounds. Therefore, a good measure should include a rationale on how and why the individual test items were included in the construction of the assessment scale. Unfortunately, all too often researchers fail to provide information on how content was decided, leaving in question the representativeness of the research measure.

In a classic statement, Norman Gronlund (1981) has offered four basic steps in the development of content validity for research scales and tests. First, a group of specialists on the topic should list the separate types of behavior included under the rubric of the subject matter. Second, the relative importance of each content area or subtopic should be weighed through some rational criteria that are spelled out for the user of the scale. Third, a table should be prepared that specifies the percentage or number of items to be included under each subtopic. And finally, items should be written according to the specifications to assure sample representativeness. Although only providing a rough check on content validity, this technique does offer a certain degree of assurance of adequate representation. However, it is ultimately up to the consumer to question or accept the thoroughness of the scale content.

▶   Some time ago, we (Munro & Adams, 1977) constructed a self-report love attitude scale to measure an individual's personal attitudes toward romantic and conjugal love preferences. To illustrate how content validity might be established in scale construction, a small segment of that research project will be reviewed. Specifically, content validity was established by reviewing popular romantic literature and past research to define the major dimensions of romantic and conjugal love. This strategy allowed the researchers to specify the major components of such love. Romantic love attitudes were defined as reflecting (*a*) idealism, (*b*) need for affiliation and dependency, (*c*) possessiveness, (*d*) emotion, and (*e*) exclusiveness. Conjugal love attitudes were defined as being (*a*) calm, (*b*) rational, (*c*) realistic, and (*d*) mutually warm and trustful. Using the five dimensions of romantic love, 31 literary quotations were used from popular romantic literature; also, 26 conjugal items were constructed using the four specifications listed above. All items were weighted equally. A panel of judges likewise reviewed the items for their appropriateness. This rough index provides the user of the instrument with a general guideline to understand how specific items were selected for use in the scale. Examples of scale items are found in Table 4.2 that can also be reviewed for face validity consideration.

Construct Validity.   Construct validity deals with assessing the degree of accuracy in measuring the underlying elements (constructs) of a scale (Messick, 1981). Does the measurement device assess the theoretical constructs that underlie the intent of the assessment technique? If a scale, for example, reportedly measures creativity, can we be assured it does not measure some other different but related phenomenon? Typically, a researcher answers such questions by examining the interrelationship of the scale items rather than examining whether they can predict other behaviors. Items measuring the

---

TABLE 4.2. Three Types of Love Scales

Factor I: Romantic Ideal
1. Love is the highest goal between a man and a woman.
2. Love is more important than any chance or opportunity for success in a profession or a business.
3. Many years of being in love deepens rather than exhausts the sense of pleasure that partners feel for each other.

Factor II: Conjugal-Rational Love
1. Erotic and romantic feelings toward another are poor signs toward indicating a long and stable love relationship.
2. It is more important to feel calm and relaxed with the one you love rather than excited and romantic.
3. A decision to marry should come from serious thinking not just a feeling of love.

Factor III: Romantic Power
1. There can be no real happiness or success in life for those in a poor love relationship.
2. There can be no genuine failure in life for those in love.
3. True love never dies; it surmounts all obstacles.

same thing should be interrelated. Furthermore, the interrelation or association between the items should follow some general theoretical assumption. For example, if a researcher has items measuring both verbal and mathematical reasoning, and wishes to use these to predict an individual's academic achievement, it would most likely be expected that: (a) *the two aptitudes are related to important activities in school;* therefore, one should expect at least a small *degree of congruency* between the two constructs, and (b) individual items measuring verbal reasoning should be more highly associated with each other than with items measuring mathematical reasoning, and vice versa. Table 4.3 provides a hypothetical example for consideration. To understand the table we need to introduce the concept of correlation.

Correlation refers to the degree of correspondence or congruence that exists between two sets of scores (Anastasi, 1988). In statistical parlance it is measured through the correlation coefficient. This coefficient ranges from −1.00 to +1.00 with values of zero possible. Let us elaborate further.

Three possible conditions can occur. There can be *no observed association* between two variables. That is, variation or change in one variable is unassociated with variation in the other. Correlations of this type are close to zero. A *positive association* can occur when variation in one variable is high and variation in the other variable is high. This association can range from +.01 to +1.00. An illustration of a positive correlation is observed when both income and purchasing power increase when inflation is nonexistent. Finally, a *negative association* can be observed. This association means as variation increases in one variable it decreases in the second variable. This statistical association can range from −.01 to −1.00. A negative correlation is observed when income increases but purchasing power decreases during a period of high inflation. Also, the stronger the positive or negative correlation, the closer the statistical value will be to + or −1.00.

As we can see from Table 4.3, the reported degree of association provides some ◄ evidence for construct validity. Beginning with the verbal reasoning items we see that each item is rather strongly associated with the total verbal reasoning score (see Column 4). Furthermore, the three items (found in the rows) are positively inter-correlated with

TABLE 4.3. A Hypothetical Example for Assessing Construct Validity

	Type of Items Verbal Reasoning				Type of Items Mathematical Reasoning			
	(1)[a] Item 1	(2) Item 2	(3) Item 3	(4) Total 4	(5) Item 1	(6) Item 2	(7) Item 3	(8) Total 4
Verbal Reasoning (VR)								
Item 1	1.00	.72	.81	.85	.36	.25	.19	.47
Item 2	—	1.00	.79	.91	.26	.30	.31	.36
Item 3	—	—	1.00	.96	.19	.20	.19	.21
Mathematical Reasoning (MR)								
Item 1	—	—	—	—	1.00	.81	.76	.84
Item 2	—	—	—	—	—	1.00	.82	.87
Item 3	—	—	—	—	—	—	1.00	.91

[a]Numbers in parentheses indicate column numbers.

one another (compare rows with Columns 1, 2, and 3), suggesting they are measuring the same type of behavior. However, as we move across the table, we see that the verbal reasoning items are not as highly correlated with the total scores and individual items of the mathematical reasoning subscale (Columns 5–8). Nonetheless, we can see in the bottom right-hand corner of the table that the individual items of the mathematical subscale are strongly associated with their total and individual scale items. Therefore, these statistics (hypothetically) provide evidence for some degree of internal construct validity wherein verbal reasoning items are more strongly associated with each other than with items measuring mathematical reasonings. Mathematical reasoning items are more strongly associated with each other than with items measuring verbal reasoning, while verbal and mathematical reasoning are moderately associated constructs.

The general technique from our hypothetical example is called the *convergent-discriminant validation* technique (Campbell and & Fiske, 1959; Cronbach & Meehl, 1955). This technique assumes that construct validity can be assessed in two ways. One is to demonstrate that the elements being measured (e.g., an attitude) *converge* with a second measure thought to be assessing the same or similar elements. The other technique is to demonstrate that the element of measurement is not measuring *(discriminating)* an element different by definition from the primary measure of consideration. In essence, one proves what something is, in part, by showing what it is not.

Samuel Messick (1981) proposed that an effective strategy in establishing construct validity is to develop two or more distinct scale constructs at the same time and to administer the combined item pool of both measures. Using correlational statistics items are then retained that correlate more highly (positive correlations) with their own purported construct scale than with the other construct. In doing so, items are selected on the basis of both convergent and discrminant evidence. Loevinger (1957) has referred to this phenomenon as substantive validity—items are supported by the construct's theory. (For more extended technical information on construct validity see Embretson, 1983, and Messick, 1981.)

Summary.   Four basic forms of validity are generally applied to measurement construction. Messick (1980) summarized the core points of these various forms. Face validity refers simply to appearance. Does the test appear to be measuring the construct underlying the items? Content validity focuses on content relevance and coverage. Are the items part of the content's domain and do the items represent the breadth of the construct? Criterion validity refers to the predictive utility and the equivalence of the assessment. Can the test be used to predict theoretically appropriate behavior and through concurrent validation can it be used to substitute for another measurement? That is, does the test measure predictably differences in behavior, and can the test be used as a substitute for actually observing these behaviors? Finally, construct validity focuses on interpretive meaningfulness or substantive consistency. Do the items show a theoretically meaningful interrelation while diverging from other constructs?

Reliability of Assessment Devices

Technically, the reliability of an assessment device deals with the degree to which responses are due to systematic sources of variance. More simply, reliability is best viewed as an assessment of the consistency in behaviors. Therefore, a highly reliable measure is one that gives the user consistent results over time, places, and occasions. Methods of assessing reliability are primarily statistical ones. Reliability is typically reported by means of a correlation coefficient which is technically called a *reliability coefficient.* A reliability coefficient is interpreted like a regular correlation: The closer the value is to +1.00 the stronger is the congruence in measurement.

Table 4.4 summarizes the three major ways in which the reliability of an assessment can be established and the types of questions they address. In determining the scientific merit of a given assessment device, the consumer of research should particularly note the procedure and samples used to establish reliability and judge the applicability of the assessment to the sample in each and every research project. One should keep in mind that a measurement may be established as being reliable with one type of sample (children) but not necessarily reliable with another sample (adults).

Test–Retest.   The test–retest method of establishing reliability entails administering the same instrument twice to the same group of individuals under equivalent conditions after some time interval has elapsed. The correlation coefficient is called the *coefficient of stability* and gives an estimate of how stable the results are over a given time period. Typically, the shorter the period of time between test and retest, the higher the coefficient. During short intervals between test and retest, participants are likely to remember how they specifically answered the first time; however, memory wanes with increasing time. If the stability coefficients are low and the researcher is predicting later behavior as a function of earlier scores, the research consumer should be skeptical about any reported relation. It is possible that an instrument with a short stability range is useless in predicting long-range behavior. For example, a child's degree of introversion may be predictive of later marital happiness; however, if the measure of introversion is not stable over an extensive period of time, that association may actually be due to some other, undefined factor. Therefore, the greater the length of time for which predictions are needed, the longer the time interval between test–retest assessment should be. Reliability estimates for two weeks are questionable for research requiring several months or years to complete, where early behavior assessments are used to predict later behavior. Frequently, stability issues are particularly difficult for developmental research in social science. When researchers are interested in the study of how people change, it becomes extremely difficult to determine when the coefficient of stability is low if the results are due to unreliability in the measurement device or a major change in one's behavior. Therefore, the coefficient of stability may be a poor index of reliability in research studying changes in people's behavior.

TABLE 4.4. Types of Reliability

Type	Research Questions Addressed
Test–retest method	Does an individual respond to an assessment device in the same general way when the test is administered twice?
Equivalent-forms method	When two forms, which are equivalent in their degree of validity, are given to the same individual, is there a strong convergence as to how that person responds?
Split-half method	Are the scores on one-half of the test similar to those obtained on the remaining half?

Equivalent-Forms. This technique involves the administration of the research instrument to the same group of people at two different times (usually in close succession) using different, but equivalent forms. The reliability correlation is called a *coefficient of equivalence*. This form of reliability tells us nothing about stability, but rather gives an indication of the general representativeness of the items in the two assessment devices. A high coefficient of equivalence suggests that both research measures are assessing similar content and, therefore, should be considered reliable samples of the subject matter being sampled.

This method can be very useful when combined with the test–retest method in which equivalent forms are administered to the same group with an extended period of time elapsing between the first and second administration period. Under these conditions, the reliability coefficient reflects both an estimation of equivalence and stability over time.

Split-Half Method. This technique is perhaps the most common of the three used in published research because it is frequently only possible for various reasons to measure a target population one time. This method calls for administering the test to a group of people and then splitting the items or behaviors in half for purposes of scoring. (Usually researchers compare the odd and even items; however, other rationales can be developed for different breakdowns.) After this procedure, the two halves are compared for degree of correspondence. The association between split-halves is called the *coefficient of internal consistency*. It provides an estimation of the degree to which the two halves are equivalent. (Why are reliability and validity important? See Tips 4.1.)

▶ *An Illustration.* In scale development in a longitudinal project focusing on identity formation we have undertaken numerous measurement studies. One effort has involved Marcia's (1964) Ego-Identity Incomplete Sentence Blank. This research instrument consists of items requiring the participant to complete a half-written sentence. One example is: "For me, success would be _____." Once completed, each item is scored on a three-point system with high scores given for specific commitments, goals, and directions to life. Items and responses are scored on a three-point scale and are summed

---

Tips for Consumers 4.1

It is essential in good science that evidence be presented on the reliability and validity of measurement. To assess whether a scientist has used reliable and valid measurements the consumer should look for evidence that

1. the assessment predicts theoretically appropriate behaviors;
2. the measure can differentiate between groups of individuals known to behave differently within the social behavior;
3. the assessment includes appropriate conceptual or theoretically based content;
4. individuals behave similarly when measured two or more times over a short period of time.

If the assessment minimally meets these four requirements the consumer can assume the measure has reasonable validity and reliability.

to arrive at an overall commitment to identity. To illustrate how all the basic forms of reliability can be estimated for a measure, we have randomly drawn 20 subjects from a large sample and have calculated reliability coefficients.

First, we asked 10 subjects to return to our lab one month after the initial interview to respond to the measure a second time. This test-retest method resulted in a *coefficient of stability* of .81. Remembering that one is likely to forget how one responded over such a length of time, this datum or coefficient of stability suggests stable reliability in the assessment of identity. Next, we compared the odd and even items to assess the *internal consistency* of this measure. The *reliability coefficient* was .94, which indicates the odd and even items are consistently measuring the same thing. Finally, we constructed 18 new items that appeared to be measuring the same construct and administered the two scales in succession to another 10 participants. The *coefficient of equivalence* between the Marcia items and the new assessment device was .84, suggesting a strong degree of equivalence of content. Collectively, the coefficients of stability, equivalence, and internal consistency can assure both the user and generator of research knowledge that the data are reliable sources of information.

SOME CRITERIA FOR BELIEVING ONE'S SOURCES: RESEARCH FINDINGS

It is essential to recognize that validity and reliability issues are important to assessing the trustworthiness of measurement, but similar issues are of equal importance in assessing the *trustworthiness of research conclusions* drawn from the context of a full study. In this section of the chapter we shall explore many of the central issues of validity and reliability as they now apply to the conclusions drawn from a research report. Research consumers should, in particular, recognize that this section provides important information for judging the worth of reported findings for application activities.

Validity of Findings

In reading a research report and judging its worth, one should look for information concerning two general types of validity—internal and external validity. *Internal validity* refers to the effects of the specific method on the reported results. More specifically, did the independent variable, which is under the control of the experimenter, actually cause a significant change in the dependent variable? Or was this change possibly due to some third variable, frequently called an extraneous variable? An *extraneous variable* is one not accounted for by the researcher and may be the actual causal factor initiating change in the dependent variable. In comparison, *external validity* refers to generalizability or representativeness of the research findings. To what group of people can the findings be generalized? In what type of settings and under what type of conditions? Thus, external validity is a matter of sampling. The broader or wider the sampling from a given population, across settings (e.g., work, home, school) and conditions (e.g., stressful, nonstressful, high-work demand, low-work demand, etc.), the greater the generalizability of reported results from the independent-dependent variable relation.

The ideal research project attempts to establish both high internal and external validity. However, due to limited monetary support, insufficient research training, inadequate facilities, and many other factors, most research projects are high on one of the factors but moderate or low on the other. There are even differences in emphasis across subfields in social science. For example, sociologists and social workers are more likely to emphasize external over internal validity, while psychologists and educators are more likely to emphasize internal validity. Therefore, when reading or doing research, the reader should assess the degree to which each general type of validity has been established. To do so, however, we must ask ourselves what are the criteria for assessing the validity of a given research finding.

Factors Limiting Internal Validity.   In a classic statement, Donald Campbell and Julian Stanley (1963; Cook & Campbell, 1979) specified several factors that limit the degree of internal validity. Keeping in mind that the major purpose of internal validity is to assure the scientist that changes in the dependent variable were actually due to the influence of specific independent variables, the presence of possible extraneous variables leads one to question if a rival cause (or alternative hypothesis) might not be as or more influential than the original stated independent-dependent variable relation. Therefore, internal validity requires the researcher to control for a number of different kinds of extraneous variables to eliminate their possible contamination of the research conclusions.

The following eight factors are extraneous variables (confounding variables), which ideally must be controlled to avoid making incorrect inferences about the effects of an experimental treatment on the dependent variable (e.g., one specific teaching method is better than another for the acquisition of reading skills).

Maturation. With the passage of time as anything under study (e.g., peer group, organization membership, individuals) matures, the internal nature or makeup of that thing changes. Peer groups enlist new members, while older members sometimes leave; organizations are supported by a particular membership that waxes and wanes with its social significance; and individuals functionally become better or worse at certain tasks or behaviors as they age (like motor coordination, manual dexterity, verbal fluency, mathematical reasoning, etc.). Therefore, studies which examine behavior at two points in time must control for changes in the unit of study (peer groups, individuals, etc.) due to mere passage of time and the maturation process that typically goes on for most things. Failure to control for maturational effects may lead the scientist to believe that the experimental treatment, through the manipulation of specific independent variables, caused the observable change in the dependent variable, while in reality it is a maturational process that accounted for the behavioral change.

▶   An illustration of this issue was made apparent in a study designed to assess the effects of a preschool intervention program on the development of empathic abilities in young children. To assess the changes in the ability to recognize and identify correct emotions for specific social contexts, DeMarsh (1979) pretested (assessed subjects prior to the educational experience) and posttested (assessed subjects after the experience) preschool-age children who experienced an early childhood education program. The data clearly demonstrated that children improved in their empathy skills. However, a comparison of other children who did not experience the preschool program maintained a similar growth pattern. Thus, maturation, not the preschool program, actually accounted for the changes.

History. Both over time and at any given data collection point, social and political events are happening. These specific events may actually cause changes in the dependent variable and, therefore, must be controlled for in social science research. For example, if we were studying political attitudes during the Watergate era, such turmoil would have likely affected political belief in the power of the presidency. The assessment of political attitudes would, in this illustration, be very historically bound, and most likely would not reflect the general attitude if a constitutional crisis was not happening. This phenomenon is sometimes called a *historicity effect.*

What if we were interested in studying longitudinal changes in high school students' political attitudes and had our first measure collected just prior to the Iran news releases? Further, suppose our second measure to assess change over time was planned to be completed one year later. In this example, a comparison would be made between the first and second assessment to measure the degree of change in political attitudes. If the tester failed to control for possible historical effects, we could never be sure if the changes were typical of normal adolescent development or were specific changes due to a strong historical event.

Differential Subject Selection. Selection and placement of research subjects into comparable groups requires some care. In placing the research participant into experimental groups (e.g., one group getting financial assistance for home maintenance versus a second group that is not financially supported), it is important that both groups are equivalent in terms of population characteristics (parameters). If not, it is possible that one group may perform better than the other on the measured behavior, not because of the experimental treatment, but because of some attribute that one group possesses which the other group does not.

An example of how this can happen rather easily to a researcher was observed in some of our own research (Adams & Cohen, 1974). In one investigation we compared "attractive" and "unattractive" children based on the frequency of teacher–student interactions they received in kindergarten as well as in the fourth and seventh grades. Attractive and unattractive children were identified, and the type, frequency, and quality of teacher–student interactions were recorded in the classroom. One of the findings was that attractive fourth graders received more teacher attention than their unattractive fourth grade peers, while an equivalent effect was all but absent for the remaining grades. However, at the close of the study we engaged in some *post hoc* examination of further data and found that the average IQ of the children in the fourth grade classroom exceeded that of the other two groups. Therefore, we cannot be sure that the reported effect between attractiveness of the child and teacher attention for the fourth grade group may not have actually been due to a differential attribute related to general brightness. Differential selection of subject effects, in particular, plagues researchers in institutional settings where individual random assignment to comparison groups cannot easily be made.

Pretesting. Not all research studies use a present measure followed by a treatment and posttest. However, when a pretest is given, it is possible that the initial experience with the test during the first assessment period can cause inflated (exaggerated) scores on the second measure. This is much like a practice effect, where experience helps one to get higher scores.

▶   An excellent example is an investigation reported by John Nesselroade and Paul Baltes (1974) in which adolescents responded to several personality measures over a three-year period. During the second session (year) a retest control group of adolescents the same age as the experimental group was also assessed. These adolescents had not been tested during the first year of assessment. Their scores were, however, compared to the scores of the young people who had both the first and second measures administered to them. For two personality measures an important retest effect was found. Previous experience taking the test resulted in high extroversion and intelligence scores. Therefore, it is possible to incorrectly conclude when using pretesting techniques that a change from pretesting to posttesting is due to the mediating experimental treatment, when it is mainly due to the initial practice with the measurement during pretesting.

Instrumentation. Many social scientists believe that the most desirable research project requires a mechanized data collection process (i.e., use of cameras, videotape, tape recorders, etc.). But even this strategy creates potential problems for internal validity. The use of such equipment can create as many validity problems as direct observation if their use is not controlled in systematic ways. Any change in the instrumental measuring process can make subtle changes in the measurement of the dependent variable. Just as direct observation can lead to incorrect findings through sloppy recording, poor timing, low competency of observer, or fatigue, mechanical equipment can create equivalent problems. Videotape equipment can malfunction, batteries in a tape recorder can begin to wear out and slow speech down, event recorders can have electrical problems, and the like. Furthermore, placing cameras at different viewing angles from one subject to the next can result in observations that are not equivalent in what they reveal to the researcher. Therefore, changes in the dependent variable can occur due to instrumentation effects if adequate controls and standardized techniques are not used.

Experimental Mortality. Even though this phenomenon is not prevalent, mortality can actually be a problem in doing research. In investigations that are completed over a lengthy period of time, individuals drop out of investigations for various reasons. Individuals can be lost due to marriage, sickness, promotion, graduation, and sometimes even death. As the researcher loses individuals from comparison groups, the differential loss may actually affect the results of the investigation.

▶   For example, one is studying the effects of group membership on personality change over the course of three years among college students. Three groups have been defined on certain theoretical grounds. One group includes athletes, another scholarship recipients, while the last includes fraternity/sorority members. Over the course of three years the initial participants in these three groups could leave for any of the various reasons we mentioned earlier (as well as others). Let us say, however, that we lost a rather large number of our athletic friends to professional contract offers. This experimental mortality may do a great deal to change our research findings over the three-year period for that group. Hypothetically, it is possible that the more aggressive or assertive members of that group may leave their college training early for professional careers. Therefore, when comparing the three groups for differences in personality, it is possible that no significant differences would appear between them on aggressive personality characteristics during the third year, even if the first year comparisons showed a sharp difference between the three groups. Thus, we might incorrectly assume that athletes mellow with age, a conclusion inaccurately drawn because of experimental mortality between comparison groups.

Statistical Regression. A complex factor limiting internal validity can occur when individuals are selected for inclusion in an investigation based on extremely high or low personal characteristics or attributes (Nesselroade, Stigler, & Baltes, 1980). For instance, a common practice in education research is to compare high and low achievement groups. In sociology, comparisons are made between high- and low-income groups, while psychologists frequently compare high-anxious with low-anxious groups of individuals. The problem with this technique is that a statistical regress to the mean (average score) can occur which may be misrepresented as an experimental effort. Regardless of experimental treatments, there is a *natural tendency* for persons to look more like the average respondent as they are measured a second or third time. That is, the high group is likely to drop in their scores over time, while the low group is likely to rise. (For simplicity our comments have dealt with one-variable-measured-on-two-occasion situations. For discussion on regression to the mean with more complex research designs we urge interested students to read the excellent article by Nesselroade, Stigler, and Baltes, 1980.)

Selection-Maturation Effects. It is possible that an interaction effect between sample selection and treatment can invalidate a research finding. That is, differential characteristics, such as motivation or interest in being a research participant, can interact with the experimental treatment in determining the results of an investigation.

To illustrate, assume we wish to study the effects of single parenting on a child's potential delinquency. One group consists of single parents, while the other consists of intact (mother and father present) family members who serve as a control group for comparison. Both groups are randomly selected from local marriage and divorce records. Children from both family types are given an equivalent social work program experience while pretest and posttest comparisons are made on their aggressiveness, assertiveness, acting-out behavior, and the like. Although randomly drawn and assigned as best as possible, there is no guarantee from this investigation that the children (or parents) from the two different comparison groups did not hold differing motivations and expectations for the investigation, the social program, and their voluntary involvement. Coupled with the actual social program experience, differential motivation may interact with the actual treatment leading to an artificial, superior performance on the dependent variables for one of the two groups.

Factors Limiting External Validity.   Information concerning external validity is essential to estimating the applicability or generalizability of the research findings. Although a number of limiting factors are important, three stand out as the most common factors likely to limit external validity.

Reactive Effects. Not only can testing or measurement affect an individual's responses to the measure, it is possible that measurement itself can *permanently change* the behavior.

Information can be given to the research participant through the measurement of behavior or attitudes that actually alter the individual's future behavior.

One of the authors worked as a psychometrist for a short period of time giving Stanford-Binet intelligence tests. It was frequently noted that subjects would look up missed items after the exam out of simple curiosity. No doubt if those individuals were reassessed on the same IQ test their intelligence scores would be higher, as they now have more correct information to offer. Thus, measurement itself can have a reactive effect on an individual's behavior.

Interaction between Selection Bias and the Experimental/Independent Variable. It is possible in selecting experimental and control groups that the sample does not adequately represent the larger population to which one wishes to generalize. Therefore, the result may only be specific to the samples used and the experimental effects on those samples. The more this particular limiting factor to external validity becomes probable the harder it is to obtain a random sample of subjects for experimentation (Campbell & Stanley, 1963). For example, research associated with highly sensitive issues such as racism or drug experimentation are particularly susceptible to this problem.

Ecological Validity. Urie Brofenbrenner (1977) has argued that broader approaches to the study of human behavior are greatly needed. Cryptically, he remarks, for example, that contemporary developmental psychology (and we add social science in general) is "the science of the strange behavior of children [or adults] in strange situations with strange adults [experimenters] for the briefest possible periods of time" (p. 513). Therefore, the relevance of a given piece of research to issues of generalizability is determined by not only the type of sampling completed, but the ecological setting in which the information is gathered. Brofenbrenner (1977) defines ecological validity as follows: "An investigation is regarded as ecologically valid if it is carried out in a naturalistic setting and involves objects and activities from everyday life" (p. 515). To engage in truly ecologically valid experimentation, the investigator must recognize several complex dimensions of behavior. It must be acknowledged that all social behavior requires a give-and-take between individuals. For example, not only does the parent influence the child's behavior but likewise the child affects the behavior of the parent. Therefore, researchers must consider the social reciprocity between individuals when they interact with each other, including the experimenter and his or her subjects. Likewise, an ecologically valid investigation recognizes that an individual's behavior is likely to be different in varying situations and settings. In summary, ecologically valid research requires a recognition of the full physical and personal ecological effect on human behavior.

Reliability of Findings

When reading individual research reports, it is rather difficult to assess the reliability of one specific finding. The question that the reader should have in mind is whether a given research method can be used more than once to replicate the findings of a previous investigation (i.e, the reader should determine if the same research results can be obtained when a specific project is completed and a second time in the exact same manner). Therefore, the reliability of research findings has to do with consistency of

---

Tips for Consumers 4.2

In a general sense a research report has its own validity and reliability. The research finding is said to be valid if

1. the independent variable clearly was shown to influence the dependent variable as evidenced by the elimination of rival causal factors;
2. the findings can be generalized to a known group of people.

Have the researchers attempted to identify and control for factors that limit internal and external validity? To begin, did the researchers recognize that there are possible factors that limit such validities? Did they introduce any controls in the study to eliminate these confounding factors? If not, can you trust the validity of the reported findings?

Is the reliability of a finding contingent on its replicability? Does the researcher indicate whether the findings are consistent with past results? If not, is it possible that due to superior research design the new findings are more accurate? Or is it possible that due to poor design the findings of past studies are not replicated?

---

results when using the same method of investigation over different geographical locations, at different times. Independent *replication* is the *essence* of reliable research.

Consumers of research should be aware that any given research report (not having a series of replications reported therein) does not assure the results are reliable. One should look for additional investigations to determine if the same type of results have been reported (when using the same method) by other investigators. Although time-consuming it is a necessary requirement in making professional decisions on how to utilize research results. *Inconsistency in findings suggests unpredictability.* If the findings are not consistent across studies, it implies that either (1) remaining factors are unaccounted for in the data results, or (2) the phenomenon is a random, unsystematic process that is not related to the experimental treatment.

Consumers of research should remember, however, that any given research project has its strengths and weaknesses (limitations). Only so many factors can be controlled for (or dealt with) in a given investigation. Therefore, two investigations replicating the same independent-dependent relationship suggest reliability, but do not assure the relationship for all time. Human behavior is complex. Multiple determinants are usually found with continuing experimentation for all social behavior. Therefore, extensive research on even the simplest of behaviors is necessary to account for the full range of variables that determine a given behavior and allows one to draw complete and reliable research conclusions. (See Tips for Consumers 4.2.)

SUMMARY

In Chapter 4 we have reviewed the major ingredients for the establishment of reliable and valid measures and the criteria for assessing the degree of reliability and validity of research results. It is our belief that the scientist is responsible for *reporting* and the consumer of research must *assess* the degree of reliability and validity of findings prior to implementing them into their professional activities. To use social science research in public policy making, building intervention programs, and implementing social changes requires wise consumers of research and well-trained and qualified social scientists alike. From the consumer end, we always urge "Let the buyer beware."

The following major points were presented in this chapter:

1. Validity deals with the truthfulness of the finding, while reliability deals with consistency. Both are needed in social science research.
2. Internal validity deals with assessing the degree of assurance one can have that the research method actually caused the effect. External validity indicates whether the results are generalizable or representative.
3. In every research report, a statement on how extraneous variables were controlled or eliminated as rival hypotheses should be found, read, and assessed.
4. Replication is the best indicator of reliability of findings.
5. Four major types of validity should be established for dependent variable measures, including face, content, criterion-related, and construct validity. Each offers a unique contribution to the validity question.
    a. Face validity refers to the common-sense content of the assessment device.
    b. Content validity refers to the representativeness or completeness of the content of the subject matter being assessed.
    c. Criterion-related validity assesses the relative validity of one assessment device by comparing it to specific criterion variables.
    d. Construct validity refers to the accuracy of assessment of the theoretical construct or element.
6. Three types of reliability are typically used in building good research assessment devices. These types include test-retest, split-half, and equivalent-forms. The time interval and content are specific dimensions that are considered in building reliable instruments.
    a. Test–retest reliability requires administering the same test to the same sample, twice, under the same general conditions.
    b. Split-half reliability assesses the degree of association between subcomponents of a test or assessment device having been administered at one time.
    c. Equivalent-forms techniques entail comparing the same sample's responses to two instruments thought to measure the same content area at two points in time.

In the chapters within the next section regarding data collection strategies, we shall review further some additional aspects of validity and/or reliability that are pertinent to each technique. In this manner we shall continue to make salient the importance of such issues to good science.

PROBLEMS AND APPLICATIONS

1. In groups of three or four individuals choose a construct and develop a scale to measure it (e.g., family violence, children's creativity, social class, the psychology of scarcity, love, or teacher effectiveness). Using the concepts of reliability and validity of measurement, outline how you

would establish both components for your scale. Present your ideas to the class and have them critique how you might improve on your ideas.

2. Read the following article: "Contemporary Views of Euthanasia: A Regional Assessment" *(Social Biology,* 1978, *25,* 62–68). As a classroom activity critique the development of the scales. What are their strengths and weaknesses? How might the information of Chapter 4 be used to continue to make the scales more valid and reliable? Since you are a consumer of research findings, how reliable or valid do you believe the findings are for use in applied program development?

3. Identify illustrations from research reports in your own major area of study which emphasize reliability of validity and vice versa. What could have been done to strengthen both components?

4. Debate in class whether one should establish reliability before validity or validity before reliability.

REFERENCES

Adams, G. R., & Cohen, A. S. (1974). Children's physical and interpersonal characteristics that affect student-teacher interactions. *Journal of Experimental Education, 43,* 1–5.

American Psychological Association. (1974). *Standards for education and psychological tests.* Washington, D.C.: American Psychological Association.

Anastasi, A. (1988). *Psychological testing.* New York: Macmillan.

Bronfenbrenner, U. (1977). Toward an experimental ecology of human development. *American Psychologist, 32,* 513–531.

Campbell, D. T., & Fiske, D. W. (1959). Convergent and discriminant validation by the multitrait-multimethod matrix. *Psychological Bulletin, 56,* 81–105.

Campbell, D. T., & Stanley, J. C. (1963). *Experimental and quasi-experimental designs for research.* Chicago: Rand McNally.

Code of Fair Testing Practices in Education. (1988). Washington, D.C.: National Council on Measurement in Education.

Cook, T. D., & Campbell, D. T. (1979). *Quasiexperimentation: Design and analysis issues for field settings.* Chicago: Rand McNally.

Cronbach, L. J., & Meehl, P. E. (1955). Construct validity in psychological tests. *Psychological Bulletin, 52,* 281–302.

Curtis, S., & Adams, G. R. (in press). The stress-response scale for adolescence. *Journal of Adolescent Research.*

DeMarsh, J. (1979). *The development of empathy, role-taking, and listening as a function of a preschool experience.* Unpublished thesis, Utah State University.

Embretson, S. (1983). Construct validity: Construct representation versus nomothetic span. *Psychological Bulletin, 93,* 179–197.

Flaugher, R. (1978). The many definitions of test bias. *American Psychologist, 33,* 671–679.

Green, B. F. (1978). In defense of measurement. *American Psychologist, 33,* 664–670.

Gronlund, N. E. (1981). *Measurement and evaluation in teaching.* New York: Macmillan.

Kirk, J., & Miller, M. L. (1986). Reliability and validity in qualitative research. *Qualitative research methods.* Vol 1. Sage Publications, Beverly Hills.

Loevinger, J. (1957). Objective tests as instruments of psychological theory. *Psychological Report, 3,* 635–694 (Monograph Supplement 9).

Marcia, J. E. (1964). *Determination and construct validity of ego identity status.* Unpublished doctoral dissertation, Ohio State University.

Messick, S. (1981). Constructs and their vicissitudes in educational and psychological measurement. *Psychological Bulletin, 89,* 575–588.

Messick, S. (1980). Test validity and the ethics of assessment. *American Psychologist, 35,* 1012–1027.

Munro, B., & Adams, G. R. (1978). Love American style: A test of role structure theory on changes in attitudes toward love. *Human Relations, 31,* 215–228.

Nesselroade, J. R., & Baltes, P. B. (1974). Adolescent personality development and historical change: 1970–72. *Monographs of the Society for Research in Child Development* (Whole No. 154).

Nesselroade, J. R., Stigler, S. M., & Baltes, P. B. (1980). Regression toward the mean and the study of change. *Psychological Bulletin, 88,* 622–637.

Saal, F. E., Downey, R. G., & Lahey, M. A. (1980). Rating the ratings: Assessing the psychometric quality of rating data. *Psychological Bulletin, 88,* 413–428.

SECTION II

Basic Research Designs

In this section, we will introduce three major types of conceptual designs that are used to direct the data collection process. These research designs provide the conceptual framework for determining the order in which data are gathered. Each of the three basic types of designs has its own individual utility, strengths, and weaknesses. First we introduce you to research designs that capture in broad descriptive terms the general patterns of human behavior. Next we will provide a chapter that details the basic observational designs that can be utilized in varying research settings. Finally, we will review the basic research designs used to assess the causes of human behavior. Collectively, the chapters in this section provide information about the three most commonly used conceptual designs that provide the structure for data collection strategies.

CHAPTER 5

Research Designs: Exploratory and Descriptive

OUTLINE

Research Design: A Definition
    Exploratory Designs
        Flexibility
        Serendipity
        Process and Activity
Functions of Explorations
    Descriptive Designs
        The Focus
        Functions of Description
        Anthropological Description
        Selectivity
        Asking Important Questions
        The Richness of Words
Data Collection: Four Approaches
    The Case Study Approach
    The Survey Approach
    The Cross-sectional Approach
    The Longitudinal Approach
Summary
Problems and Applications
References

KEY TERMS

Research design
Exploratory research
Serendipity
Descriptive research
Verbal description
Numerical description

Selectivity
Case study research
Survey research
Cross-sectional research
Longitudinal research

STUDY GUIDE QUESTIONS

1. What is meant by the notion of research design? What are the main functions of design in conducting quality research?
2. In thinking about descriptive studies, what are the main features of this research design?
3. In thinking about exploratory studies, what are the main features of this research design?
4. How can researchers employ the concept of "serendipity" in conducting day-to-day research in the broad spectrum of social science?
5. Contrast the main features of cross-sectional research with those of the longitudinal approach. Do you believe that taking all things into consideration, one approach is inherently superior to the other?
6. What are the key characteristics and functions of survey research?

Role of the Scientist

A clearly defined purpose and the appropriate design to fit the problem place the researcher in a good position to successfully complete research. Exploratory and descriptive designs have been used widely in social science research and continue to be of extreme importance for many important research problems. A good working knowledge of these designs is necessary for the functioning social science researcher. A good working knowledge of exploratory designs permits one to engage in creative and pioneering research, while competence in dealing with descriptive designs permits one to provide the rich detail and "color" associated with insightful research.

Role of the Consumer

The competent consumer of research in the broad area of social science will probably be exposed to more exploratory and descriptive research than any other types, hence the critical importance of being able to assess the conclusions of research in terms of the design employed. A research design tells us much about the purposes of a study and whether the right design was used for a specific problem. Knowing about exploratory and descriptive designs will facilitate critical reading, study, and application of knowledge from these studies to everyday living in society. The consumer of research needs to be able to understand the limitations and strengths of these two designs so as to read and interpret a variety of designs. Decision making is an elaborate process, and these two designs have direct bearing on many decisions made in the daily life of the consumer.

RESEARCH DESIGN: A DEFINITION

To a significant degree, completing successful research depends on having a clearly defined purpose and access to useful data pertinent to that purpose. Certainly, various problems require that different strategies be employed in successful research. The strategy employed, the approach, or the particular research tools involved relate to the idea known as design or research design. A *research design* refers to a plan, blueprint, or guide for data collection and interpretation—sets of rules that enable the investigator to conceptualize and observe the problem under study. A research design can be defined as a collection of guides or rules for data collection. Kerlinger (1964) notes two basic purposes of designs: (1) to control for variations and (2) to provide answers (data) to questions being researched. As Kerlinger further notes, the design "tells us, in a sense, what observations to make, how to make them, and how to analyze the quantitative representations of the observations" (p. 276). The purpose or intent of a study defines the type of design that should be used.

Two very common designs in the study of social institutions and human behavior are the exploratory and descriptive research designs. These designs will be treated in some detail in the sections of this chapter, and illustrations will be provided to clarify what they are, how they work, and when it is appropriate to use one as opposed to the other. Following these two major sections, we will briefly cover four research strategies associated with, or commonly used in doing, exploratory and descriptive research: (1) case studies, (2) surveys, (3) cross-sectional, and (4) longitudinal studies. Their similarities and differences will be assessed.

Exploratory Designs

The concept of exploration brings to mind the tremendous feats of Columbus, De Soto, Ponce de Leon, and modern-day explorers such as John Glenn, Neil Armstrong, and recently Sally Ride, the first American woman in space. These explorers were seeking new information, new insights, and were dedicated to making observations about colonization, terrain, natural resources, atmosphere, and the like. For example, the explorer John C. Fremont set out to map, describe, and "live in" the mountain West in his five explorations of the West. In 1843, caught up in the beauty of his surroundings, he described his feelings as being awed, perplexed, and thoroughly thrilled. His wife, Jessie Benton Fremont, did much of his writing as he dictated, and she is credited with bringing to the reader in a popular form (see Fremont, 1988) much of the richness and insight of his explorations. Thus, the ability to explore that which is important and then describe it clearly and accurately is an important craft.

While preliminary goals guided their studies, these explorers were not locked into a rigid design or ultimate outcome. So it is with the social scientist working within the context of the exploratory design. The very purpose of *exploratory research* is to seek out new insights, ask questions, and assess phenomena in a different perspective. Exploratory studies are less structured, which permits the researcher to seek new insights. The less developed an area, the more likely the exploration should be the design used. It will become apparent that exploratory research serves three main purposes: (1) to satisfy curiosity, (2) to build methodology that might be used in later, more tightly designed research, and (3) to make recommendations regarding the likelihood of continuing with additional research on the topic.

Flexibility.   By their very nature, exploratory designs allow considerable flexibility in answering or exploring the problem in question. This freedom is vital if the investigator is to observe, talk, listen, question, and evaluate a given situation. One cannot be locked into an "iron-fisted" design and still be free to challenge a problem or to deal more broadly with an "I wonder what would happen if" type question. A keen observer in the broadest sense will almost always obtain new insights by using the main elements of exploratory designs. These may be in the form of hints, apparent inconsistencies, a dearth of information, but hardly ever anything as formalized as a hypothesis. Exploratory designs often provide provocative questions that can be followed up in other studies or have a formal hypothesis as an end goal.

It will be useful for the reader to view an exploratory design as a process of discovering the most general information about a research problem. Note that exploratory studies typically involve three components: a review of literature (see Chapter 3), discussion with experts, and involvement with case studies. By being open, probing, and seeking the *why, how, what,* and *where,* the researcher can minimize personal bias and maximize the gaining of new perspectives.

Serendipity.   Researchers in exploratory work should have heightened awareness of the familiar, a sharper appreciation of the unfamiliar, and a spirit of intellectual inquiry. They must be open to flirting with serendipity— the "serendipity pattern refers to the fairly common experience of observing an *unanticipated, anomalous* and *strategic* datum which becomes the occasion for developing a new theory or for extending an existing theory" (Merton, 1968, p. 158). Merton notes that the happy event of serendipity is typically unanticipated, is surprising, and often can be very important.

▶ *Process and Activity.*   In August of 1868, Othiel Charles Marsh, a Yale paleontologist, came West on a train to learn more about a well full of ancient bones that had been discovered. Professor Marsh remarked at the time:

> I could only wonder if such scientific truths as I had now obtained were concealed in a single well, what untold treasures must there be in the whole Rocky Mountain region. This thought promised rich rewards for the enthusiastic explorer in this new field, and thus my own life work seemed laid out before me. (Marsh as quoted in Goetzmann, 1966, p. x)

Goetzmann (1966), in reference to Marsh, noted that exploration is much more than adventure or discovery; the essence of exploration deals with process and activity.

> It is the seeking. It is one form of the learning process itself, and...a branch of science which resulted in a discovery at a place trod many times over by previous generations of explorers bent on their missions in days gone by (p. xi)

Although Goetzmann is referring to historical exploration of the West, his emphasis on process and activity are very pertinent to methodology used in the exploratory design in social science. Even though the exploratory design is open and negotiable by definition, it is not without purpose.

Asking the Creative Question. A detailed example of an exploratory study will help to illustrate the design of this approach, the questions involved, data collection, and the results from a specific study. Adams and Cromwell (1978) present their work in attempting to more fully understand morning and night people in a family context. They point out their work is preliminary; in fact, the idea for the research came out of a brainstorming session by the authors. They had made personal observations of personality matches and mismatches in regard to "morningness" and "nightness" among couples, they had wondered about the consequences of these relationships on marital stability, reviewed the available literature, and finally had carried out a small pilot study of 28 married graduate students.

The initial work convinced the authors that people were capable of defining themselves, their spouses, and other family members in terms of rhythms and hour of the day. Four categories emerged: (1) husband and wife as morning persons; (2) husband and wife as night persons; (3) wife as night person, husband as morning person; and (4) husband as night person and wife as morning person. From a series of explorative questions, Adams and Cromwell gained broader understanding of the two categories of body activity—nightness and morningness. As an example, one person said, "I consider myself a morning person because, when I get up, I am filled with energy and a desire to complete planned activities before evening" (Adams & Cromwell, 1978, p. 7). Under the category of matched couples, one person remarked,

> We both like to do things at night, stay up late, etc. Our mornings are not times of great communication. In fact, we've decided if we had to face each other in the morning, our relationship would never survive. He gets up and fixes breakfast for the family while I get ready for work, then I clean up while he gets ready. Our sex life is definitely a night thing except on weekends. Even on camping trips we stay up late and sleep late. (p. 10)

These authors conclude their observations by attempting to form guiding questions for additional research. In Category 1 (matched couples), they believe that night couples are more likely to be highly involved in family networks than morning couples, that morning couples enjoy greater job satisfaction when their work is regular daytime scheduling as opposed to night work, and that morning couples are likely to engage in sexual intercourse in the mornings and night couples at night. In Category 2 (mismatched couples), the researchers assert that out-of-time-phase couples will spend less time in conversation, shared activities, and sex than matched couples. Mismatched couples will have poorer marital adjustment, and finally, mismatched couples with better couple adjustment are more likely to enjoy greater flexibility and adaptability than matched couples. And last, in Category 3 (matched and mismatched families), the authors claim that the most difficult parent–child adjustment will occur when a *morning couple have one or more night-oriented children.*

Thus, we see the emergence of additional questions for more extensive research on body rhythms and time routines in the family setting. The authors also commit themselves to complete additional research on the topic. In summary, a novel question about day and night rhythms is readily addressed by using an exploratory approach.

FUNCTIONS OF EXPLORATIONS

We can understand more about the function of exploratory studies by assessing major motives in any type of exploration work. In assessing the fifteenth and sixteenth century era of extensive New World exploration, certainly *economic gain* was a major motive, but a *vibrant curiosity* about what lay beyond the next cape or mountain had to rank high as well. Some explorers came in search of *new homes* for *surplus population,* while *military campaigns* or *missionary activity* prompted others to explore a world not yet well understood. Many explorers came for *scientific purposes,* and these were typically sponsored by a society or the State. These explorers seeking to assess the New World, like contemporary social scientists, employed *multiple* or *mixed purposes* as they carried out the exhaustive, and sometimes heroic, work. And finally, the social scientist, like the famous mountain climber, simply engages in some exploratory research because the question is there!

Denzin (1970) states that exploratory designs are for areas unknown or unfamiliar to us. Further, we should use such designs to help us sharpen lines of inquiry so that we focus, direct, analyze, and interpret within the context of a guiding theory. We agree with Denzin here and add that one can avoid trivial or fragmented research by using, whenever possible, some guiding theory or framework; however, in exploratory research, we should not be burdened with a theory—it should only be a guide.

In summary, then, exploratory designs are purposeful and flexible. The researcher must be constantly adaptable, willing to change, and open to impact from the data. The flexibility inherent in exploratory research does not mean absence of direction to the inquiry; rather the flexibility means that the focus is initially broad and becomes progressively smaller as the research goes on. The user of the exploratory design would do well to ask all kinds of questions about the phenomenon being researched, even if some of them appear to be ridiculous. Being alert for observations that seem odd or interesting and events that make you question previously held beliefs should be a regular format for those who successfully engage in exploratory research. (See Tips 5.1.)

Descriptive Designs

Once we have obtained sufficient insights and useful information we can move to *descriptive studies,* a design of research in which the main goal is to portray an accurate profile of persons, events, or objects. In descriptive studies the investigator is typically concerned with providing a profile of variables such as age, race, religion, occupation, and marital status. Selltiz, Lawrence, Wrightsman, and Cook (1976) note that descriptive

---

Tips for Consumers 5.1

Some of the most important and intriguing studies in the social science world would be classified as exploratory research. Characteristics of exploratory research useful to consumers include

1. asking the good question at the appropriate, even critical time;
2. going into the research situation with an open agenda—letting the phenomena or data "speak to you";
3. approaching exploratory studies by trying to arrive at good questions, not necessarily answering questions;
4. opening up new areas of research to help point the direction for new problems with instruments that are flexible enough to be modified often.

---

studies require extensive previous knowledge of the problem to be researched or described. This is in contrast to the exploratory study in which this assumption is not made. It is further assumed that the investigators will be able to measure as appropriate the concepts or problem under study. Since we have considerably more information and direction in the descriptive research, the design is less flexible. We are not as free to probe, explore, and "shotgun" around in descriptive research.

The Focus.   Descriptive research usually focuses on events that are in process or that have already taken place; hence, the investigator may vary methods of observation and description, but not the actual events in a situation. Descriptive designs involve much more than merely gathering data and analysis. They involve interpretation, contrast, classification, and integration of findings. Descriptive research uses words and numbers to describe *what is.* In the use of *verbal descriptions,* validity is heavily dependent on the ability of the investigator to use the right words and clear writing style. In *numerical descriptions,* the researcher is obliged to present an accurate profile of the situation with descriptive statistics (typically measures of frequency, central tendency, and dispersion).

Functions of Description.   Hyman (1955) notes that a descriptive study attempts to make a precise measurement of a dependent variable in a population, whereas in an explanatory study the goal would be to uncover the effects of independent variables. The purpose then is not to predict, but to describe. Good (1972) helps to clarify the purposes of descriptive research in stating that this type of research seeks to acquire evidence concerning a situation or population, it identifies norms or baseline information which can be used for comparative purposes, and finally, it serves to determine how and if one is to move to another type of research. Viewed in this context, descriptive research is akin to historical study—recording history as it occurs.

Storehouses of descriptive research are available, since most of the research in the social sciences is more of a descriptive type than any other design. Examples of disciplines that have made extensive use of description include child development, cultural anthropology, and sociology.

▶ *Anthropological Description.*   This example comes from anthropology and continues a long history of descriptive designs being used extensively and with richness by this discipline. Women, symbolic roles, and ritual are depicted in the practice of southern lay midwives as specialists in childbirth.

> My sister-in-law gave birth to her son. He came to the world, he was what you call, it's not a normal delivery, he came foot foremost. Aunt Susie had quite a time getting him to live. I was with her and she found that this baby was coming foot foremost so she taken it over. It was my first experience seeing a baby born that way. She was nervous herself. She had quite a lot of luck because she was a Christian woman. She believed in prayer. She said that was the only thing that was going to save that baby was prayer. So she prayed to the Lord that this baby might live. He was gasping for breath and he was so tired. The smaller parts of the baby come and then the head come. The baby had a chance of losing his life on account of the fluids there, but somehow through the will of God, she was prepared to take care of that baby. I just know it was the Lord's will because lots of times they die in that condition. (Dougherty, 1978, p. 155)

Dougherty presented the midwife's own natural verbal description of the birth event and is successful in depicting the stress of the midwife in her first delivery of this type and how she attributes success to her fervent prayer. Dougherty, using verbal description, catches the stress, trauma, and relief in this situation and shares the potential fate of mother and baby with the reader. Descriptive research can be aimed at the smallest of details in a situation or can be sweeping in scope; in this case, the focus is on mother and baby "captured" in historical time and triumph.

Selectivity.   Regardless of the level of description—focusing on small details or merely touching with broad brush strokes—the ultimate burden is on the ability of the descriptive researcher to be selective in what is presented. One must focus on some events at the exclusion of others and emphasize some factors while only briefly mentioning others. Hopefully, an investigator's discipline training and specific preparation for a project will help in determining what points will be selected for observation and what will be disregarded. One must keep in mind that the outcome of a project is potentially very important, as descriptive research is most often used to *inform*, as a basis for *decision making,* or as a *fact-gathering* stage in order to support or pursue additional research objectives. (See Tips 5.2.)

▶ *The Hijacker Profile.* Our next example had its origin in the crisis that grew from the onslaught of air piracy so frequent in the troubled 1960s. This example is used to illustrate how descriptive designs can capitalize on reports and data already gathered (for other specific purposes). In 1969, the most intensive year for plane hijacking, a total of 40 attempts were made to hijack aircrafts in the United States, and the hijackers achieved some degree of success in 33 of these attempts. The alleged motive in hijacking aircraft has included such extremes as fleeing with a child who was in the legal custody of the other parent, dropping political leaflets on other countries, for example, Lisbon and Caracas, and for political asylum in Castro-ruled Cuba (Turi et al., 1972).

Hubbard (1971) presents a descriptive profile of the American skyjacker as about 29 years of age, a native-born white man at the lower end of the economic ladder, apolitical,

---

Tips for Consumers 5.2

Four very common modes of data collection and strategies for conducting research are (1) the *case study research,* (2) the *survey approach,* (3) *the cross-sectional approach,* and (4) the longitudinal approach. Each of these strategies has both strong points and some limitations. Be aware that most polls such as Gallup or Harris employ a cross-sectional approach in which 1,000 to 1,600 people are interviewed in a restricted time period. Time is very important in a national poll tied to prediction or decision making because of data stagnation or spoilage.

Very few longitudinal studies have been completed in the arena of social science. Time, resources, human motivation, and cooperation are reasons that result in little longitudinal research. Gallup, as well as other pollsters, have polled a national sample on the same topic for several years so that one can assess trends year to year. While this is very useful and justified, keep in mind that the data generated through this approach are not longitudinal. To be longitudinal, the data must be from the same subjects, dealing with the same topic over a period of time. In this context, one can assess both the impact of social time as well as maturational time with human respondents.

---

emotionally detached from public causes, and conservative in dress, ideas, and customs. At the personality level, Hubbard depicts this person as weak, fearful, and generally ineffective. He has few close friends and is not successful in business, sexual, or marital relationships. The skyjacker is typically aware that air piracy is not likely to achieve the desired goals but, nevertheless, seizes on this adventure with tenacity to show the world that for once in a miserable life cycle, he will succeed and bring fame and fortune to himself.

This composite profile of aircraft hijackers was developed after intensive analysis of several dozen descriptive cases that came from intensive interviews with hijackers, their family members, their friends, and former employers. The data further indicate that the great majority of the United States skyjackings have gone to Cuba, that the incidents have been cyclical, that they have occurred in flurries, and that a significant number of skyjackers were mentally disturbed and in strainful relationships with authorities.

It should be obvious that exploratory or descriptive designs would be the main types to use in studying similar phenomena. For a number of reasons, it would not be practical, legal, or ethical to manipulate or alter events to engage in some controlled studies of this type. Turi et al. (1972) explain their methodological approach to this research and the skyjacker profiles:

> The purpose of this study is to prepare a descriptive study of all aspects of the phenomenon known as "skyjacking." This study compiles the latest statistics on skyjacking, i.e., number of incidents, type of aircraft, type of weapons, disposition or status of skyjackers. It also reviews the legal aspects, both national and international, related to this crime. The personality and emotional state of the skyjacker are also examined. The preventive measures taken by both the government and the airline industry are examined. Included in the preventive measures are the sky marshal program, the pre-boarding screening process and the latest developments in electronic detection devices. (pp. 2–3)

This important descriptive research has been widely used in coping with a real problem of health, safety, and national security. Many of the points presented, as well as recommendations given, have become implemented to cope with the problem of skyjacking. The Turi et al. (1972) research has been used for information, decision making, and policy implementation—major outcomes of descriptive research. This example helps to clarify the assertion that descriptive research is much more than merely gathering data—it involves the skillful analysis, interpretation, and implementation of the data.

▶ *The Longitudinal Case of Anna.* We move now to another example of descriptive research, which has become a classic in the study of child socialization in the context of extreme deprivation. This descriptive study focuses on Anna, a girl five years of age found tied to an old chair in a second floor storage room of a farmhouse in Pennsylvania. She was born March 6, 1932, found by authorities in February 1938, and died of hemorrhagic jaundice $4^1/_2$ years later. Anna had the misfortune of being the second illegitimate child born to her mother, and since the mother still lived with her father and other relatives in the family household, her father was extremely upset and rejected the baby. This impasse forced the child to be reared in an extreme state of isolation and deprivation. Kingsley Davis became familiar with the case through the press and became involved at once with observation and assessment of Anna. After preliminary assessment and testing he described Anna and her situation in the following manner:

> Since Anna turned her head slowly toward a loud-ticking clock held near by, we concluded that she could hear. Other attempts to make her notice sounds, such as clapping hands or speaking to her, elicited no response, yet when the door was opened suddenly she tended to look in that direction. Her feet were sensitive to touch. She exhibited the plantar, patellar, and pupillary reflexes. When sitting up she jounced rhythmically up and down on bed—a recent habit of which she was very fond.... She neither smiled nor cried in our presence, and the only sound she made—a slight sucking intake of breath with the lips—occurred rarely. She did frown or scowl occasionally in response to no observable stimulus; otherwise she remained expressionless. (Davis, 1940, pp. 556–557)

Anna was unable to drink from a cup, had no interest in toys (many toys were sent to her from sympathetic readers of her case), but did exhibit a liking to having her hair combed. Several months after removal from her wretched environment and receiving intensive care, improvements were evident. Her case is remarkable in the study of human development as she made dramatic growth for a child who for all practical purposes had missed six years of nurturance and socialization. In the period before her death she was able to follow directions, identify a few colors, string beads, build with blocks, and display a good sense of rhythm. She loved dolls. Anna was clean about her clothing, talked mainly in phrases but attempted to carry on a conversation. Davis commented about her progress at this point.

> Her improvement showed that socialization, even when started at the late age of six, could still do a great deal toward making her a person. Even though her development was no more than that of a normal child of two or three years, she had made noteworthy progress. (Davis, 1949, p. 205)

Thus Anna's tragic circumstance of birth and brief traumatic life have been described in detail by a number of investigators who have sought to assess the causes behind her six-year captivity and the profound and lasting impact it had on her development. She was tested extensively by social workers, psychologists, sociologists, nutritionists, and medical personnel. Her case is a good example of an event that lends itself clearly to the facility of the descriptive design—her situation had already occurred and our task is to describe the *what*.

Best (1970) refers to descriptive research as it applies to cases like Anna in the following terms.

> At times, descriptive research is concerned with how *what* is or *what* exists is related to some preceding event that has influenced or affected a present condition or event. (p. 116)

Furthermore, the example of Anna is a case study, and as we shall explain later in this chapter, case study approaches often use description.

As noted, although descriptive studies are useful in making inferences about causality, they do not address that concern directly. Descriptive studies, perhaps more than other types of studies, are concerned with taxonomy building, providing profiles, showing the emergence of phenomena, and the general relationship between events, persons, or objects. The purpose of research is to seek truer knowledge, and the purpose of descriptive studies is to provide profiles and understandings about relationships in the social world.

Asking Important Questions. Descriptive designs, as noted, can deal with both qualitative and quantitative issues. Good and Scates (1954) note that if a researcher chooses a descriptive design to complete a research project, it should be because this design is best in answering the questions under study. Numbers or lack of numbers is not what makes or breaks science; asking important questions and using appropriate designs coupled with appropriate methodology to answer the questions is a mark of good science. Reynolds (1971) states that even an approximate answer to a significant question is more useful than a precise, elegant, and quantified answer to a trivial or nonsensical question. These cautions are mentioned here because often exploratory and descriptive designs are relegated to the ranks of unscientific designs because they often deal with word pictures and qualitative data. We agree with C. Wright Mills, who in *The Sociological Imagination* (1961) chided social scientists for primarily studying questions for which there was ready methodology. He challenged researchers to ask the significant and important questions and then develop the necessary methodology to deal with those questions. We see descriptive designs playing a most significant role in this kind of questioning process.

Coca Leaves: Describing a Culture. The major purpose of descriptive research is to portray situations and events, and in this regard it is very similar to historical research. A descriptive study may read very much like a historical report, with the exception that a descriptive study in science deals with present time, whereas history deals with the past as it reflects the present. We shall now provide an illustration of descriptive research in the study of human behavior which focuses on coca leaf use in southern Peru. This example illustrates application of descriptive study in a field context. Hanna (1974) was concerned with the consequences of coca leaf chewing by the high mountain dwellers in the Andes. Chewing of the coca leaves is widespread in the Andean region of South America, and a number of researchers have commented on possible functions that chewing the leaves serves, including providing energy, ritual, sacrifice, medicine, mythology, and divinity. Chewing coca leaves is similar to tobacco chewing, since the user takes a given amount of leaves and chews it until it forms a wad. This wad of leaves is then held in one side of the mouth for a period of time and then chewed or rechewed as necessary; the juice and up to 70% of the leaves may be swallowed as this process continues. The coca leaves contain cocaine, and evidence indicates that the chewing process will remove up to 80% of the cocaine. Multiple investigations have pointed out that the Andean cultures do not experience the ecological disturbance over the use of this drug as people often do in a culture like the United States.

Hanna goes on to describe the variations in the use of coca leaves with Indians at various altitude levels in the region, noting that the higher the altitude, the more likely the Indians are to use the leaves. The following profile provides additional understanding regarding the utility of coca leaf chewing.

> Perhaps the most economical manner of coca acquisition is to circumvent the formal network by making direct contact with one of the smaller coca producers in the foothills. Each year some men sometimes with their families travel to the foothills, taking with them their animals, meat, potatoes, and cereals from the Altiplano [high plateau]. These they can trade for coca as well as for the other tropical products to be used and sold when they return to Nuñoa [community]. In some cases, the traveler may remain and aid in the cultivation of fields in the coca producing regions. The system is viable because it avoids the more costly distribution network and its taxes, but, more importantly, the individual farmer can realize a multiplier effect on the materials that he transports. The meat and potatoes could be sold to a local Nuñoa store, but they are worth far more when transported to lower altitudes. Similarly, the coca and other products of the foothills are more valuable when taken to Nuñoa. The traveler thus receives a double advantage: A multiplier operates upon the goods he takes to the jungle and upon the products he brings home to Altiplano. (p. 291)

Hanna believes that the practice of coca leaf chewing results in an increase of maximum working time of a laborer, helps a person function at the extremely high altitudes, promotes retention of body heat in the cold climate, stimulates the multiplier economic function mentioned, is an important medium of exchange, and lastly, serves as an important economic factor in regard to production, trade, and tax revenues.

It is clear that this rich descriptive study has a great deal of application in the current "drug wars" between the United States and Bolivia, Colombia, and Panama. It is also clear that eradication is very difficult because of the cultural significance at the level of origin as well as consumption.

▶   Flinn (1988) provides a rich and detailed account of mate guarding in a Caribbean village. Competition for mates involved a great deal of hostility and was based upon the amount of resources available to the male and reproductive ability of the female. He concluded that guarding of mates was a vital part of the social structure for these villagers.

Descriptive classification and causal inferences emerge in these studies, and once classification and description are sufficiently complete, one can move from questions of relationship to more complex causal linkages resulting in a more complete explanation. Without the initial classification and description, these latter processes are not possible.

The Richness of Words.   As contrasted with exploratory research, our goal in descriptive ◀ research is to provide accurate, complete, and informative profiles that reflect data about size, number, habits, relationship systems, or whatever dimension our purpose dictates. The imagery, richness of detail, and cultural contrast of this design are well-known and illustrated in the following profile of the people of Bali, an Indonesian island.

> The Balinese, who can be numbered in hundreds of thousands, not in a few thousands like the Samoans or a few hundreds like the New Guinea peoples, are not a primitive people, but a people whose culture is linked through Asia with our own historical past. Light, graceful, wavy-haired, with bodies every segment of which moves separately in the dance, they have a highly complex and ordered way of life that in its guilds and Hindu rituals, its written records and temple organizations, its markets and its arts, is reminiscent of Middle Ages in Europe. Crowded on a tiny island with a beautiful highly diversified, changing landscape, they have turned all life into art. The air is filled with music day and night, and the people, whose relations to each other are light, without enduring warmth, are tireless in rehearsal for a play where these disallowed feelings will be given graceful stylized expression. (Mead, 1955, p. 49)

Note the number of facts contained in this brief paragraph and the contrasts coming out of a comparative approach the famous anthropologist Margaret Mead used. One can see the clear, dramatic contrast between this compacted statement of description and the probing, searching, more hesitant statements that are characteristically associated with exploratory studies.

This difference in utility and outcome of the descriptive design as compared to the exploratory design necessitates that samples or populations for studies be selected with great care in the descriptive research undertaken. An adequate sample is perhaps more important in descriptive research than in any other, as the goal is to describe *what* is and *how* it is. Therefore, errors in sample make-up (e.g., a distortive segment of a population could be selected) can be disastrous in thwarting this goal. Readers are well aware of the detail that Gallup, Harris, and other pollsters employ in taking a representative sample of the citizenry in order to describe how they feel about issues such as abortion, the legalization of marijuana, or the use of women in active combat. An accurate profile or description can only emerge if we have the appropriate segments of the population to permit this type of profile to be depicted. Furthermore, the first descriptive study is critical in setting the stage for additional research that may follow.

The focus, the importance, and the theoretical relevance often determine the impact a study can make. Kaplan (1964) notes the observation of Sigmund Freud in regard to the importance and role of descriptive research: "The true beginning of scientific activity consists...in describing phenomena and then in proceeding to group, classify and correlate them" (p. 78).

DATA COLLECTION: FOUR APPROACHES

There are a variety of ways to use exploratory and descriptive designs to obtain data, and many different methods of data collection can be used within each type of design. The *case study* and research *survey* are heavily used by the mass media and are, therefore, quite well-known. Less known to the public, but certainly common in research, are the *cross-sectional* and *longitudinal* approaches to research and data collection. We will now define each of these strategies, state their major functions and contributions to social science research, and examine some of their limitations as well as how each compliments the other. The student should take particular note of what each approach contributes to research. From an integrative perspective it is also evident that case studies have a lot in common with longitudinal designs, while cross-sectional and survey approaches are really variations of the same design.

The Case Study Approach

A *case study* is confined to one or a few subjects (cases), the focus is usually broad in the type and quantities of variables that can be studied, and the approach tends to be in-depth and comprehensive. Since a case study includes only one or a very few cases, it can afford to deal with all pertinent information or aspects of the cases or situation. A case study, such as that of Anna, typically views the individual, family, community, or the entire subject focus. The case study approach has been used extensively in the field of social work, law, medicine, psychiatry, education, counseling, sociology, psychology, and economics, to mention just a few.

In contrast to a survey approach, the case study attempts to thoroughly assess a cluster of factors by focusing on a small number of cases. The case study approach usually assesses the world or unit as it exists, in a natural, unaltered setting. Since the focus is on a single case or limited number of cases, the problem of generalization is a major difficulty with the case study method. In addition, bias might be manifest in the very cases that were selected for study as well as the open-ended nature of the case approach, which may allow the investigator to influence the nature of the case under study.

The example of the skyjacker (Turi et al., 1972; Hubbard, 1971) shows how individual cases were accumulated to build a more comprehensive profile than any of the separate cases could by themselves. In contrast, the mother in a difficult breech delivery situation (Dougherty, 1978) illustrates the richness of the case study method to assess specific profiles, but likewise we have little idea how representative this case is as compared to the total birth experiences attended to by the southern midwife.

The Survey Approach

The term *survey* is used in a variety of ways, but a main feature refers to the gathering of data or information from a sample or specific population, usually by questionnaire, interview, or telephone survey. The researcher does not manipulate independent variables or apply control conditions to the subjects under study. In many ways, the survey approach to data is very akin to descriptive studies, but of course survey data can be used in a variety of ways such as for explanation and testing of hypotheses. Samples tend to be large in surveys, and the emphasis is not usually on individuals in a sample but rather on the generalized profiles or statistics derived from all the individual cases. A survey is usually a cross-sectional study and should stem from a random sampling base. It is the primary base for data collection in the social sciences and should involve a clearly defined purpose, problem, and objective.

In our previous research examples in this chapter, the attempt to understand the synchrony or lack of synchrony in the lives of 28 graduate married couples (Adams & Cromwell, 1978) was an example of the survey at work (see pp. 104–105). Through interview and questionnaire the authors surveyed these couples in an attempt to acquire profiles of *morning* and *nighttime* couples to assess the meaning of these body rhythms for daily family and marital interaction. To a lesser degree, even Othiel Charles Marsh, who searched for ancient bones in the West by means of a train ride to the Rocky Mountains in the nineteenth century, was using the survey method (Goetzmann, 1966).

The Cross-sectional Approach

Surveys with no element of longitudinal design are referred to as *cross-sectional* studies, meaning that the focus is on the make-up of the sample at one point in time. A cross-sectional approach also indicates that the research attempts to present a broad picture with analysis on a large group in regard to such variables as age, sex, race, education, religion, and the like. Cross-sectional studies usually involve large samples and are typically collected by personally administered or mailed questionnaires, personal interviews, or telephone interviews. The large sample size, coupled with the control of "freezing" all respondent information at a specific time, makes the cross-sectional approach to data collection a very useful and widely used method, especially in the field of sociology. Not only should the sample be sufficiently large in a cross-sectional study, the emphasis is also on a random sample in order to depict accurately the characteristics of the cross-section at one point in time.

Accurate and swiftly gathered data to determine the reaction or status of some event at one point in time makes cross-sectional studies a useful approach on a wide variety of topics and across several disciplines. Also, fewer resources, less time, and little or no control over the sample are needed if it is of the random type. The cross-sectional approach is obviously not as useful as the longitudinal design to assess change or development, but a number of inferences about change can be properly assessed within the constraints of this approach.

For example, one can assess the attitudes of freshman students and compare these with the measured attitudes of seniors at the sample institution and make certain statements about change due to students' experiences and class in school. The Gallup poll and related polls have shown a number of charted attitude changes on issues such as abortion, drug usage, or confidence of the population toward certain institutions in society. In short, the cross-sectional approach has specific limitations, but for many research problems, the advantages of less time, fewer resources, larger samples, a large array of variables, and the versatility of the cross-sectional approach indicate its central utility in social science research.

Mead (1955) made the assumption that her vivid word picture of the people in Bali was a representative cross-section view of these island people. This is not a very good, or clear, example of a cross-sectional research, nor is Hanna's work (1974), but these two illustrations come closer than any of the other examples presented to cross-sectional research. The famous Kinsey et al. study (1953) on the sexual behavior and attitudes of American females stands as a classic illustration of a cross-sectional study in which the researchers assessed a large sample of women on a broad range of questions specific to their sexual attitudes and behavior.

The Longitudinal Approach

An individual or group that is studied over a period of time constitutes the basic idea of *longitudinal* research, since the goal is to describe or assess the change and development of some process (i.e., weight, height, prejudice, love, adjustment to surgery, or recovery from illness). Intervals of time are of primary importance in this approach, since the major goal is to determine what occurs or changes over time. Advantages of this approach are that one observes or studies the same issue and same people or events over a long period of time; thus one is able to maintain considerable control over the variables being studied. Because the longitudinal approach does use the same persons or elements in the sample over time, these persons or elements are viewed as "identical" with regard to the study variable, assuming that they are not influenced by the study process itself. Hence, one can have greater control and ultimately more precise measurement with a longitudinal design since one can administer repeated measurement, and the sample is a matched type group (Goldstein, 1979).

A problem associated with the longitudinal design is the expense of following a population over time, and this expense often dictates that a smaller unit is employed. The validity of a study may also suffer due to some people dropping out of the study due to "research fatigue," or even if they stay with the study, the process of repeated measures and contact with the investigator may create some unwanted effects with the sample member. Additionally, an investigator may become sufficiently involved in the research that a "spill over" occurs and this may influence the responses or behavior shown by the subjects in the sample.

Our examples in this chapter involved three cases of longitudinal research: the case of Anna, the use of coca leaves by the Andeans, and mate guarding by Caribbean villagers. Of the three, the case of Anna is perhaps the best example, as the main goal by Davis was to assess her developmental changes over time, specifically to determine if the previous six years of extreme deprivation could be reversed with intensive intervention (Davis, 1940, 1949).

For a more detailed coverage and excellent discussion of both cross-sectional and longitudinal approaches we suggest the works of Baltes and Shaie (1973) and Goulet and Baltes (1970).

SUMMARY

1. Two major research designs in social science are exploratory and descriptive. The strength and limitations of these two designs were noted and illustrated in several research examples.

2. Exploratory designs are most appropriate for preliminary work in a new area where the main goal is to obtain insights and to gather information that may be useful in continuing more in-depth research on a given problem.

3. In contrast to exploratory research, descriptive design assumes that one already knows a good deal about the problem under study, and the goal now is to provide a clear profile—verbal or numerical—of the research problem. Carefully completed descriptive research not only provides a clear profile, it can also provide understanding and at times a valid explanation as well.

4. Careful planning to have random samples is important in a good descriptive research. If we fail to test a representative sample, we run the high risk of giving distorted pictures of a situation.

5. The following four research approaches are closely associated with exploratory and descriptive studies.

   a. *The case study approach* is an in-depth study of one or a limited number of cases in which each case is treated as a whole. The case study approach is particularly helpful when deeper understanding is needed and when there is little concern about generalizing to a large population.

   b. *The survey approach* is a collection of data from a sample, typically a large sample, to a set number of defined questions. The survey is usually a cross-section of a stated population, with the emphasis on generalizing statistics to the population, not on the individual, as is the focus in case studies.

   c. *The cross-sectional approach* is a design presenting a broad picture with analysis of a large group on multiple variables. The subjects are studied at one point in time with no attempt to assess developmental change. Data in this approach are most often collected by interview, by questionnaire, or by telephone contact.

   d. *The longitudinal approach* involves studying an individual or a small number of units over a period of time. The goal of this approach is to describe or measure the change or development of some process. This approach provides high control over variables and is the design to use when the primary goal is to understand change or developmental patterns.

PROBLEMS AND APPLICATIONS

1. Define the notion of a research design and why designs are important in *planning* and *conducting* social science research.

2. Explain the main features and uses of exploratory research.

3. Explain the main features and uses of descriptive research.

4. Relate your own major area of study to exploratory and descriptive research. Which type of design has been used the most and why? What should be the direction of future designs as applied to your own major area of study?

5. Select an issue of a journal in your area of study and determine how many of the articles used an exploratory or descriptive design. Was the design appropriate for the problem under examination?

6. What type of design as well as mode of data collection covered in this chapter is most often used for studying issues that have direct impact on consumers of research? What are your recommendations in this regard?

REFERENCES

Adams, B. N., & Cromwell, R. E. (1978). Morning and night people in the family: A preliminary statement. *The Family Coordinator 27,* 5–13.

Baltes, P. R., & Schaie, K. W. (Eds.). (1973). *Life-span developmental psychology: Personality socialization.* New York: Academic Press.

Best, J. W. (1970). *Research in education.* Englewood Cliffs, N.J.: Prentice-Hall.

Davis, K. (1940). Extreme social isolation of a child. *American Journal of Sociology, 45,* 554–565.

Davis, K. (1949). *Human society.* New York: Macmillan Company.

Denzin, N. K. (1970). *Sociological methods: A source book.* Chicago: Aldine.

Dougherty, M.C. (1978). "Southern lay midwives as ritual specialists." In J. Hock-Smith & A. Spring (Eds.), *Women in ritual and symbolic roles.* New York: Plenum Press.

Flinn, M. V. (1988). Mate guarding in a Caribbean village. *Ethology and Sociobiology, 9* (1), 1–28.

Fremont, J. C. (1988). *The exploring expedition to the Rocky Mountains.* Washington, D.C.: Smithsonian Institution Press.

Goetzmann, W. H. (1966). *Exploration and empire.* New York: Alfred A. Knopf.

Goldstein, H. (1979). *The design and analysis of longitudinal studies.* London: Academic Press.

Good, C. V. (1972). *Essentials of educational research.* New York: Appleton-Century-Crofts.

Good, V. C., & Scates, D. E. (1954). *Methods of research: Educational, psychological, sociological.* New York: Appleton-Century-Crofts.

Goulet, L. R., & Baltes, P. B. (Eds.). (1970). *Life-span developmental psychology: Research and theory.* New York: Academic Press.

Hanna, J. M. (1974). Coca leaf use in southern Peru: Some biosocial aspects. *American Anthropologist, 76,* 281–296.

Hubbard, D. G. (1971). *The skyjacker: His flights of fantasy.* New York: Macmillan Company.

Hyman, H. (1955). *Survey design and analysis.* Glencoe, Ill.: The Free Press.

Kaplan, A. (1964). *The conduct of inquiry.* San Francisco: Chandler Publishing Company.

Kerlinger, F. N. (1964). *Foundations of behavioral research. New York: Holt, Rinehart and Winston.*

Kinsey, A. C., Pomeroy, W. B., Martin, C. E., & Gebhard, P. H. (1953). *Sexual behavior in the human female.* Philadelphia: Saunders.

Mead, M. (1955). *Male and female: A study of sexes in a changing world.* New York: The New American Library-Mentor Book.

Merton, R. K. (1968). *Social theory and social structure.* New York: The Free Press.

Mills, C. W. (1961). *The sociological imagination.* New York: Grove Press.

Reynolds, P. L. (1971). *A primer in theory construction.* Indianapolis: Bobbs-Merrill.

Selltiz, C., Lawrence, S., Wrightsman, S., & Cook, W. (1976). *Research methods in social relations* (3rd ed.). New York: Holt, Rinehart and Winston.

Turi, R. T., Friel, C. M., Sheldon, R. B., & Matthews, J. P. (1972). 'Descriptive study of aircraft hijacking.' *Criminal Justice Monograph, 3* (5), 1–171.

CHAPTER 6

Research Designs: Field Studies and Field Experiments

OUTLINE

Introduction
Field Studies
    Perspectives on Field Research
    Doing Field Research
        Field Research Example: Nurses and Mental Patients
        Field Research Example: Running Away
        Field Research Example: Times Square and Sex Shops
Field Experiments
        Field Experiment Example: Music in the Supermarket
        Field Experiment Example: The News Media and Public Policy
        Field Experiment Example: Authority and Compliance
        Field Experiment Example: Discrimination and Bumper Stickers
Summary
Problems and Applications
References

KEY TERMS

Field

Field research

Field experiment

Field entry

Observation

Note taking

Data analyses

Natural situation

Rapport

Taxonomies

Dependent variable

Independent variable

STUDY GUIDE QUESTIONS

1. What is a field study and where does one typically conduct field research?
2. How does one enter "the field" in order to carry out a successful research project?
3. What does it mean to preserve one's data in conducting a field study? What are some key ways of preserving data?
4. Define the idea of a regular field experiment. What is a main difference between a field study and a field experiment?
5. Are there specific or particular strengths and weaknesses of field studies and field experiments?
6. What is the main mode of collecting data in using field study or field experiment designs?

Role of the Scientist

Field research and field experiments afford powerful methodological flexibility and rigor in conducting research. Because of these utility features, these two designs have been extremely popular for nearly a century. Understanding the strengths and limitations of these approaches with field designs is necessary for one to be an effective researcher.

Role of the Consumer

Field research designs are especially well suited to assess or evaluate issues in the everyday life of people in society. The consumer of research should know basic strategies for field research versus field experiments and what these two approaches have permitted science to accumulate in terms of understanding people in the everyday world of actors in social situations. Occupations and roles are especially well suited to study by field designs.

INTRODUCTION

One of the oldest and most widely used research designs in the social sciences is referred to as *field research*. This approach has been used heavily by sociologists and especially by anthropologists. Going into "the field" is a phrase used to describe such diverse activities as using the university semester to do student teaching, interning at the local mental health clinic, touring to a foreign nation to refine language skills, or going on a field trip to study hunting and gathering practices of the Australian Bushman. Nye (1964) notes several methodological referents in regard to field studies: descriptive research, a method of obtaining data, a study design, sample size, and then the development in detail of a particular treatment of survey and cross-sectional designs as special application of field research.

FIELD STUDIES

The most common, as well as the most useful, definition of field research is the one used in such classical works as William F. Whyte's *Street Corner Society, Tally's Corner* by Elliot Liebow, or *Life in a Mexican Village* by Oscar Lewis. Field research in this context refers to a place where research is conducted, such as work, play, street life, or training situations. Several formal definitions from various sources may help to sharpen the perspective on what is labeled as field research and the components of this research design.

Perspectives on Field Research

View One. "Direct or indirect observation of behavior in the circumstances in which it occurs without any significant intervention on the part of the observer" (Kaplan, 1964, p. 165).

View Two. "Field research is the design, planning and management of scientific investigators in real-life settings" (Fiedler, 1978, p. vii).

View Three. "The field researcher concerns himself less with whether his techniques are 'scientific' than with what specific operations might yield the most meaningful information. He already assumes his own honesty, rationality, and scientific attitude; therefore, he is not ready to concede in advance the superiority of certain types of 'instrumentation' over his own abilities to see and to make sense of what he sees" (Schatzman & Strauss, 1973, p. 8).

View Four. "Field work is carried on by immersing oneself in a collective way of life for the purpose of gaining firsthand knowledge about some facet of it" (Shaffir, Stebbins, & Turowetz, 1980, p. 6).

View Five. "The *first* principle of the qualitative strategy approach is that social data are appropriately collected by means of intimate familiarity by which is meant close, detailed, dense acquaintanceship with a particular locale of social life based on a free-flowing and prolonged immersion. This immersion, first and ideally, may take the form of direct, bodily presence in the physical scenes of the social life under scrutiny, either in any indigenous role or in the role of someone known to be studying that world" (Lofland, 1978, p. 7).

From these five views some common factors stand out in both location of the *field* and *how* data are gathered in the field according to the field research approach. First of all, it is clear that the *field* location is wherever *social behavior* is occurring; it is with *real life situations* and the conditions or events are *natural* (i.e., as they would unfold in everyday life). Our second question of *how* data are collected in field studies is likewise clear in showing that this approach is *not highly structured* in which questionnaires or set strategies are imposed; rather it primarily relies on *observation* (i.e., the investigator is there on a *firsthand* basis, becomes *immersed* in the situation or lives of the people, but is able to maintain a *basic objectivity* due to *training* and specific preparation before entering the field). In sum, our definition of *field research* as presented in this chapter refers to the study of interaction of social situations as they naturally occur through the use of participant observation.

Most of us have an intuitive feeling for the basic goal of field research and how it is done. Through participant observation we have been observing people interact with one another as we have been growing and living in our situation and have undoubtedly made statements such as "she is that way because of job pressure," "he is rich because of his family," or "all truck drivers are super macho." We arrive at these assertions through observation and experience. In none of them did we directly use test questions to arrive at our conclusions. Our conclusions may or may not be correct, and we can hardly defend them because we did not arrive at such conclusions through a systematic analysis. Gaining results through systematic observation in a field context is the purpose of our deliberations in this chapter. The skills to develop and the knowledge to utilize, along with the common sense to employ this combination in the study of human interaction, constitute the essence of the field approach. As Matza (1969) observed, "naturalism in the study of man is a disciplined humanism" (p. 8).

Doing Field Research

The data for almost any topic out "in the field" are there, but obtaining or even getting access to data becomes an important concern in doing field research. Furthermore, it is the ultimate goal that whatever data are obtained will be valid. Fiedler's assertion—"field investigators create the conditions under which valid research can be done" (Fiedler, 1978, p. vii)—is the reason why we must know what these conditions are and how we can create them. As with all designs, a clearly defined purpose is a prerequisite, and then for the field study our main operating question is one of *getting into our field.* "Getting in" requires permission in some studies while in others such as Humphreys' study (1970) of sexual encounters in public park restrooms, may not require permission as such, but negotiation must be in force before access to, and legitimacy in, the field are attained. Getting into the field can be accomplished by writing letters to appropriate persons, making personal visits, having people negotiate the entry or gain the permission for you, and joining forces with an agency or group to help them achieve certain needs as you accomplish your own goals in the proposed field study.

You can facilitate your legitimacy by using your university affiliation, your business credentials, or letter of recommendation; by showing that you have the necessary training to do the study; and by making sure that people are aware that you are genuinely concerned with the topic under investigation. Negotiation, articulation, and permission seeking are parts of a process, not events to be accomplished just one time. Entry to the field is, in fact, a *"continuous process"* (Schatzman & Strauss, 1973, p. 22).

A second step is *gaining* and *building* trust with actors in the field situation to achieve a functional level of *rapport.* Obtaining rapport with people in the situation involves reduction of the investigator's inhibitions, learning the "language" and day-to-day work habits of the people, and being genuinely committed to putting yourself into the situation. Lofland (1976) talks about this process as becoming "intimately familiar with a sector of social life...to have easy, detailed, dense acquaintanceship with it based on free-flowing and prolonged immersion" (p. 8). In short, Lofland is talking about a process of being accepted in the research setting. It is a process of entering directly or requesting that others help you build the relationship that will lead to trust or *rapport* while in a field setting.

Creating rapport is heavily tied to the first step of entry, as our entry credentials can do much in achieving rapport by establishing what you are and eliminating false beliefs that you are a spy, a government undercover person, or some sly reporter. Thorough preparation, such as learning how to speak the "language" (street talk), how to dress, and generally how to blend into a situation, is helpful in achieving this step.

The third step in field research is referred to as *obtaining* and *preserving the data*. This is a central step in field research and has been elaborated in very detailed accounts (Johnson, 1975; Lofland, 1971, 1976; Schatzman & Strauss, 1973), but our treatment here will be much briefer. We have already established that the primary data collection device is *observation*—watching, listening, and reading the people and situations. A common reaction in a new situation is to "tune in" to all stimuli, which is good because one notices these things at first and then gradually blends into the situation. A good balance of keeping open to all events and having a seasoned "eye" as to what to look for and what to ignore are important principles in observing.

As noted in Chapter 4, one has to guard against the investigator altering the situation being studied, as this can lead to observing and recording events that are distorted by being in that setting. Establishing trust, rapport, confidence, and being "one with the actors" are some ways to accomplish this, and these traits should be continually buttressed by a sensitive awareness of this problem by the investigator. One can watch events from the outside, or one can become an insider, depending on the study and the negotiations that can be accomplished with the people to be observed. One's identity can be completely open or it can be hidden, at least for a phase of the project.

As to *preserving* what we see and hear in field research, we can elect to *take notes* on everything, take no notes, use a tape recorder continuously or selectively, plus a variety of combinations in addition to these. Most observers take very brief notes in a situation, using a key word, phrase, or statement, and then write complete field notes after that episode or at the end of the day. Schatzman and Strauss (1973) note that what an observer needs is "recording tactics that will provide him with an ongoing, developmental dialogue between his roles as discoverer and as social analyst" (p. 94).

Taking notes as soon as possible is important in order to increase the validity and coverage of events witnessed. Further, one needs to be willing to do this on a regular basis. Lofland (1971) notes that often an investigator will spend as much time recording notes as was spent in observing the events that took place. Schatzman and Strauss (1973) note that various trade-offs are involved whether one uses a typewriter in writing up notes or dictates them onto tapes. While the mode is important, arranging and managing the notes are far more important. The notes should be legible, permanent, and in great enough detail that one can still effectively use them months or years later.

In sum, notes are necessary, since few people can remember all that went on without effective record keeping, and furthermore, notes properly prepared give a framework and order to the research. Field notes will be used heavily in preparing final written reports for publications, agencies, and other organizations for individuals. Schatzman and Strauss further emphasize the importance of good notes by stating that notes are not " 'soft data';

they are as hard and true as he [the researcher] could make them from his experience" (1973, p. 106).

After one finishes the data-gathering process (observation and recording in the field), one leaves the field and is faced with step four, *analysis of the data*. If one has managed notes carefully and put them in useful order, the major task now is to reduce the many pages of notes to profiles, flow charts, or *taxonomies* (sets of ideas organized according to dimensions). "The most fundamental operation in the analysis of qualitative data is that of discovering significant *classes* of things, persons and events and the *properties* which characterize them" (Schatzman & Strauss, 1973, p. 110). Typically, labels and classes are richly abundant in field notes, some from persons being studied, while others may be coined by the researcher. Classifying the data according to some meaningful scheme and then linking or "hooking" the classification together constitute the major task. The central purpose of the study can be illuminated as necessary by examples from notes. Distinguishing questions that are clearly answered from those only partially answered will be part of the process; and, of course, new questions raised by the research itself will emerge from the data analysis. In sum, data analyses in field research involve classification, organization, integrating the categories, illustrations, and a synthesis of the data to give direct response to the research purpose. A final step is writing the research report (see Chapter 18 for strategies helpful in writing up most kinds of research for various audiences). (See Tips for Consumers 6.1.)

People live in two main spheres, the animal world of biological activities and the more complex world of symbolic interaction with the self, others, and the social world. McCall and Simmons (1966) make a very useful contribution to field research in the symbolic environment of mankind and we refer readers to this work for a detailed treatment. In a more recent monograph, McCall (1978) outlines additional steps in the field research process as related to the areas of crime and the criminal justice system. Tips on field entry, field conduct, and broad coverage on the *who*, the *what*, the *where*, and the *when* of field research will be of specific use to both researchers and consumers of research.

Another major type of field study is the field experiment, but before we present this

---

Tips for Consumers 6.1

Much research in the social sciences is subject to extensive criticism because of alleged problems with reliability and validity. Human and social behavior are often very difficult to study because of the nature of the subject matter as well as the fact that human beings are both dynamic and reactive in nature. Field studies and field experiments are special types of designs because we study people on their level, in their work, love, play—in short, in a "natural environment." Additionally, in field experiments we can engage in unobtrusive intervention or let this intervention occur under natural conditions.

Field studies are particularly useful in helping to solve such problems as discrimination, conflict resolution, and a variety of school-related problems. Field studies, perhaps more than other designs, are specifically oriented to the who, what, where, and when of events. These dimensions are particularly important for consumers to be aware of and use in a variety of ways.

approach, a few examples and illustrations concerning regular field research will help to further clarify major goals of the chapter—defining, specifying the steps, and understanding the overall mission of field research.

The first example comes from the medical-nursing patient ward of a hospital and is useful in illustrating the type of setting which can be understood in field research. Please note the complexity of the setting and the personal dynamics impacting on this field setting. Also, note that the problem of field entry is minimal due to the background of both investigators.

Field Research Example: Nurses and Mental Patients.   The book *The Nurse and the* ◀ *Mental Patient* (Schwartz & Shockley, 1956) emerged as the end result of a two-year study in a mental patient ward in which the sociologist team member observed directly or participated in the ward and made notes on the many interactions which occurred. Shockley, a psychiatric nurse and formerly director of nursing education at the hospital, worked with Schwartz in observing, interviewing, and reviewing the many incidents occurring over a two-year period of intensive study to examine the ways in which nurses interact with patients and to modify these relationships in order to improve patient mental well-being. The ward in which the research took place was filled with patients who were judged as being least able to care for themselves in a regular manner and were also designated patients prone to injure themselves or others in the ward. The ward had an average of 15 patients. Shockley, as a long-time nurse in the hospital and one who had administrative experience in the setting, obviously had no difficulty in obtaining entry into the field study setting. In a similar manner, Schwartz, as a sociologist, had taught graduate courses for nursing students and supervised various research projects that several students had participated in while in the hospital setting. Thus, both authors, because of professional assignment and location, enjoyed excellent *logistics* to complete research in a hospital setting focusing on the interaction of nurses and mental patients.

A situation presented by Schwartz and Shockley illustrates how a nurse introduced a self-fulfilling prophecy to the ward and how this situation had far-reaching influences on other nurses and patients. A new nurse to the ward believed that patients "became assaultive" and blew up at the "full of the moon" (p. 22). Previous experience in the ward indicated that a full moon influence was not a concern, but soon after the nurse in question arrived, this notion permeated the hospital personnel. "At the next full moon there was a noticeable increase in violence" (p. 22). The nursing personnel talked about the next full moon as it approached and developed strategies for coping with the anticipated patients' assaults, which in fact did occur with the appearance of the full moon. This new pattern continued for a six-month period: "Each month the nurses dreaded the full moon and expected patients to become violent, and each time they did. By this time personnel were convinced of the inevitability of these outbreaks" (p. 23).

During the course of the study, another nurse seriously questioned the alleged causal relationship between the full moon and patient difficulty, and when other nurses argued that violence did increase with the full moon she countered that the increase could be nothing more than response to the fact that the nursing staff were fearful and anticipating the outbreak. This nurse was successful in convincing many nurses of their *cycle* of conflict and to take a different, more relaxed posture during the next full moon. The nurses discussed the full moon much less, and refrained from mutually stimulating fear, which, in turn, showed up at the patient level—"assaultiveness was not greater than at any other time of the month" (p. 23).

Field entry and legitimacy were extremely important in this example. Trust, rapport, and singularity of purpose stand out in this field study. Field studies, as illustrated in this example, are especially flexible, and can be sensitive to both process and structure of the field setting.

▶ *Field Research Example: Running Away.*   During the course of a two-year period, Palenski and Launer (1987) interviewed young people who had run away from home. At the time, the senior author was the research director for a youth advocacy group and had been previously employed as a New York City youth worker. He was thus able to draw upon former friendships and associates to contact and establish rapport with the youth. In addition, the researchers were able to contact youth through runaway shelters and friends who knew the runaways and were able to visit with them on a number of occasions while they were living out of the home. Since the investigators were already "in the field," they were able to gather in-depth information regarding family life, peer relationships, school problems, and individual perspectives of the runaway youths.

▶ *Field Research Example: Times Square and Sex Shops.*   Another example of field research and getting into a life situation is provided by Karp (1980) in his study of behavior in crowded public places such as Times Square, specifically to study social interaction and behavior in adult bookstores and movie theaters. This research is particularly interesting for the reader to learn about problems, obstacles, and unexpected happenings connected with field research in urban public settings.

The applications for researcher and consumer of research from this type of study are diverse, ranging from those interested in certain types of deviancy, inner-city social problems, and coping styles of youth group organizations who may express concerns about the impact of sexual materials in such establishments. Karp shows that planning and preparation are necessary, but he also shows that field designs call for flexibility and adaptability. This necessity for planning and yet logical adaptability constitutes what we have earlier referred to as both the method and art of research methodology.

Karp spent about two years in this field project and describes in detail the stress in defining the physical boundaries of the public area, the behavioral boundaries of the project, and the day-to-day operations in being an observer with the great variety of regulars and tourists in a place like Times Square. After some time in the field, he noted

> there is no logical progression of events that uniformly occurs in participant observation. The choice of behaviors for observation is particularly arbitrary at the beginning of the research . . . as the research progresses . . . the choice of events and persons for observation became increasingly focused. (p. 88)

Certain difficulties arise in observing a public place, such as how long to stay in a porno bookstore, whether to tell the manager about the study, how to interact with other customers, how to approach people who might provide valuable data for the study, and whether to merely observe or actually participate in certain situations. Karp notes that investigators doing research in public places are faced with the task of piecing together information from sources such as "observation alone, personal introspection, deliberate intervention in a situation, and casual conversation" (p. 93). Most of Karp's data come from observing people interact in a public place. Elaborating on this point, Karp says:

> Although I did participate in both movie and bookstore behaviors, there were certain areas of the sexual scene that I never learned about. Although interested in the relations of prostitutes and clients, I never became a total participant in this aspect of sexual activity. (pp. 95–96)

In contrast to *The Nurse and the Mental Patient,* Karp is faced with a major problem of field entry and legitimacy once in the field. Additionally, his skill in handling questions, probes, and personal feelings about sensitive issues stands out in this report.

FIELD EXPERIMENTS

If field studies are aimed at understanding naturally occurring interaction in a particular context, *field experiments* are aimed at understanding how *intervention* of some type *influences behavior* in a *natural setting.* One of the main reasons for study of intervention in a natural setting as compared to a lab experiment is the argument for validity—to see how people or events actually behave in the "real world." A field experiment may be appropriate when a researcher does not want to or cannot control the experimental variables in a lab nor can subjects be assigned to random groups; it is in this context that field experiments can provide fairly valid data, even though control is not of the same rigor as in the lab. It is the belief of many investigators that what one loses in lack of lab rigor is gained by an increase or validity by conducting the research in a real ongoing life context. A *field experiment* may be defined as a *procedure in which the investigator manipulates the independent variable in a natural setting and then studies the consequences of this manipulation on a dependent variable.* The main advantage of this is control of understanding causal factors. A field experiment can take advantage of *naturally occurring manipulations* of the independent variables or ones introduced by the investigator.

Swingle (1973) asserts that experimental studies "of social behavior are our most powerful tool for developing an understanding of human social behavior" (p. 5). We will now provide examples of field experiments to provide additional clarity and understanding in regard to this design. (With the major exception of manipulation of independent variables, the same review of steps in research for a field study also apply to completing research with field experiments; therefore, these steps will not be repeated here.)

Field Experiment Example: Music in the Supermarket.   Smith and Curnow (1966) ask ◀ the simple question: Does music or type of music played in a supermarket have any influence on the amount of time one spends shopping? This is an interesting and useful question, as we have all thought about mood music, whether it be in the supermarket, the reclining posture of the dentist's office, or on the radio as we drive down the freeway. In this field experiment, the investigators were specifically interested in testing an idea called the "arousal hypothesis," which postulates various levels of noise will influence activity (i.e., soft music slows people down while loud music increases activity).

Smith and Curnow collected data on 1,100 shoppers on several Friday afternoon and Saturday morning shopping times in two different large supermarkets where music was played either loudly or softly *(independent variable)*. The dependent variable included the amount of time spent shopping and the amount of each sale. The investigators followed up with questions to the shoppers focusing on awareness of the background music, their evaluation of the music loudness, and how they rated the favorability of the music. The results indicated no important differences in the amount of money spent per shopper when comparing the loud with the soft music group. In regard to the time question, shoppers completed the shopping duty more rapidly under the influence of loud music, thus confirming the notion of the arousal hypothesis. In short, people buy about the same volume of supermarket items, but they do it more rapidly under the influence of loud music. These investigators suggest that results of this type could possibly be applied to supermarkets by varying the level of music in various areas of the store to help control traffic flow and prevent shopper traffic jams in certain areas.

The Smith and Curnow research is a clear example of a field experiment, since they focus on one variable of manipulation—loudness of music—and how this in turn influences rate of shopper activity. One could, of course, compare male and female shoppers in such a study, weekday with weekend shoppers, and adults with children versus those with no children. To add further design factors, one could vary music from loud to soft in the same store to overcome objections if someone were to argue against comparing two different supermarkets as did Smith and Curnow. It is also clear that we have little to say about the influence of any stimuli other than music. The strength of the study is that it was done in a natural environment, and the results appear to be potentially useful in many consumer settings.

Furthermore, supermarkets and music are in process and the scientist can execute a thoughtful field experiment by working within this ongoing activity. Validity is likely to be high in this type of naturally occurring setting.

▶ *Field Experiment Example: The News Media and Public Policy.*   Protess and his associates (1987) illustrated how journalism and the news media impact the public and policymakers. In a project targeting toxic waste, the investigators used a pretest, posttest field experimental design. A television series, "Wasted Time," disclosed that potentially hazardous waste products were being stored under classrooms at the University of Chicago. The program was aired as a three-part broadcast. Pictures of previous fires and chemical explosions were included as part of the series. It was suggested that federal, state, and local agencies were not carrying out their responsibilities properly.

Attitudes of the general public and public administrators were examined both before and after the broadcast of the investigation. Although the impact of this particular study was modest, the authors concluded that if investigative reports are timely and are focused on a topic of interest (i.e., rape, police brutality, etc.), they are not only able to sway public opinion, but also to influence policymakers to respond.

▶ *Field Experiment Example: Authority and Compliance.*   What happens to the professional judgment of nurses in a hospital setting when directed by a doctor to administer nonlethal overdoses of Valium to patients? Rank and Jacobson (1977) guessed that when nurses were thoroughly *familiar* with the drug and also had opportunity to *discuss* the directive with other nurses, the nurses would change their dosage administration from the amount ordered. Of the 18 nurses given this directive, 16 refused to administer the volume of Valium directed by the doctor. In addition to nurses' familiarity and opportunity to talk with other nurses about the order, the investigators suggest that increased willingness of hospital personnel to challenge the doctor, rising self-esteem of nurses, and fear of potential lawsuits might have increased noncompliance.

The Rank and Jacobson study vividly shows how scientists can manipulate critical variables in the natural world to test very significant questions, the ramifications of such being important for both patient and professional. The patients in this study were probably safe, as the directed Valium level was not lethal, and it would appear that nurses would not be influenced by patient awareness of their refusal to follow doctor's orders. This example in particular and field experiments in general are important to carefully assess in terms of ethical issues as we covered in Chapter 2.

Actually, this example is a good one to assess the impact of authority figures in our lives and what factors in our experience or training best equip us to cope with authority (see research by Milgram, 1963). How many other applications of these findings can you think of? What other types of controls would you have sought to use in this study? A field experiment of this type shows how occupations are influenced by the law, shifts in sex role behavior, and new perspectives in regard to authority figures in the medical world. (See Tips for Consumers 6.2.)

Field Experiment Example: Discrimination and Bumper Stickers.   Our final example ◄ of field experiment research takes place with Black Panther Party members, police reaction, and the political climate in the 1960s. Note how quickly evidence for a specific problem can be gathered using a field design. Furthermore, this example helps to illustrate the need and difficulty of controlling for other variables that may influence the dependent variable. As you review this study, try to deal with effective ways of bringing more rigor and control to this type of research activity.

Tips for Consumers 6.2

What type of research design should be employed within the context of field studies—a regular field study or a field experiment? If one desires to observe and document the "natural unfolding" of human events, then the regular field study would be preferred. However, if one wants to assess intervention in the "real world," then use of the field experiment is the design to employ.

Consumers of research should keep in mind that field studies focus on the social situation or setting. Getting access to the field and building rapport with the members in the field are two major steps. In contrast to a field study, researchers conduct field experiments in order to manipulate one or more independent variables in a natural world or let the manipulations occur naturally. Field studies of both types permit us to be better observers of our personal world and how that world is impacted by other major social institutions in society.

Heussenstamm (1971) reports that members of the Black Panther party in Los Angeles were extremely upset with citations and general harassment by law enforcement, and this concern brought them to the realization that they all drove cars with Panther Party bumper stickers. In order to test the relationship of this type of bumper sticker on one's car and the likelihood of arrest, Heussenstamm carefully screened 15 drivers from a pool of 45 for additional study. Of these drivers 5 were black, 5 were white, and 5 were of Mexican background; 3 males and 2 females comprised each of the 3 groups. All of these students were regular commuters to a large university, averaging about 10 miles per round trip drive. All 15 of these participants had unblemished driving records, attested by means of sworn statement that they had received no "moving" traffic violations in the past year, and each driver also agreed that he or she would continue to drive in strict compliance with all traffic regulations. Heussenstamm also requested that each driver sign a statement testifying that they would engage in no behavior that would make them prone to attract the attention of law officers in the Los Angeles area. All the cars were judged to be free of defects, although one car was a "hippie van" painted in "flower child" style.

> The appearance of the drivers was varied. There were three blacks with processed hair and two with exaggerated naturals, two white-shirt-and-necktie, straight Caucasians and a shoulder-length-maned hippie, and two mustache- and sideburn-sporting Mexican-Americans. All wore typical campus dress, with the exception of the resident hippie and the militant blacks, who sometimes wore dashikis. (p. 32)

Each car was fixed with a bright orange and black sticker depicting a panther with large "Black Panther" lettering. The first student received a ticket less than two hours after the experiment started for making an "incorrect" lane change on a freeway, and this was followed by a flurry of tickets by other students for failing to yield right of way, driving too slowly, following too closely, and so on. "One student was forced to drop out of the study by day four, because he had already received three citations" (p. 33). Arresting officers ranged from polite to very aggressive. One white girl was questioned as to why she was supporting the "criminal activity" of the Black Panther party, and why she had the sticker on her bumper.

The 15 students in the study received citations on an equal basis; race, sex, appearance, or ethnicity seemingly had no impact. Heussenstamm concludes that "it is statistically unlikely that this number of previously safe drivers could amass such a collection of tickets without assuming real bias by police against drivers with Black Panther bumper stickers" (p. 33). He also recognizes that some citations were probably deserved, and it should also be mentioned that bias on the part of the driver might influence the way one would drive. If this study were to be repeated, we would attempt to control for additional conditions, such as color, year, and make of car. Furthermore, we could more tightly control self-presentation of the drivers as well as vary routes the drivers might use in arriving at a specified destination. Heussenstamm also notes that after a student was seated in the car and ready to drive off, one could attach a "Black Panther party" or "America Love It or Leave It" sticker in a random fashion, thus preventing any driver from knowing what message was being carried on the bumper.

This example is particularly useful in illustrating how complex it is to obtain a useful and valid response to a seemingly simple question of potential prejudice because of a symbol attached to a car bumper. This study also shows how it is profitable to intervene in a situation with an ongoing history. The dependent variable in this study is easy to measure—one receives a citation or drives on with no citation. The study of social problems is particularly clear in this example—giving further evidence to the versatility of field experiments. Examples such as this illustrate in part why researchers would do well to use this design in more of their research and rely less on survey approaches.

SUMMARY

Two major approaches in the study of everyday life in natural settings have been presented—*field studies* and *field experiments*.

1. Field studies focus on the social setting or situation and the events that occur in that situation as people carry on their particular activities. A field study is a design for the study of human behavior in which one obtains understanding about a situation by becoming close to the people in that situation.
2. A field is a place where the activity occurs, and, as noted, this can range from the freeways of Los Angeles to a psychiatric ward of a community hospital. A field as opposed to a laboratory is the "natural place" where people spend their day-to-day life, whether it be in a patient's ward in a hospital, in a school classroom, on the urban streets, or in the supermarket. A field is connected with other fields or units in society, and the investigator may or may not be aware of this fact, since a researcher by necessity focuses on a specifically defined field for a particular study.
3. Main activities in field research involve *entering* into a field, having a clearly defined *purpose* and organization for the purpose, *observing* those interactions vital to understanding the social situation, *listening* to obtain understanding, *recording* what one hears and sees, and finally, *analyzing* the field notes to create integrated profiles of the field setting.
4. The field experiment, in contrast to regular field research, takes advantage of assessing social situations and the people in these natural ongoing life situations, and in addition, manipulates one or more independent variables to determine the impact of such intervention in a natural environment. The main argument for field experimental research focuses on validity—to assess events in the natural world. Also, many field experiments take place in settings where the intervention is occurring in a natural way, such as the school classroom, the community hospital, or community roadways.
5. The implications of this design for researchers and the application of findings from various field studies for both researcher and consumer of research are readily apparent. As Schwartz and Shockley (1956) noted, a nurse can only become more effective in working with patients by engaging in acute observation, being constantly curious, and maintaining a habit of questioning the "why" of events in the situation. We likewise would recommend this same type of directive to both researcher and consumer of research. The essence of field research is to immerse oneself into social reality, sympathetically observe, and then critically analyze results to arrive at more accurate profiles of human behavior.

PROBLEMS AND APPLICATIONS

1. What are the advantages of a regular field design versus an experimental field design when the results are to be applied to solving human problems?

2. Contrast the main advantages of serendipitous "payoffs" in research using field designs versus the precision and rigor of more experimental designs.

3. In collaboration with other student groups in the class, design a field study in which you will collect longitudinal data and one for cross-sectional data.

4. Discuss with team members in the class how you carry out research to test the effectiveness or customer appeal of a new product to be sold in a supermarket setting. What design would you use? Why?

5. Provide a critique of the research example focusing on nurses and mental patients. What are the two or three main strengths and weaknesses of this study?

6. Form discussion groups and talk about the payoffs of field studies and field experiments for consumers of research in society. What are the common elements of the main points discussed?

7. Working with a team of three other students, design a field study that would provide new insights and understanding to your area or focus of study.

REFERENCES

Fiedler, J. (1978). *Field research*. San Francisco: Jossey-Bass.

Heussenstamm, F. K. (1971, February). Bumper stickers and the cops. *Transaction, 8*, 32–33.

Humphreys, L. (1970). *Tearoom trade: Impersonal sex in public places*. Chicago: Aldine.

Johnson, J. M. (1975). *Doing field research*. New York: The Free Press.

Kaplan, A. (1964). *The conduct of inquiry*. San Francisco: Chandler Publishing.

Karp, D. A. (1980). "Observing behavior in public places: Problems and strategies." In W. B. Shaffir, R. A. Stebbins, & A. Turowetz (Eds.), *Fieldwork experience: Qualitative approaches to social research*. New York: St. Martin's Press.

Lewis, O. (1957). *Life in a Mexican village*. Urbana, Ill.: University of Illinois Press.

Leibow, E. (1968). *Tally's corner*. Boston: Little, Brown.

Lofland, J. (1971). *Analyzing social settings: A guide to qualitative observation analysis*. Belmost, Calif.: Wadsworth.

Lofland, J. (1976). *Doing social life: The qualitative study of human interaction*. New York: Wiley.

Lofland, J. (Ed.). (1978). *Interaction in everyday life: Social strategies*. Beverly Hills, Calif.: Sage.

Matza, D. (1969). *Becoming deviant*. Englewood Cliffs, N.J.: Prentice-Hall.

McCall, G. J. (1978). *Observing the law: Field methods in the study of crime and the criminal justice system*. New York: The Free Press.

McCall, G. J., & Simmons, J. L. (1966). *Identities and interactions*. New York: The Free Press.

Milgram, S. (1963). Behavioral study of obedience. *Journal of Abnormal and Social Psychology, 67*, 371–378.

Nye, F. I. (1964). "Field research." In Harold T. Christensen (Ed.), *Handbook of marriage and the family*. Chicago: Rand McNally.

Palenski, J. E., & Launer, H. M. (1987). The "process" of running away: A redefinition. *Adolescence, 22* (86), 347–362.

Protess, D. L., Cook, F. L., Curtin, T. R., Gordon, M. T., Leff, D. R., McCombs, M. E., & Miller, P. (1987). The impact of investigative reporting on public opinion and policymaking. *Pubic Opinion Quarterly, 51,* 166–185.

Rank, S. G., & Jacobson, C. K. (1977). Hospital nurses' compliance with medication overdose orders: A failure to replicate. *Journal of Health Social Behavior, 18,* 188–193.

Schwartz, M. S., & Shockley, E. L. (1956). *The nurse and the mental patient.* New York: Russell Sage Foundation.

Schatzman, L., & Strauss, A. L. (1973). *Field research: Strategies for a natural sociology.* Englewood Cliffs, N.J.: Prentice-Hall.

Shaffir, W. B., Stebbins, R. A., & Turowetz, A. (Eds.). (1980). *Fieldwork experience: Qualitative approaches to social research.* New York: St. Martin's Press.

Smith, P. C., & Curnow, R. (1966). "Arousal hypothesis" and the effects of music on purchasing behavior. *Journal of Applied Psychology, 50,* 255–256.

Swingle, P. G. (Ed.). (1973). *Social psychology in natural settings.* Chicago: Aldine.

Whyte, W. F. (1955). *Street corner society.* Chicago: University of Chicago Press.

CHAPTER 7

Research Designs: Experimental–Causal

OUTLINE

Introduction
Unconfounding the Confounded
The Basic Experimental-Control Group Designs
The Pretest–Posttest Control Group Design
The Solomon Four-Group Design
The Posttest-Only Group Design
Between versus Within Research Design Question
Strengths and Weaknesses of Laboratory Experimentation
Summary
Problems and Applications
References

KEY TERMS

Confounding factors
Experimental control
Experimental group
Control group
Pretest–posttest control group design
Solomon four-group design

Posttest-only control group
Between-subjects design
Within-subject design
Practice effect
Sensitization effect
Carry-over effect

STUDY GUIDE QUESTIONS

1. What is meant by experimental confound?
2. How can one study cause and effect in a laboratory setting?
3. What are the basic experimental research designs?
4. How are the various experimental research designs similar? How are they different?
5. One distinction of some importance in understanding experimental designs centers around the notions of *between* versus *within* subject design. What is meant by these terms?
6. Are there particular strengths and weaknesses to laboratory experimentation?

Role of the Scientist

Scientists seek information regarding cause and effect. They are often interested in identifying what factors caused a certain event, behavior, or outcome to occur. To study causality the scientist draws upon experimental and control groups. Several techniques are available with their own strength and utilization. In this chapter we summarize the basic research designs that are used in social behavior research. You will read in this chapter about the major components of experimental design, review the strengths and weaknesses of laboratory experimentation, and be presented with a discussion of subject use in experimental contexts.

Role of Consumer

Considerable information is presented to consumers under the umbrella concept of cause and effect. For example, several sports columnists have often stated that athletes who appear on the cover of *Sports Illustrated* are jinxed, suggesting that this publicity lowers performance. A similar suggestion has been made in psychology, where some have suggested that appearing in *Psychology Today* (a popular magazine on psychology issues) results in lower academic performance in regards to publications in peer-referred scientific journals. However, such notions can only be tested through the use of experimental research designs. In this chapter we shall show why a knowledgeable consumer of research should recognize when facts are based on true experimental designs that test causality.

INTRODUCTION

The laboratory experiment has been heralded as the epitome of science at its best, primarily because it is the only major research design that assesses cause and effect. Frequently, beginning research methods texts either ignore the importance of the laboratory experiment or inundate the student with the complexity of experimental research design. Rather, we contend, it is best to direct new students to four basic components of experimentation during their beginning study, leaving many of the more complex issues to advanced training. Therefore, we shall simply address, in this chapter:

(1) the concept of "confounding" and how experimentation deals with it; (2) a description of the three most frequently used "true" experimental designs; (3) a review of how researchers go about choosing either a "between" or a "within" research design; and (4) a brief summary of some of the strengths and weaknesses of laboratory experimentation.

UNCONFOUNDING THE CONFOUNDED

In Chapter 4, we reviewed several issues related to the reliability and validity of research findings. In particular, we examined possible extraneous variables which, if left unchecked, may lead to incorrect inferences about the effects of experimental treatment on the dependent measure. These extraneous variables are more appropriately called *confounding* factors or variables. Therefore, if a study is said to be confounded with some factor other than the independent (treatment) variable, this means we cannot be sure if the independent variable manipulation is the cause for changes in the dependent variable, or if some other extraneous (third) variable actually accounted for the dependent variable change. You will recall some of these confounding variables include aspects related to maturation, history, pretesting, instrumentation, experimental mortality, regression, and sample selection effects, to name a few.

The ultimate goal of science is to identify a "pure" relationship between the independent and dependent variables in such a way as to document and verify the assumption of cause and effect. To perform such an important activity, the scientist must engage in the use of *experimental control*. That is, the researcher must design investigations in which the potential effects of confounding variables can be systematically eliminated through appropriate research designs, experimental manipulations, and control group comparisons. Seldom, however, and perhaps never, are we capable of eliminating all potential confounding variable effects in a given experiment. Rather, we attempt to eliminate the most obvious first, and through additional replication–extension studies attempt to verify that other possible confounding variables are not having an influential effect on the reported independent-dependent variable relation.

The assessment of cause and effect, or causality, in the study of independent-dependent variables relations requires several basic conditions. First, a temporal relation must be established between the independent and dependent variable, where the causal independent variable *must* precede the dependent variable. That is, if the antecedent is a cause of a consequence, the antecedent must precede the consequence. Second, to establish a causal relationship, the researcher must control for extraneous events that might confound the proposed independent-dependent relation. Finally, the scientist must demonstrate concomitant variation or demonstrate that variables x and y covary together. The more fully a researcher can meet these three basic conditions the more assurance one can have in realizing a cause-and-effect relationship.

In summary, to document a cause-and-effect relationship, potential confounding or extraneous variable influences must be eliminated. These confounding variable influences are best removed through experimental control. We shall now turn to three of the most common research design techniques used in controlling and eliminating possible extraneous variable influences.

The Basic Experimental-Control Group Designs

For years Campbell and Stanley (1966; Cook & Campbell, 1979) have been cited as the classic review of experimental research design. Since little improvement on their excellent treatise has been made, we shall draw heavily on their work in outlining the three major experimental research designs. But prior to examining each individual design, we shall begin by outlining the major conceptual similarity between the three research designs. Table 7.1 provides this outline.

As mentioned earlier in Chapters 2 and 4, the independent and dependent variables are the workhorses of hypothesis testing. The independent variable is the variable that is directly manipulated and controlled by the researcher. The dependent variable is the measure of behavior. In using the experimental design, a formal hypothesis is constructed with some form of an "if-then" statement. The "if" refers to the independent variable and the "then" to the dependent variable. Therefore, the hypothesis is a formal statement indicating that "if" a certain independent variable is introduced to a group of people, "then" it is expected to have a certain effect or outcome (change in the dependent variable).

To test the if-then relation, a true experimental design must, at a minimum, have at least one *experimental* group and one *control* group. Simply put, the experimental group receives a specific treatment, which is controlled by the experimenter through manipulation of the independent variable. In contrast, the control group receives no such treatment and is allowed to behave in their own typical way, or is given an experience, devoid of immediate influential effects. Therefore, as can be seen in Table 7.1, the experimental process is a straightforward one. A sample of people is identified. Half are randomly placed in the experimental group. Individuals in both groups are assessed on the dependent variable at the beginning of the study. The experimental group is given a treatment (i.e., the independent variable is introduced), while the control is not directly manipulated. This process allows a comparison between a group that has a special treatment experience with one that has not. And finally, individuals in both groups are reassessed on the same dependent variable. Thus, the experimental laboratory process is complete. The matter of determining whether the experimental treatment has an "if-then" effect is a straightforward process. Through the use of statistical analyses, the experimenter then attempts to show that the scores on the average for the experimental group are different (either higher or lower, depending on the hypothesis) than those of the control group.

TABLE 7.1. Basic Components of the Experimental-Control Group Design

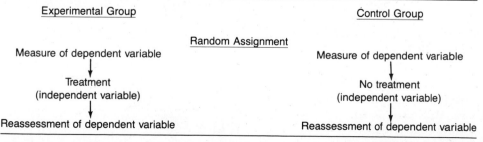

In summary, through the use of experimental and control groups, hypotheses are tested to determine if the independent variable has an effect on the dependent variable measure. Control groups allow us to determine if the independent variable had a true experimental effect, or if some extraneous variable might be confounding the proposed if-then relation. In our examination of three specific experimental designs we shall deal more with the issue of using control groups to eliminate confounding factors.

The Pretest–Posttest Control Group Design.   This design is the most frequently employed experimental design in social science research. The power of this design is that it eliminates numerous extraneous confounding variables through its control group comparison. The design matches that outlined in Table 7.2.

To briefly describe the table we begin with two randomly determined groups. True randomization eliminates differences between the groups on the assessment of the dependent measure at Time 1 and thus assures equivalence between the two groups. However, the pretest at Time 1 allows a check for equivalence. The researcher can compare the average scores for the two groups to verify that they are approximately the same. Next, the time that elapses between Times 1 and 2 is held constant for both groups. However, the experimental group receives some special treatment prior to the posttest. Dependent variable measures for the two groups are then compared at Time 2.

But how does this design eliminate potential confounding variable effects? Given the same amount of time elapses for both groups between the first and second test of the dependent variable, maturation and historical effects are ruled out. If such effects are influencing the behavior of individuals in each of the two groups, they should be doing so equally since the same amount of time has elapsed for both groups. But how about testing effects? Could the pretest be accounting for the changes from Time 1 to Time 2? While pretest effects might be influencing behavior, once again because both groups are having pretest experiences, the potential influence should be the same (on the average) for both groups. Further, the problem of subject selection is eliminated through random assignment to the two experimental groups, so that on the average each group is actually equivalent to the other. Therefore, the pretest–posttest control group design eliminates a number of potential confounding extraneous variables, including maturation, history, testing (instrumentation), and subject selection.

▶   Recently, in our research laboratories, we have used this technique to study the effects of social skills training on enhancing problem solving among conflict-laden

TABLE 7.2. Basic Elements of the Pretest–Posttest Control Group Design

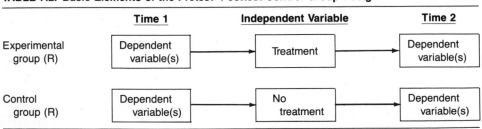

	Time 1	Independent Variable	Time 2
Experimental group (R)	Dependent variable(s)	Treatment	Dependent variable(s)
Control group (R)	Dependent variable(s)	No treatment	Dependent variable(s)

Note: R = randomization.

parent-adolescent dyads (Noble, Adams & Openshaw, 1989). In this investigation we identified families with conflict-laden interactions, randomly selected a sample from a larger population, and then randomly assigned the families to either an experimental or control group. We pretested all subjects on a problem-solving measure. We then had the experimental group complete a social skills training program while the control group remained untreated. We followed this up with a posttest assessment of problem solving. We first compared the experimental and control groups on problem-solving ability using the pretest data and found no differences. Then we compared the experimental and control group on posttest data. We observed that subjects in the experimental group, who received social skills training, showed significantly more problem-solving abilities than were observed in the control group, even though both groups manifested similar abilities at pretest time. This evidence can be used to support the hypothesis that social skills training can influence problem-solving abilities among conflict-laden parent-adolescent dyads. Given the design strengths, one can further eliminate the effects of history, maturation, testing, and selection of subjects as possible rival hypotheses or confounding variable effects. Thus, such a design has strong internal validity, as we discussed in Chapter 4.

The Solomon Four-Group Design.   An improvement on the pretest-posttest control group design is advanced in the Solomon four-group design technique. Specifically, through the addition of two more control groups an increase in external validity is gained. This design is shown in Table 7.3.

The design includes the strength of the experimental and control groups of the pretest–posttest control group design, with the added utility of two additional groups. A second experimental group is included where the subjects who were randomly assigned to that experience are not given a pretest but do experience the experimental treatment and the Time 2 dependent variable measurement. Further, a second control group is included

TABLE 7.3. Basic Elements of the Solomon Four-Group Design

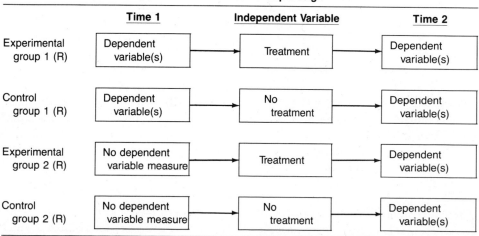

	Time 1	Independent Variable	Time 2
Experimental group 1 (R)	Dependent variable(s)	Treatment	Dependent variable(s)
Control group 1 (R)	Dependent variable(s)	No treatment	Dependent variable(s)
Experimental group 2 (R)	No dependent variable measure	Treatment	Dependent variable(s)
Control group 2 (R)	No dependent variable measure	No treatment	Dependent variable(s)

Note: R = randomization.

that is not given the pretest or the experimental treatment, but is measured during the final posttest period.

In addition to controlling for the possible confounding effects of maturation, history, testing, and subject selection, the additional two research groups help the researcher to eliminate the extraneous variable effect of testing and the possible interaction of testing with the treatment. In that the second experimental group did not receive a pretest, the measurement of the dependent variable at Time 2 is unaffected by any possible pretesting effects. Therefore, a comparison of the Time 2 measure between Experimental Groups 1 and 2 allows the researcher to assess for possible test–retest effects that might confound the independent-dependent variable relation. Further, the same comparison could be made between the two control groups to assess for possible test–retest effects.

▶   An illustration of the utility of the Solomon four-group design is highlighted in a report by Harvey Parker (1974). Parker was specifically interested in the application of "contingency management" in classroom settings on elementary schoolage children's self-concepts. Through a review of the research literature this investigator documented that effective use of classroom behavior modification techniques can lead to positive changes in children's classroom behavior. However, he argued that such techniques should likewise have positive effects on children's self-concepts, but such an assumption had not been adequately demonstrated by experimental research. Therefore, this investigator used a Solomon four-group design to test, over an eight-week period, whether contingency management by elementary school teachers can have a predicted positive effect on self-concept development of disruptive children. In the experimental groups, rewards were given for (1) raising a hand to speak, (2) staying in one's seat, and (3) completing classroom work. Also, children who were unable to control themselves were sent to a "time-out booth" where they were isolated from their peers for short periods of time. The control group children were, in comparison, housed in classrooms of a traditional nature where contingency management was not utilized. On several of the self-concept posttest measures it was found that children who experienced the contingency management classroom experience showed more positive self-concepts than those children from the control groups. Thus, a comparison of the dependent variable measures from the Experimental Groups 1 and 2 were appreciably higher than those from Control Groups 1 and 2. The investigator rightfully concludes that the application of behavior modification techniques with children can have a positive effect on children's self-concept development.

In summary, the Solomon group-group design is an improvement over the pretest–posttest control group design in that it can further eliminate possible testing or test x (by) treatment confounding effects. Also, it offers further credibility to the "if-then" relation through multiple experimental and control testing. Therefore, one would expect similar results between experimental groups, while differing from control groups—whose average scores would be expected to be similar. However, in all due honesty, this design is the least commonly used in social science research due to the extensiveness (and expense) of the technique.

The Posttest-Only Group Design.   Campbell and Stanley (1966) have noted that while scientists are thoroughly entrenched with the security of using pretest measures (which can be compared to assure group equivalence at Time 1), the use of randomization in the placement of research subjects into the different experimental groups makes such a practice unnecessary. Randomization does serve the same purpose of pretesting for equivalence in eliminating initial biases between research groups. Further, on common sense grounds, there are many cases in which pretesting is either unfeasible or too costly. Therefore, where true randomization is possible, the posttest-only control group design is an adequate substitute for the two research designs discussed previously. This design is shown in Table 7.4.

Subjects are randomly placed into 1 of 2 research groups based on a total random chance criterion. One group is given a treatment; the other is not. Both groups, at the same point in time, are given the assessment for the dependent variable.

The posttest-only design has recently been used to study the effects of criminal sanctions on recidivism. For example, in one investigation (Baker & Sadd, 1981) 650 felony defendants were randomly assigned to an experimental and control group. The experimental subjects were offered job service training during a four-month pretrial release period, while the control group subjects were provided no such assistance. Subjects were then tracked regarding dismissal of charges. The experimental subjects were observed to have 72 percent of their charges dismissed, while only 46 percent were dismissed for the control group. As the investigators note, the dosage of criminal sanctions were substantially lowered for the experimental versus control group. It might be noted, however, that a follow-up one year later revealed no differences between the groups in rearrest rates. Therefore, the experimental program influences court decisions but not actual criminal behavior over a one-year follow-up period.

In a related study reported by Sherman (1988), 1,600 apprehended shoplifters, in a department store experiment, were randomly assigned to a release (no treatment) versus visit to the police station (treatment) condition and recidivism rates were assessed. In this posttest-only study no differences were observed even when comparisons were made for age, sex, race, and income differences.

In summary, the posttest-only control group design, while not receiving as wide a recognition as it warrants, is an appropriate experimental design when complete randomization is possible. In particular, it is appropriate where pretesting is unfeasible, and additionally it eliminates any possible contamination of pretest effects. (See Tips for Consumers 7.1.)

TABLE 7.4. Basic Elements of the Posttest-Only Group Design

| Experimental group (R) | Treatment | → | Dependent variable |
| Control group (R) | No treatment | → | Dependent variable |

Note: R = randomization.

Tips for Consumers 7.1

The basic experimental research design has two fundamental groups. These two groups include

1. an experimental group that is given a pretest and a posttest;
2. a control group that is given a pretest and posttest.

While several variations of this basic design are used, the two basic groups are an absolute necessity. However, placement into each group must be random to be maximally effective. Has the researcher drawn a sample of a known population? Were the subjects randomly placed into the two basic groups? Is there evidence that the experimental group made greater change from pre- to posttest assessments than did the control group? The basic notion of causality in an experimental design requires that (1) evidence of change be found from pre- to posttest for the experimental group, and (2) substantial differences be observed in the posttest behavior between the experimental and control groups.

Between versus Within Research Design Question

Beyond the choice of which experimental design to use, an added problem emerges when the scientist has to face the choice of whether he or she wishes to have subjects experience more than one possible experimental treatment. When research participants experience only one treatment, such that an individual participant is either in an experimental or control group, it is called a *between-subjects* design. The between-subjects design designation implies that the comparison is made "between" subjects from different groups. However, there are cases in which the researcher exposes the same subject to two or more (perhaps all) experimental treatment conditions. This design is called the *within-subject* design. Hence, the subject responds to each experimental treatment and comparisons are made within the subject for changes in behavior over treatment conditions.

For example, a between-subjects design might be used in the study of the effects of dieting techniques. A group of volunteers might be randomly placed into either an exercise-oriented program or one using a special medical treatment. Average weight loss might be compared between the two dieting techniques. Conversely, a within-subject design might be used when a specific type of individual is being studied.

Let us assume that we believe heavy males differ from females in their underlying reasons for obesity and that dieting may be better than exercising for one sex than the other. Thus, both obese males and females are introduced to both dieting techniques. The effectiveness of each technique is compared for each subject. Usually such a design requires a counterbalancing strategy. Half of each sex would experience the exercise program first, followed by the dieting procedure. The other half would experience the techniques in the reverse order. In this manner, the counterbalancing would allow the researcher to assess whether the order in which the treatments were delivered had any meaningful effect on making one treatment more effective than another.

But when should a researcher use one strategy over the other? And how might we as consumers be sure the researcher chose the right technique? Anthony Greenwald (1976), in a review of the literature, has concluded the following guidelines might be used in answering these two questions. It must be recognized that the within-subject design is more economical than the between-subjects technique. In the within-subject design each subject is given two or more treatments, and hence only half of the subjects are needed in comparison to the between-subjects design technique in which each experimental group is filled with different subjects. Further, in the within-subject design each subject provides data for two or more treatments and thus serves as his or her own control. In summarizing this first point, Greenwald recommends the within-subject design, due to its economic nature, be used when per-subject cost is extremely expensive while treatment costs are very low. An extreme illustration of this might be one in which an experimental drug is available at very low cost, but the subject's risks might be very high. Therefore, the researcher may have to pay the subjects a great deal of money to take the risk, but the actual costs attached to the production and administration of the experimental drug may be very modest. In contrast, when treatment costs are high, but subject costs are low, the between-subjects design may be the most appropriate.

The second guideline in choosing a *between* versus a *within* design has to do with the issue of *practice effects*. In making a choice, the researchers must predetermine their relative interest in the study of treatment effects that either minimize or maximize practice effects. If the investigator is interested in understanding the effects of a given treatment, independent of practice, then a between-subjects design is called for. As noted, in this design the subjects are given only one opportunity to perform. However, if the researcher wishes to understand how the treatment effect works across a range of practice levels (as is the case in many learning and developmental studies), then the within-subject design is in order. However, when the presentation of one *condition sensitizes* the subject *to treatment variations,* which may result in the subject guessing what the experimenter is looking for (the hypothesis), then the within-subject design, which offers several treatment variations to the subject, is not useful and should be avoided.

When *carry-over effects* are possible, such that one treatment may have effects that are still apparent when the next treatment is given, the within-subject design is undesirable. For certain types of social behavior manipulations the effects may be maintained for some time after measurement; and assuming another treatment is given to the same individual during this period of time, the effects measured after the second treatment may be due to either the first treatment condition, the second treatment, or a combination of the two. Hence, the findings would be confounded. Therefore, when treatment effects are likely to carry over into an unknown period of time and the researcher does not wish to take that risk, the within-subject design is not a useful technique. Rather, the researcher should utilize the between-subjects research design technique.

In summary, the between-subjects design is the preferred technique when (1) treatment costs are high but subject costs are low, and (2) when practice, sensitization, and carry-over effects are probable. In comparison, within-subject or repeated measures designs are more appropriate (1) when subject costs are high but treatment costs are low, and (2) when treatment effect: at different levels of practice are to be studied. Therefore, when subject cooperation and access are difficult, time is limited, and expense is high in running experiments, between-subjects strategies might be the most practical answer to the *between* versus *within* question. (See Tips for Consumers 7.2.)

Tips for Consumers 7.2

A between-subjects design uses different subjects for each research group. The within-subjects design uses the same subject in each of the research groups. To assess the appropriateness of using one design over the other, consumers should ask whether

1. practice effects are possible and whether they are worthy of study;
2. the cost of research subjects precludes the use of a between-subjects design.

Does the researcher recognize these problems? How does the scientist deal with the two issues? Are the research facts hampered by the design chosen?

Strengths and Weaknesses of Laboratory Experimentation

The major strength of experimentation in laboratory-type settings is in the researcher's ability to utilize control. One form of control involves the use of randomization. The researcher can be sure that each research group is equivalent at the beginning of the study. Hence, posttreatment measures can be assuredly due to treatment differences and not initial differences between groups before they experienced the treatments.

A second major type of control is the manipulation of the treatment itself (the independent variable). Laboratory experimentation allows the researcher to carefully define and control the specific form of experience. Hence, one can specifically state what the causal agent of behavior is like (i.e., what it consists of). Through the use of randomization and control in laboratory experimentation when true experimental designs are employed, the scientist can eliminate confounding variables as potential elements of rival hypotheses. Thus, experimentation, more than any other design, provides the best assessment of causality.

The major weakness of experimentation in laboratory settings centers around our previous discussion in Chapter 4 on ecological validity (i.e., behavior in natural contexts). Most behavior occurring in strange laboratory settings is likely to be suspect of poor ecological validity. It is very difficult to establish a "real-life" atmosphere in a laboratory setting; thus, it is difficult to remove the feeling of artificiality that most subjects experience when participating in laboratory experimentation. However, we have shown in Chapter 2 a case in which simulation techniques within a controlled laboratory-type environment might be utilized to reduce the sense of artificiality. The Zimbardo study, while occurring in a laboratory setting, was far from creating an artificial atmosphere. Therefore, through the use of props and environmental design a great deal can be done to minimize the weakness of ecological validity in laboratory experimentation.

SUMMARY

Laboratory experimentation is considered one of the best strategies for the study of proposed cause-and-effect relations. Effective experimentation requires the application of research design in eliminating confounding variable effects. As we have indicated, its major strength is in control and manipulation, while weakness can appear in establishing ecological validity.

The central points made in this chapter are

1. Confounding or extraneous variables in experimentation are eliminated through appropriate research designs utilizing control group comparisons.
2. Three basic "true" experimental designs are available. These techniques include the pretest–posttest control group design, the Solomon four-group design, and the posttest-only control group design. The first two designs utilize pretesting while the latter design does not.
    a. In the pretest–posttest control group design both experimental and control groups are pretested and posttested. By effective randomization in subject placement no pretest differences should be observed. Therefore, any differences between the two groups on the posttest should be associated with treatment effects.
    b. The Solomon four-group design involves adding two control groups to the basic pretest–posttest control group design. These control groups provide important information on possible pretesting effects to either the experimental or control group responses.
    c. The posttest-only design can be used when full randomization in sampling and in placement into the experimental and control group can be assured. It is an effective and cost-effective design when all conditions can be met.
3. Another important design issue has to do with the use of subjects. A researcher can utilize a between-subjects design strategy in which different samples are used in the experimental and control groups, or the investigator can use a within-subject design technique that offers two or more treatment conditions to each subject. In most situations, the between-subjects is preferred over the within-subject design technique.

PROBLEMS AND APPLICATIONS

1. Using the outline provided in Table 7.1, design a small experimental study to see if the delivery of a small lesson about sex education is best taught by reading of materials, lecturing, or a combination of both. Begin by agreeing on the content of the lesson and the audience for which it is directed. How will you design the control group in such a study?
2. If you were asked to determine if a lifesaving procedure (e.g., therapy or medication) were truly effective, which of the experimental designs would you most want to use to be sure of your conclusions? Why?
3. How might a sociologist use an experimental research design to study group or organization behavior (e.g., social compliance or conformity)? Why do psychologists use experimental techniques in the study of clinical treatment effects? When should educators or nurses use the experimental technique in their practice with students or patients?
4. What are the strengths and weaknesses of using laboratory experimentation to study such behaviors as

    moral action
    academic achievement
    violence
    political behavior?

REFERENCES

Baker, S. H., & Sadd, S. (1981). *Diversion of felony arrests.* Washington, D.C.: National Institute of Justice.

Campbell, D. T., & Stanley, J. C. (1966). *Experimental and quasi-experimental designs for research.* Chicago: Rand McNally.

Cook, T., & Campbell, D. (1979). *Quasi-experimentation.* New York: Rand McNally.

Greenwald, A. G. (1976). Within-subjects designs: To use or not to use? *Psychological Bulletin, 83,* 314–320.

Noble, S., Adams, G. R., & Openshaw, D. K. (in press). Interpersonal communications in parent-adolescent dyads: The effects of a social skills training program with conflict-laden families. *Journal of Family Psychology.*

Parker, H. (1974). Contingency management and concomitant changes in elementary school students' self-concepts. *Psychology in the Schools, 11,* 70–79.

Sherman, L. W. (1988). Randomized experiments in criminal sanctions. In H. S. Bloom, D. S. Cordray, and R. J. Light (Eds.), *Lessons from selected program and policy areas.* New Directions for Program Evaluation. No. 37. San Francisco: Jossey-Bass.

SECTION III

Elements of Measurement and Sampling

To become a knowledgeable consumer and generator of scientific information it is essential that you understand the primary elements of social science measurement and be familiar with how one obtains adequate research samples. You will find in the measurement chapter that scientific measurement has multiple levels of conceptions. The same phenomenon can be studied on a simple or highly complex dimension of measurement. Likewise, we shall argue, among other things, that obtaining a sample technique does not necessarily imply a poor or a weak strategy. Rather, we shall argue that the complexity of the task is determined, in part, by the rigor, objectivity, and conceptual basis of the research endeavor. Also, you will find that complexity in measurement and sampling does not automatically assure quality. In summary, Section III presents information on measurement and sampling issues that accompany the research design and provides the underlying essential precursors of all data collection strategies.

CHAPTER 8

Levels of Measurement and Scaling

OUTLINE

Measurement in Everyday Life
    Elements in Measurement
    Cultural Origins of Measurement
    Functions of Measurement
Levels or Types of Measurement
    Nominal Measurement
    Ordinal Measurement
    Interval Measurement
    Ratio Measurement
Scales and Measuring Devices: Tools of the Trade
    Summated Scales
    Cumulative or Unidimensional Scales
    Semantic Differential Scale
    Sociometric Measurement
Summary
Problems and Applications
References

KEY TERMS

Measurement	Level of measurement	Properties of scales
Instruments	Nominal	Summated scales
Attributes	Ordinal	Cumulative scales
Inference	Interval	Semantic differential scales
Scales	Ratio	Sociometric measures
Standards	Static phenomena	Item analysis
Probability	Dynamic phenomena	

STUDY GUIDE QUESTIONS

1. What are the main elements or features of measurement in science?
2. In reviewing scientific research, it appears that researchers are continually attempting to develop more precise measurement devices. Why?
3. Most social science research is carried out with measurement being conducted at what level?
4. For a researcher to argue that measurement is being carried out at the interval level, what conditions must be met?
5. Why have the social sciences made such heavy use of summated scales in conducting research?
6. What are the main features and utility of sociometric measures in conducting social science research?

Role of the Scientist

Science is strongly devoted to the measurement of objects, events, situations, and behavior as these exist or occur in the "real world." To engage in science or research is to engage in a process of measurement from which one obtains data, information, and eventually understanding. The researcher utilizes measurement and its tools to obtain truth.

The development of measurement tools, seeking effective ways to use such tools, and the continual refinement of the measurement process is a main activity of most researchers. The object of measurement and the type of measure employed are determined by the problem involved. The researcher is obligated to know much about the element or issue to be measured as well as how to construct and use measurement apparatus.

Role of the Consumer

Fair practice, money's worth, honesty, truth telling, and a host of other important concepts emerge when we think about consuming or using that which is produced by research. Additionally, the consumer of research is influenced by reports claiming one outcome is more valid than another. Should an overweight person refrain from drinking soft drinks sweetened with saccharin? Should babies be fed foods prepared with cyclamates? How truthful or believable is the research about seat belt use or impact airbags? How safe are infant car seats? What are the causal links in the correlation between tobacco use and the development of lung cancer? Will attitudes shift in regard to alcohol use as a result of mandatory labels as was the case with tobacco products?

The questions and arguments go on, and a good number of the debates deal with measurement and testing—were they valid, appropriate, and administered correctly? Is it possible to measure an attitude, prejudice, adjustment, stress, and so on? One thing is certain: the consumer of research must know about measurement and testing to survive in a modern world. Both applied and basic research involve the use of measurement and awareness of levels of measurement.

MEASUREMENT IN EVERYDAY LIFE

Measurement begins with the idea of quantity, condition, property, or other characteristics of the issue or property to be considered. Measurement helps to answer the questions of how many, how much, or how often. Broadly defined, measurement can be made by unaided human senses. It consists of estimates of distance, dimension, temperature, attitude, weight, identification of colors, estimates of chemical composition via smell or taste, or evaluation by touch. However, unaided human estimates are subject to gross error. Therefore, mankind's measurement capability needs to be extended and refined by *instruments—measurement devices specifically developed* to obtain more precise, objective, and useful information. For example, a teacher typically has a "feeling" for how students are doing in a course, but a test is really a measure to determine who knows or does not know the material, or who prepared or failed to prepare. Therefore, a *test* is a way of objectively assigning some letter grade based on class performance.

One of the oldest recorded examples of a "test" to measure some aspect of human behavior was that of Gideon, a judge and popular hero of the Israelite tribe of Manasseh, who delivered his people from the oppressive control of the Midianites (Judges 7:2–7). Apparently some 32,000 prospective warriors were anxious to go into battle against the enemy with Gideon as the leader, but Gideon was instructed to greatly reduce this number lest the Israelites vaunt themselves up and take claim for victory rather than giving credit to the God of Israel. The first *measure* employed by Gideon was to dismiss all men who evidenced *fear and trembling* as they thought about the prospects of battle. Apparently Gideon was capable of observing these characteristics as he dismissed 22,000 men from the ranks using this criterion. Gideon was still left with 10,000 soldiers, a marching force much too large for the specialized mission he was instructed to head, and he was once again instructed to reduce the ranks by having the men obtain a drink of water from a nearby stream. His task was to *carefully observe* the *manner* in which they *drank water* and to divide them into groups—those who *lapped up the water as a dog* and those who *knelt down and drank directly from the stream*. Gideon observed that 9,700 men knelt down and drank from the stream while only 300 prospective warriors raised water to their mouths with their hands and lapped as a dog. The *water test* gave him the needed 300 men who brought victory on the battle field. While this measurement strategy may sound strange, our daily use of height, sex, weight, hair color, skin color, and age as criteria for making decisions is also unusual. Decisions about our social and economic world are made using these variables in ways not dramatically different than the criteria employed by Gideon.

Attribute is another important dimension in understanding the idea of measurement. Physical things are often perceived through their properties as attributes, and it is in this context that a parent may directly sense the property called body temperature by feeling an infant's forehead. One cannot directly observe colicky feelings nor share the infant's experience of stress or hunger. The parent must infer such unobservable private activities from hearing a baby cry, watching the baby squirm, or noting apparent discomfort in the child's face or posture. More broadly speaking, much of what we refer to as measurement comes as the result of *inference,* the process of making a decision or judgment based on a manifestation of behavior or attitude thought to be related to the issue under focus. To infer is to draw a conclusion from known facts applied to something not known. An attribute is the activity or property used to make an inference.

Elements in Measurement

To measure a property or attribute is to assign it a specific position along some kind of dimension or numerical scale. In the Gideon example, the attributes were apparently simple to measure: fear and trembling, and the posture in which water was drunk. Concerns about size, height, depth, length, weight, and strength (to mention just a few dimensions) have been issues of interest to mankind for a long time. In the study of social behavior, data telling the age of subjects, marital status, birth order, educational attainment, and political party affiliation represent various indicators about subjects that would be derivable from measurement. For example, the question "How old are you?" is a measurement question; when answered correctly it can supply information about chronological age. If there is little need for pinpointed accuracy or fine discrimination in decision making, then extremely fine measurement does not appear to be especially important. However, social science has invested heavily in measurement and is zealously committed to a precision-oriented understanding of human behavior and social processes. The old saying, "Even a stopped clock is right twice per day," may be a clever observation about measurement, but the current emphasis on refinement is oriented to develop measures that are accurate each time one wants to use them, not just two times per day.

▶ All measurement involves two elements—units and numbers. To make accurate measurements people have invented instruments or measurement tools such as clocks, scales, tape measures, thermometers, and other devices. To use these tools, one compares some phase of the object or event being measured with the units marked on a standardized tool. For example, the Babylonians used sundials to divide the time from sunrise to sunset into 12 parts, which were later referred to as hours. By the 1700s, clocks were sufficiently developed and accurate to further divide time into smaller units than hours, and the hour was divided into 60 units called minutes and the minute into 60 units referred to as seconds. In the twentieth century, time can be divided still further using an atomic clock measurement tool, which was developed to present extremely refined measures of time. An atomic clock is capable of dividing (measuring) time by counting the number of vibrations made by atoms of the element cesium. These atoms vibrate 9,192,631,770 times per second—a far cry from the innovative sundial that earlier revolutionized the Babylonian world.

Cultural Origins of Measurement

Measurement is with us all of the time in each phase of life, not just in research, the lab, or in using a measurement device. As Phillips (1976) reminds us, "measurement is a process by which the individual obtains information, and as such is fundamental not only to the cybernetic process in science and everyday life but also to life itself" (p. 137). To think about measurement of any property necessitates that one make reference to some type of *standard* that is essentially *a community agreement* arrived at by scientists, government, and people in a situation in which they will by *authority use that standard for future references.* This standard is applied when one makes reference to length, weight, time, color, and to a lesser degree when we refer to attitude or group stability of some type. All of these measurement standards or devices make use of a *scale* of some type which can be defined *as a representation* or a *characteristic* of an event or object when the device is applied against some characteristic, object, or event. As an example, the plains Indians measured warrior status by engaging in coup counting, and they believed that coup was a sensitive indicator of all-around warrior capability—the greater the number of scalps, the greater the warrior's status in the group. Thus, warrior status was in part determined by this form of measurement.

Where would such a practice come from, how did it gain community support as a standard, and why would still other groups make reference to measurement standards such as a foot, yard, the pound, or bust size? At first, a foot was just that—the length of the human foot—but later it was measured against the foot of the ruler or chieftain. With continued use and tradition, standards were established with the Romans who introduced the unit of the foot to Britain, and Britain in turn brought the concept to America in the colonial period. Standardization was viewed as being so useful and important for the conduct of daily life that *standards* were frequently placed in the temples for preservation. Precision, which came from the English standard, can be greatly refined by the use of the metric system of measurement, which many countries have now adopted or are using in some form. (See Tips for Consumers 8.1.)

Almost all questions or scientific enterprises necessitate measurement of some type, and this involves the task of comparing objects or human factors and assigning numbers to these properties where appropriate in order to represent certain relationships between them. Measurement, as noted, can range from being a loose or general guess, to the atomic clock with an accuracy of more than a billionth part of a second. In contrast to this fine type of discrimination, social science research works in a world of *probability*—a world where we estimate the likelihood that some event will occur. Measurements in this context are usually not precise or as precise as in the world where events are deterministic. It is clear, though, that social science as a part of the scientific enterprise in a modern world, shares the truth-seeking mission of science in general. As Blalock (1974) notes, "If every variable were perfectly measured by a single indicator there would be few difficulties. But research always consists of a series of compromises in design, measurement, and analysis" (p. 2).

Tips for Consumers 8.1

Many scientists would adhere to the statement that rough measurement of an important issue is more critical than precise measurement of trivia. Of course the goal of quality research is to have precise measurement applied to critical events in the same study. As you read and evaluate research be aware of documentation, claims for differences, magnitude of differences, and applications of findings.

Newspapers, magazines, and other journals are filled with claims and counterclaims. Beware of statements such as "they," "science says," "researchers found," for they are key phrases coming from the methodological activity of researchers at work. These are turn-on words and one must press people or the written word to verify, to document, and supply the data and clarity to go along with the assertions.

We live in a world of testing, tryouts, evaluations, and experiments. It is important to evaluate, interrogate, and apply from this world in order to create the necessary links from the generation of "truth" to the application of "truth."

Functions of Measurement

The roles of measurement and research design (see Chapters 5, 6, and 7) are closely intertwined, and it is, of course, impossible to complete useful research without implementing the best design for a given problem. Further, one must have sensitive, accurate ways of measuring the phenomena under study within the parameters of that design. This process forces the scientist to clearly (1) establish precisely what is to be measured, and (2) decide on, and then use or construct, a device for measuring whatever has been established as the thing to be measured. Thus, measurement is very important in scientific work and helps to accomplish a variety of useful functions:

1. Measurement produces data for the scientist.
2. When data are analyzed, the scientist will have information usable in a variety of ways.
3. Measurement is the process by which the scientist attempts to understand the properties of objects or events.
4. Measurement is the mechanism for helping the scientist view the relationship of one property to that of another.
5. Through measurement we test hypotheses, propositions, and theories.
6. Measurement helps to establish whether some factor is present or absent and to what degree either state exists.
7. Measurement ties methodological concepts to the world of reality—or simply put, we are able to make meaningful observations about reality.
8. Measurement helps promote the world of discovery.
9. Measurement is a detailed way of looking at or assessing certain aspects of the data-collection process.

In the research setting and in everyday use or application of research, measurement or reference to measurement is very much a part of conversation, habits, and decision making. To live is to measure, calculate, judge, discriminate, and make conclusions based on the evidence one has reviewed. The scientist and the consumer of research are much closer than they often think in regard to measurement and judgments based on measurement. If the scientist has a primary role of developing measures for testing relationships it would seem that the consumer of research has a primary role of critically evaluating research reports at both the personal and societal level.

LEVELS OR TYPES OF MEASUREMENT

To measure a property or issue is to assign it a unique position along some kind of dimension or numerical scale. When numbers, names, and words are used to merely identify or label individuals, objects, or classes, they constitute a *nominal scale*. When a set of numbers or words reflect only the order of things—bigger than or smaller than— they constitute an *ordinal scale*. An *interval scale* has equal units and a zero point that was determined in an arbitrary manner (e.g., the Fahrenheit scale). The fourth type of scale, *ratio,* has equal units and, in addition, an absolute or true zero point. These four types of discrimination are called *levels of measurement*.

Not all issues or properties can be measured in the same way or use the same rules. Thus, various levels of measurement exist which science uses in assessing the world. Each type of measurement follows different rules and makes different assumptions about the measurement process. Each level of measurement has utility. Our purpose here is to define and illustrate the utility of each type as applied to the social sciences.

Nominal Measurement

Measurement at the *nominal level* is, as the name implies, a *naming* or *labeling process*. One uses names or labels to classify people, objects, or events as they exist in some context. Data obtained at this level represent a classification of some type and reflect a difference in kind rather than amount or degree. Classification of people in a classroom according to their home state or country of origin would be examples of nominal measure. Researchers often attach a number to the names or classes established for nominally measured concepts, but it is important to keep in mind that the numbers are also only labels. For example, the social security numbers held by most Americans are merely labels and have no imputed difference one from another other than they must all be different. The telephone number, the jersey number on the football player, and classification of people according to political party are still further examples of nominal measurement. This is simple measurement, to be sure, but think of the great utility and daily usage of this type of measurement: gender status, religious preference, type of occupation, home state, political party, eye color, or day of the week.

Variables or objects at the nominal level of measurement must be capable of simple categorization, apply to all phenomena being named, and also be discrete. The problem of classification at this level can become very complicated. For example, how does one deal with borderline cases if the task is to divide the social world of a community into those who are church attendees and those who do not attend? Some people who seldom attend might realistically be assigned to either camp.

Nominal measures serve the important function of letting one tell items apart, to discriminate between objects on a reliable basis. The researcher is able to assign observations and descriptions to classes, categories, or "pigeonholes," as we sometimes say. For example, college teachers may be classified as professors, associate professors, assistant professors, instructors, and lecturers, and in all such cases a person is only a member of one subset or set and all others in that category would have the same defined characteristics. To summarize, nominal measurement is classification, and no ordering of the categories is permitted—it is simply exhaustive and mutually inclusive.

Ordinal Measurement

In many avenues of research it is possible not only to classify objects but, in addition, to *order* them in some manner, such as "more than" or "less than." Thus, *ordinal measurement* is a *ranking operation,* such as first, second, third, fourth, fifth, and so on. Measurement at the ordinal level is simply order, and the differences between any one rank and another may not be equal, but simply more or less. Measurement at this level involves the same rule of nominal measurement—unique classification, and in addition, a new rule, namely, *ordering or ranking the objects on some dimension.* Ordinal measurement employs the mathematical operation of greater than or less than, and to order things one has to have evidence that someone or some object truly has more or less of a property. Applied to common elements in the social world, we might say one mother is more protective of children than another; one scientist is more competent than another; one student has more ability than another; or one citizen has a higher social class than another. The exact amount of difference in all of these examples is not known, nor is it generally possible to ascertain such with this type of measurement. It should be clear that this scale or level of measurement supplies the idea of *more or less only* and not the idea of *how much more or how much less.*

In an ordinal scale we have the element or rule of *classification*—all properties or objects with this characteristic may be so categorized, and we develop as many classes or names as needed to account for all observations. Secondly, we then are permitted to compare all events, say boys and girls on some level of athletic ability, but it could be any common property we might be interested in for comparison. As we compare, it is clear that differences will be observed and properties will be ranked (ordered) in some way. This illustrates a third characteristic of ordinal measurement, the rule of *asymmetry*—if category *B* is larger than *A,* then *A* cannot be larger than *B.* Thus, the properties in ordered ranks cannot be reversed. The fourth truth rule indicates that if *A* is larger than *B,* and *B* is larger than *C,* then *A* is also larger than *C*—the rule of *transitivity.*

We often assign numbers to ranks, and this serves a useful purpose, but again, it is necessary to keep in mind that the numbers do not permit analysis as if the ranks had equal distance between one another. The numbers in this case merely represent which objects have more or less ranking information only. Ordinal scales represent the most frequently used measurement level in the social sciences since it is possible to order a great many important properties, but in most cases our measurement tools do not permit us to state the magnitude of difference between properties.

Observations such as academic or military ranks known as private, major, colonel, or general are examples of nominal measurement and ordinal ranking. Thus, ordinal measurement retains all the power or characteristics of nominal measurement (classification) and, in addition, adds the property of order to the observations.

Interval Measurement

Interval measurement may simply be defined as an ordinal scale in which the *distance between two rankings* is a *known,* and this distance is a *constant* interval. At this level of measurement, the observations (data) may be added, subtracted, multiplied, and divided. In short, one may carry out mathematical functions because data measured at this level have objective quantification that can be expressed in constant and equal appearing units of classification. Any scale or measurement tool capable of quantifying data into fixed intervals (equal distances in the order) can be regarded as an interval scale.

All the social sciences are interested in interval measurements and use them when a study involves variables such as time, geographical distance, population density, height and weight, or income. Temperature as expressed in either centigrade or Fahrenheit is a classical example of interval measurement.

In regard to the temperature example, it is clear that a reading of 72° represents a specific or a *different* observation than a reading of 80°; hence, this is *nominal* level datum. It is also *ordinal* since 80° is *higher than* 72°, and it is *interval* in nature since the 8-degree difference between 72° and 80° can be broken down into units of *equal value.* Further, the *interval* between 72° and 80° is the *same* at the interval between 42° and 50°.

The interval scale is a most useful scale in research, even though it is not routinely used in the bulk of social science research. Even with all of its attractive characteristics and the difficulty of achieving this type of measurement, it does have some limitations in terms of scientific utility. It has an arbitrary zero point; that is, there is not a fixed or true zero point in our examples of temperature. In a Fahrenheit thermometer a reading of zero is arbitrary, as this does not reflect the ultimate in coldness. Zero on this scale is only a reading that says it is now 32° colder than freezing, which started at 32°.

Ratio Measurement

The new and unique characteristic of *ratio measurement,* not found in the three previously defined levels of measurement, is the addition of *an absolute* or *fixed zero point.* When a true or real zero point is added to the measurement, then one can measure or arrive at decisions of a ratio judgment. Research using geographical distance, time units, and weight or height would provide further examples of this level of measurement. Measurements such as length, time, weight, pressure, or voltage are all clear examples of this type of measurement. A scientist studying observations with any of these measures with a value of zero is reporting a true zero, meaning a zero amount of the variable. Forty pounds is twice as much as 20 pounds; 6 feet is twice as high as 3 feet. The Kelvin Scale, named after the British physicist and mathematician, uses a scale of temperature measured in degrees centigrade from an absolute zero of -273.18, thus constituting a classical example of this type of scale. When it comes to attitude, IQ, religiosity,

TABLE 8.1. Typology of Levels of Measurement for Research

Level of Measurement	Different-Same; Equal-Unequal	Greater-than or Less-than	Constant Measured Unit	True Zero Point	Extent of Use in Social Science	Example of Research Concept of Variable
Nominal	Yes	No	No	No	Very common	Gender, marital status
Ordinal	Yes	Yes	No	No	Common	Social class
Interval	Yes	Yes	Yes	No	Uncommon	IQ, Fahrenheit
Ratio	Yes	Yes	Yes	Yes	Very uncommon	Birth rate, age[a]

[a]It is clear that these variables are somewhat different from temperature on the Kelvin Scale, pressure or other variables from physical science, but they do represent variables treated at the ratio level of measurement in several of the social science areas. (*Source:* H. W. Smith. [1975]. *Strategies of social research.* Englewood Cliffs, N.J.: Prentice-Hall, p. 44.)

liberalism, or marital adjustment, it becomes clear at once that the notion of ratio measurement has no reality or meaning given the characteristics of measurement in regard to these variables. Table 8.1 provides a summary of the levels of measurement, highlighting their various characteristics as well as illustrating their utility and type of concept or variable as examples of research.

SCALES AND MEASURING DEVICES: TOOLS OF THE TRADE

Instruments or measuring scales in the social sciences are the counterpart of the measuring tape, weight scales, thermometer, and various scopes used in other types of scientific research. IQ measurement is perhaps the best known example of a measure that is standardized to assess some capacity of the individual, but even in this instance IQ tells us almost nothing about motivation, drive, and overall dedication of the individual, all of which may be of equal importance.

We are faced with an additional problem in the measurement of social phenomena that the geologist, chemist, and physicist do not have to face, and that is the nature of the objects being measured. The physicist, for example, measures properties that are more likely to be *static*—masses or forces in a state of *equilibrium,* forces at *rest,* forces in a *motionless state.* In this context, a sophisticated instrument directly compares some aspect of an object under study with the standard scale or calibrated meter contained within the instrument. It is assumed, and rightly so, that the numerical values represented by the tool will correspond closely to properties of the real variable being measured.

Contrast this measurement approach with that of the behavioral sciences in which the properties being assessed are *dynamic* in nature as opposed to static. By dynamic, we mean that the elements or forces are in a *constant state of flux* and *full of movement.* It is this world of dynamic change into which the social scientist enters. To further complicate matters, social scientists know that the measurement process has further impact on whatever they measure—people, groups, and organizations have reactive properties that create additional problems whenever some aspect of behavior is being measured.

Notwithstanding the very extensive hurdles in the measurement of social phenomena, considerable success has been achieved in measuring dynamic properties in the

---

Tips for Consumers 8.2

To measure a property is to assign it a specific position along some kind of dimension or numerical scale. Four types of measurement that have profound impact on society include

1. *nominal measurement:* This is a category or some label attached to a category. It is useful measurement, but it is classification only.
2. *ordinal measurement:* In addition to categories, ordinal measure also orders or ranks the events under study. One can merely state "greater than" or "less than." No claim or basis for mathematical manipulation is possible. Most measurement and research in the social sciences goes on at this level. Assess the claims carefully when a report states that a higher level of measurement was used.
3. *interval measurement:* At this level we categorize, rank, and in addition have equal units between elements as well as an arbitrary zero point.
4. *ratio measurement:* This level of measurement, which is rarely used in the social sciences, employs categorization, ranks, equal intervals, and has an absolute or true zero point.

Each of these four types of measurement has utility for various types of research. One level is not necessarily more scientific or less scientific than another. They are rather different, carry different assumptions, and should be sensitively used for the appropriate research topic and level of measurement.

---

social world, and many believe that we are at a stage of scientific development in the social sciences where considerable success will now be attained.

Several types of scales or measurement devices have been developed and used widely in the past three to four decades. The specific goals of such scales have been to provide more refined measurement of social phenomena and to overcome the gross inadequacies inherent in general estimations (see Lodge, 1981, for application of magnitude scaling and related issues as an example of new direction in scale construction). It is important for students to understand the notion of measurement as reflected in specific scales and to be aware of the difficulties involved when attempting to construct conceptual scales to provide refined measurement for the fleeting and seemingly elusive dynamic social concerns. (See Tips for Consumers 8.2.)

Our goal in this section is to illustrate selected types of measurement by briefly reviewing four types of scales that have been widely used in the social sciences. Becoming familiar with the nature and utility of these four types of scales, now widely used, will enable researchers and consumers of research to increase their utility and understanding skills regarding measurement in social science. Our coverage in this section should not be interpreted as a status report of measurement in social science. Rather, it is more properly a profile of past and present measurement applications.

Summated Scales

A *summated scale* is an approach to measurement by which one creates a set of items designed to reflect very favorable to very unfavorable responses to some issue or idea with items reacted to by individuals in a sample or population. Respondents give their reaction to such items by some degree of agreement or disagreement. This approach to measurement was devised by Likert (1932) and is perhaps the most widely used approach to measurement in the social sciences today. The basic idea in constructing a Likert-type scale is rather straightforward. The steps in developing a Likert-type scale are as follows (Edwards, 1957):

1. A pool of items that appear to be related or important to the problem under study is developed. These items should reflect both a positive and negative stance in regard to the problem under study. Extremely positive or negative statements should be avoided because this type of scale permits respondents to give their degree of agreement or disagreement to each item. Statements are judged and classified into either a favorable or unfavorable category, with the goal of having about the same number of items in each type. The favorable and unfavorable items should be randomly mixed in a completed scale.

2. A response category for each item is provided, typically a 5-point response composed of (1) strongly agree, (2) agree, (3) undecided, (4) disagree, (5) strongly disagree. Most Likert-type scales use a 5-response category, although fewer or more categories have been used. It is generally advisable to have an uneven number of item responses to provide a clear midpoint.

3. Some items are stated positively and others negatively, as this approach serves to reduce the tendency of respondents to select a choice without carefully reading and pondering each item.

4. A usable instrument should be around 20 to 30 items—select the best statements from your original pool of items, which, of course, might contain several dozen (and sometimes well over a hundred) different items.

5. Administer the instrument to the designated population and collect the desired data.

6. Analyses of the data can be accomplished by scoring the various responses and summating them—the reason for calling this a summated scale. A summated score is possible by assigning a numerical value to each response—usually a value of 1 to 5 so that a summated response represents the most favorable attitude under measurement. Once the scoring procedure has been devised, one simply determines each subject's score by adding the individual numbers for each item. This procedure results in a score for each subject who responded to the Likert-type scale. Respondents can then be ranked according to the score obtained if desired.

7. In addition to using the scores or data from the scale in testing a question or hypothesis in a study, one should determine which of the items in the scale are effective versus those that had little discriminating power. *Item analysis* is the typical tool used to accomplish this, where the researcher wants to know which items discriminate between high scorers and low scorers on the scale. Item analysis is carried out by comparing the responses of the upper 25% with those of the lower 25%. Then, one retains only those items in the scale that were able to discriminate between these two groups. By eliminating those items that *do not* discriminate between high and low scores, the scale is made more useful and reflects a higher level of internal consistency in all of the "good" items. We make the assumption, and attempt to verify the assumption by test evaluation, that each item in our scale represents a slightly different aspect of the dimension being

measured. However, all retained items in a scale possess some shared characteristic being measured. The Likert-type scale is an ordinal scale and is widely used because of the ordering factor, plus its great flexibility and relative ease in construction. (See McIver and Carmine, 1981, for more detail on scale construction.)

One example of a Likert-type scale comes from Fibel and Hale (1978) in their attempt to construct a scale capable of measuring a Generalized Expectancy for Success Scale in life (GESS). The scale is composed of 30 items, 17 stated in the positive or in the direction of success and 13 items in the negative or failure direction. The negative and positive items are randomly ordered in the scale. Respondents are directed to circle a number on a 5-point scale from 1 (highly improbable) to 5 (highly probable) for each item. The complete scale is shown in Figure 8.1.

Scores of GESS for each respondent are summated in the direction of success. Thus, a high total scale score indicates a high belief or attitude toward the expectation for success in the future. The possible range of scores was from a low of 30 to a high of 150.

These 30 items represent the best of several items originally developed by these researchers. With continued use of this summated scale on various samples and over a period of time, the scale may be further modified. The dependent variable measured by this Likert-type scale is the expectancy for success in life. The various items in the scale are designed to tap or measure the profile of characteristics that people use in estimating or projecting what they see happening in their lives and careers. When the GESS is scored for various populations, the investigator would analyze the data according to sex, age, religion, political affiliation, occupation, marital state, and perhaps other background variables in order to increase the precision of measurement and understanding about expectancy for success.

The Sense of Coherence Scale (Antonovsky & Sourani, 1988) is another example of a Likert scale. The investigators were interested in whether or not a sense of coherence was associated with successful coping to various family stressors. Items were scaled from 1 to 7, with 1 indicating that there would be a full understanding from family members and 7 meaning that there was no understanding or acceptance by family members. Examples of items included, "Is there a feeling in your family that everyone understands everyone else well?" (p. 91) and "When you are in the midst of a rough period, does the family always feel cheered up by the thought about better things that can happen. . . . feel disappointed and despairing about life?" (p. 91)

A third example of a Likert-type scale is the Marital Instability Index used by Edwards, Johnson, and Booth (1987) to predict the chances of marital dissolution. Responses were rated on a 4-point scale ranging from "never" to "almost always." Questions included such items as, "How often do you eat your main meal together?" (p. 170), and "How often do you work together on projects around the house?" (p. 170). The researchers concluded that the instrument was a highly valid predictor of marital dissolution.

Cumulative or Unidimensional Scales

A *cumulative scale,* as proposed by Guttman (1944), claims to yield a single score, based on the notion that all items in the scale are measuring a single dimension. You will recall that in the Likert-type scale ordinal measure was achieved in terms of the responses (strongly agree—strongly disagree), while in a Guttman-type scale one achieves ordinality through the items themselves. Respondents react to a series of *ordered* items, but typically only agree or disagree; they do not vary in degrees of attitudinal intensity. The items are constructed in such a way that each item evidences a respective rank in regard to the variables being measured. Some of the statements should be worded in a positive stance and some negative so that a scale will be composed of 10 to 15 statements. The scale items are then submitted to a group of respondents who are asked to agree or disagree with each of the respective items. In scoring the completed scales, a value of 1 is

---

Highly Improbable   1   2   3   4   5   *Highly Probable*

In the future I expect that I will:

1. find that people don't seem to understand what I am trying to say.
2. be discouraged about my ability to gain the respect of others.
3. be a good parent.
4. be unable to accomplish my goals.
5. have a successful marital relationship.
6. deal poorly with emergency situations.
7. find my efforts to change situations I don't like to be ineffective.
8. not be very good at learning new skills.
9. carry through my responsibilities successfully.
10. discover that the good in life outweighs the bad.
11. handle unexpected problems successfully.
12. get the promotions I deserve.
13. succeed in the projects I undertake.
14. not make any significant contributions to society.
15. discover that my life is not getting much better.
16. be listened to when I speak.
17. discover that my plans don't work out too well.
18. find that no matter how hard I try, things just don't turn out the way I would like.
19. handle myself well in whatever situation I'm in.
20. be able to solve my own problems.
21. succeed at most things I try.
22. be successful in my endeavors in the long run.
23. be very successful in working out my personal life.
24. experience many failures in my life.
25. make a good impression on people I meet for the first time.
26. attain the career goals I have set for myself.
27. have difficulty dealing with my superiors.
28. have problems working with others.
29. be a good judge of what it takes to get ahead.
30. achieve recognition in my profession.

Figure 8.1. Generalized Expectancy for Success Scale. (*Source:* B. Fibel and W. D. Hale [1978]. The generalized expectancy for success scale—a new measure. *Journal of Consulting and Clinical Psychology, 4* [5], 924–931. Copyright 1978 by the American Psychological Association. Reprinted by permission.)

given for all items receiving agreement and 0 to all items in which the respondents express disagreement. We would often eliminate items on which complete agreement was attained, whether it be positive or negative, because of the belief that these items are not working for the scale. In a similar fashion, items on a true and false test that everyone gets correct are doing little to tell us about the capability of students taking the test.

Since the items in a completed scale would reflect order, it is assumed that a ◄ respondent who agreed with Item 3 would also have agreed with Items 1 and 2. For example, Reiss (1964) illustrated the utility of assessing premarital sexual permissiveness using a Guttman scaling approach. Both males and females were instructed to respond in terms of agreement or disagreement to 12 items, some of which are shown in Figure 8.2. The nature of these items clearly illustrates the order differential between each item and how response to a "higher" commitment item is an excellent predictor of one's attitude response on an item of lesser intensity—in this example, attitude toward premarital sexual permissiveness.

While most individuals do reflect an accumulative quality to their score, there are persons who "break" the logical sequence of response in their score and make a "mistake." Guttman assumed that a scale should have at least a .90 *coefficient of reproducibility,* which means that one can tolerate up to about a 10 percent error in response with regard to the order of agreement or disagreement with the items and still have a legitimate basis for claiming that the scale is accumulative, thus tapping an order or single dimension scale.

The Guttman-type scale has been used widely in social science, especially in the areas of race relations, power and authority structure, housing, and other attitudinal dimensions. The notion of *tapping* a single dimension (i.e., all items in a scale refer to the same concept) is one of the main features of unidimensional scales. This unidimensional characteristic constitutes one of the main differences between this approach to measurement and a Likert or summated scale. Researchers and consumers of research in the broad spectrum of social science activity should know about Guttman-type (unidimensional) scales and the contribution they bring to measurement. (See Gordon, 1972, for detailed analysis.)

AGREE   DISAGREE

1. I believe that kissing is acceptable for the male before marriage when he is engaged to be married.
2. I believe that kissing is acceptable for the male before marriage when he is in love.
3. I believe that kissing is acceptable for the male before marriage when he feels strong affection for his partner.
4. I believe that kissing is acceptable for the male before marriage even if he does not feel particularly affectionate toward his partner.

The items continue up through Number 12:

12. I believe that full sexual relations are acceptable for the male before marriage even if he does not feel particularly affectionate toward his partner.

Figure 8.2. Premarital Sexual Permissiveness Scale. (*Source:* I. L. Reiss. [1964]. The scaling of premarital sexual permissiveness. *Journal of Marriage and the Family, 26,* 188–198. Copyright 1964 by the National Council on Family Relations, 3989 Central Ave. N.E., Suite #550, Minneapolis, MN 55421. Reprinted by permission.)

Semantic Differential Scale

We now move to a third example of measurement and scale construction in the study of social phenomena. While the semantic differential scale is not as well known or as widely used as summated or unidimensional scales, it does appear to be a flexible and innovative approach to many of the variables of interest to researchers and consumers of research.

▶   The semantic differential scale is extremely flexible and can, with very minor adaptation, be used to measure a variety of attitudes. The semantic differential scale attempts to measure respondents' attitudes toward some phenomena by having them check a point along a continuum between two words or concepts. The basic rationale of the semantic differential scale is to measure respondents' reactions to some *property* using *bipolar adjective ratings*. This measurement scale was developed in 1957 by Osgood, Suci, and Tannenbaum and uses a 7-point differential category between two bipolars, such as good–bad, hot–cold, and so on. Smith (1975) notes that it is possible to measure the response of individuals to virtually any subject with 9 to 12 bipolar adjective scales. These bipolars consist of verbal opposites that are defined or illustrated with adjectives. The three major dimensions reflected in the Osgood, Suci, and Tannenbaum work are: (1) *evaluation* (clean–dirty; beautiful–ugly); (2) *activity* (fast–slow; active–passive); and (3) *potency* (strong–weak; large–small). Figure 8.3 is a typical format used in reaction to this particular approach to measurement. This example comes from the original work of Osgood et al. (1957, p. 81) and shows how this scale is presented to a respondent. A respondent is instructed to check one of the seven categories for each of the bipolar sets in regard to the main notion of "Lady." All judgments are to be made strictly on the basis of what the word means to the respondent, and no one else should be considered. Checkmarks are to be placed in the middle of the spaces as shown in Figure 8.3. A respondent's score on a given concept is the sum (or one can also use the average) of the rating on the concept being evaluated. The scale and the scoring for this measure make the assumption that each pair of polar adjectives is an approximation of the meaning contained in a hypothetical pair of adjectives that can be taken as a pro- or anti-view of the variable being rated (Upshaw, 1968).

While this brief example from the original work of Osgood et al. illustrates the basic format of this type of measurement scale, we shall move to a more detailed presentation of an example focusing on the semantic differential scale.

▶   Religion and religiosity have been studied widely and constitute important factors in predicting and explaining attitudes and behavior. The work of Muthen, Pettersson, Olsson, and Stahlberg (1977) is an interesting illustrative study using the semantic differential (SD) to assess religious attitudes toward six stimulus concepts: (1) altar, (2) the conciliating Christ, (3) love, (4) prayer for God's help, (5) the crucified Christ, and (6) God. The 120 university students in their sample reacted to these six concepts with some 60 bipolar adjective sets, some of which are presented in Figure 8.4 as one would use the sets in reacting to one of the stimulus concepts, God.

We believe that the semantic differential scale has real merit, as the scale is easily administered and understood as well as widely applicable. It stands as one of the very novel attempts to measure social and cognitive concerns and, therefore, is important to assess if one is to achieve an understanding of research methods.

In sum, the semantic differential seeks to understand behavior by studying language concepts and the meaning projected on the concepts. Most social scientists agree with the

LADY

rough	____	____	____	✓	____	____	____	smooth
fair	✓	____	____	____	____	____	____	unfair
active	✓	____	____	____	____	____	____	passive

Figure 8.3. Semantic Differential Scale. (*Source:* Reprinted from *The measurement of meaning* by C. E. Osgood, G. J. Suci, and P. H. Tannenbaum, © 1957 by the Board of Trustees of the University of Illinois, by permission of the University of Illinois Press.)

GOD

Temporal	____	____	____	____	____	____	____	____	Eternal
Light	____	____	____	____	____	____	____	____	Heavy
Present	____	____	____	____	____	____	____	____	Absent
Dull	____	____	____	____	____	____	____	____	Excited
Masculine	____	____	____	____	____	____	____	____	Feminine
Dishonest	____	____	____	____	____	____	____	____	Honest
Just	____	____	____	____	____	____	____	____	Unjust
Redeemed	____	____	____	____	____	____	____	____	Damned
Valuable	____	____	____	____	____	____	____	____	Valueless
Moral	____	____	____	____	____	____	____	____	Immoral
Unbelieving	____	____	____	____	____	____	____	____	Believing
Meaningful	____	____	____	____	____	____	____	____	Meaningless

Figure 8.4. Semantic Differential Scale. (*Source:* B. Muthen, T. Pettersson, U. Olsson, and G. Stahlberg. [1977]. Measuring religious attitudes using the semantic differential technique: An application of three-mode factor analysis. *Journal for the Scientific Study of Religion, 16* [3], 275–288.)

notion that how a person behaves in a situation is dependent on one's perception of the situation, and the semantic differential is particularly useful in measuring this type of meaning.

Sociometric Measurement

Our final example of a scale focuses on a widely used type of measurement referred to as sociometry. *Sociometric techniques* comprise the measures designed to *assess interaction patterns* among close associates in a variety of groups. It is a very versatile approach that can be used with preschool children (Peery, 1979), adolescents (Horrocks & Benimoff, 1966), or prison groups (Killworth & Bernard, 1974). Questions such as, "Who do you like best?", "With whom would you rather sit?", or "With whom would you rather go to the movies?" represent items frequently used to generate important data on social relationships in such groups and the expectations held by members in the groups.

Further, as Selltiz, Wrightsman, and Cook (1976) report, the interaction assessed can be "behavioral, or it may only be desired, or anticipated, or fantasized" (p. 322). Data may be collected by interview, observation, or questionnaire, but the questionnaire method has been used most frequently.

▶   Horrocks and Benimoff (1966) in a study of high school youth in a Midwestern city found that peer groups are in a state of change, as indicated by their use of a sociometric measure administered two times to the same group of youths (n = 749, first administration; n = 549, second administration). The test contained one instruction: "List below the names of your best friends, both boy and girl." Space was provided so that three names could be listed for each sex. The researchers found that a large number of youths at any one time failed to receive any nominations as a best friend, that youths reflect a lot of fluidity in nominations as a best friend, that youths reflect a lot of fluidity in nominations from Time 1 to Time 2, and that a small group of both boys and girls did not receive nominations as friends in either of the two test times.

▶   In a similar study, a sociometric measure was utilized by Francis and Ollendick (1987) in their examination of peer group entry behavior by popular and unpopular fourth- and fifth-grade children. Each child rated the other members of the class to the extent to which they desired each child to be their friend. The researchers noted that those children labeled as unpopular by their peers tended to hover outside of the group, took longer to enter the peer group, and were often ignored by the other children.

▶   Another illustration of this technique (Cunningham and associates, 1950, p. 172) shows the range of group acceptance of two youths (Table 8.2) in a specific classroom. Responses to the five items in reference to the most accepted child and the least accepted child provide interesting profiles of group interaction. Note in particular Items 1, 2, and 5 which reflect the greatest differences in how children perceive and respond to these two children. As a group study technique, this social acceptance sociometric measure generates very useful data for researchers interested in assessing popularity, isolation, cliques, and general friendship patterns. Teachers, counselors, school administrators, and parents can profit greatly from the type of information generated from this type of scale.

▶   In a much more detailed use and analysis of sociometric measures, Killworth and Bernard (1974) present complex groupings of prisoners in cottage settings. One such configuration from Group 9 shows a white inmate (4) in relationship to a prisoner (49) who functions as the chore officer, as shown in the sociogram in Figure 8.5. Data derived from this measure and illustrated in the sociogram leave little question as to the clout and centrality of Prisoner 49 in the cottage setting. Furthermore, this example illustrates the great diversity of situations in which sociometric measures may be profitably applied.

Still another and very common way to present a group relationship is with the use of a sociometric matrix, as shown in Table 8.3. From our hypothetical data, it is clear that Ezekial enjoys the most peer acceptance among these six boys, as evidenced by the tallies of the number of times each boy was nominated by another.

Thus, one can rather straightforwardly analyze data using the sociometric matrix or the sociogram. The validity of such data is directly related to the content and logic of the generated nominations. A question designed to tell us who would be most often selected

TABLE 8.2. Range of Social Acceptance of Two Pupils

Items on Scale	Checks for Child 1 (*Most Accepted*)	Checks for Child 2 (*Least Accepted*)
1. Would like to have him as one of my best friends.	20*	2
2. Would like to have him in my group but not as a close friend.	7	15
3. Would like to be with him once in a while but not often or for a long time.	3	4
4. Don't mind his being in our room, but I don't want to have anything to do with him.	1	3
5. Wish he weren't in our room.	1	8

*N = 32. (*Source:* Reprinted by permission of the publisher from Cunningham, Ruth, and Associates, *Understanding Group Behavior of Boys and Girls.* New York: Teachers College Press, © 1951 by Teachers College, Columbia University. All rights reserved, p. 172.)

as a movie-going companion tells us little about athletic or scholastic standing in the group. Also, this technique does not really provide an understanding of why a phenomenon occurs; it only tells us about nominations or selections.

Measurement in social science arenas has been a very active process in the past years, and interest in the construction and refinement of scales continues, as evidenced by the variations of the sociometric approach. It is clear that we need scales to measure different types of phenomena as well as specific applications of certain scales for special issues.

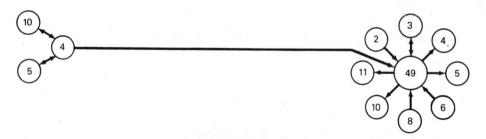

Figure 8.5. Sociogram of Prisoners in Group Nine. (*Source:* P. Killworth and H. R. Bernard. [1974]. Catij: A new sociometric and its application to a prison living unit. *Human Organization, 33* [4], 335–350. Reproduced by permission of the Society for Applied Anthropology.)

TABLE 8.3. Group Relations as Shown in a Sociometric Matrix

	Harry	Ezekial	Cannon	Bill	Paul	Joe
Harry	0	1	0	0	0	0
Ezekial	1	0	0	0	0	0
Cannon	0	1	0	0	0	0
Bill	0	0	0	0	1	0
Paul	0	1	0	0	0	0
Joe	0	0	0	0	1	0
Total	1	3	0	0	2	0

SUMMARY

1. Measurement is a process by which decisions are made concerning the size, depth, weight, impact, consequence, or importance of objects or events which occur in society.
   a. It is a process to determine answers to the questions of how many, how much, or how often.
   b. Measurement of a crude type can be made without help of instrumentation, but refined and discriminating judgments have created a need for measurement tools capable of producing data not possible without such tools.
2. The concern and need for measurement are as old as mankind, but the scientific activity of researchers in more recent times has been instrumental in building revolutionary devices, such as the atomic clock on the one hand and social science scales on the other, to measure properties such as attitude and adjustment, properties that were judged to be too personal or too elusive to measure.
3. Measurement in research serves the important functions of producing data, deriving information from the data through careful analysis, testing hypotheses, assessing the importance of issues, and promoting the world of discovery. To measure a property or issue is to assign it a specific position along some kind of dimension or numerical scale.
4. Four different types of measurement were presented:
   a. *Nominal* scales consist of labels or names, a classification system for events or situations.
   b. A set of numbers or observations reflecting only the order of things, such as bigger than or smaller than, constitutes an *ordinal* scale.
   c. In contrast to nominal and ordinal measurement, an *interval* scale is substantially different, as it has equal units between points and a zero point that is determined in an arbitrary manner.
   d. Finally, a scale seldom used in most social science research, the *ratio* scale, has equal units and an absolute or true zero point.
5. Scales or measurement tools developed for research in social science include the following:
   a. Likert-type scales are a very common form of summated scales and are widely used to assess attitudes. They typically consist of responses ranging from strongly agree to strongly disagree.
   b. The cumulative scale also uses a series of items to measure some social dimension but attempts to do this with a single dimension scale. The items in the scale are ordered so that a respondent demonstrates increasing commitment with each successive item.
   c. Semantic differential scales are particularly useful in measuring cognitive and situational meanings to people. The semantic differential scale is composed of a series of stimulus concepts to which one reacts using a series of bipolar adjectives (e.g., hot–cold).
   d. Sociometric scales seek to measure interaction patterns among close associates. Data derived from these scales are usually presented in the form of a sociogram or a sociometric matrix.

6. Measurement as a process in the social sciences presents some very difficult problems for researchers due to the fact that the phenomena under study are dynamic in nature as opposed to the more static properties that the geologist or physicist faces in the study of deterministic matters. Social science is highly committed to the development and use of measurement tools that probe into social relationships not understandable without such fine measures. The ultimate goal is to develop and systematically use measuring devices that produce valid and reliable data so that the truth-seeking mission of science is continually advanced.

PROBLEMS AND APPLICATIONS

1. Review with other class members the extent and types of measurement you use in a typical day. Also, as applied to work you have done, what type of measurement was used? Were the measurement techniques employed effective?

2. Contrast the function of measurement for consumers versus the functions of measurement for scientists. In your opinion, who benefits most from measurement—consumers or researchers?

3. Review various research journals in your area of specialization and identify a study using nominal measurement, one using ordinal measurement, one using interval measurement, and one employing ratio measurement.

4. What are the main advantages of sociometric measures for social science research? What type of research might you conduct in which a sociometric measure would be helpful? What are the main limitations, if any, of using sociometric measures in the study of human behavior?

5. Either develop or use an existing summated measure from some research publication and critically evaluate the instrument. Identify the strengths and weaknesses of the summated scale instrument.

6. Illustrate the use of a Guttman-type scale in class. Involve other students and have them complete items in a scale so as to demonstrate function and scoring of the scale.

7. Have a class panel debate the strengths and limitations of scales use in the study of human and social phenomena.

REFERENCES

Antonovsky, A., & Sourani, T. (1988). Family sense of coherence and family adaptation. *Journal of Marriage and the Family, 50,* 79–92.

Blalock, Jr., H. M. (1974). *Measurement in the social sciences: Theories and-strategies.* Chicago: Aldine.

Cunningham, R., & Associates. (1951). *Understanding group behavior of boys and girls.* New York: Bureau of Publications, Teachers College, Columbia University.

Edwards, A. L. (1957). *Techniques of attitude scale construction.* New York: Appleton-Century-Crofts.

Edwards, J. N., Johnson, D. R., & Booth, A. (1987). Coming apart: A prognostic instrument of marital breakup. *Family Relations, 36,* 168–170.

Fibel, B., & Hale, W. D. (1978). The generalized expectancy for success scale—A new measure. *Journal of Consulting and Clinical Psychology, 4* (5), 924–931.

Francis, G., & Ollendick, T. H. (1987). Peer group entry behavior. *Child & Family Behavior Therapy, 9* (1/2), 45–54.

Gordon, R. (1977). *Unidimensional scaling of social variables: Concepts and procedures.* New York: The Free Press.

Guttman, L. (1944). A basis of scaling quantitative data. *American Sociological Review, 9,* 139–150.

Horrocks, J. E., & Benimoff, M. (1966). Stability of adolescents' nominee status over a one-year period as a friend by their peers. *Adolescence, 1,* 224–229.

Killworth, P., & Bernard, H. R. (1974). Catij.: A new sociometric and its application to a prison living unit. *Human Organization, 33* (4), 335–350.

Likert, R. (1932). A technique for the measurement of attitudes. *Archives of Psychology, 140.*

Lodge, M. (1981). *Magnitude scaling: Quantitative measurement of opinion.* Beverly Hills: Sage.

McIver, J. P., & Carmine, E. G. (1981). *Unidimensional scaling.* Beverly Hills: Sage.

Muthen, B., Pettersson, T., Olsson, U., & Stahlberg, G. (1977). Measuring religious attitudes using the semantic differential technique: An application of three-mode factor analysis. *Journal for the Scientific Study of Religion, 16* (3), 275–288.

Osgood, C. E., Suci, G. J., & Tannenbaum, P. H. (1957). *The measurement of meaning.* Urbana, Ill.: University of Illinois Press.

Peery, J. C. (1979). Popular, amiable, isolated, rejected: A reconceptualization of sociometric status in preschool children. *Child Development, 50,* 1231–1234.

Phillips, B. S. (1976). *Social research: Strategy and tactics* (3rd ed.). New York: Macmillan.

Reiss, I. L. (1964). The scaling of premarital sexual permissiveness. *Journal of Marriage and the Family, 26,* 188–198.

Selltiz, C., Wrightsman, L. S., & Cook, S. W. (1976). *Research methods in social relations* (3rd ed.). New York: Holt, Rinehart and Winston.

Smith, H. W. (1975). *Strategies of social research: The methodological imagination.* Englewood Cliffs, N.J.: Prentice-Hall.

Upshaw, H. S. (1968). Attitude measurement. In H. M. Blalock, Jr., & A. B. Blalock (Eds.). *Methodology in social research.* New York: McGraw-Hill.

CHAPTER 9

Samples and Uses of Sampling

OUTLINE

Introduction
Sampling as a Way of Life
Type of Sample: Does It Really Matter?
The 1936 Presidential Election: The Need for a Random Sample
Truman versus Dewey, 1948: The Need for a Fresh Sample
Business and the Consumer—The Edsel Case: Avoiding Sample Bias
The Sex Research of Kinsey and Associates: The Need for a Random Sample and Description
      Example: The Share Hite Report on Women and Love
Malformed Infants—The Case against Thalidomide: The Need for Complex Samples
Sampling Terminology
Advantages of Sampling in Research
Types of Samples
Probability Samples
Nonprobability Samples
Size of Samples: How Big?
Investigators in Search of Samples
The Nurse Image in Films: A Nonreactive Sample
A Theory of Imitation—Suicides and Automobile Accidents: A Sample Design for Those Unable to Talk
Neonatal Death: A Public Relations Sample
Remembering High School Classes
Americans at Leisure

Helps in Obtaining Samples
Summary
Problems and Applications
References

KEY TERMS

Uses of sampling
Sampling error
Population
Element
Sampling unit
Sample
Probability sample

Simple random sample
Systematic random sample
Cluster probability sample
Stratified random sample
Nonprobability sample
Snowball sample
Convenience sample

Purposeful sample
Quota sample
Homogeneous sample
Heterogeneous population
Sample size
Degree of precision
Content analysis

STUDY GUIDE QUESTIONS

1. Why is sampling so important in conducting quality research?
2. What kind of sampling approaches are most commonly used by social scientists? Is this good?
3. What is the main difference between a probability and nonprobability sample?
4. How big should a sample be? What are more useful guides in determining sample size?
5. What is a cluster sample and in what type of research would one be likely to use such a sample?
6. If a researcher was struggling to obtain a sample for a research project, what helps or resources might he or she turn to?

Role of the Researcher

To engage in research is to engage in sampling. Without data it is impossible to do original research, and original research is impossible without having data. Data are obtainable through some type of sampling process. The type, size, composition, and nature of the sample are dependent on the purpose of the study, the population available, research design, and the resources available to the researcher. To obtain appropriate samples for research, the investigator must know methodological rules and procedures about samples, plus cultivate the human interactional skills necessary to obtain support, cooperation, and public belief in the importance of the work to be completed. Sampling is the art of assessing the whole pattern by looking at only a part of the pattern. The concept is old, but refinement of sample strategies for science is relatively new.

Role of the Consumer

Safety, utility, truthfulness, and *longevity* are all terms that rush to the forefront when one discusses the sample types and adequacy in consuming research or products and the decisions coming from sampling activities. If one is to obtain useful results, one needs a quality sample. A quality sample is one that is sufficiently large and representative of the population under study. A consumer of research must know types of samples, how they are obtained, and limitations of sampling decisions for various studies or it is impossible to make the judgments necessary to be a competent consumer of research or the products derivable from the research.

Problems with measurement and sampling have great impact on consumers of research. What to eat, to wear, to spray, to sleep on, and related questions have both short- and long-term consequences for the population as a whole.

INTRODUCTION

Sampling is a process whereby one makes estimates or generalizations about a population based on information contained in a portion (a sample) of the entire population. It is the goal of quality research to have a sample that is truly representative of the total population from which the sample has been selected. A *sample*, then, is an estimate of something else. Generally, the larger the sample, the more accurate the estimate becomes. In social science research, sampling is very important, since one collects data via a sample; the counterpart in physical science would be to conduct an experiment on some elements or matter. Specific types of samples, definitions, illustrations, and applications of sampling follow in various sections of this chapter.

SAMPLING AS A WAY OF LIFE

Sampling as a practice is very old and has probably been used for as long as people have engaged in hunting, planting, business, and evaluation of their world. In the world of commerce, merchants have conducted much of their business transactions by using samples (i.e., a piece of cloth, a taste of cheese, or examination of precious stones). Today, people grow up in a world permeated with sampling or the consequences of sampling. For example, the courtship period and mate selection in the Western world represents a sampling strategy—dating widely to select "the one" and then a period of steady dating, engagement, or living together is still another type of sampling process to see if marriage seems appropriate or workable. The "test drive" of a new automobile is a designed sample that hopefully leads to the purchase of a new car—if the car performs well in the test run, the generalization is made that it is a good car. The shopper in a supermarket is often confronted with multiple invitations to sample sips of the latest brand of orange juice, or bite-size pieces of cheese, pizza, crackers, or sausage. The invitation of the sales person in the chic boutique to model a new dress contains the basic element of sampling—if it feels and looks good during the "try-on" sample, one can generalize it will be a good buy.

It is, of course, common knowledge that major industries such as coffee, tea, or wine producers have long engaged in extensive taste analysis of their products so that skilled taste samplers will ensure that consumer-preferred tastes are achieved before products are placed on the market. The "preview of coming attractions" at your favorite movie theatre is nothing more than a sample designed to lure you back later for the full movie. Space explorations during the past decade have scooped up various samples of rocks and soil from the moon and returned these to the earth where scientists have analyzed these samples to increase our understanding about the nature and origin of the moon. And when one takes prize-winning canned goods or a delicious cake to the local county fair, it is understood that judges will make their decisions about the texture and taste of the entries on the basis of a sample.

Sampling and decisions based on sampling are with us on a regular basis. In this chapter we wish to define sampling types, their use, terminology, and show how research is carried on with samples in the general social science arena. We will show that sampling has several real advantages over the assessment or study of the entire population. It will further be the goal of this chapter to illustrate various types of samples, what type to use in a particular study, and the relative advantages of one type of sample versus another. Given the previous illustrations of samples in everyday life, it should come as no surprise that the chapter will directly assess sampling in research and illustrate the utility of knowing about sampling in the consumption and completing of research.

TYPE OF SAMPLE: DOES IT REALLY MATTER?

If one is predicting outcome, describing a situation, or testing an event of supreme importance to society, a well-defined probability sample is a must. Furthermore, one must take precautions to keep sampling current—some findings can become stale very quickly, further testimony that social science subject matter is dynamic, not static.

In regard to the following illustrations to help answer the question, "Does sampling really matter?" please note certain problems that could have been averted if more attention to sample detail had been employed. The main elements of sample breakdown occurred because samples were not random, they were biased or stale, incorrect questions were asked to people in poorly defined samples, sampling procedures were given without enough detail, and subjects were not sampled over a developmental period as well as in complex interactive situations. Sampling error is costly to researchers, corporations, drug companies, political parties and presidential candidates, and the general population of consumers of research.

The 1936 Presidential Election:
The Need for a Random Sample

▶ One of the classic examples in research was the inadequate sample employed by the *Literary Digest* poll in which they predicted a defeat of Franklin D. Roosevelt based on a huge sample of ten million contacts. How could one ever go wrong with such a large sample? In this case, the *Literary Digest* went wrong by taking their sample from automobile registrations, telephone directories, and other related sources for generating names for the survey. Unfortunately, only about 20% of the respondents returned their mailed forms. Furthermore, these sampling techniques resulted in a heavily biased response in favor of the affluent and higher-educated individuals. This unrepresentative group did not vote for Roosevelt, and they did not reflect the mood of the majority of voters at that historical time. Samples do make a difference, and in this case nonprobability sampling and a low rate of response spelled doom for the 1936 presidential prediction.

Truman versus Dewey, 1948: The Need for a Fresh Sample

A similar situation in regard to sample error occurred in the fall of 1948 when Thomas ◄
Dewey challenged Harry Truman for the presidency. The Gallup poll predicted that Dewey would win the election. However, Gallup was incorrect due to the fact that polling stopped too early in the race and thus did not reflect the apparent heavy change in voting mood that occurred just before the election. This was a quota sample (obtaining a given number of respondents in a specific setting) as opposed to a probability sample (where each person would have the same probability of being interviewed). This would of course contribute to a sampling error leading to the well-known distortion of findings (Som, 1973). Sample error due to quota sampling and stale data created a combined error leading to a failure of prediction.

Business and the Consumer—The Edsel Case:
Avoiding Sample Bias

As early as 1948 the Ford Motor Company began the extensive work that was to eventually ◄
result in a new 1958 Edsel introduced into the showrooms of America in the fall of 1957. Millions of dollars were spent on this new car, which was designed to successfully compete for a larger share of the market and specifically to attract car buyers in the middle range (those who bought Buicks, Pontiacs, Oldsmobiles, Chryslers, and Mercuries). The new Edsel was a big car, longer, highly powered, adorned with chrome, and filled with accessories. This is what consumer research had indicated that the car public wanted. These consumer assessment studies were conducted over a long period (from 1955 to 1956, and were still in process in 1957 on the eve of the new car's debut).

The Edsel was, of course, not well received by the public for a number of reasons, and the economic recession of 1958 was a major one, but sampling and research design problems also entered the picture. Research questions focused on status, ego, car personality, and product snobbery as opposed to questions that tapped reactions to car price, cost of upkeep, parking and garage problems due to size of cars, and the automobile as a transportation machine. This type of sample design and research question failed to determine the important concern, "Is there a group of car buyers who are inadequately served by the present car menu?" Furthermore, the projected attraction to the medium-priced field of cars was apparently gone by 1957, the very year Edsel was introduced, and the new consumer appeal was starting in the compact field (Deutsch, 1976).

We believe that in addition to asking the wrong questions, problems in sample make-up, and stale responses from several years of consumer research, the Edsel case also reflects an unwillingness to objectively assess the data. Personal investment of ego, reputation, and power bases sometimes allows decisions to be made in spite of data indicating another direction.

The Sex Research of Kinsey and Associates: The Need for a Random Sample and Description

▶ The classic research on sexual behavior of humans conducted by Kinsey and his associates (1948) was compromised by sampling errors. Specifically, geographical convenience, access to college students, and reliance on volunteers comprised the main ways for obtaining respondents. In addition, information was not forthcoming about the sample—how it was done, size, and what data were used (Cochran, Mosteller, & Tukey, 1954). Generalizations to the population are severely thwarted when dealing with primarily a volunteer-convenience sample, and particularly when facts about the population are not well articulated to the reader.

Example: The Shere Hite Report on Women and Love.   In 1987, Shere Hite published her book, *Women and Love, a Cultural Revolution in Progress,* documenting the findings of her third study on human sexuality and love. She concluded that women are fed up with the male species. In addition to being oppressed and abused by men, the women in the Hite study reported that their love relationships were unsatisfying. Communication problems, infidelity, willingness to divorce, and general dissatisfaction with their partners was the norm for the women polled by Hite. The overwhelming majority of this sample expressed rage and hostility towards the opposite sex.

Although the report caused a stir in the general population, closer examination of the study reveals major methodological problems. Questionnaires were mailed to women's organizations (feminist groups, religious organizations, garden clubs, etc.), thus limiting the sample to only those women who were motivated to join such organizations. Only 4,500 of 100,000 questionnaires were returned for a response rate of 4.5%. Most social science researchers are reluctant to generalize their findings to the population if the response rate is not at least 70%. Further, in order to make the sample more representative, Hite made demographic comparisons from the first 1,500 responses and then filled in the blank spots.

Those supporting Hite's view state that although the women in the sample are not representative of the population in general, they may be speaking out in a way that the majority of women are reluctant or unable to do. However, the findings present an extreme view of women as absolute victims, and men as possessing the ultimate shortcomings leading to the unhappiness of their feminine partners. Not surprisingly, given the sampling bias of this study, Hite's conclusions were at odds with other major studies addressing human intimacy.

Malformed Infants—The Case against Thalidomide: The Need for Complex Samples

▶ One final example to show that design and sample make a critical difference focuses on the tragic consequences of the use of a sedative drug by thousands of European women in 1962. This drug was called thalidomide, and if taken by a pregnant mother in the stage when arms and legs were developing it had the unfortunate consequence of arresting

---

Tips for Consumers 9.1

If the sample is inappropriate it is a sure conclusion that the research is flawed. Elaborate statistical analysis, detailed reviews of literature, and beautiful prose do not do away with problems of flaws in the sampling part of completing a quality piece of research. Consumers of research should be constantly aware of the following questions in regard to sampling issues:

1. How big was the sample? Was the size adequate for the study?
2. What type of sample was used?
3. Was the sampling type appropriate for the purpose of research?
4. Was the sample still "fresh" or was it on the "stale" side?
5. Did the research report give sufficient detail and clarification regarding the sample and the general conditions under which it was selected?

---

development in these limbs. The drug caused such damage because it was capable of crossing the placental barrier between the mother's and the baby's blood vessels. This tragedy prompted the United States government to pass the Kefauver-Harris Amendments to provide a more adequate protection against such an incident (Proger, 1968).

Thalidomide had undergone considerable testing with a wide sample range, but the breakdown occurred in terms of samples that would permit assessment in a developmental and interactional context. Sample makeup and testing were needed to determine the interaction of the drug and stage of pregnancy. This example dramatically illustrates that sampling and breakdowns in sampling design can have long-lasting consequences.

To summarize, we have invested considerable time and space in attempting to build a case for the importance of sampling in research as well as in consumer behavior in everyday life. Sampling does make a difference. It is true that animals in the laboratory serve as subject samples on a regular basis and they are sometimes sacrificed "for the good of science." But whether a rat is being killed, a mother is taking a dangerous drug, a corporation is losing millions, or the sexual behavior of Americans is being somewhat distorted, sampling is the process for collection of data on which social science research is performed. This chapter seeks to increase understanding about samples, their use, the types, and some examples of how samples are obtained and used in a variety of research areas. (See Tips for Consumers 9.1.)

SAMPLING TERMINOLOGY

It is necessary to offer some brief definitions and illustrations of terms used in the sampling procedures. Definitions will be covered only for the more general terms, and technical terminology will be kept to a minimum.

1. Concept: *Population* refers to the entire group having some common characteristics that justified reference to the population. These entire groups or populations may be people, objects, materials, events, and so on. The size of such populations may range from exceedingly large to a specific sample number.

2. Concept: *Element* refers to a single case or object in a sample. The element is the actual unit on which we perform measurement or we take measurement from it of some type. In a study of college basketball players, a single case interview would constitute an element in the population.

3. Concept: *Sampling units* may be defined as collections or clusters of elements from the populations that do not overlap. In a statewide study to assess attitudes of school board members toward some issue, each school board as a group would be the sampling unit and the members as individuals would be the elements. If a sampling unit only contains one element of a study population, then the sampling unit and the sampling element would be the same.

4. Concept: A *sample* is defined as a grouping or collection of sampling elements or units from a specified population. The sample comprises an aggregate of elements that is studied in order to make inferences to the whole by examining only a part. A statewide group of 700 prospective voters to obtain views on the upcoming senate race would be an example of a sample.

5. Concept: *Sampling frame* refers to a list of the sampling units from which the investigator draws the sample.

ADVANTAGES OF SAMPLING IN RESEARCH

We have already illustrated the need for, and the utility of, current probability samples in regard to elections, marketing, decision making, health, and understanding of sexual behavior. Probably most researchers and consumers of research will not focus on predicting presidential elections or test the safety of certain drugs, but they will be faced with problems of budget, time usage, generalization, coordination, and educating various groups.

Certainly one of the main reasons to use samples in research is just plain *economics*—the *cost* involved in measuring a sample is considerably less than that required if we were to assess all elements in a population. Since most research is carried out under conditions of limited resources, this economic factor is a very important advantage.

A second major advantage of sampling over assessing the entire population comes down to *time*. The 700 telephone calls to the voters in the state senate race represent a substantial investment of time and resources, but relatively little when compared to the amount of time necessary if one were charged to contact all eligible voters in the state.

As noted in other chapters on measurement, design, and methods for obtaining data, we seldom obtain "perfectly measured" data. We do not argue that data obtained in a sample are free of errors or distortions as opposed to data collected in the measurement of the entire population, but it is reasonable to assert that better quality control can be exercised at the sample level of measurement. Since the goal of research is to promote accuracy, then carefully executing samples is one of the important ways to obtain more accurate data.

Sampling serves a very important function in research and has specific advantages. If the research goal demands that every element in a population be measured, then obviously sampling a part of that population would not be appropriate. Likewise, if the population is small to begin with, such as all skyjackers in the United States in a given year, it would behoove the researcher not to sample, but to measure the entire population.

TYPES OF SAMPLES

As noted previously, a sample represents a portion of a whole, a part of a greater population. A sample is always a portion of the whole and it is possible to obtain that portion in a variety of ways. For example, one can study the national character of the United States by touring and interviewing people as Sir Richard Burton did in the nineteenth century (Brodie, 1967), or one can come as a scientist in the same way that Gunnar Myrdal did (1944) in *An American Dilemma: The Negro Problem and Modern Democracy.*

Samples may be scientific or unscientific, random or haphazard, based on probability or nonprobability techniques, to mention just a few. A sample, when properly selected, offers an unbiased, practical, and valid method of describing various aspects of the entire population (Frankel & Frankel, 1987). When persons on the street refer to selecting something at random, they are referring to a process in which little or no control was exercised in picking and choosing—it was more "impulse." This use of the word *random* in the lay context is strikingly different than the use of *random* applied to sampling in the social sciences. *Random* as used in the latter context refers to a *probabilistic sample,* which is a sample with each element or groups of elements having an equal probability of being included.

All samples that do not determine the probability that a given element will be included are referred to as *nonprobability samples.* If you were to interview the first 25 people entering a large department store, the first 15 students leaving the university library, or the individuals who vote in the last hour before the polls close, you would be dealing with nonprobability samples. These samples may have utility to obtain insights, to obtain "a feel for how things are going," or simply to describe the activities of these people, but it is clear that one would not be justified in describing the whole population or making generalizations about the whole based on these nonrandomly selected portions.

Probability Samples

Now that we have defined a probability sample at the general level we shall be more specific and define types of probability samples. The most basic and common type of probability sample is the *simple random sample,* which can be defined as a sample in which all elements or groups of elements have the same chance of being included. If one were to select a sample without replacement, it would be in violation of this definition since each succeeding selection would have a higher probability of being included, such as drawing 10 numbers from a hat. To make this a simple random sample, one would have to draw the various numbers after the first one while replacing the numbers back into the hat to assure that each number had the same probability of being drawn.

Another type of random sample widely used in social science research is the *systematic random sample,* defined as selecting every *n*th unit from a population after having selected the first by a random method. For example, suppose we were interested in evaluating 40 juvenile court records from a file containing 400 such cases. If the cases were numbered, a systematic random sample approach would dictate that we use every 10th case to comprise our final *n* of 40. We need every 10th case, hence we would select the first case by randomly choosing a number between 1 and 10, say case 7, and then every 10th case thereafter—17, 27, 37, and so on until we obtained 40 cases.

A *cluster* probability sample is also a probability sample in which the researcher is interested in selected groups or clusters of units to be included in a final study sample. For many studies the elements are so scattered that it would be very expensive and time-consuming to attempt to draw a simple random sample from the population and proceed to contact each one. In cluster sampling, one can reduce some of the logistic problems by selecting units and then working with elements in each of the representative units rather then covering elements randomly distributed throughout the area.

In a 1970 research report by Schvaneveldt, the goal was to interview in depth 100 aged family units in a rural setting and 100 in an urban setting. To reduce time and cost of interviewing, especially in the rural area, it was established that there were 23 towns or rural communities that should be addressed in the sample and 7 communities (clusters) were drawn in a random fashion for the sample. Our research in this example contained an additional reason for using a cluster sample—namely, we had no listing of the family units in the whole population to begin a sample selection. Thus, use of cluster sampling reduces the whole into clusters, and from the clusters it is possible to identify separate elements that can be selected by simple random fashion or systematic sampling.

Stratified random sampling constitutes a fourth common probabilistic method of selecting a sample for research. In this sampling technique, the population is divided into parts or *strata* according to some characteristics (say religion, race, or social class), and then one selects a random sample from each of the defined strata. This sampling technique requires that the researcher be somewhat knowledgeable about the whole population or it would not be possible to divide the population into defined homogeneous strata. Mendenhall, Ott, and Schaeffer (1971) note three major advantages for using stratified random sampling: (1) it produces more homogeneous data within each stratum, (2) the logistics of collecting data within the specified strata reduce the cost of the sample, and (3) since data are collected within each of the separately defined strata, it is possible to obtain separate estimates of population characteristics from each stratum.

Stratified random sampling also permits one to select cases within each stratum in a variety of ways as well as in different proportions. Additionally, this approach to sampling virtually guarantees that the subgroups in a population will be represented. Stratified random sampling is an efficient and high quality data-producing sampling device. Its major disadvantage is, perhaps, the need to be more highly informed about the population as a whole than is the case in a simple random sample.

Nonprobability Samples

As noted earlier, not all samples are probability samples, and in some studies it may not be necessary to use probability samples to gather useful data for certain types of decisions. Since nonprobability samples may be useful, economical, and especially since they are so widely used in social science research, it is important to understand the types and features of these sampling approaches. All of the examples in this section are *nonprobability samples* because it would not be possible to indicate the probability that a given element would be in the sample. Nor would one be able to tell if each element had the same chance of being selected. Since these dimensions are not known, it makes it difficult, if not impossible, to make certain inferences about the population based on the sample or to describe a sample with a high degree of assurance that the description will hold for the entire population. These are important limitations, for as Smith (1975) notes, chemistry or physics may not need to be concerned about the question of representativeness, but the social sciences in general must always be concerned with this question.

Snowball sampling may be defined as obtaining a sample by having initially identified subjects who can refer you to other subjects with like or similar characteristics (Bailey, 1978; Eckhardt & Ermann, 1977). If the population is unknown to you or others, then the snowballing approach is about the only way to find subjects. One may run an ad in the newspaper in which you call for people with certain situations or characteristics to help you in a research project. If 14 people respond to your ad and you are able to successfully interview them, you would seek to have each of the 14 identify as many people as possible who are similar to them in their situation or characteristic. If each of the people could supply you with 4 new names, you would have 56 new persons to interview. The stages could theoretically go on until you were satisfied that a sufficiently large sample for conducting the desired research had been achieved. As social science steadily obtains acceptance in communities and as the need increases to more fully understand patterns of deviance, topics of taboo, or just ill-understood, sometimes nonvisible populations, the use of snowball sampling will significantly increase as a strategy for locating and conducting research of these respondents. If one is successful in getting the initially identified small group to grow in successive stages to a large sample, one has seen the "snowball" grow from a small unit as it is "rolled" into a larger and larger unit.

Convenience sampling is the oldest and perhaps most frequently used sampling technique for a variety of pilot projects, student exercises, thesis or dissertation work, or for the process of generating some quick and "dirty" data. As the name implies, you gather data from anyone who is convenient—your family, roommates, neighbors, classmates, and, of course, the captive audiences which always seem to be available in the large sections of psychology, sociology, social work, political science, nursing, and home economics.

The technique is also referred to as an accidental (Selltiz, Wrightsman, & Cook, 1976) or incidental sample (Meyers & Grossen, 1974). Regardless of what it is called, the main features are availability, convenience, and accessibility. The "man on the street" interview as often seen on television is an example of convenience sampling. Researchers often claim that their samples with this strategy are representative of the greater population. Most social scientists have very little basis for making this claim, but it is very important to at least be aware of the advantages as well as the limitations of convenience samples.

Purposeful sampling may be defined as a procedure for building a sample based on cases, individuals, or communities judged as being appropriate or very informative for the purpose of the research underway. Cases are handpicked to achieve some specific characteristic that will *illuminate* the purpose of the study. Pollsters have identified key states, towns, or regions that are particularly accurate in picking the winner in a presidential election. Going to one of these towns (a purposeful sample) would be a logistically useful way of obtaining very sensitive information about a possible political outcome.

As Bailey (1978) notes, researchers can make good use of their special knowledge about some events, groups, or research skills in using a purposeful sample to achieve some particular goal. It is clear that a purposeful sample is still a nonrandom sample no matter now carefully selected. As Som (1973) notes, such samples are personally selected and thus subject to that bias.

Quota sampling may be defined as a special edition of stratified sampling in which one attempts to include the various elements in a population in a final sample. The researcher will often attempt to include the various quotas in relationship to their size in the whole population. Som (1973) notes that while one may be able to collect data about the quota (sex, religion, social class, etc.), the actual people selected are left to investigator choice. In short, quota sampling is a procedure in which the investigator defines the characteristics of the desired sample as related to the purpose of the research and then proceeds to select respondents to reflect the specified characteristics previously defined. The tendency of interviewers to obtain data from people they know or find easily accessible, or to obtain respective quotas by convenient or easy methods, adds limitations to this sample approach in terms of actually filling the defined quotas. (For further reading, Sudman [1976] provides an informative coverage of quota versus probability sampling. Of particular interest is the discussion of probability sampling with quotas.) (See Tips for Consumers 9.2.)

Tips for Consumers 9.2

The most common and popular groups of people used in social science research are students and housewives. Traditionally these two groups have been used extensively because of their availability and convenience. Much of the research with these two groups has been extremely valuable but the ability to generalize to other important parts of society may be severely limited.

Consumers of research need to be concerned about makeup of samples because of the following notions:

1. Drugs such as thalidomide brought serious problems to consumers because of a lack of strict testing and problems with sampling design. Some foods or drugs have interactive effects and these need to be assessed in the sample composition.
2. Predictions as noted in various examples can be wrong because of sampling error or stale data.
3. Social class, religion, race, ethnicity, sex of respondents, and age are all critical elements in a quality sample. Were these concerns clearly presented in the study?
4. Was a sample the proper approach to the study or should the entire population have been used?
5. Were the sampling procedures and characteristics sufficiently clear that another researcher could repeat the same type of study?

SIZE OF SAMPLES: HOW BIG?

Abraham Lincoln allegedly replied to the question, "How long is a piece of string?" by saying, "It is as long as it needs to be." It is tempting to give this same answer to the question, "How large should a sample be?" Invariably the size depends on the purpose of the study, design, data collection method, and type of population available for the research problem. There are, however, a number of useful guidelines about sample size.

   If a research population is completely *homogeneous,* it stands to reason that a sample of *one* would be sufficiently large to carry out necessary research. One moon rock may be representative of all rocks on the moon. In blood analysis, one drop is typically a sufficient amount to qualify as a good sample for making generalizations about the entire body supply. But in the study of social phenomena *one* is hardly ever large enough. On the other hand, more or bigger is not always necessarily better. It is possible to provide one guiding rule about sample size at this point—the *more homogeneous* the population under study, the *smaller* the sample needs to be *to accurately reflect* the characteristics of that population, assuming random selection procedures.

   It should be clear that the smaller the difference between sample size and population size, the smaller will be the *sampling error* in actually being an accurate "mirror" of the entire population. This is especially true in a probability sample. If time, resources, and other conditions exist for obtaining a larger sample, then the incentive is to decrease sample error and subsequently increase both the *internal* and *external validity* by obtaining a larger sample. Survey and descriptive research have been especially concerned with sample size because of a desire to increase validity of findings.

   The *method* of *data collection* is also an important factor in considering ultimate sample size. Some collection methods are very expensive while others are relatively inexpensive. If interviewing is the method, then expense per unit will be high in comparison to a mailed questionnaire. This is one of the advantages of cluster sampling reviewed earlier, for it is one very strategic way of reducing cost in an interview or observational study. For most research, cost is a factor, and the investigator should be prepared to project expenses, determine total resources, and weigh these concerns along with data collection method and desired sample size. However, some designs and research topics must employ a certain data collection method, and here one has to face the cost–sample size ratio.

   Another factor in determining sample size is the *degree of precision* needed or *desired* in final results (see Slonim, 1960, for detailed treatment of this concern). Relative to the question of precision is the issue of how many or what type of *variable questions* will be analyzed in the data. If the goal is to subdivide the sample into multiple categories in order to relate these to some dependent variable, then sample size must be considerably larger than if one were to deal with only one or two relationships. This issue must be addressed in the study design stage and when decisions about sampling are in the planning stage. If you wish to compare Chicanos or blacks with whites on some issue, you must have a sufficiently large sample to assure that these groups are represented in large enough numbers to make analysis possible. Blalock (1960) indicates that in terms of just statistics an *n* of 50 is a minimum size; Champion (1970) for the same reason notes that 30 is the very minimum, and still others call for considerably larger samples if one is to control for certain variables and lay claim that the sample accurately "mirrors" the population.

One final concern in determining sample size relates to a research proposal as it is reviewed by some funding agency. In this case it is the ideal situation if this decision can be jointly arrived at by the investigator and someone from the agency reviewing the proposal. An agency will often recommend a smaller sample than that proposed by the investigator as one way of making decisions about competing grants for fixed amounts of money available for funding research (Sudman, 1976). Sudman notes that for projects receiving funding, agencies are primarily interested in relationship of the cost per unit in the sample and the value of the information from each unit as related to the ultimate mission of the funding agency. It is typically a strategic move to include a fairly large sample so that one can cope with the sample error, have sufficient cases to analyze subgroups, and still experience a reduction in sample size from a funding agency to reduce the cost of a project.

It is no doubt wasteful to obtain a larger sample than is necessary, especially if it is not a probability sample. Since time, resources, logistics, and the short life of several populations and problems impact on most researchers, it is very important to give careful consideration to both type and size of sample. It may be true that some data are better than no data, but we believe researchers should be careful what they do with "some data" when sample design and size are not appropriate.

INVESTIGATORS IN SEARCH OF SAMPLES

Next to working out the design of a study, we often hear our students and colleagues comment that obtaining a workable sample is one of the most challenging events in completing social science research. If one is blessed with planning ability, optimism, public relations skills, or willingess to learn about this trio, then a major part of the task of obtaining samples has been accomplished. Doing research calls on the scientist as well as the artist—this dualism is needed in obtaining good samples. The following examples from a variety of sources are presented to help illustrate how samples are closely tied to research purpose and design. Furthermore, both researchers and consumers need to know about public relations skills in obtaining the cooperation of others, the variety of avenues for research, and the creative ways in which samples can be forthcoming.

The Nurse Image in Films: A Nonreactive Sample

Our first example of sampling focuses directly on a *process* for obtaining a sample coupled with a *novel* source of sample for historical-developmental study of the nursing image. Our examples up to this point might lead one to believe that only living people in social structures are interviewed in some way to achieve a certain sample. Movies constitute our sample in this illustration, and each movie represents a sample element. Believing that movies are a powerful medium for influencing perceptions about events, roles, and occupations, Kalisch, Kalisch, and McHugh (1980) were prompted to analyze some 200 major movies released between 1930 and 1979 to determine how nurses are depicted in films and how this image may have varied over a 50-year period. To be included in their sample, the film had to have one or more nurses as major characters in the story. Then, through content analysis (analyses of documents—films, books—by using systematic coding and making inferences about the content of the material) each of the films was viewed by at least one of the investigators with a coder assigned to complete the detailed content analysis. Three major tools were employed in this process: *the unit analysis tool* dealt with dominant impressions of nursing, the *nurse character analysis tool* was used to collect data on individual nurse characteristics, and last, *the physician character tool* was used to contrast nurse and doctor on specific characteristics.

The major findings from this elaborate content analysis revealed that nurses in films were depicted as young (76% as 35 years of age or younger), unmarried (78%), female (99.5%), and childless (91%). The factors in film media contributing most to a positive image of nurses and the nursing profession dealt with a portrayal of the nurse as humanitarian, character building, and one who is self-sacrificing. Over time the data show that films portray nurses in an ever-increasing negative image during the past decade and in selected aspects of the role over the past 20 years. Figure 9.1 presents data on film portrayal over time to help illustrate this particular sampling approach leading to the Kalisch et al. finding. The figure clearly shows the dramatic shift that started in 1950 and became pronounced in the last two decades.

The authors conclude by noting that "film content must be understood as symbolic representations about social roles and relationships, human types, life chances and risks, norms for behavior, and other roles of life" (p. 552). They also note it is paradoxical that as the need for well-trained nurses reached new heights in the 1970s, the image of nurses in motion pictures deteriorated at an alarming rate. The authors believe that the denigration of nursing in the movies will sustain a negative image to prospective nurses, thus adding to the already major shortage of nurses in the United States.

We have given considerable detail to the analysis and use of the data in the nursing image historical study. Several points in regard to this type of sample now need to be

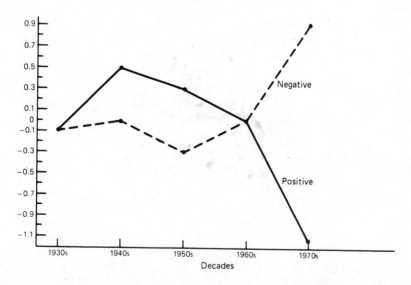

Figure 9.1. Historical Status of Nurses as Portrayed in Films. (*Source:* B. J. Kalisch, P. A. Kalisch, & M. McHugh. [1980]. Content analysis of film stereotypes of nurses. *International Journal of Women's Studies, 3* [6], 531–558.)

stressed. First of all, it is a novel way of obtaining a sample. One does not have to rely on the cooperation or goodwill of people; one can circumvent this hurdle and work directly from reviews and catalogs. Thirdly, the sample is historical since the 200 films used spanned a period of nearly 50 years. This historical-developmental dimension is important, as change can be more readily assessed through this type of sample than a "one-shot" survey. Finally, film as a medium is nonreactive—it is a frozen imprint on celluloid and whatever was put on the film is still there 50 years later.

The degree to which one can generalize from this type of sample is questionable. There is no assurance that the sex role and occupational images placed on celluloid reflected reality even when the film was done, but that is the assumption of the researchers in this example. Also, content analysis is a useful, but very time-consuming, approach to research, and one problem in particular emerges in this study. What is the probability that content analysis becomes distorted due to the political times and sex role questions during the time of the study?

▶ Ascione and Schvaneveldt (in review) conducted an entirely different type of study focusing on specific characteristics of couples in interfaith marriages. Their investigation utilized the total population of marriages performed in a Mountain West Diocese over a 31-year period. The sample drawn from this population included every interfaith marriage sacramental record for the 1959, 1974, and 1986 years. The final sample consisted of 502 cases collected from these three time periods. To develop this type of sample, it took seven weeks to examine 35.3 linear feet of file cards in 10 drawers. Approximately 46,640 sacramental cards yielded the 502 cases that were later analyzed.

A Theory of Imitation—Suicides and Automobile Accidents: A Sample Design for Those Unable to Talk

▶ The impact of a certain theory sometimes becomes the impetus for research, which is the case in the next example dealing with the theory of limitation. To what degree are we motivated or influenced by what we see in the press, in our community, or on the campus? *Suggestion* is a most intriguing notion, a notion that prompted D. S. Phillips (1979) to apply this theory to the traumatic act of suicide initially and later to the relationship between suicides as publicized in the press and the spillover influence on the increased rate of automobile accidents, which might be argued as accident–suicides.

It is obvious that one cannot contact people who were successful in suicide to determine if they were influenced by the power of suggestion stemming from well-publicized suicide cases. We must seek a sample or a population in a different vein. The one proposed by Phillips constitutes an innovative use of data probably greatly underused by social scientists (see Chapter 14 for more details).

Phillips argues that the national level of suicides rises dramatically after a suicide is covered heavily in the press, especially in the geographical area where the suicide took place. Secondly, he notes that the increase in suicides takes place only if a great deal of publicity is given to the suicide. Thirdly, the higher the amount of press coverage to the suicide event, the more the national levels of suicides increase. As an example, Phillips notes that the American suicide rate temporarily increased by 12% right after Marilyn Monroe committed suicide in 1963. He contends that the increase in suicides after a highly publicized story holds even after one takes into account seasonal, yearly, and random fluctuations regarding the suicide levels.

Motor vehicle accidents rank as the fifth leading cause of death. Since many people believe that a number of these accidents are not really accidents but truly suicides, it should be possible to further test the theory of suggestion by assessing motor vehicle accidents right after a suicide story—in short, to treat it as a special brand of suicide. Phillips reasoned that if suggestion occurs, the increase in automobile wrecks should go up in a significant manner. Using California as a study base (since it publishes a daily motor vehicle fatality list), he sent out to test this hypothesis. Cases of suicide were obtained by engaging in an exhaustive search of front page suicides as reported in the *Los Angeles Times* and the *San Francisco Chronicle* for the years 1966–1973. This search produced a sample size of 23 cases in which large amounts of publicity were given and the appropriate control periods could be applied for analysis. Phillips does not technically have a sample. He uses the entire population of 23 cases in which large amounts of publicity were given. True, he did not sample from all major newspapers in California, the West, or certainly the United States as a whole, but within the defined sampling frame the 23 cases represent more of a population than a sample. In addition, the sample for this study is composed of people who imitated the suicide publicity using the automobile. As you continue to read and study this example note the two levels of sampling involved—the suicide cases in the press and the automobile drivers involved in imitation.

It was necessary for Phillips to account for month of the year and match up the experimental group with the control group. This was also done for day of the week, since vehicle fatalities vary greatly by day of the week. Also, the presence or absence of a holiday weekend was noted. Specifically, if the experimental period contained a holiday or weekend, then efforts were made to match these with similar time frames at the control level. The converse of the matching was also done for these variables. The experimental group was defined as those motor vehicle deaths in a certain time period following a publicized suicide (a specified number of days) and the control group defined as the same type of deaths by automobile in a matched time frame when no suicides were publicized.

Data indicate a significant increase of fatal automobile accidents following a publicized suicide story, adding support for the theory that drivers of motor vehicles are indeed affected by what they are exposed to in the press. These drivers appear to be influenced by the stories about suicide. One way to further understand this relationship was to analyze data in the control and experimental groups by calculating how long it took a person to die. Phillips reasoned that a true accident victim would be braking to prevent an accident, whereas a potential suicide victim would be stepping on the accelerator to increase the chance of death in a specific situation. Data indicate that the experimental group was much more likely to die rapidly (average: 1.016 days) as compared to the control group (4.131 days).

Is there a relationship between the age of the suicide victim in the paper and the age of people who imitate this type of behavior in the automobile? This hypothesis was put to test, and the data show that stories about young people in suicide tend to be followed by single vehicle crashes with young drivers, and when the newspaper story tells about an older person dying by suicide this is likewise followed by single-vehicle crashes of older drivers.

Phillips analyzed these data in one other dimension to further understand the relationship between publicized suicides and a significant increase of automobile fatalities in matched time periods. If the story is about pure suicide—nobody else involved—then automobile accidents in the experimental period involve a single-car accident–suicide. On the other hand, if the story tells of a murder–suicide event, then this is much more likely to be related to multiple-vehicle accidents involving other passengers, some of whom are also killed.

In terms of the Phillips (1979) sample, the *n* is not really large, but this does not appear to be a real problem due to the nature of the data and the types of analysis carried out. Phillips is primarily attempting to test suggestion theory in a novel way, and there is relatively little concern with generalization to the whole society. Furthermore, the data are secondary (not directly generated by Phillips for research) and seemingly waiting for a creative application of theory applied to significant questions about life and death. This sample or population would be most likely labeled as *purposive,* as there is really no other way to generate a sample for this type of research. Problems of cooperation, interviewing, completing questionnaires, and so on are completely avoided in the sample for obvious reasons.

There are some parallels with the Phillips study and the nursing image in films research. Both studies rely on secondary data or documents for samples, both use a form of content analysis to extract data for the sample, and both represent a novel use of social science data and sampling to assess the topics of occupational sex roles and imitation behavior.

The Phillips sample would involve a large investment of time, but little cost is involved otherwise. One does not have to obtain cooperation of subjects, reactive effects do not exist, and this type of sample lends itself to an experimental design. In addition, this type of sample will be available in a few more years and the study can be replicated using content analysis of these two newspapers or others as appropriate. The innovative type of sample, the application of research from this sample, and the application of suggestion theory to this sample are some of the features of this strategy that are very important.

Neonatal Death: A Public Relations Sample

▶ The next example of sampling illustrates the idea of *snowballing* to a degree, as well as the role of *publicity* in obtaining respondents for research. In the 1980 work, *Motherhood and Mourning: Perinatal Death,* Peppers and Knapp relate that personal experiences with stillbirth and miscarriage in their own marriages stimulated their interest in this area. Further, one of the spouses, while waiting in a doctor's office, read an article in *Today's Health* about a group of mothers in the St. Louis area and their involvement with an organization called AMEND (*A*id to *M*others *E*xperiencing *N*eonatal *D*eath). Peppers and Knapp made contact with this group and readily completed 42 interviews with respective mothers who had experienced fetal or infant deaths. Their main goal at this point was to do exploratory work and pretest their interview schedule. But they report that they received such a rich source of data and an abundant amount of material that they released summary findings from this analysis to United Press International. The response from this story was overwhelming as they received hundreds of letters from around the world in which women and men gave very lengthy accounts of their own experience on this issue. This response enabled the researchers to engage in additional interviewing on the topic and specifically to do systematic interviewing with the AMEND chapter in Los Angeles.

The nature of the dependent variable invites potential subjects to participate in this sample. The researchers, who were initially motivated to do this type of research because of their spouses, were further influenced by reading an article, and developed the sample and research design additionally because of sample response. In addition to being a snowball sample, this example illustrates the art and evolution of a research project. It would be traditional for us to say that each piece of research is systematically planned and evolves in a logical step-by-step fashion, but it is clear that neither the design nor the sample in this study followed that pattern. We hasten to add that this pattern is quite typical in most studies of unusual populations.

Remembering High School Classes

The next two examples of sampling involve random probability samples. The first takes place in Texas and focuses on the use of consumer education, while the second example illustrates a Gallup (1980) probability sample on leisure activity. The first study (Bell & Durr, 1983) not only illustrates a random sample, but in addition focuses on how consumers use education over time in a variety of personal, family, and community settings.

Bell and Durr (1983) studied the responses of 912 students who had enrolled in consumer education and home economics classes in various sized high schools in the state of Texas. The sample was proportionally stratified on the basis of school size and the Athletic Conference designations were used to classify school size. The 1979–1980 Athletic Conference designation noted that 31% of Texas high schools were 4 and 5A (large city schools), 12.5% were 3A, 16.5% were 2A, and 40% of the high schools were 1A (the small rural schools).

The research team of Bell and Durr used these percentages in computing the sample stratification of 1,440 questionnaires which were sent. A total of 912 usable forms were returned and the rates of response were essentially the same among the various sizes of schools. The final sample of 912 respondents was composed of 11th and 12th grade students currently enrolled in a high school consumer and homemaking course (54%); students who had previously enrolled in this type of course in the 5-year period 1975 to 1979 (25%); and 21% came from students who had been enrolled in high school during the 1969–1974 period.

In summary, the schools were sampled using a stratified sampling approach based on size of high schools for the state of Texas. The actual sample of respondents was obtained by selecting current and former students who had enrolled in a consumer and homemaking education class. Schools were selected in proportion to their existence in the state system and students were selected by a random procedure within each selected school. It is of interest to note that former students rated consumer concepts higher than currently enrolled students, suggesting that the realities of life beyond high school create situations where ideas are both tested and used. Furthermore, child development concepts were ranked the most useful by all three groups within the sample and home management ranked second in utility.

Americans at Leisure

▶ Our final example of sampling procedure is a *national probability sample;* it is carried out with precision and swiftness, and meets most of the sampling recommendations covered in the first part of the chapter. It is a large sample when compared to the sample populations of 200, 23, and 42 in our other three sampling illustrations. This example illustrates the concepts of sampling error, broad generalization, and the process by which each of the elements was selected.

The *Gallup Poll* of June 1980 revealed an interesting profile of leisure time and exercise activities of a national probability sample of adults 21 years of age and over. Gallup uses a standard sampling device for each of the monthly published reports on a variety of topics concerning politics, the economy, crime, the family, the Equal Rights Amendment, and so on. The design of the sample produces a representative profile of the entire American population and the national surveys are based on interviews with a minimum of 1,500 adults. A sample of 1,500 adults produces a *sampling error* with a tolerance of 3 percentage points 95% of the time. Remember that the sampling error is the difference between what occurs in a sample versus what would occur if the entire population were interviewed. The Gallup data are usually published within $1\frac{1}{2}$ to 2 weeks after they are collected in the field interview. Note that while this time lag is very brief in comparison to most social science data, it would create a significant problem of stale data if one were attempting to depict something as dynamic as presidential preference.

Getting back to Americans and leisure exercise activities, Gallup found that Americans showed a decline in participation in many sports and outdoor activities and indicates that this may reflect in part the energy crunch. For example, motor boating declined dramatically compared to 1972. Bowling showed a general decline going back to 1964 (31% in 1964 versus 24% in 1980). In contrast tennis showed an increase from 4% in 1959 to 14% in 1980. Roller-skating also showed a big increase in popularity, moving from 5% in 1972 to 12% in 1980.

Swimming was the sport with greatest appeal (37%) followed by bicycling (27%), bowling (24%), hiking (21%), fresh water fishing (20%), and camping (19%). Out of a very long list of activities, the four with lowest appeal are surfing (2%), surfcasting (2%), scuba diving (1%), and squash (1%).

All respondents in this interview were presented with a list of 47 sports or activities and asked to respond to each in terms of the question, "Which of these sports and activities have you, yourself, participated in within the last 12 months?" (Gallup, 1980, p. 26).

On the exercise dimension, Gallup reports that 46% of Americans exercise on a regular basis, up dramatically from 24% in 1961. Those most likely to exercise are college educated, in the upper and upper-middle classes, and in business or other white collar settings. In terms of age, it is not surprising that those under 30 are more likely to exercise most and further, men do more than women, and people in the Northeast and far West exercise more than those in the Midwest or in the South. As might be expected, jogging is extremely popular, with 12% reporting this as a regular activity. Analysis of this type reflects the need for a large sample as noted earlier in the chapter. An *n* of 1,500 is sufficiently large that Gallup could theoretically test the dependent variables on almost any demographic factor conceivable.

HELPS IN OBTAINING SAMPLES

The Gallup Poll.   The Gallup Poll, published on a monthly basis, is an example of a useful data source for a variety of topics. The sample of 1,500 adults comes from 320 locations and uses a probability design. At each location an interviewer is provided with a map, a starting point, and instructions for completing the interviews.

The Current Population Survey.   The Current Population Survey in the United States is conducted monthly by the Bureau of the Census. The sample comes from 449 areas which comprise 863 counties and independent cities. In terms of size, 60,000 households are sampled each month. This large and carefully controlled sample provides the monthly estimates of total employment and unemployment and a detailed profile on personal characteristics of the total population, which is a running census between the decennial censuses.

The Detroit Area Study.   The Detroit Area Study is operated by the Survey Research Center at the University of Michigan and conducts a major project each year. A probability sample of at least 500 is contacted in the Detroit area.

National Opinion Research Center (NORC).   This center, located in Chicago, is a widely known and widely used source of samples (for example, Reiss, 1964, as noted in Chapter 8, used NORC to conduct a national probability sample on sexual attitudes). This is a versatile organization and will take on specific projects on a variety of topics for a fee.

There are other useful sampling helps on a variety of topics that students may wish to investigate. A check with the reference librarian and discussions with your research professors may help identify sources useful for your particular projects. A variety of other polls are also published, such as the Harris, Roper, and Nielsen reports.

SUMMARY

Sampling is one of the most important events in the whole research process, since it is the method for obtaining data on which analysis, information building, and decisions are made. A good sample should be the type and size that will reflect an accurate profile of the population from which it is drawn. In this case, the type should be a probability sample, since it is possible for one to make statements about representativeness and precise chances of specific elements being selected. When a probability sample is selected, one can use the appropriate statistical procedures in analyzing the sample, describing it, and making necessary inferences about the population from which it was drawn. And as noted by Lazerwitz (1968), a sample should be no larger than is needed for precision, should be as economical as possible and gathered as quickly as possible under the constraints of budget and measurement logistics. Some samples "spoil" or become "stale" very rapidly, as was illustrated with various examples. Therefore, it behooves the researcher to make sure that analysis and findings are presented on samples that are still "fresh" (Gallup, 1980).

The following are brief descriptions of the main ideas of this chapter:

Concepts

1. Population—the entire group. All items of interest in a particular study (i.e., individuals, households, etc.).
2. Sample—a selected portion of the population representative of the entire population.
3. Element—a single case or object in a sample.
4. Sampling units—collections or clusters of elements that do not overlap.
5. Sampling frame—a list of the sampling units from which the sample is drawn.

Samples

1. Probability samples include:
   a. simple random samples
   b. systematic random samples
   c. cluster samples
   d. stratified random samples
2. Nonprobability samples include:
   a. convenience samples
   b. snowball samples
   c. purposeful samples
   d. quota samples
3. Sample size—the sample should be as large as necessary to reduce the sampling error.
4. Purposes of sampling—to produce valid data economically and swiftly to enable the investigator to precisely describe or test some concern.
5. Sampling leads to economy, a shorter time lag, higher quality work, and the completion of certain projects that would never be possible if one had to assess the entire population.

PROBLEMS AND APPLICATIONS

1. Enumerate and clarify three examples or situations in which you should have used some type of sampling procedure to arrive at a decision.
2. Complete a sample workup for a study dealing with the effect of minimum wage on employment-unemployment rates for teenagers. What are the limitations of your sampling type?
3. Design and talk about a study that could utilize a snowball sample.
4. Review and discuss various ways in which the notion of probability and probability sampling can be useful in addressing the problems of consumership and decision making in the daily commerce of people.
5. What are the most common samples, sample sizes, and type of sampling procedures used in your respective field of specialization? Why? What, if anything, should be changed in terms of sampling as used in your area of specialization?

REFERENCES

Ascione, D., & Schvaneveldt, J. D. (in review). *Trends in Catholic interfaith marriages in Utah: A comparative study.*

Bailey, K. D. (1978). *Methods of social research.* New York: The Free Press.

Bell, C. G., & Durr, G. E. (1983). Usefulness of consumer education concepts as perceived by current and former homemaking students. *Home Economics Research Journal, 11,* 215–222.

Blalock, Jr., H. M. (1960). *Social statistics.* New York: McGraw-Hill.

Brodie, F. M. (1967). *The devil drives: A life of Sir Richard Burton.* New York: W. W. Norton.

Champion, D. J. (1970). *Basic statistics for social research.* Scranton, Pa.: Chandler.

Cochran, W. G., Mosteller, F., & Tukey, J. W. (1954). *Statistical problems of the Kinsey Report on sexual behavior in the human male.* Washington, D.C.: Greenwood Press.

Deutsch, J. G. (1976). *Selling the people's Cadillac: The Edsel and corporate responsibility.* New Haven: Yale University Press.

Eckhardt, K. W., & Ermann, M. D. (1977). *Social research methods.* New York: Random House.

Frankel, M. R., & Frankel, L. R. (1987). Fifty years of survey sampling in the United States. *Public Opinion Quarterly, 51,* S127–S138.

The Gallup Opinion Index. (1980, June). Leisure activities. *The Gallup Poll.* Princeton, N.J.: Report no. 178.

Hite, S. (1987). *Women and love, a cultural revolution in progress.* New York: Knopf.

Kalisch, B. J., Kalisch, P. A., & McHugh, M. (1980). Content analysis of film stereotypes of nurses. *International Journal of Women's Studies, 3* (6), 531–558.

Kinsey, A. C., Pomeroy, W. B., & Martin, C. E. (1948). *Sexual behavior in the human male.* Philadelphia: Saunders.

Lazerwitz, B. (1968). Sampling theory and procedures. In H. M. Blalock, Jr., & A. B. Blalock (Eds.), *Methodology in social research.* New York: McGraw-Hill.

Mendenhall, W., Ott, L., & Schaeffer, R. L. (1971). *Elementary survey sampling.* Belmont, Calif.: Wadsworth.

Meyers, L.S., & Grossen, N. E. (1974). *Behavioral research.* San Francisco: W. H. Freeman.

Myrdal, G. (1944). *An American dilemma: The Negro problem in modern democracy.* New York: Harper & Row.

Peppers, L. G., & Knapp, R. J. (1980). *Motherhood and mourning: Perinatal death.* New York: Praeger.

Phillips, D. P. (1979). Suicide, motor vehicle fatalities, and the mass media: Evidence toward a theory of suggestion. *American Journal of Sociology, 84* (5), 1150–1174.

Proger, S. (1968). *The medicated society.* New York: Macmillan.

Reiss, I. L. (1967). *The social context of premarital sexual permissiveness.* New York: Holt, Rinehart and Winston.

Schvaneveldt, J. D. (1970). *Family member interaction in a rural and urban aged population.* Research Foundation Report, Utah State University, Logan, Utah.

Selltiz, C., Wrightsman, L. S., & Cook, S. W. (1976). *Research methods in social relations* (3rd ed.). New York: Holt, Rinehart and Winston.

Slonim, M. J. (1960). *Sampling in a nutshell.* New York: Simon & Schuster.

Smith, H. W. (1975). *Strategies of social research.* Englewood Cliffs, N.J.: Prentice-Hall.

Som, R. K. (1973). *A manual of sampling techniques.* New York: Crane, Russak.

Sudman, S. (1976). *Applied sampling.* New York: Academic Press.

SECTION IV

Data Collection Strategies

In addition to specifying the research design, measurement, and sampling procedures of a study, a social scientist makes decisions on the practical issues of how data will be collected. Obtaining sound data (facts) is perhaps the most practical and demanding aspect of the research process. In this section, we will review six major data collection strategies. First, you will be introduced to the most common data collection strategies involving questionnaire and interview techniques. Next you will have an opportunity to become acquainted with four major observational strategies. Third, the basic steps of laboratory research will be examined. Fourth, you will be introduced to the basic elements and use of projective or indirect measures in clinically oriented research. In the fifth chapter of this section, you will find out how historical documents and archival information can be used to address important research questions. Finally, you will have an opportunity to see how all of the varying data collection techniques and research designs can be used in practical evaluation studies in social agencies. In summary, this section introduces the major strategies for obtaining data in social science research.

CHAPTER 10

Obtaining Data: Questionnaire and Interview

OUTLINE

Talking and Testing for Science
The Questionnaire as a Research Tool
   Open-ended Questions
   Closed-ended Questions
Response Rate and Sensitive Questions
   Obtaining a High Return on a Mailed Questionnaire
Constructing Your Questions
Obtaining Sensitive Information
Arrangement and Layout Guides
Style and Types of Questions
The Interview and Interviewer
   The Interview
The Nature and Type of Interview
   The Focused Interview
   The Nondirective Interview
   The Clinical Interview
   Telephone Interviews
   Administration of Questionnaire and Interview
The Art of Interviewing
   Presentation of Self
   The Door Approach
   Conducting a Quality Interview
   Rapport and Morale Level
   Probes

To Record or Not to Record: That Is the Question
Perspective Taking about Questionnaires and Interviews as Methods for Collecting
Data
  Issues in Validity and Reliability
Summary
Problems and Applications
References

KEY TERMS

Questionnaire	Mailed questionnaire	Focused interviews
Interview	Personally administered	Nondirective interviews
Data collection device	questionnaire	Clinical interviews
Structured and	Double-barreled	Telephone interviews
unstructured	questions	Rapport
Open-ended questions	Response set	Probes
Closed-ended questions	Question order	Recording strategies
Response rate	Funneling	
Sensitive questions	Style of questions	

STUDY GUIDE QUESTIONS

1. What data collecting device has been used most often in the wide area of social science? Why?
2. What is a closed-end question and where would one likely use this format?
3. Contrast the main advantages and disadvantages of questionnaires versus interviews in collecting data. What is your conclusion?
4. In interviewing human subjects, what are some main "dos and don'ts"?
5. How does one conduct a quality interview?
6. What are research probes and why are probes used in interviewing respondents?

Role of the Researcher

Questionnaires and interviews can be likened to the use of the stethoscope or surgical tools in medicine in that these research devices represent the two most common modes of data collection in all of the many branches of social-behavioral science. Both of these modes are highly flexible and adaptable to a variety of research designs, populations, and purposes. Questionnaires and interviews can be highly structured or very unstructured, as well as reflect varying degrees of structure between these two polar types. The social scientist needs to know how to use these devices, how to construct them, and the conditions that would lead to the use of selected styles of the questionnaire or interview. The limitations and strengths as well as the expenses involved in using either of these data collection devices must be understood by the researcher. With the availability of VCR cameras and other related video technology, it will be interesting to see the impact of these on the interview and questionnaire in future social science research.

Role of the Consumer

It is almost impossible to grow up and function in modern society without being asked to complete a questionnaire or respond to interviews on a fairly regular basis. The consumer uses the interview and questionnaire in both a formal and informal manner to shop, make decisions, create new projects, and engage in social interaction on a broad scale. In addition, the consumer of research studies consumes or uses a great variety of ideas, products, and facilities that originated in someone's questionnaire or interview session. Knowing the conditions for using these two data collection devices, as well as the various types of questionnaires and interviews, becomes increasingly necessary if one is to make intelligent decisions in the context of competing alternatives. Knowing what to believe about research is often related to understanding the utility of either the questionnaire or interview in a respective piece of research.

TALKING AND TESTING FOR SCIENCE

Just as there are various ways to obtain cash from a bank (withdrawal from savings or checking accounts, obtaining a loan, or even robbing a bank), so there are several ways to obtain data about the social world. Earlier chapters have focused on observation, field studies, and experimentation as specific methods for obtaining data, information, and understanding about certain conditions or relationships. Two central methods for obtaining data, *questionnaires* and *interviews,* can be used in a variety of designs, research settings, purposes, and samples. These two strategies, perhaps more than any others, are the "workhorses" of social research. Most of the research conducted or published involves one or both of these data collection devices. Please note the phrase, *data collection devices,* because it is important to understand that these are not research designs, analysis procedures, or purposes as such, but rather modalities for allowing people to share information about their attitudes, behavior, history, future plans, or current situation.

Interviews and questionnaires can be extremely rigid or very open. The most distinctive thing about an *interview* regardless of type or form is that the respondent is orally presented with questions—whereas in the *questionnaire,* regardless of type or form, the respondent is presented with a written question to respond to directly. Each data collection device has merit and utility; the ultimate decision for using questionnaires over interviews would among other things depend on the purpose of the study, type of information needed, size and makeup of the sample, resources for conducting the study, the variable(s) to be measured, and certainly the measuring device would be an important determinant. Webb, Campbell, Schwartz, and Sechrest (1971) note that the interview is probably the most flexible device for data collection, and if strictly limited to one device, then the interview is the clear choice.

Since the basic mission of this text is to inform prospective researchers and consumers of research about the central processes and methodology and to illustrate these methodological principles with applicable examples, this chapter attempts to provide this level of coverage for questionnaires and interviews. A careful reading and clear understanding of these principles will enable one to conduct and understand research using these two data collection devices, but of course we will not be able to provide a full coverage of the many types, styles, criticisms, and applications on which several full-length volumes have appeared on questionnaires and interviews (i.e., Berdie & Anderson, 1974; Converse & Schuman, 1974; Hyman, 1954; Metzener & Mann, 1952; Oppenheim, 1966; Parten, 1966).

THE QUESTIONNAIRE AS A RESEARCH TOOL

D. L. Phillips (1971) reported that about 9 of every 10 articles published in two major sociological journals, the *American Sociological Review* and the *American Journal of Sociology,* use either questionnaires or some type of interview as the main device in collecting data. This vast usage testifies to the utility of questionnaires, their flexibility, and the degree to which scientists believe them to be the best method for data collection or else the questionnaire has become so conventionalized that researchers do not pursue the use of either better or more creative devices. Questionnaires' high use may be habitual indeed, but the degree of their use also testifies to high utility and flexibility.

We may define a *questionnaire* as a list or grouping of written questions which a respondent answers. It is, in the words of Smith (1975), "a self-administered interview" (p. 170). A questionnaire is a data-gathering device that elicits from a respondent the answers or reactions to printed (pre-arranged) questions presented in a specific order. Questionnaires can be group administered, self-administered, mailed, long, short, open-ended or closed-style questions. The purpose for which a questionnaire is used can range from exploring-probing type research to a highly structured lab experiment. The following treatment illustrates many of these particular types, styles, and uses of questionnaires. (See Belson [1981] for a review of literature on questionnaires and detailed illustrations.)

Open-ended Questions

In this question format the respondent is free or open to supply answers or information in an unstructured manner. For example, one might be presented with the question, "What do you think should be done about illegal aliens in the United States?" Space is provided for the answer by the respondent. The advantage of this question format is that one has the opportunity to openly express what he or she believes, feels, or recommends. One is not confined to a pre-arranged response category that forces you to agree or disagree, a "yes" or "no" response, or one in which you check some degree of reaction to questions. An open-ended question should be carefully worded so as to present a standardized question to all respondents. Standardization is important because you will want to compare the responses, and this is meaningful only if you have assurance that all respondents were in fact reacting to the same question and that the responses are comparable in that context.

A greater depth of response is allowable in the open-ended question; and since no clues are given for the answer, it would seem to invite a respondent to give authentic information to a question. But since the response is open, it does take effort and high motivation for a respondent to react to the items and complete the instructions provided by the questionnaire maker. The investment of time, motivational level, and attentiveness needed to supply responses for open-ended items typically lead to a low level of response from a sample, especially if it is a mailed questionnaire. If one has a captive audience, such as a classroom of students for example, then this problem is largely eliminated. The open-ended question used in this context is essentially an essay question, a style of question most readers are extremely familiar with after many years of testing in school.

It is particularly appropriate to use open-ended questions when one desires to know the respondent's frame of reference or the level of information possessed. In a closed-question format, we sometimes force respondents to choose from a number of response categories, none of which may really apply to their situation or frame of reference. Obviously this can lead to distortion of validity and to an overuse of the response "don't know."

Closed-ended Questions

This question format allows the respondent to answer items by checking categories or by providing a brief written response. A marking of "yes" or "no," checking an item from a list of possible responses, or a very short response would be the three main ways in which one answers questions posed in a closed-ended style. An investigator will often supply the respondent with a category such as "other" to permit the respondent some latitude in frame of reference, thus allowing some individuality in response while hopefully getting at what is truly most important for the respondent.

The major advantages of this question style include

1. ease of completing the questions
2. brevity of response time
3. specification of the frame of reference for the subject
4. promotion of objectivity
5. ease in scoring, coding, and tabulation

If a main goal of the research is to classify or rank an individual's attitudes or behavior on some concern that is well understood and would have a common frame of reference to respondents, then closed-style questions are the appropriate format. Additionally, a respondent may be quite willing to check response categories asking for sensitive information about income, sexual behavior, or other personal habits, but would not be willing to write out answers to such questions. Somehow checking a fixed-alternative response or a number which stands for some value in relation to the question provides distance, neutrality, or anonymity for the respondent. In addition to time and motivational factors for using a closed style is the advantage of mechanically responding with a check or circling a category. Bailey (1978) suggests that some respondents may have a difficult time writing an answer that reflects their feelings even if they are motivated and willing to participate, hence the need for closed-ended questions.

It should be clear that each question format has distinct advantages and disadvantages. For exploratory work or research in which feelings, attitudes, or type of behavior are not known or well understood, the open-ended questions would be better than the closed type. On the other hand, in terms of return rate, time, expense, objectivity, ease of scoring and analyses, the closed-ended type (fixed-alternative) question is much superior. This fixed-alternative question can be more directly applied to a hypothesis because the data are quantifiable with much less effort. The fixed alternative question reduces data to a common dimension that can be more easily applied to the testing of a specified hypothesis.

▶   A recent survey by Wright and Rogers (1987) illustrates not only the flexibility of a questionnaire, but also the importance of the way in which the questions are worded. The researchers polled 840 undergraduates regarding their attitudes towards abortion. The study took place just prior to the 1984 elections when the subject of abortion was a hot issue. Those participating in the study completed a self-administered questionnaire designed to ascertain if they would approve or disapprove of abortion under the following circumstances: (1) if a young woman accidentally got pregnant during her first year of college, (2) if a woman had several children and was unable to provide financially or emotionally for another child, (3) rape, (4) if the pregnancy created a life-threatening condition for the prospective mother. By use of the questionnaire, the participants' backgrounds and attitudes were also assessed. The authors were able to conclude from the results of the questionnaire that women, those affiliated with anti-abortion churches, and younger respondents were more conservative in their replies.

        In comparing the present study with research done in 1982 and 1985, the investigators found that the campaign issues did not seem to influence the attitudes of the participants. However, they did determine that wording of the questions had a dramatic influence on pro-choice or pro-life attitudes of the respondents. In the 1982 study reviewed (Henshaw & Martire, 1982), 69% of the women surveyed agreed or agreed strongly that "a pregnant woman should have the right to decide whether she wants to terminate a pregnancy or have a child" (pp. 521–522). By dividing the question of abortion into four specific situations, the present study elicited favorable responses by 84% to 99% of those polled, depending upon the specific question.

Tips for Consumers 10.1

The episode of the questionnaire
As a consumer of research, you are invited to reflect on the following points:
1. In the course of a typical year, how many and what type of questionnaires are you requested to complete?
2. How do you feel as you complete questionnaires for researchers, political, or consumer-oriented groups? Do you fill them out and return them?
3. The next time you receive a questionnaire we sincerely hope that you will complete it and even critically review it for the sender. Write marginal notes and make observations on what you like and do not like about the form, but then be kind enough to send it back to the researcher. This is one of the key methods for the consumer to have a direct bearing on what the researcher is doing.
4. What rewards or incentives have you received for cooperating in the completion of questionnaires from various groups? Did you feel that the experience of completing the form was a sufficient reward? What kind of incentive levels would you like in order to complete questionnaires?

A 1985 *Newsweek* poll was also cited wherein the question "Do you think abortion should be legal under all circumstances, only certain circumstances or illegal in all circumstances?" (p. 522) was asked. In response to the question, 21% of the participants indicated that abortion should be illegal under all circumstances. Yet in the present study, only 3% of the participants were against abortion in cases where the mother's life might be endangered. The authors concluded that the results could be skewed dramatically simply by the manner in which the questions were worded.

This example shows the great flexibility of a questionnaire as well as clear documentation that wording style of a question definitely influences type of response. As we move into other sections of this chapter, a number of detailed explanations will be provided to help clarify many of the points made in the Wright and Rogers example. (See Tips for Consumers 10.1.)

RESPONSE RATE AND SENSITIVE QUESTIONS

Bradburn and Sudman (1979) have shown that questions about leisure time and sports create little apprehension in respondents, whereas questions dealing with income, drinking, and gambling are moderately threatening. However, questions dealing with sex and illicit drug use had high threat potential. Table 10.1 provides a detailed account of response rate potential as related to various topics. Bradburn and Sudman found that how a person believes an item might produce threat in another person is highly related to that person's reports about engaging in the same kind of behavior, leading to the conclusion that a respondent's perception of how others might be threatened about certain types of questions is a useful indicator of respondent threat.

On the basis of their research, Bradburn and Sudman (1979) suggest that investigators carefully assess threat potential before data collection. In particular, "when more than 20 of the respondents feel that most people would be made very uneasy by talking about the topic" (p. 166), researchers should either modify or carefully monitor data collection. When this perceived threat rate is between 10% and 20%, an investigator should be alert to distortion in responses. These authors report that several factors can be introduced to increase the likelihood that people will give valid information about sensitive areas. These factors include: (1) a longer discussion–introduction concerning the research and why a respondent should participate; (2) an open format response rather than fixed alternatives; and (3) freedom for the respondents to select their own words in talking about sensitive areas. Use of these strategies when measuring threatening topics can lead to a two- or three-fold increase in reporting behavior as compared to the more traditional questionnaire format according to Bradburn and Sudman.

Bradburn and Sudman have also found that the presence of others when an interview is being conducted can have direct impact, depending on who the "others" are. Their data show small effects for the presence of a child (but children make adults more uneasy about discussing threatening activities) and the presence of an adult third party contributes to the refusal rate. In the very few cases in which young respondents were interviewed in the presence of their parents, the data indicate a strong inhibiting influence.

TABLE 10.1. Percentage of Respondents Who Feel Most People Would Be Very Uneasy or Not at All Uneasy about Topic

Topic	Very Uneasy	Not at All Uneasy
Masturbation	56.4[a]	11.8
Marijuana	42.0	19.8
Intercourse	41.5	14.5
Stimulants and depressants	31.3	20.2
Intoxication	29.0	20.6
Petting and kissing	19.7	26.3
Income	12.5	32.7
Gambling with friends	10.5	39.7
Drinking	10.3	38.0
General leisure	2.4	80.8
Sports activity	1.3	90.1

[a]$N = 1,172$, but actual n varies slightly from question to question. (*Source:* Norman H. Bradburn and Seymour Sudman. [1979]. *Improving interview method and questionnaire design.* San Francisco: Jossey-Bass, p. 17.)

Obtaining a High Return on a Mailed Questionnaire

Obtaining a high return on mailed questionnaires can be challenging. Some of the methods that have proven to be effective in increasing the rate of return are briefly presented and we also provide extensive references here and throughout the chapter to facilitate the reader interested in more detailed coverage.

1. The standard use of stamped, addressed, return envelopes for respondents to use in returning the completed form results in a higher return rate than a conventional business reply envelope and, of course, higher than providing nothing (Warwick & Lininger, 1975).
2. The use of first-class mail has proven to be an effective method for obtaining a higher return rate (Gullahorn & Gullahorn, 1963).
3. The use of follow-up post cards or letters in which the investigator reminds the respondent of the need to cooperate, complete the questionnaire, and return it is suggested.
4. After a follow-up post card or letter, it is recommended that the investigator phone respondents and make a personal request for cooperation in the research.
5. A suggested deadline can be helpful if used skillfully. One should avoid creating the idea that if not returned by a certain date it would be worthless to return the questionnaire. Perhaps a return date used as a guide would be better.
6. Personally typed or written letters with official letterhead are useful. Roeher (1963) found that using an official title (Director of Rehabilitation) resulted in an 81% return versus only 55% when he used just a plain signature.
7. The use of small denomination stamps of various colors positively influences the rate of return (Roeher, 1963).
8. The more personalized attention shown to the respondent, the greater the likelihood that the response will be positive. Several of the above factors speak

to this point (stamped envelope, type of stamps, signatures, or personalizing names).

9. The greater the interest or potential utility of the study to subjects, the greater the participation rate.

CONSTRUCTING YOUR QUESTIONS

There are many parallels between constructing a clear exam for a class and a questionnaire for a research project. These parallels include the need for clarity in meaning, simple language, questions that are easy to read, and items that reflect the subject under examination or investigation. A good questionnaire should create a feeling of importance in the respondent, a feeling that the research is relevant, and that cooperation is vital. The following suggestions for writing useful questionnaires offer many practical guides for clear writing in general, while stressing that clear writing is particularly important in communicating with subjects. (The work of Warwick and Lininger [1975] is heavily referred to in this section.)

1. Wording for the items in a questionnaire should be *clear* and presented in a style that will be familiar to all respondents. Attention should be focused on directness and simplicity in structure and word usage. This is not the place to impress respondents with social science jargon or your own flair for long, compound sentences. Equally inappropriate is the use of sentence structure and style which offends the reader by "talking down." A sensitivity to region of the nation, ethnic or religious patterns, educational level, and unique speech patterns should be carefully assessed as a questionnaire is prepared.

2. Double-barreled or double meaning items are confusing in any context, but they are particularly difficult in questions designed to obtain reliable and valid information from respondents. The question designer should review each item to determine if double meanings exist in various items such as, "Do you like school and do you study on a regular basis?" "Do you miss your father or your mother since leaving home?" The structure of such items does not enable a respondent to focus on a specific aspect of the question, hence answers are either unclear, skipped, or lack validity. The solution to this problem is in the need to reduce a double-barreled question to an item containing one specific dimension to which one can respond.

3. Avoid questions leading to a certain point of view or that are loaded in meaning or suggestion. These questions lower validity and eliminate the objective goal of science by pushing or suggesting answers to a respondent. For example: "Most people believe...," "Most Americans want...," "...wouldn't you agree?"

Loaded questions incorporate some, but not all, of the information relating to a certain issue under study. Questions such as, "How do you feel about American relations with countries in the Middle East, say Iran, as related to energy policies?" or "How do you generally spend your free time, watching television, or what?" illustrate the problem (Warwick & Lininger, 1975). The problem is in supplying partial information and its distorting implications. Common sense in solving this problem tells us that we should offer all of the issues involved by merely asking the respondent to react to the central question.

Warwick and Lininger (1975) also caution against using loaded questions that contain emotionally charged words. Some examples would include *big business, powerful labor, moral majority, socialists,* and so on. These are all "red flag" words (or referents), and people react in specific ways to them because of media influence or socialization regarding certain ideologies.

4. Will the question apply to all respondents in the sample? This is a difficult one to cope with, but a few rules can largely eliminate problems like: "Where do you work?" "How long have you been married?" "How many children do you have?" or "How many times have you moved in the past three years?" In these cases we are guilty of categorizing or assuming that all people have certain things in common rather than allowing respondents to merely report what is true for their situation. Some people will distort their response to comply with a felt need to oblige the investigator in these types of items. One can readily cope with this problem by using a category such as "not true for me," "does no apply," or "If no, skip or go directly to the next item and continue on with your responses." A *skip* or *filter* type question screens the respondent, guiding him or her to those items that do apply and avoiding those that might be irritating or distorting because they do not apply to the respondent or to the situation.

5. Some people have a tendency to answer questions in terms of a *response style*. That is, they may generally *agree* with terms or answer "yes" to questions even if the investigator has reversed the content of the item. This is a *response set* problem, a problem for many people who reflect agreement, a need to be positive, to be supportive, or to be on the "yes" or agreement side of life rather than on the "no" or the "disagreement" side. One can avoid a tendency to want to agree by eliminating agreement in the answer categories. For example:

▶ "In your opinion has fulfullment in your sex life gone up, gone down, or stayed about the same in the past six months?

Up   Down   Same   Don't know

A response category of this style forces the respondent to select one that hopefully reflects reality rather than a tendency to agree or disagree with a statement about sexual fulfillment during the last six months. Since most of us want to appear normal, doing well, or adjusted, a researcher must guard against using questionnaire items that place the respondent in a position where distortion is easy or inviting.

6. Long, complex, and encumbered sentences should be avoided. A rule of thumb says that a question should be no longer than 20 words, and questionnaire makers should carefully edit to reduce excess words, statements, or jargon. A short, clear, and direct item should be the goal.

7. Is the meaning of the question clear and can it be easily read by the respondent? Warwick and Lininger (1975) note that the main or key idea should come at the end rather than at the first of the question to prevent the respondent from focusing on it rather than listening or focusing on the conditions in which the key part applies. For this reason, the second of the following questions is better because of the location of the key clause. Question 1: "What region of the nation would you rather be transferred to if your company

asked you to relocate?" Question 2: "If your company asked you to relocate in a company transfer of employees, what region of the nation would you prefer?"

The Berdie and Anderson (1974) study of student evaluation of graduate assistants illustrates a variety of important issues in editor questionnaire form. Various styles are illustrated in Figure 10.1 with specified items (pp. 112–115).

Response categories in the example include a simple dichotomy of answers such as "yes" or "no," a satisfaction rating, a 5-point Likert-type response, and very broad open-ended items at the conclusion. Please note that undergraduate students have the sophistication, and probably the incentive, to complete such a form, but this combination of items may present very serious problems for the more general public.

Study each of the items in Figure 10.1 to determine if the questions are free of loaded intent, double-barreled points, if they are too long, and if the language is sufficiently clear. Note that on Item 3, Berdie and Anderson (1974) include a response category of "I

Please indicate your response by *circling* the appropriate alternative.

1. Do you believe most teaching assistants (TAs) have a sincere interest in the undergraduate students in their classes?   Yes   No

2. Have teaching assistants in your classes been: (*Circle one only*)

   | Generally satisfactory | Sometimes satisfactory | Sometimes unsatisfactory | Generally unsatisfactory |

3. When you have gone to teaching assistants for help about classwork, have they usually been helpful?   Yes   No   I have not gone

4. Do you feel free to take your academic problems to teaching assistants?   Yes   No

5. How often have you experienced the following in regard to teaching assistants?

	Never (1)	Seldom (2)	Sometimes (3)	Often (4)	Always (5)
A. They were too busy to see me	1	2	3	4	5
B. They kept appointments	1	2	3	4	5
C. They had office hours	1	2	3	4	5
D. They kept their office hours	1	2	3	4	5

6. What suggestions do you have for improving the effectiveness of teaching assistants ? (*Please discuss below*)

7. In what ways have you found teaching assistants most helpful? (*Please discuss below*)

Figure 10.1. Question Styles. (*Source:* D. R. Berdie and J. F. Anderson. [1974]. *Questionnaires: Design and use.* Metuchen, N.J.: Scarecrow Press).

have not gone" so as to make the question applicable to all respondents, since not all undergraduates would be motivated to see their teaching assistant.

Item 5 is a Likert-type question and attempts to measure *the degree* to which respondents have experienced 4 different types of reactions in making contact with teaching assistants. Item 5 is a good illustration of funneling, of becoming much more specific as one moves from Questions 1, 2, 3, and 4 to this measurement of intensity and frequency.

The last two questions illustrated here are open-ended, very broad in scope, and are presented to obtain "anything else, tell us the specifics of your experience, fill us in on what has happened to you" levels of additional understanding concerning the interaction with teaching assistants. Considerable open space should be provided for the respondents to react to both of these items.

Given the central meaning of these two items, one can assume that students would be motivated to respond since their education and professional development are directly influenced by their interaction with teaching assistants.

OBTAINING SENSITIVE INFORMATION

We have already noted that it is a good practice to use some warm-up items at the beginning of the questionnaire, then move to the main body of items, which should be organized in logical, topical flow. This order should facilitate the respondent's thinking and item completion. We made reference to the notion that many researchers believe that sensitive items should be left to the end of the questionnaire. This is to avoid arousing hostility in the respondent early in the questionnaire, and it is important to orient the respondent and build up confidence before requesting more detailed, sensitive data. However, Warwick and Lininger (1975) assert that categorically putting such items at the end of the form amounts to a "hit-and-run" strategy (p. 150). They caution against this approach, arguing instead that it amounts to a questionable ethical practice and the respondent is often tired at this point and may either ignore the items or give a superficial response. They recommend that sensitive items not be automatically introduced at the end of the form but at that point where it is likely that the respondent has "developed trust and confidence in the interviewer and the study" (pp. 150–151). Another guide for the placement of those items relates back to content organization—simply place them where they fit. Finally, Warwick and Lininger recommend that sensitive items be introduced after warming up a respondent with items related to sensitive items, but that they be factual and perhaps less threatening than the more sensitive ones to follow.

ARRANGEMENT AND LAYOUT GUIDES

A questionnaire should be attractive in appearance, easy to read, and clear to follow by either the interviewer or the respondent. Size of print should facilitate easy and accurate reading. Investigators often try to "get it all on one page" and have to use a very small letter size to do this. It is questionable whether the appearance of a shorter form is worth the strain on a respondent, and hence, the chance that quality of data is lowered. Not only is size of print and layout important, but spacing between items is also important for encouragement of completion. Visual clarity and spacing also promote accuracy in assuring that respondents put responses in categories fitting with the appropriate questions. It is important to provide space for "other," "additional," and "comments" from respondents, including the invitation to write on the back of the form.

Funneling refers to the process of beginning with general, more open questions in the first part of the questionnaire and gradually moving to the items referring to more specific and detailed information. This is a usual strategy for many questionnaires, but should not always be the rule for placement of sensitive items (deferring them to the end), as noted in the previous section.

We recommend that the items be numbered consecutively throughout, regardless of sectional content, or how long the questionnaire is either in pages or number of items. Such a procedure facilitates completion of the form with fewer omissions and certainly makes the preparations and the coding process more straightforward.

STYLE AND TYPES OF QUESTIONS

Again, the purpose of the study, the size and type of sample, measurement goals, and method of data collection (interview, interview with questionnaire, or mailed questionnaire) are all determinants of the style of question to be used. Our goal here is merely to illustrate and define types and remind the reader that what is appropriate in one setting may need to be very different for another purpose and study population.

In the chapter on scales we reviewed one of the most common styles employed in questionnaire construction, that being the *Likert-type* scale in which respondents react to items in varying degrees of intensity, typically from "strongly agree" to "strongly disagree." An example of this style is presented in Figure 10.2.

Another common style is often referred to as a "cafeteria-style" questionnaire in which the respondent is requested to check or indicate as many items as applicable to his or her situation. (See Figure 10.3.) For this type, one can instruct the respondent to check all those that apply to his or her situation or merely respond to the *one* which best describes their situation.

Pets are just as important as people in making a family a fun place to live. (*Check the one response that best reflects how you feel about this statement.*)

_____ Strongly agree

_____ Agree

_____ Uncertain

_____ Disagree

_____ Strongly disagree

Figure 10.2. Likert-type Scale Response Format

Please check any of the following that apply in your family:

_____   My father is no longer living.

_____   My mother is no longer living.

_____   My mother and father are divorced.

_____   My mother and father are separated.

_____   I live with just my mother as a parent.

_____   I live with just my father as a parent.

_____   I live with both my mother and father.

Figure 10.3. "Cafeteria-style" Question Format

▶   In addition to intensity of attitude and the "cafeteria-type" question, one can refer to the amount or quantity of some behavior or activity. A typical way to measure this dimension is to use the following style of format as illustrated in the Gregory (1939) Law-Abidingness scale (in *Scales for the Measurement of Attitudes* by Shaw and Wright, 1967).

> *Directions:* This study is being conducted to find out which of these behaviors are being performed by the largest number of people. You are asked to help in finding the prevalence of these behaviors by *underscoring* the answer that most accurately describes your behavior in each of the situations named. (p. 259)

> In filling out forms or stating information verbally when applying for work, any kind of license, bonus, relief, etc., about how often have you omitted or reported facts incorrectly? (p. 262)

> (a) Never
> (b) Rarely
> (c) Sometimes
> (d) Frequently
> (e) Always

In this style of question Gregory (1939) was attempting to understand the things that people do in varying degrees and specifically find out which behaviors are carried out most often by the largest number of people.

▶   The semantic differential scale (Osgood, Suci, & Tannenbaum, 1957), presented in Chapter 8, illustrates still another format for question style. This format uses a 7-point rating scale placed between two adjective words or phrases. The respondent rates a stimulus word or concept in terms of what it means by placing a check mark on one of the 7 points between the polar-type dimensions. An example from their original work illustrates the format (p. 136).

My Mood Today

Good ____ √ ____ ____ ____ ____ ____ ____ ____ Bad

One very common style of question has to do with supplying the respondent with a series or list of items and asking the respondent *to rank the items* from high to low, important to unimportant, or between a range of numbers on some attitude dimension such as frequency or importance. Figure 10.4 from the work of Parten (1966) illustrates the ranking or the *order-of-merit method* (p. 188). Most people experience difficulty in meaningfully ranking more than six items, and this fact should be considered when using a ranking format.

A final and very standard style question has to do with the process of extracting *demographic* or *objective* information from respondents, such as education or income. Common examples of questions that seek factual or demographic information are found in Figure 10.5.

Depending on the nature of the question, demographic or objective information questions can be used appropriately with a percentage check as in Figure 10.5, or respondents can be asked to write in the answer that best fits the point of the question. Questions dealing with work, education, family, previous employment history, age,

---

How important to you are the following features in a good glove? Place (1) beside the most important, (2) next in importance, etc.

( ) Its color

( ) Its fit

( ) Its style

( ) Its quality

Figure 10.4. Order-of-Merit Method

In my family there are _____ boys and _____ girls. I am number:

1 2 3 4 5 6 7 8 9 (*Circle one.*)

or

Of the various applicants who apply for positions at this institution, what percent are American Indians?

0– 5% _____

5– 25% _____

25– 50% _____

50– 75% _____

75–100% _____

Figure 10.5. Demographic-Objective Information Format

health, and leisure time are all examples of items that would be used in objective-demographic type questions.

THE INTERVIEW AND INTERVIEWER

One of the real methodological differences between the use of questionnaires and gathering data by interview is the presence of the interviewer and the possible interactional effects that can influence both the quality as well as the quantity of the interviewee response. And the interview, like the questionnaire, can vary from a highly structured event to a very unstructured conversation. The interview setting, skill, and training of the interviewer, openness and frame of mind of the respondent, the subject under study, and a host of other mood-situational factors enter into the process of collecting data via the interview. Since the respondent is supplying the needed information orally to the investigator, a number of factors can influence the face-to-face interchange, including manner of speech, dress, grooming, age, sex, race, and personality-interaction skills. In the following section we will talk about the interview as a tool of research and then follow it with a section on the interviewer as a person.

The Interview

If the setting is appropriate, the respondent motivated and willing, the interviewer skilled, and the instrument well prepared, the interview has the potential to be an extremely sensitive device for the acquisition of reliable and valid data. Most people are more willing to talk and verbally react than to write responses to questions. Because of cost and time factors, the interview is not used as often as the questionnaire, but it has some very specific and particular advantages as a data-gathering device. (See Stewart & Cash, 1982, for detailed treatment.)

1. *Explanation.* One of the main advantages of the interview is that the *interviewer can explain* the *purpose* of the *study,* discuss the interview, and respond to any questions a respondent might have. This process of explaining, establishing rapport, and giving information has a number of "spillover" influences that become specific advantages of the interview, one of them being *cooperation rate.*

2. *Cooperation rate.* While the typical low return rate of the mailed questionnaire is one of its main limitations, the *participation rate* with the interview becomes one of its main advantages. It is particularly effective in this regard because:

The investigator can establish rapport, which leads to trust and willingness to participate.

It takes less effort for the respondent to talk than to read and write, so the participation goes up accordingly.

A mailed questionnaire makes the assumption that a respondent can read, but if this is not always the case, there is no easy way to obtain a valid response from respondents who have minimum reading and writing skills.

3. *Quality of data.* A skilled interviewer can "read" people, assess their mood, probe, clarify, and seek additional information in a variety of ways—all representing

conditions somewhat specific to the interview as a data-collecting device. It is possible to seek the same information in a different way or at a later time in the same interview, thus one can more readily determine the truthfulness of responses. *Quality data* from first grade children would not be possible at all with a questionnaire, while an interview would prove to be a useful device for understanding some phenomenon with this age group.

4. *Observation of respondents.* In addition to flexibility already noted above, one particular quality of the interview has to do with the fact that one not only can listen to responses, one can *observe the respondent* as he or she talks throughout the interview. Facial expressions, body language, mood, and other observable expressions can prove to be very valuable in understanding the totality of the interview. Marginal notes concerning such behavior can be very useful in later analysis, and, of course, such gestures may serve as the cue for the interviewer to refocus or clarify some question or comment.

5. *Motivation and rapport.* A face-to-face interaction can be instrumental in establishing the needed *rapport,* and this often leads to a higher level of *motivation* from a respondent. If the motivation level can be established and maintained, a higher participation rate will be attained, respondents will feel better about participating in the study, and the quality of data is likely to be superior to that obtained when subjects are participating out of "pure" obligation or pressure. In completing a questionnaire or responding to an interview, once the respondent accepts the situation as nonthreatening, the more likely the response will be open, candid, and insightful. This is more likely to occur with the interview since it is personally monitored. As noted by various researchers (Adams, 1958; Converse & Schuman, 1974), it may be necessary at times to limit comments, stories, or details that seem to endlessly spill forth from a respondent, a problem very seldom, if ever, encountered in the mailed questionnaire.

6. *The communication process.* There is good evidence that people *enjoy talking* (Adams, 1958; Converse & Schuman, 1974), and this is a real advantage of the interview as a data-gathering device. The interviewer comes prepared with questions to ask, and hopefully the respondent is in a frame of mind to want to respond to such questions. The interview then is a specific type of communication. As Adams states:

> If the interviewer will remember that he and the individuals he interviews are communicating with each other his task should be greatly facilitated, for many of the principles of interviewing are in reality principles of communication. (1958, p. 6)

This statement helps to establish the fact that the interview is very much an *artful process,* a process in which a sensitive and skilled practitioner can make it easier for respondents to use communication to forward the goals of scientific understanding as well as serve as a very rewarding process through directed conversation.

7. *Sensitive and emotional topics.* The interview is particularly valuable in obtaining information about *sensitive, personal,* and sometimes *perceived deviant data.* Some topics may be perceived as too sensitive to put them on the paper of a questionnaire, but people will talk about these topics to a skilled and sensitive interviewer once trust has been established. Since the interviewer is present, additional assurances can be given to stress that anonymity is guaranteed, that the respondent's help is needed, and that the world will be a better place if the insights and experiences of the respondent are shared through the scientific process. (See Tips for Consumers 10.2.)

Tips for Consumers 10.2

The episode of the interview
We invite consumers to take the following attitude test regarding the interview in their lives.
We are using a 5-point Likert-type scale for this instrument. Please respond honestly to each
item, using the following format—*SA*, strongly agree; *MA*, mildly agree; *U*, undecided; *MD*,
mildly disagree; *SD*, strongly disagree.

1. I enjoy being interviewed by a researcher more than complet-   SA MA U MD SD
   ing a questionnaire form.
2. Sex, race, and social class of an interviewer have almost no   SA MA U MD SD
   bearing on whether I cooperate with a request to be inter-
   viewed for some research project.
3. I seldom ever question the motives of an interviewer.   SA MA U MD SD
4. In my opinion, data are much more valid if they come from   SA MA U MD SD
   an interview setting than from a questionnaire.
5. It has been my observation that men are better at completing   SA MA U MD SD
   questionnaires, whereas women respond better in an inter-
   view situation.
6. Generally, I would rather submit to an interview situation for   SA MA U MD SD
   free than do the same in a questionnaire situation.

THE NATURE AND TYPE OF INTERVIEW

Interviews, like questionnaires, vary widely in form and purpose. The interview can be
very structured, so that all questions are read verbatim, always in the same order using
strict standardization; or the interview can be very permissive, amounting to a free-
flowing conversation between the interviewer and the respondent. As noted previously, the
type of interview used will depend on the purpose of the study, the nature of the
population, the setting, and the topic for the interview. We will now cover some of the
major types of interviews and review some guides in using various types.

The Focused Interview

Merton, Fiske, and Kendall (1956) provide detailed coverage of a style of interview known
as the *focused interview*. The wording of the questions is not strictly specified, but the
interview is nevertheless focused since information is sought on an area experienced by
the respondent. The interviewer comes to the situation with goals in mind, objectives to
be attained, and the questions to be used in accomplishing these purposes. The
researcher is informed and knowledgeable about the focus of the interview and this
enables the interviewer to guide, direct, and interpret the process to achieve the express
purpose of the focused interview, namely, to focus research attention on the background
and experience of the respondent as related to the purpose of the study. As noted by
Merton et al. (1956), certain respondents are sought out for interview because they are

known to have experience (life, school, lectures, films, books, accidents, or political situations) that can provide insight and understanding to a topic in question. The interviewer's knowledge about the situation under study coupled with information about a specific respondent's experience enables the interviewer to guide the interview to achieve certain purposes.

Schneller (1976) in a focused-type interview sought to understand the impact of a ◄ spouse's incarceration on the wife and children through interviews with these family members. The families were contacted and interviewed in their respective homes with an instrument made up of the Locke Short Marital Adjustment Test and the Family Change Scale (the latter scale being constructed for this study). The study involved 93 couples with a total of 236 children, making an average of 2.5 children per couple. Schneller notes that most of the wives were very polite and helpful, expressing gratitude that someone was doing research on this topic, which was, of course, very important to them, and "most of the women talked openly of their personal problems" (p. 38).

We will present four different items from the Family Change Scale with the responses to illustrate type of items and responses to research on a rather sensitive topic. The first item (Table 10.2) focuses on kinship contacts. The second item (Table 10.3) deals with a specific element in everyday life—clothing—and seeks to assess the impact of imprisonment of the husband on the remaining family members in regard to clothing. Sexual relationships with the spouse was the content of the third item (Table 10.4). The final item (Table 10.5) is a follow up of the above item and attempts to understand how the spouse at home would feel about the possibility of having conjugal visits with the husband in prison.

This investigator had a letter of endorsement from the prison and was working "somewhat within the system" to have access to names, addresses, and support to do the research. It is also clear that the interview setting with structured items was helpful in obtaining cooperation and trust to complete the research. The first item from the Family Change Scale presented here focuses on kinship and simply seeks to assess how contacts with kin have fared since the spouse was sent to prison. Responses to this item indicate no dramatic change in lifestyle or daily interaction; sameness is the most common reaction to the husband being at Lorton. The question focusing on clothing, a rather personally tangible factor, elicits a very different reaction from the wives. While the majority say things are about the same as before, a very sizable number report that clothing is now a real problem as compared to before the husband was sent to prison.

As we move from kinship and clothing adequacy to that of sexual relationships, the response reaction to the husband being in prison changes dramatically. Overwhelmingly, the wives miss sexual relations with their husbands and would opt for at least weekly conjugal visits if such were available at Lorton. Schneller (1976) explained what conjugal visits were, talked about help with baby sitting and transportation, as well as making such visits convenient. It seems certain that this type of explanation not only provided clarity for the question, but probably also contributed to the enthusiastic endorsement of such a practice. Schneller's data and methodology do not permit one to determine how much each of these factors (baby sitting, transportation, and convenience) contributed to the response pattern of the wives. This question is a good one to illustrate the point in research that hopefully one obtains at least what one asks, but seldom does one ever receive something in an interview or questionnaire unless it is specifically measured.

TABLE 10.2. Contacts with Family Members While Spouse Is in Prison

*How have your relatives reacted to you since your husband went to Lorton?**

Responses	Number of Families
The relatives are much more helpful or friendly now.	7
The relatives are more helpful or friendly now.	8
The relatives are about the same as before.	57
The relatives are less friendly or helpful now.	8
The relatives are much less friendly or helpful now.	13

*Lorton is the name of the prison.

TABLE 10.3. Family Clothing Status as Related to Impact of Prison

Is the family's clothing different now that your husband is at Lorton?

Responses	Number of Families
Family clothing is much better now.	8
Family clothing is a little better now.	3
Family clothing is about the same as before.	35
Family clothing is not quite as good now.	13
Family clothing is not nearly as good now.	34

TABLE 10.4. Desire for Conjugal Visits with Imprisoned Partner

How often do you miss having sexual relations now that your husband is at Lorton?

Responses	Number of Families
Do not miss sexual relations at all.	5
Miss sexual relations very little.	6
Miss sexual relations about as much as when he was here.	11
Miss sexual relations more often now.	13
Miss sexual relations much more often now.	58

TABLE 10.5. Desired Frequency of Conjugal Visits with Imprisoned Partner

If conjugal visits were allowed at Lorton, how often would you make these visits?

Responses	Number of Families
Would never like to have conjugal visits.	21
Would like conjugal visits once or twice a year.	2
Would like conjugal visits once a month.	8
Would like conjugal visits once a week or oftener.	53

The Nondirective Interview

As the name implies, this interview strategy is not highly structured, but unlike the focused interview, the nondirective interview does not purposefully guide the interview process with some specific goal in mind. Seeking new information or understanding is a desired outcome, but the process is permissive, the direction and type of areas covered are in the respondent's control. It is hoped that a safe and permissive environment for the interview will enable the respondent to express feelings, ideas, and information without fear of being wrong, deviant, or out of place.

Carl Rogers (1951) and others who have promoted client-centered and nondirective counseling have popularized this approach to interviewing and understanding the respondent. As seen by Rogers, the counselor's or interviewer's purpose is to provide a safe setting, a dialogue framework for interaction, but the respondent sets the pace, tone, mood, and is responsible for the content of the interview. The skill of the interviewer is manifest by inviting the client to talk, to express, to explore. Furthermore, the interviewer does not approve or disapprove, but is merely supportive of the respondent through warmth, acceptance, alertness, and empathic understanding.

The Clinical Interview

The clinical interview (Hyman, 1954; Selltiz, Wrightsman, & Cook, 1976) is very similar to the focused interview and finds its most frequent usage in social casework, counseling, and prison work settings where it is commonly known as a personal history interview. This type of interview is flexible and moderately unstructured as the interviewer will map out a domain of interest for the interview, but it is the client who controls direction and intensity. Introductory questions inviting the client to "Tell me about your family," "What about your early years of school," or "Help us understand what your peer group was like" are all examples of this approach, and the interviewer would typically be searching in these areas for their potential to shed light on a variety of research questions such as homosexuality, assassination potential, or runaway disposition.

While the clinical interview has some focus, it is perfectly acceptable for the respondent to mention other factors and elaborate on such; in fact, this is one of the strong points of the clinical interview. These new points of view may turn out to be very useful in making some prediction, diagnosis, or prognosis concerning a person or situation. The purpose of the study or planned usage determines the direction, the type of guide questions, and the areas of content covered in the clinical interview.

Telephone Interviews

Telephone interviews are extensively used in such activities as polls, market research, and other survey projects. The rapidity with which contact can be established and data gathered constitutes the main advantage of telephone interviewing. Furthermore, one does not have to leave the work setting and venture out to find people; one merely needs a directory, questions, and the phone to obtain extensive amounts of research data.

We have noted that the questionnaire is less expensive to use than the interview, and the cost factor becomes an additional advantage of the telephone interview since it is even less expensive than the questionnaire. Unless one is paying for long-distance calls, the additional use of already existing phones for extensive interviewing generates no additional phone expenses. Parten (1966) notes that one can complete about 30 calls per hour on selected topics if the calls are brief. She notes that the telephone is particularly useful in assessing listening habits for radio research. Furthermore, the refusal rate in telephone work tends to be very low, and it is rather easy to standardize the questions and approach to be used by the interviewer.

Along with these inviting reasons for using the telephone as a device for interviewing come disadvantages—sample representativeness is of particular concern. Not all potential respondents can be reached, because they do not have telephones or else they have unlisted numbers. Thus, people not available for telephone contact are the very poor who cannot afford a phone in their home and the well-to-do who do not wish to be "bothered" by unsolicited telephone contact.

Parten (1966) notes that it is difficult to obtain detailed or lengthy information by phone, as most people expect a phone call to be short. Respondents quickly lose their motivation and desire to cooperate if the interview goes very long. A long interview may easily push someone to hang up or give distortive responses as a way of "getting even" with you for bothering them. The telephone interview, like a mailed questionnaire, does not make the interviewer capable of observing anything about the person or the interview situation. Visual cues do not exist, and few symbolic factors other than voice tone can be picked up on the phone.

The interviewer is often placed at the mercy of the respondent to cooperate, as a good number of people are apprehensive about getting "a sales pitch" on the phone and have little incentive to stay on long enough for you to establish sufficient credibility to state your real purpose. Again, the extent of misinformation is very hard to detect.

Administration of Questionnaire and Interview

In addition to the types of interviews just reviewed in this section, the reader is invited to apply the advantages, disadvantages, and rules of application from the questionnaire section to the interview section since we are essentially dealing with the same process. Unless a questionnaire is mailed, it must be given to somebody personally, and this personal contact is typical in an interview situation or a captive audience such as a class or group gathering. Questionnaires can be handed out in a supermarket, street, convention, or other setting with instructions for the respondent to mail them, place them in the "box," or give them to the door attendant. It is important to keep in mind that the questionnaire as an instrument may be the same whether it is mailed or used in an interview situation. Furthermore, questionnaires are sometimes administered personally by an interviewer who introduces himself or herself, the purpose of the study, and then gives the form to the respondent to complete while the interviewer waits. The advantage to this approach is that one is available to answer questions, give directions, and offer support, but the respondent is free to work at his or her own pace rather than the pace set by the interviewer. Additionally, the setting can be more thoroughly controlled if the interviewer is present, and this is especially important in family research where both spouses are instructed to complete a questionnaire separately. The presence of the interviewer is about the only way that independence of response can be assured. In the Schvaneveldt (1970) study of rural and urban aged populations, two interviewers would call at a home (appointments were made ahead of time), and the male interviewer interviewed the husband in one room and a female interviewer interviewed the wife in another room. The age, health, and anticipated education level of this population dictated that this was the most appropriate method for obtaining valid and reliable data. The personal contact, rapport, and secondary comments proved this approach to be a useful strategy.

THE ART OF INTERVIEWING

There is not a single predictable formula that can be used to assure that a person will be successful as an interviewer. Type of study, composition of a population, and historical-social factors all impinge upon success and failure in the interview process. Our goal here, then, is to review major guides proven to be useful in successful interviewing.

Presentation of Self

One often hears that common sense should prevail, but we would like to briefly add some pointers to the realm of common sense in *dress* and *grooming*. The key goal is that of appropriateness, and this perhaps should be a state of neutrality in clothing and grooming. Excesses should be avoided whether they be clothing, makeup, and accessories, or general physical appearance. The first impression is important and the interviewer should not present a self that is so startling, disruptive, or negative that the respondents resist or refuse to cooperate. Knowing one's audience is important, and then one should dress and present the self to complement that audience. Adams (1958) notes that "the first impression the interviewer makes should leave him 'nameless,' and the impression should be maintained throughout the interview" (p. 17). Knowing one's audience will do much to instruct the interviewer regarding hair style, length of hair, beards of men, and other factors of physical presentation of self.

The goal in presenting the self should be that of making a good impression, or appearing neutral, to complement or blend into the setting of the interview, and to invite people to help you in your goal of getting the information necessary to make the interview successful. Any part of dress or presentation of self that runs the risk of causing people to form inappropriate impressions of you and your task should be avoided.

The Door Approach

Knocking on the door or ringing the door bell should be done in a pleasant manner, being careful to avoid an impression of aggression, compulsion, or impatience. Waiting a reasonable amount of time before a second knock or ring should be done to avoid the impression of aggression or impatience. The opening remark to the person answering the door should be pleasant and friendly—the appropriate greeting for the time of day followed by a brief statement in which you tell the respondent what you are doing, whom you represent, and what you would now like from the respondent. Avoid giving a "big" speech at this point: opening remarks should be brief, but informative enough to let the respondent know that you are not selling, it is anonymous, it is harmless, and it will only take *x* amount of time. Parten (1966) cautions against using the word *investigation* or *investigator* at the door and suggests that one use a more neutral label such as *study*, *survey*, or *opinion poll*.

Self-confidence, belief in the importance of your work, the scientific merit of the research, and the value of talking to this particular person should all be a part of the "door approach and greeting to a respondent." We recommend that the interviewer maintain a constant assumption that people will talk, be helpful, find the interview to be interesting and will be somewhat flattered to be selected for the interview. This frame of reference by the interviewer will help to eliminate self-defeating introductions and approaches that invite a potential respondent to turn you down, such as "Do you have a few minutes to help?" "Would you mind helping me on this study?" or "If you are not busy now, I would like to talk to you." A friendly greeting, clear statement of purpose, followed by a positive invitation to help in the study, and then moving directly to the first question will greatly increase the cooperation rate. We recommend an approach something like: "Good evening. I am completing a survey to determine how people in the community feel about water distribution in the region. In general, how do you feel about the proposal to permit more water to be distributed to the other region?"

Conducting a Quality Interview

Treating people with respect and courtesy will go a long way toward making the interview a professional experience for both the interviewer and respondent. There are no direct or easy ways to accomplish this, but we do have a number of "dos and don'ts" to share in helping to achieve this goal. Being aware that *time* is very important to both you and the respondent and then using time as efficiently as possible are two important ways to make the interview a quality experience. Meeting and working with people on their own level, in their own setting, and making them feel good about that setting and themselves are also important. The friendly greeting can be appropriately followed by sincere observations concerning hobbies, yard, flowers, decoration, or other points of conversation to "break the ice" or "warm people up" for the interview to follow.

    Converse and Schuman (1974) relate the following episode about ego involvement versus professionalism in the interview setting:

> I found the temptation to handle situations in such a way that respondents would like me was overwhelming. In most cases it had nothing to do with the gluey term *rapport*. I just wanted people to like me—for my own ego. So I nodded like mad, murmured encouraging sounds, looked terribly interested, laughed at all jokes, patted all dogs, said hello to all children, etc., because those seemed to be good ways to get people to like me. (p. 11)

As this example illustrates, the desire to be liked or accepted in a situation can sometimes get in the way of doing a professional job; there is nothing wrong with that desire, but it should not contaminate or bias the interview process.

The quality interview allows the respondent to react, to speak out, to give responses and opinions without censorship from the interviewer. Facial expressions are very important in this context, and verbal comments represent just one way to inappropriately influence the respondent. If your own feeling is a positive one regarding some question and you are nodding your head "yes" in anticipating the respondent's answer, you are definitely violating the rule of neutrality in working with a respondent. One should continually stress to the respondent that there are really no right or wrong answers to the questions, just varying degrees of attitudes, or whatever holds "true" for you, and then allow the respondent to function within that context throughout the interview.

If it is a highly structured questionnaire used in the interview, then the interviewer is professionally committed to follow the schedule as outlined, including the question order, working on directions, and uniformity for possible response categories. If this process is not followed, then the major purpose of using the structured form has been violated, namely, the need to have comparability between answers. If the interviewer is seeking data on church membership and one interviewer asks, "What church did you grow up in?" another asks, "What church do you now attend?" and a third interviewer asks, "What church do you currently belong to?" we have a clear example as to why the question must be framed exactly the same in all three cases. Responses to these three questions as presented are worthless if one truly wants to know about church membership across a sample.

Related to the question of sequence and exact wording is the need to ask all respondents all of the questions. Unless the question is a factual question that has already been answered, the interviewer should ask all questions. It is certainly permissible to preface asking a repeated question with a phrase such as, "We have covered this in part earlier," or "I know you dealt with this area just a minute ago, but let me ask you...." Such phrases tell the respondent you are sensitive to what is going on and that you recognize his or her vital role in supplying responses to the series of questions. Additionally, you must not skip over a question because you feel you know the answer the respondent would give or skip and item because the interviewer feels uncomfortable asking the question. Sometimes questions about race, income, sexual activity, or other personal questions are glossed over because the interviewer does not feel comfortable asking such items.

Rapport and Morale Level

Some interview sessions can be very lengthy, involved, and highly complex, and in such a setting the interviewer has a special obligation to keep the pace moving, thank the respondent as you go along, and be involved with the process along with the respondent. It is sometimes tempting to go through the form like a recording which communicates a nonpersonal feeling to the respondent. A personal, caring, sensitive, and appreciative attitude is very important if motivation is to remain high and if rapport is to be established and maintained throughout the interview.

To cope with fatigue it is appropriate to digress for a brief period and talk about something else of interest to the respondent. One can then get back to the form with a variety of statements such as, "That is a most interesting topic, but we must move on in order to finish in the next few minutes." It is also important to remind the respondent that his or her point of view is vital to understand the whole "picture," or that his or her responses will be blended in with others and no individual answers will be used. Such statements help to remove the personal nature or the burden of response from the respondent and help to increase a willingness to "stay with you just a little while longer."

Probes

A probe is a clarifier, "another run at the questions," or a way of helping the respondent to see the question or supply an answer for a given type of question. Sometimes instructions on a form will instruct the interviewer to probe if necessary, but probes may also be necessary on other items, and a sensitive interviewer should be ready. Adams (1958) says the two types of probes, *those which are printed in question form* and those which *arise spontaneously in the interview,* are vital to obtaining quality data. *Questionnaire probes,* the first type, are specific questions to obtain more detailed information following a more general question. *Interviewer probes,* the second type, require that the interviewer "read" the respondent and interview setting to determine when and if additional questions are needed to obtain full and clear responses.

Six types of probes (Adams, 1958) will be very briefly presented for the benefit of understanding the "what" and the "how" of probes in completing quality interviews. First, the *completion* probe is an invitation to expand to give more, and to round out the response already given— "Anything else?" (p. 25). The second type of probe, *clarification*, is primarily concerned with explaining something in more detail, which, of course, also renders more information— "Please go over that one more time." A third type is called a *channel* probe and is used to determine the origin or uncover the source of a comment made by the respondent—if the respondent says "they say" or "I have heard" in response to a question asked in the interview, a channel probe might be, "Would you please indicate the identity of *they*?" The purpose of a channel probe is to get at the origin of who *said* or *did* something alluded to by the respondent.

Hypothetical probes are useful when it is important to understand alternatives or variations of attitude that a respondent may hold on a given point, for example, the question, "Do you believe all guns should be outlawed?" If a respondent were to say, "I don't think that outlawing *all* guns is the answer to preventing crimes," a hypothetical probe to this response might be, "What guns should be outlawed in your opinion?" A fifth type, *reactive probes,* are designed to bring out additional "affective reactions or feelings to situations which have been mentioned by the respondent" (p. 26). To a question on gun control a respondent might say, "Our community does not want gun control in any form." The interviewer could profitably use a probe here to obtain a reaction, such as, "What is your *own* personal attitude toward gun control?" and the respondent might reply, "All *handguns* should be totally banned from the general public." The last type of probe is a *high-pressure* type to challenge a respondent or push a respondent for the ultimate truth as he or she really sees it. This type of probe should be used only when rapport is very high and then only with caution. A probe of this type helps to push a respondent to be more candid when there is some reason to believe that responses are "good polite responses" and do not reflect true feelings. Questions about hiring minorities, women, or anti-Semitism are often met with very general "all is well" answers, and here the interviewer might directly ask, "Do *you* personally approve of that practice?" (p. 27).

TO RECORD OR NOT TO RECORD: THAT IS THE QUESTION

If it is a highly structured questionnaire with straightforward response categories, then it is a simple and direct process to record all responses as given, and this should be done. Even the best of interviewers cannot remember well enough to go back and fill in missing data at the end of the interview, or worse yet, at the end of the day. All other things being considered equal, it is best to record fully and accurately in the situation as the data emerge.

If you are working for an agency, the directions and training for the project should instruct you regarding the recording question. Since you as an interviewer are really a "go between" for the agency and the respondent, it is very important that you follow the instructions given. For open-ended items or probes, it is important to record statements just as given, especially if responses are short. For long and involved responses, it is important to capture the main substance of the responses, and if the exact wording is needed then it may be necessary to use a tape recorder to obtain a verbatim copy of what is shared. If a recorder is to be used, it should be cleared with each respondent and used in an unobtrusive manner.

Clear, precise, and legible responses are needed if the information is to have optimum utility. If some items have missing responses, the interviewer should write in the reason for no response ("does not apply"; "subject would not answer"; etc.). *Do not just leave the item blank with no explanation.*

Interviewers for a project should find out if comments should be made in the margins, on the back, or both, and then follow such procedures. Such comments should be clear and tied to specific questions so that coders will be able to interpret and use comments in the most fruitful manner. It may be advisable that all probes given by the interviewer be recorded in parentheses. If this practice is strictly followed, then it is relatively easy to interpret the frequency and type of probes used throughout the interview (Adams, 1958).

Regardless of the ease of the recording process for the interviewer, we believe it is a good idea to tell the respondent that you are completing a form, checking responses, or attempting to "capture" the main line of thought. This sharing process helps to maintain cooperation, assures the respondent as to what you are really doing, and promotes trust. If the interview situation permits for proximity seating, you may want to let the respondent actually see you mark responses as the interview continues. Openness, trust, and truthfulness can be developed only if the respondent sees the interviewer as a truthful and open person. The appearance of trying to hide, conceal, or "be sneaky" can raise havoc with the interview situation.

In sum, interviewing is a useful process for collecting a broad range of data from a wide array of respondents. If a respondent can talk, then the potential for a successful interview exists. If the respondent is motivated to help and the interviewer is successful in establishing rapport, then a quality interview is probable. Three factors function to make a successful interview: (1) having a thoroughly tested questionnaire or interview form from which to work, (2) being familiar and "wise" in the interview process, and (3) treating respondents with trust, respect, and courtesy. Interviewing is a *methodological operation* because one can learn and use certain guides in the procedures for successful interviewing. A parallel claim is that interviewing is an *art,* because insight, creativity, personality, adaptability, flexibility, tact, graciousness, and friendliness are needed if the interview is to be successful. The successful blend of *method* and *art* is the goal of interviewers dedicated to obtaining quality data for successful research.

PERSPECTIVE-TAKING ABOUT QUESTIONNAIRES AND INTERVIEWS AS METHODS FOR COLLECTING DATA

These two strategies have no close competitor in terms of their utility and frequency of use in social science research. They are flexible, yet can be most specific. They contrast with observation, which focuses on behavior as it emerges; the questionnaire and interview more often than not are used to collect data on attitudes, behavior, or information from the past. Hardly any data collection approach avoids the use of one or both of these strategies, again noting the great flexibility of questionnaires and interviews. Questionnaires can be mailed and interviews can be conducted on the phone, two specific attributes which contrast with the collection modes of observation or the use of documents. A major limitation of the two modes is the necessity for the respondent to either talk or write about themselves or a situation. (See Zeisel, 1981, for a review of issues concerning questionnaires and interviews.)

Issues in Validity and Reliability

If we can safely assume that individuals, groups, and classes are willing and capable of talking to us or completing various forms, then we have the potential of great research utility with interviews and questionnaires. If we can furthermore assume that people are honestly supplying requested information, then both of these avenues for data collection can be both highly reliable and valid. The interview is probably more sensitive than the questionnaire in terms of coping with issues of validity. They are the two most common types of data collection devices in general social science and the most highly criticized for lacking sufficient reliability and validity. No instrument should be used unless it has some basis for coping with or establishing information concerning both reliability and validity.

SUMMARY

Questionnaires and interview procedures remain long-established devices for the collection of data in all realms of social science. This high degree of usage is attributed in part to the great flexibility of these devices, the nature of where the data are located (in the experiences and memories of people), the ease of collection (mailed questionnaires and captive student-like audiences), and professional training (social scientists know more about using these approaches). Either of these devices can be highly structured or rather unstructured in construction, and the style of question within both questionnaires and the interview can range from closed-ended to open-ended, simple "yes" and "no" responses, frequency and intensity, semantic differential rating scale, and ranking to that of the objective information style used to collect demographic data about respondents. Highlights of this chapter include:

Questionnaires

1. A questionnaire is a grouping or list of written questions that a respondent answers. It is a data gathering device that elicits from the respondent answers or reactions to printed (pre-arranged) questions.
2. Questions may be open-ended allowing the respondent to supply information in an unstructured manner, or closed-ended in which the respondent checks categories.
3. Constructing a good questionnaire is important in order to elicit cooperation of the subject as well as to gain relevant information. Suggestions include the following:
    a. The questionnaire should be attractive in appearance, easy to read, and clear to follow.

    b.   Wording should be clear and presented in a style familiar to all respondents.

    c.   Avoid double-barreled questions and loaded questions leading to a particular point of view.

    d.   Design questions to apply to all respondents in the sample.

    e.   Guard against using questionnaire items that lead to response set problems.

    f.   Consider using warm-up items to prepare the respondent to answer more sensitive questions, but avoid leaving sensitive questions until the very end.

4.   Style and types of questions include the following:

    a.   Likert-type scale—Respondents check items varying in intensity ranging from low to high.

    b.   Cafeteria style—The respondent checks all items that are applicable.

    c.   Questions referring to the amount or quantity of a particular activity or behavior (Example: The Law-Abidingness Scale).

    d.   Semantic differential scale—This format uses a rating scale placed between two adjectives which have polar dimensions (Hot–Cold).

    e.   Ranked items format or order-of-merit method. Avoid as much as possible using more than six items.

Interview

1.   Advantages

    a.   The interviewer is present to explain, clarify, and correct any misinterpretations.

    b.   It is possible to observe the respondent.

    c.   People are more willing to talk than write.

2.   Disadvantages

    a.   Time

    b.   Cost

    c.   Interviewer bias

3.   Types of Interviews

    a.   Focused—the researcher has specific goals in mind and guides, directs, and focuses the interview.

    b.   Nondirective—the process is permissive, and the direction and type of areas covered are controlled by the respondent.

    c.   Clinical—the interviewer maps out the domain of interest, but the client controls direction and intensity.

    d.   Telephone—popular due to low cost and easy to accomplish. Most successful when brief.

4.   The Art of Interviewing

    a.   Presentation of self

        1.   common sense in dress and grooming

        2.   pleasant manner

        3.   self-confidence

    b.   Treat respondents with respect and courtesy.

    c.   Maintain neutrality during the interview.

    d.   A caring, sensitive, and appreciative attitude facilitates the interview process.

    e.   Thank the respondent for participating.

Probes

1. Probes are devices that clarify or stimulate the respondent to focus a certain way.
2. Categories
    a. structured questionnaire probes
    b. interviewer probes
3. Types
    a. completion
    b. clarification
    c. channel
    d. hypothetical
    e. reactive
    f. high-pressure

PROBLEMS AND APPLICATIONS

1. Conduct an intensive, unstructured interview with some person in your community and a structured interview with another. Contrast the instrument and the type of information derived from these two types of interviews. Which type was the most difficult for you? Why?

2. Talk with a personnel director, head nurse at the local hospital, or the research bureau director on your campus setting. In your talks with these people, find out their main points on successful interviewing of people, what to do, what to avoid.

3. Contrast the main advantages and disadvantages of questionnaires and interviews. What is your overall conclusion?

4. Survey several recent studies published in your major area of study, determine what types of questionnaires and interviews have been used most frequently. Rationalize why your major area uses the data collection it uses.

5. What would you do to obtain a higher rate of questionnaire return or increase the response cooperation in an interview study?

6. Have a panel of students debate the strengths and weaknesses of interviews and questionnaires in conducting quality research in the social sciences.

REFERENCES

Adams, J. S. (1958). *Interviewing procedures: A manual for survey interviewers.* (Chapel Hill, N.C.: The University of North Carolina Press.

America's abortion dilemma. (1985, January 14). *Newsweek,* pp. 20–25.

Bailey, K. D. (1978). *Methods of social research.* New York: The Free Press.

Belson, W. A. (1981). *The design and understanding of survey questions.* Aldershot, Hants, England: Gower Publishing Company.

Berdie, D. R., & Anderson, J. F. (1974). *Questionnaires: Design and use.* Metuchen, N.J.: Scarecrow Press.

Bradburn, N. M., & Sudman, S. (1979). *Improving interview method and questionnaire design.* San Francisco: Jossey-Bass.

Converse, J. M., & Schuman, H. (1974). *Conversations at random: Survey research as interviewers see it.* New York: Wiley.

Gregory, W. S. (1939). Ideology and effect regarding "law" and their relation to "law-abidingness." Part 1, *Character and Personality, 7,* 265–284. In M. E. Shaw & J. M. Wright, (Eds). *Scales for the measurement of attitudes.* New York: McGraw-Hill.

Gullahorn, J. E., & Gullahorn, J. T. (1963). An investigation of the effects of three factors on response to mail questionnaires. *Public Opinion Quarterly, 27,* 294–296.

Henshaw, S. K., & Martire, G. (1982). Abortion and public opinion polls: Morality and legality. *Family Planning Perspectives, 14,* 53.

Hyman, H. H. (1954). *Interviewing in social research.* Chicago: The University of Chicago Press.

Merton, R. K., Friske, M. O., & Kendall, P. L. (1956). *The focused interview.* New York: The Free Press.

Metzener, H., & Mann, F. (1952). A limited comparison of two methods of data collection: The fixed-alternative questionnaire and the open-ended interview. *American Sociological Review, 17,* 486–491.

Oppenheim, A. N. (1966). *Questionnaire design and attitude measurement.* New York: Basic Books.

Osgood, C. E., Suci, G. J., & Tannenbaum, P. H. (1957). *The measurement of meaning.* Urbana, Ill.: University of Illinois Press.

Parten, M. (1966). *Survey, polls, and samples: Practical procedures.* New York: Cooper Square.

Phillips, B. S. (1966). *Social Research: Strategy and Tactics.* New York: The Macmillan Co.

Phillips, D. P. (1971). *Knowledge from what: Theories and methods in social research.* Chicago: Rand McNally.

Roeher, G. A. (1963). Effective techniques in increasing response to mailed questionnaires. *Public Opinion Quarterly, 27,* 299–302.

Rogers, C. R. (1951). *Client-centered therapy.* Boston: Houghton Mifflin.

Schneller, D. P. (1976). *The prisoner's family: A study of the effects of imprisonment on the families of prisoners.* San Francisco: Rand Research Associates.

Schvaneveldt, J. D. (1970). *Family member interaction in a rural and urban aged population.* Research paper, Research Foundation, Utah State University, Logan.

Smith, H. W. (1975). *Strategies of social research.* Englewood Cliffs, N.J.: Prentice-Hall.

Selltiz, C., Wrightsman, L. S., & Cook, S. W. (1976). *Research methods in social relations.* New York: Holt, Rinehart and Winston.

Stewart C. J., & Cash, W. B., Jr. (1982). *Interviewing principles and practices.* Dubuque, Iowa: Wm. C. Brown.

Warwick, D. P., & Lininger, C. A. (1975). *The sample survey: Theory and practice.* New York: McGraw-Hill.

Webb, E. J., Campbell, D. T., Schwartz, R. D., & Sechrest, L. (1971). *Unobtrusive measures.* Chicago: Rand McNally.

Wright, L. S., & Rogers, R. R. (1987). Variables related to pro-choice attitudes among undergraduates. *Adolescence, 22,* (87), 516–525.

Zeisel, J. (1981). *Inquiry by design: Tools for environment-behavior research.* Monterey, Calif.: Brooks/Cole.

CHAPTER 11

Obtaining Data: Observational Techniques

OUTLINE

Introduction
A Classification of Observational Methods
    Observational Research with Low Environmental Structure
        Participant–Observer Methodology
        Nonstructured Field Observation Methodology
    Observational Research with High Environmental Structure
        Structured Field Experiment Study
        Laboratory Observation Studies
        Summary
The Technology of Observation
Observation of Behavior through the Unobtrusive Technique
    Validity and Reliability Issues
Summary
Problems and Applications
References

KEY TERMS

Formal and informal rating techniques	Reactivity
Structuring of environment	Subject bias
Participant–Observer	Tape recorder
Nonstructured field observation	Event recorder
Field notation	One-way mirror

Frequency, duration, and latency
Time and event sampling
Trait rating
Structured field experiment
Laboratory observation
Inter-rater reliability
Observer bias

Camera filming
Videotaping
Obtrusiveness/Unobtrusiveness
Archival data
Physical traces
Transcontextual validity

STUDY GUIDE QUESTIONS

1. Observational techniques vary according to the type of rating of behavior used and the degree to which the researcher attempts to provide structure to the research setting. Using these two dimensions how can we conceptualize four basic types of observational techniques?
2. What is meant by participant–observer methodology?
3. How does a nonstructured field observation research technique differ from that of a structured field experiment? How do both of these techniques differ from the laboratory observation study?
4. What are the basic observational technologies used in contemporary observational research?
5. What is meant by an unobtrusive observational technique? How do such techniques differ from the more conventional observational research strategies?
6. How does a researcher deal with issues of internal validity in observational research strategies?

Role of the Scientist

Observational techniques, like rating scales, are essential measurement skills in the scientific process. In this chapter, we review four well known and frequently used observational techniques. Several specific suggestions regarding appropriate strategies are provided. Students in training for scientific careers should understand the basic differences and similarities between the four types. Further, they should recognize the advantages and the disadvantages of each technique for research in their own interest areas.

Role of the Consumer

All forms of research involve gathering accurate information through some form of observation—be it direct or indirect. Information gathered through observation of behavior (versus indirect descriptions from such things as surveys, scales, or interviews) provides "direct" evidence. Such evidence, however, can be based on qualitative descriptive accounts or from quantitative numerical-based observational strategies. In utilizing observational research, consumers should come to understand how the information is obtained and how results are comparable (or not) across observational strategies, while recognizing the strengths and limitations of reported findings from each observational technique. Further, consumers of observational research should understand how each technique deals with internal and external validity and reliability of measurement.

INTRODUCTION

Many classic works of social science have come to us through observational strategies. Such notable works as Bronislaw Malinowski's cultural comparisons of sexual behaviors and attitudes *(Sex, Culture and Myth,* 1962), Margaret Mead's observations of psychological and social behavior of primitive youth in Samoa *(Coming of Age in Samoa,* 1928), ethnological observations on the cooperation and competition of such diverse cultures as the Arapesh of New Guinea, the Eskimo of Greenland, the Ifugao of the Philippine Islands, or Zuni of New Mexico (Mead, *Cooperation and Competition among Primitive Peoples,* 1937), Ruth Benedict's work on cultural relativism of small primitive tribes *(Patterns of Culture,* 1946), Masters and Johnson's vivid detail of the human body and its response to erotic stimulation *(Human Sexual Response,* 1966), Kenneth Keniston's detailed commentary on alienated youth *(Youth and Dissent,* 1971), Liebow's observations of street behavior *(Tally's Corner: A Study of Negro Street-Corner Men,* 1967), and Oscar Lewis' observation of five Mexican families *(Five Families: Mexican Case Studies in the Culture of Poverty,* 1959) are just a few of the many vivid illustrations of observational methodology in its classic form.

While observational strategies are excellent primary techniques for gathering data, it can be difficult to understand the differences between the many utilized strategies. Therefore, we begin this chapter by providing a conceptualization that delineates four basic types of observational strategies commonly utilized in social science research.

A CLASSIFICATION OF OBSERVATIONAL METHODS

Any student, examining the various research reports in the professional social science literature, will appreciate the variety of observational techniques there are to be utilized in collecting data. However, most of the currently used observational methodologies actually fit into one of four basic methods. These four methods are depicted on two-dimensional figural axes in Figure 11.1.

Observational methods can be analyzed on two simple dimensions. First, researchers must make a decision about the use of *formal* or *informal rating techniques.* A rating technique is simply the manner in which information is gathered and recorded. Informal rating techniques are less structured and allow more freedom in recording information. Typically, such strategies consist of note taking, diary keeping, gathering informant information, and the like. Information gathered in this manner is less structured, richly complex, and highly divergent but requires the researcher to synthesize, abstract, and organize the data content. Formal rating techniques, in comparison, place a great deal of structure or direction on what is to be observed. This latter technique requires the

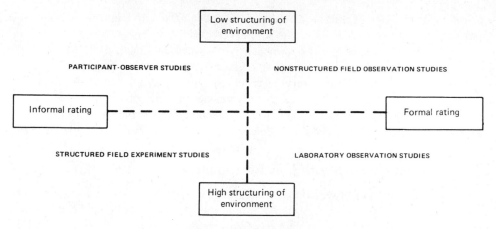

Figure 11.1. A Two-dimensional Conceptualization of Observational Techniques

researcher to attend to only observable behavior of a specific nature (kind). All other behavior, not concretely specified in the rating form, is treated as irrelevant and nonessential information. In contrast to the informal rating technique, the formal rating strategy provides more specific information, is limited to only those behaviors delineated by the rating form but requires less synthesizing and organizing by the researcher. Perhaps it can be seen, given the issues outlined in Chapter 4 on reliability and validity, that the informal rating technique, while providing much richer and more complete information about a behavioral setting, is more difficult to utilize with a high degree of reliability and validity. (This is not to imply that the latter is impossible, only more difficult.) In comparison, formal rating strategies can be more readily documented as having acceptable levels of reliability and validity, but are greatly limited in the scope (breadth or range) of behavior observed. In general, a good rule of thumb is, the more structure or direction provided by rating scales that focus the observer's attention on specific observable behaviors, the greater the chance of establishing high levels of reliability in measurement.

The second dimension that can be utilized in defining the four predominant types of observational methodologies has to do with the degree of structure placed on the behavioral setting. Behavioral settings, as defined by Barker (1968), consist of an ecological unit in which commonplace behavior of an everyday nature occurs. Such ecological units, in our minds, have been either highly specified, and thus extremely structured, or left unspecified, and thus low structured. In the case of high structure, the setting in which behavior is observed is very specific and usually highly detailed in the research report. In low structuring studies, the environment or ecological unit is very broad, frequently expansive, and defined in only general terminology. For example, a highly structured observational study would be one where the researchers report watching behavior on benches adjacent to bus stop locations. A low structured study would be one where an individual is observed in normal activities over a typical day, which might include observations at home, work, or church, during recreational periods, with friends or strangers, in town, out-of-town, and so forth. This latter dimension might likewise include observations dealing with cultural or subcultural environments, social class settings, or behaviors observed across several independent behavioral settings.

Through the use of the two dimensions, outlined in Figure 11.1, four specific observational strategies can be noted which have a relatively high frequency of use in social science research. While serving a heuristic (or analytic) value, the beginning student should not view this figure as the only manner in which observational techniques can be differentiated. Rather, its use has been intended to assist the student in making a meaningful distinction between the various extreme types of observational techniques.

Observational Research with Low Environmental Structure

There are two types of observational strategies that place few limits on the structural elements of a behavioral setting (Weller & Romney, 1988). These techniques can be called the *participant–observer* and the *nonstructured field observation methodologies*. Both strategies allow behavior to flow in its natural ecological sense (i.e., place few limits on the specifics of the behavioral settings, allowing behavior to move from one ecological area to another, or from one space to another). However, the two strategies differ greatly on the types of observational rating techniques that are used. Participant–observer research is typically more informal, while the nonstructured field study is usually highly formal in its rating strategy techniques. More specific details of each methodology will be briefly summarized in the following sections.

Participant–Observer Methodology.   Historically the participant–observer methodology has been the most acceptable form of observation—particularly among sociologists and anthropologists. As the term participant–observer implies, the researcher is located in an intimate relationship with the subjects. Bogdan (1972) has characterized participant observation research as "a prolonged period of intense social interaction between the researcher and the subjects, in the milieu of the latter, during which time data, in the form of field notes, are unobtrusively and systematically collected" (p. 3). Hence, the researcher engages in observation of people's behavior in everyday life activities to understand individuals' social relations and behavior within the broad social ecology in which they live.

Perhaps the role of the observer takes the most important or central role in this methodology (Fielding & Fielding, 1986). The observer can assume the role of *complete involvement* where the observer attempts to become an accepted member of a specific group for the purpose of scientific study, without making this intention known to the infiltrated group. Or the researcher can make the *role as observer* completely *open* and clearly stated as to intent to the observed group membership. Certain cautions have been advanced about the role of the observer (e.g., see Fine & Sandstrom, 1988). Junker (1960) maintains the participant-as-observer, as the phrase conveys, may err toward subjectivity and sympathy due to personal involvement with the research subject, while the observer-as-participant is more likely to lean toward objectivity with empathy. This distinction is an important one, for the investigator must always remain objective about the task and, to do so, must be cautious not to become so involved in the daily personal transactions of people as to lose sight of the objective research goals. This, of course, is always the problem of the complete involvement technique. Thus complete involvement, due to unconscious biases, may result in threats to gathering reliable and valid data.

Denzen (1970a,b), in a description of the features of participant observation, has pinpointed the three central assumptions of participant observation research. First, as we have already noted, the researcher shares an intimate relationship with the subject(s). Second, and perhaps much more difficult for the researcher, is the assumption that the investigator will share the "symbolic world" of the subject–participant. That is, the researcher will learn the language, symbolism, social conventions, and nonverbal communications of the individuals under observation. Finally, the researcher must establish a role within the context of the participant–observation setting. This may be seen as using some degree of ingenuity at utilizing one's personality and past experiences in defining an individual role identity. Collectively, these three methodological assumptions are demanding in time, energy, and know-how. They require the researcher to submerge himself or herself into the social world of the participant—a task which many researchers are not capable of or prepared to assume.

The participant–observer experience is both an intimate and intense one (Pearsall, 1965; McCracken, 1988). Specific research phases have been identified by Bogdan (1972) and Olesen and Whittaker (1970). In particular, the latter researchers have delineated the four phases of social interactional exchange which occur between the researcher and the participant. Each of these phases contains elements of reciprocity in the roles of coming to understand the circumstances under which the participant lives. During the early phase a "surface encounter" begins where the researcher and the participant merely make initial contact and begin to build a tolerance for each other. The second phase of the role-making process becomes the first crucial stage of the participant–observer process. During this phase, the participant and observer begin to clarify each other's roles through invited questions and answers. Furthermore, certain rules and regulations emerge during this period as to what form the communication will take (i.e., acceptance of profanity, certain types of gestures, communicative styles, etc.). The third phase primarily consists of the researcher and participant accepting mutually agreed upon "meaningful" definitions for their roles during the research experience. Closure to the third phase results in stabilization and the sustainment of interpersonal exchange based on mutually acceptable definitions of researcher roles. Information gathered at each of these four phases may actually be qualitatively different information, with latter phase information more likely to be sensitive and in-depth. Prior to the fourth phase the data may be primarily descriptive and superficial; however, after the fourth phase is completed the participant may offer important insight as to the dynamics of social relationships, group organization, or such factors as social costs and benefits.

But how are the data actually gathered in this technique of observational research? While several strategies have been employed in participant–observer research, the primary tools consist of watching, asking questions, and "eavesdropping." Once mutual reciprocity is obtained between the participant and observer, the researcher maintains an unassuming role, the observer watches and asks certain nondirective questions. Through questions, elaborations and clarifications are sought. While eavesdropping is not typically acceptable social behavior, subtle eavesdropping can be very informative. In fact, eavesdropping may be an unfair description given an open involvement participant-observer technique. In this technique, an understanding of the ground rules makes listening and observing a legitimate and acceptable activity.

Recording of the data in participant–observer research typically takes one of two forms. The most common technique is the *field notation* strategy where the researcher records notes as soon as possible after a social contact. These notes are kept in systematic and objective manners with all the necessary information about the behavioral setting recorded along with descriptive information about the event, the actors, and verbatim comments where appropriate or possible. While typically these notes are recorded in privacy, a second technique has been used by some investigators in which notes are recorded in the field—visible to the participant, but not obviously so. For example, participant–observer research in school systems lends itself to field notes. Taking notes during educational experiences is a common practice and thus would not stand out as an unusual behavior. However, following a brief contact with an observer (researcher) in the grocery store taking notes might be rather obtrusive and undesirable in attempting to maintain trust and rapport with the participant.

Bogdan (1972) has offered several excellent hints on recording data from an observational period or event. Three essential guidelines from this rather lengthy list include (1) recording the notes soon after the observational experience, (2) recording notes prior to discussing them with anyone, and (3) taking great care in recording the sequences of events, the social setting, the actors, and important conversation. To this list we add the importance of recording information about the data, time of day, transitional flow between what had previously occurred and what is about to occur or followed. This latter information places the event in its proper time perspective.

It is common practice during notetaking to make a distinction between "data" and "interpretive" notes. Data notes are merely descriptive of the event. They are clearly written to summarize the event by occurrence. Guides to fieldnote taking suggest that double quotations (" ") be used to indicate verbatim quotes, single quotation marks (' ') be used for paraphrases, parentheses ( ) be used for contextual information and interpretations, while angle brackets (< >) be used for emic lexicon, solid lines (_____) for partitions of time, and slashes (/) for denoting emic contrast (see Kirk & Miller, 1986). Interpretive notes in comparison consist of inferences made by the researcher. Usually these inferences consist of proposed cause-and-effect assumptions and underlying social dynamics.

▶   A brief illustration is warranted at this time on classic participant–observer methodology. Humphreys (1970) has reported the use of this observational technique in the study of "impersonal sex in public places." While utilizing a multi-method strategy, a significant portion of Humphreys' research involved the use of participant–observation where the researcher's intentions were undeclared. Humphreys infiltrated a specific subcultural group of which he was not a member. Specifically, to study "tearoom trade" (impersonal sex between homosexuals and/or bisexuals in public restrooms), the observer played the role of the "watchqueen" in public restrooms frequented by males who engaged in acts of fellatio (mouth-to-genital sexual behavior). The watchqueen, usually voyeuristic in nature, stands by the window and watches for police or unknown strangers and signals with a cough when such individuals are found to be approaching the restroom. During this time, and in the role of watchqueen, Humphreys observed the sexual activity of the restroom inhabitants and on several occasions struck up a conversation with the participants outside the restroom where he subtly quizzed them on their life-style and other matters. When feasible he would return to his automobile and tape record his observations for later interpretive study. Outside of the participant–observation period, several individuals agreed to be extensively interviewed. Further, Humphreys reports he recorded, when possible, the license number of the participants' cars and followed them for further study in their neighborhoods and used the license number to retrieve public archival data. Through this technique, he was able to utilize his observational data to identify the most likely environment for tearoom sex, note the interaction and impersonal silence of such unusual sexual behavior, and ultimately through interview data and archival information delineate four types of adult males who engage in such behavior and the personal crisis of aging that affects an individual's role in the fellatio act.

While the participant–observer technique in this study is an important one, the ethical issues are immense. The individual's privacy is invaded during the infiltration process; in this example, he is deceived by the role of the unannounced researcher. One might say he is watched by the voyeuristic watchqueen–sociologist. His life is scrutinized through his automobile license with archival data retrieved through his identification with an automobile. His impersonal behavior is opened up to public scrutiny through the report of the scientists. Many subjects feel betrayed when finding out about such scientific reports, thus questioning the appropriateness of unannounced infiltration techniques. On the other hand, open involvement is less likely to create such ethical dilemmas and has been shown to be an equally efficient manner of observation.

Nonstructured Field Observation Methodology.

The nonstructured field observation study, like the participant–observer methodology, utilizes the normal social ecology with the study of typical behavior in common behavioral settings. Because researchers use commonplace settings in the typical ecology of everyday life, many social scientists (particularly psychologists) call this type of investigation a "naturalistic observation study."

In the nonstructured field observational technique a particular, but general, setting is chosen in which individuals are to be observed. However, the researcher does not tamper with the environment. Rather the environment is allowed to influence behavior within its own normal social boundaries. Thus, individuals are observed in "their natural habitats" such as in school, at home, on the playground, or in one's neighborhood (Hutt & Hutt, 1970). The major distinction between this method and that of the participant–observer study is the manner in which the behavior is observed and data recorded. Rather than notetaking after an observational period, a formal rating form or scale is used to record each datum (usually as it occurs). Thus, researchers using the nonstructured field observation methodology study behavior in normal social ecology settings through the use of very specific observational rating forms.

In the nonstructured field observation study, the type and form of behavior to be studied are predetermined before the observational period. During the observational period only the behaviors delineated on the observational rating form are treated as relevant target behaviors to be observed and recorded. All other behaviors are treated as irrelevant and are ignored by the observer.

The most common measure used in the application of a formal rating form is a measure of *frequency,* that is, how often a particular form or type of behavior occurs. This measure simply requires counting the number of behaviors. The second most frequent measure is one of *duration.* Through the use of a timing mechanism (usually a stopwatch) the observer records the length of time a particular behavior is engaged in with another. A third and less frequently used observational measure is that of *latency.* Latency refers to the time that elapses between events or behaviors. That is, how much time passes between one thing and another, or one behavior and another. Hence, observational techniques that utilize formal observation rating strategies allow the researcher to count the number of behaviors that occur, discover how long they last when they do occur, and report the length of time that elapses between one behavior and another. Thus the nonstructured field technique is more precise than the participant–observation strategy, but is more narrow in focus and less descriptive of the full range of behavior within the general social ecology.

Let us turn to two brief examples of nonstructured field observation studies.

▶   For many of us controlling our waistline is a continuous battle. Numerous social science studies on obesity indicate the widespread concern with the control of "fatty tissue." Marston and his associates (Marston, London, Cohen, & Cooper, 1977) have, for example, been interested in understanding the eating patterns of obese and thin individuals. Previous research had suggested a possible relationship between eating rates and obesity, which these investigators wished to verify in common daily eating patterns. Therefore, using a free field observation technique these investigators identified a public cafeteria where individuals, who were either obese or thin, eating alone or with a group, were observed during an evening meal. The observer sat close to each research subject and, unbeknownst to the individual, made a series of observations during their meal time. Using a formal observational rating form, four different periods of time (three minutes each) were included in the observational period of each subject and behavior was recorded as it occurred. The major objective of the study was to determine if extraneous behaviors (e.g., toying with food, using a napkin, etc.) were associated with a possible slower eating rate for nonobese subjects.

During the observation periods the observer recorded the number of extraneous food behaviors, counted bites and chews, estimated the size of each bite, and rated perceived tension, mood, and food enjoyment on Likert-type scales (see Chapter 8 for a discussion of Likert-type scaling). A clear pattern emerged for the thin subjects. They took smaller bites, used a much slower rate of biting, engaged in more frequent extraneous food behavior (such as picking up and putting down utensils, hesitation between bites), left more food on their plate, and spent less time sitting at the table once the meal was apparently finished. No observed differences were noted in perceived tension, mood, or food enjoyment between the obese and thin subjects.

▶   Another example of nonstructured field observation methodology is found in a study of age segregation during adolescence. Based on the notion that adolescence is a period of high peer contact, and that differing social structures are more or less likely to encourage same-age peer contacts, Montemayor and Van Komen (1980) studied the age composition of naturally occurring adolescent groups in in-school and out-of-school settings. On specified hours over a course of seven days an observer noted the formation of peer groups and recorded the date, time, and setting (in-school or out-of-school). Each group was then approached wherein the observer asked the age of each group member. General locations included a park, a downtown setting, a fast-food restaurant, a shopping mall, and the school grounds of two high schools. The most salient finding was that while age segregation was extensive, it was most prevalent in school settings. Data summarized in Figure 11.2 indicate that for all ages the school setting had less variability in age of peers than was noted in out-of-school peer groups. Other findings indicated that adolescents were most often seen with adolescent friends, next with adults, and least with children.

In field studies of this nature three specific types of formal rating techniques are commonly employed (Lamb, Suomi, & Stephenson, 1979). Wright (1960) has labeled these techniques as the time sampling, event sampling, and trait rating strategies of

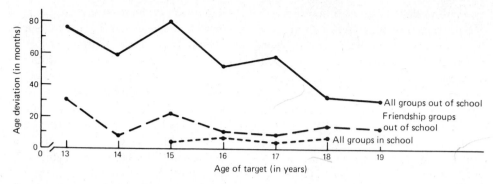

Figure 11.2. Age Comparisons for Adolescent Groups Observed in and out of School Settings. (*Source:* R. Montemayor and R. Van Komen. [1980]. Age segregation of adolescents in and out of school. *Journal of Youth and Adolescence, 9, 371–381.*)

recording behavior. In the *time sampling* strategy of data gathering, specific behaviors are watched for and counted if they happen during precise time limits. In our previous illustration on the study of obesity, the time limit consisted of three-minute spans over four observational samples for each subject. The *event sampling,* in comparison, does not include a limiting time factor, but specifies behavioral events which are thought to be within a given general class of behaviors that are observed when they occur regardless of the time which passes prior to enactment. Thus, the researcher–observer stations herself or himself where the behavior is most likely to occur and waits for it to happen. Therein the observer records behavioral occurrence (and if desired, all of the apparent causes and consequences of the behavioral event).

For example, if one were interested in studying aggression using a time sampling technique, observers would locate themselves in a setting where it is likely to happen (e.g., a parking lot) and if aggressive acts (e.g., hitting, or verbal anger) occur, record the full behavioral stream of that event. For example, Mr. X drives into Mrs. Y's car, Mr. X gets out of his automobile and strikes Mrs. X's car with a large blunt object which looks like a handle to a jack. Event sampling was used in the age segregation study by Montemayor and Van Komen to identify the age structure of naturally occurring groups that included adolescents. Finally, the *trait rating* strategy defines particular dimensions of behavior and requires the observer to make judgments about their apparent extensiveness in the individual behavior pattern following an extended period of observation time. This was illustrated in our earlier example of the obesity study where perceived tension, mood, and food enjoyment were rated after four three-minute observations of eating. (For an elaboration on the history of levels of research analyses that can be used in each of the sampling strategies interested readers should examine Kessen, 1983.)

Observational Research with High Environmental Structure

As Figure 11.1 indicates, there are two specific types of observational techniques that use a highly structured environmental setting. These techniques have been labeled the *structured field experiment* and the *laboratory observation study.* Both techniques require a substantial degree of control or manipulation of certain properties of the social environment. However, the rating techniques are less formal in the field experiment than they are in the laboratory observation study. Manipulation of the environment, which is usually treated as the independent variable, requires the identification of certain elements or properties within the environment that are thought to maintain a strong impact on behavior. For example, conceptual differences may be drawn between physical and psychological space as found in the study of animal social behavior (Lamb Suomi, & Stephenson, 1979). In many research studies two or more levels of the same property of the social environment are constructed and half of the subject population (sample) experience one level while the remainder of the population experience the other. Individuals are then observed to determine if different values of the same independent variable are associated with the appearance of behavior (Runkel & McGrath, 1972; Cairns, 1979).

Structured Field Experiment Study.   Field experiments are important investigations that offer increased experimenter control on the independent variable but maintain an important sense of reality to the situation. Many times the subjects are unaware of the actual manipulation and thus behave in manners which are typical to the situational context in which they find themselves.

Berkowitz (1975) offers one illustration of a hypothetical field experiment. Previous information offered through a UPI news release indicated that telephone bomb threats were found to increase after the showing of a movie called *The Doomsday Flight.* Further, each repeated showing resulted in an ever increasing number of threats. Berkowitz argued that a field experiment study could be completed to test the effects of such a movie on bomb threat behavior. Two versions of the same movie could be made, one where the extortionists escape, the other where they are arrested and punished. With the cooperation of the FCC, arrangements could be made with the two networks to show one of the two versions. Following airing of the two versions of *Doomsday,* the number of telephone threats could be recorded and compared on the influence of viewing arrest or escape outcomes. Such a field experiment would offer important information on the likely postviewing behavior of individuals watching unpunished and punished versions of terrorism–extortion.

The rather important distinction to be made with this illustration is the care one must take in locating realistic and meaningful environmental units which can be manipulated by the researcher. Once a particular hypothesis is generated the researcher is called on to identify an environmental manipulation which can be used to assess a possible independent-dependent variable relation. Further, the measurement of observed behavior is determined more by the situation than by the researcher. That is, naturally occurring behaviors are the unit of study. Let us turn to a classic example of field experimentations to make these points clear.

Sherif and associates (Sherif, Harvey, White, Hood, & Sherif, 1961) completed a series of structured field experiment studies which have come to be called the Robbers Cave experiment (named after the isolated summer camp in the state of Oklahoma where the study was conducted). These social scientists, using an interdisciplinary theoretical perspective, focused on intergroup relations in the form of conflict and cooperation. A 3-stage field experiment was conducted with 24 12-year old boys from Protestant middle-class families. The general hypothesis was that intergroup attitudes (interpersonal judgments) and behaviors (discrimination) are a function of the nature of relations between groups (i.e., common goals are conductive to intergroup cooperation and positively shared attitudes between groups.) To test this assumption (hypothesis) young adolescents at a summer camp were unknowingly put through a 3-stage field experiment and were observed by their senior camp counselors.

During Stage 1 of this study, in-groups were formed between adolescents who were previously unacquainted. Adolescents engaged in a wide variety of activities that included a trip to Robbers Cave, group work activities, cooperative game playing, backpacking, and so forth during the first stage of the study. By the close of this phase each adolescent had developed a specific status position and role in his group with a clearly stabilized pattern of behavior as identified by the counselor–observers.

Previous to Stage 2, each group of adolescents was unaware of the other group in the camp. However, during Stage 2 they were made aware of the other camp group and immediately wished to enter into competition with them. Therefore, as an experimental condition to enhance conflict between groups, a camp tournament was announced and the trophy, prizes, and medals for victory were exhibited. This formal announcement merely heightened an already strong urge for competition. The two groups took on the names of the Rattlers and the Eagles during this stage. The tournament consisted of such contestant events as baseball, tug-of-war, football, tent-pitching competition, and staff-judged events like inspections, skits and songs, and a treasure hunt. The staff-judged events were included in the field experiment to keep the teams appearing close in points throughout the Stage 2 manipulation to maintain high motivation and hopes of winning (i.e., the counselors actually juggled the apparent outcomes, unbeknownst to the boys, to keep them close in points). Score values were recorded for the Rattlers and the Eagles on a rising thermometer that was used as an official score sheet.

Intergroup attitudes and behavior were measured through several techniques. The primary technique was that of observation by the camp counselors. The influence of the tournament was to elicit name calling, fights, and raids on each other's personal possessions between the Rattlers and the Eagles. Further, a measurement of friendship choice between in-group and out-group members revealed almost exclusively Rattlers chose Rattlers (94% of the time) and Eagles chose Eagles (93% of the time) as their best friend. Thus, a statement of competition and frustration was observed, in a structured natural setting, and was found to induce an in-group solidarity. Further, the lower status boys within their own group were observed to increase their physical and verbal aggression toward the other group as a means of hopefully improving their status with the in-group.

The third and final stage of this field experiment consisted of reducing intergroup friction. Two techniques were employed to test their effectiveness in changing intergroup behavior. First, a series of intergroup contacts were arranged in a noncompetitive setting (e.g., during a brief stereotype rating session, watching a maritime movie, eating breakfast, a Fourth of July ceremony). However, such contact was not found to lead to any apparent (observed) improvement in group relations. Second, a series of problems common to both groups were introduced to the adolescents (both groups simultaneously); these included superordinate goals and required interaction between the groups (cooperation) for successful solutions. For example, the available drinking water was disrupted which created a common deprivation for all the boys, the securing of a movie for viewing depended on sharing the costs, a campout was held where the truck stalled and the boys needed to pull it to get it started. Through observations by the camp counselors it was verified that groups in friction can develop better working relations, attitudes, and behaviors through contact where a superordinate goal requires a group effort to achieve success—thus reducing group tensions.

Hence, the Robbers Cave experiment entailed a great deal of care in designing field manipulations that were related to the hypothesis under consideration. Conflict and cooperation conditions were constructed within the normal social ecology of adolescent camp life. The behaviors exhibited by the adolescents were not predetermined by the counselor–observer, but were allowed to occur in their natural unfolding manner and were observed and recorded as they occurred. Hence, the independent and dependent variable relationships studied in this example were due to the effects of what appeared to be a normal behavioral setting as it influenced typical behavior by in-groups following tension and frustration or cooperation for a common good.

Laboratory Observation Studies.   The fourth type of common observational technique involves the greatest amount of experimental control of the four observational techniques. Both the rating form and the environment are under control by the experimenter. Typically, these studies are conducted in laboratory observational rooms where specific properties of the room are under the control of the experimenter at all times. Usually, but not exclusively, the laboratory observation study is conducted by researchers who are studying specific hypotheses related to interpersonal relations.

This observational technique not only includes a very careful manipulation of the environment, but is usually reported in great detail by the investigator. Nonetheless, this detailed information is useful in understanding what the specific functional relationship is between the independent and dependent variable(s). A great deal of attention is given, in this technique, to observational measurement. *Interrater reliability* (reliability or agreement as to what has been observed between two independent observers) is highly emphasized. Many times the behaviors are videotaped and two observers record behavior from the tapes. Other times they record behavior as it actually happens. While there are many ways to check interrater reliability, the most frequently reported technique is a percentage of agreement strategy where the number of agreements between the raters are divided by the number of total possible agreements or disagreements (Johnson & Bolstad, 1973). To assure reliability over the whole course of the study, at a minimum, the researcher should provide a "spot check" on interrater reliability for research subjects observed early, midway, and late in the investigation.

Several types of influences can affect the reliability of the observational data. Johnson and Bolstad (1973) have summarized a number of factors which can create observer errors. Two sources of *observer bias* that can confound the results of an observational study include problems in recording and expectancy biases by the observer. Careless recording, in particular where numerous behaviors are being observed at one setting, can lead to low reliability and invalid data. Expectancy effects are perhaps even more discomfiting.

Robert Rosenthal (1973), in his study of the self-fulfilling prophecy, has shown that expectancy for particular behaviors can be influential in obtaining such behaviors by the research subjects. That is, if a researcher expects a participant in an observational study to behave in specific ways, through subtle communication the research subject may discover such expectations and perform accordingly.

Observational laboratory research can create another source of confounding through *reactivity*. Under observation it is possible that people may behave in ways different from their normal manner. Hence, observational reactivity effects may limit the generalizability of findings because of the influences of knowing that one is being watched as a research subject. For example, the more conspicuous the observer, the more one is aware of being watched. Hence, behavior in this situation may be narrowly defined, guarded, and atypical. Or personal attributes of the observer may lead the observee to act in unusual ways. A host of early studies on children's social behavior have shown that permissive adult observers are more likely than nonpermissive observers to elicit antisocial behavior in children during free play periods.

Finally, Johnson and Bolstad (1973) point out that the *observee (subject bias)* may likewise offer confounding factors. In particular, the subject, under a state of observation, may behave according to a response set and "fake good." While all three types of observational confounding effects (observer bias, reactivity, and subject bias) are possible in laboratory observational studies, they are as likely to occur in the previous three observational methodology techniques, too. Rather, laboratory researchers are more likely to deal with them as possible confounding variables due to their advantage of having greater experimental control on both the environment and the rating technique in a laboratory setting.

Let us turn to an example of laboratory observation research that we completed   ◀ sometime ago in our own laboratories (Adams & Hamm, 1973). Attempts were made to show how children's imitation of an aggressive adult model, when reinforcement for such action is not visibly present, may actually be due to the child's previous history of reinforcement for imitation behavior. Our major hypothesis was that children who have a history of reinforcement for imitating adults' behavior, in comparison to children who do not, will be more likely to show imitative behavior although reinforcement for such actions is not present in the immediate environment.

To test this hypothesis a laboratory research trailer was moved to a local elementary school where kindergartners were used as subjects. The research trailer consisted of two rooms with a one-way mirror between them which allowed the researchers to watch the children at all times. One room was designated the reward–control room. It contained a small table with two chairs with an electrical training box on the top of the table. Also located in this room was a videotape television monitor and several small rewards for the children (marbles and trinkets). The second room in the trailer contained a Bobo doll, some balls, a mallet and pegboard, a cap gun, cars, toy kitchen utensils, plastic animals, a fire engine, a baseball bat, and dolls. This room was named the playroom.

The research procedure was a simple one. Prior to watching a television show on the television monitor, half of the children were put through either a training condition where they received small rewards for imitating the adult on the electrical training box (a gadget which involved lighting up a series of colored lights to match the experimenter's lights), while the remaining half were not given reinforcement for imitation of this task. Two conditions were constructed: (1) half of the children now had an immediate history of reinforcement for imitation of adult behavior, and (2) the other half did not. The next phase of the study involved having children watch a special television show in which an adult actor physically and verbally attacked a Bobo doll. All of the children were attentive to this brief film. During this filmed scene, the adult performed some very unusual behavior toward the Bobo doll. First, the adult pushed the Bobo out of his way and said,

"Out of my way, Bobo." Second, he pushed the Bobo down, sat on top of it, and said, "Pow, right in the nose." Finally, the adult grabbed the toy mallet located in the playroom and knocked the Bobo doll down while saying, "Sockeroo, stay down."

After viewing this rather unusual television program, each child was taken into the playroom. This room was identical to the room in which the adult model was filmed displaying his aggressive behavior toward the Bobo doll. (Now keep in mind, half of the children prior to watching the television violence were reinforced for imitating adults, the other half were not.) Each child was left alone to play in the room for eight minutes during which time unknown to the child any aggressive behavior was observed and recorded. Particular behaviors of interest included exact imitation of the physical (e.g., hitting the Bobo doll with a mallet) and verbal (e.g., saying, "Sockeroo, stay down") aggression or partial imitation where half of a sequence matched the adult's behavior but the remaining portion was novel or specific to the child. Further, all other forms of novel aggression not modeled by the adult were also recorded. The results clearly showed that having a history of reinforcement for imitating adults was associated with a high degree of aggression following the viewing of an aggressive television show. Specifically, children who were given training and reinforcement for matching or imitating adult behavior and were then shown a violent television program were more likely than the other children to imitate physical and verbal aggression from a television viewing session.

In this laboratory observation study the environment was extremely structured. Both the experiences with the researcher and the television program were highly structured to test a very specific hypothesis. Further, the kinds and types of behavior to be observed were very narrowly defined to the hypothesis under study.

Summary.   Four types of observational techniques are commonly employed by social scientists. Each, if used appropriately, can be a reliable and valid research technique. Foremost, each technique offers a useful tool in understanding and describing social behavior. However, the participant–observer and structured field experiment methodologies offer a wider perspective, while the nonstructured field observation and laboratory observation methodologies are more narrowly focused in the range of behavior studied. A similar distinction can be made between the low- and high-structured continuum. Observational techniques employed in high-structured settings are more narrowly defined and limited to the behavior setting, while low-structured field research has broader generalizations and applications. In utilizing research in one's professional endeavors, these distinctions should be noted. Care should be taken not to overgeneralize the implications from any of the four observational techniques summarized. Likewise, the reader should continually keep in mind that replication between independent studies (ideally by different researchers) is the primary factor in determining valid generalizable scientific fact (external validity). (See Tips for Consumers 11.1.)

THE TECHNOLOGY OF OBSERVATION

Observational research methodology offers a challenge to the recording of behavior. To accomplish the goal of observation, five basic types of research tools are available at most educational or research institutions. These observational tools include tape recorders, event recorders, one-way mirror rooms, motion pictures or film, and videotaping.

Tips for Consumers 11.1

To understand the fundamentals of an observational technique reported in a book or research report the consumer can use the dimension of *type of ratings* and *level of structure* placed on the research setting to conceptualize the strategies used. In assessing the report the consumer should ask the following questions:

1. How did the researcher enter the research setting?
2. Did the researcher manipulate or change the environment to provide a necessary structure to assess the independent-dependent variables?
3. Does the researcher assess only a predetermined set of observed behaviors? Or are all behaviors noted and studied?

These basic questions can provide the necessary information to determine if the observational strategy evolved around the use of formal or informal observational techniques within a high- or low-structured environment.

Once the appropriate observational technique is identified can you, in reading the report, find how the researcher established reliability and validity in observational assessment? Is there evidence to suggest the observational techniques have a minimal level of both?

Excellent elaborative discussions of the details for specific methodologies related to the utility of these have been provided elsewhere (e.g., Hutt & Hutt, 1970; Lamb, Suomi, & Stephenson, 1979; Sackett, 1978). We will merely introduce you to some of the basic facets of these five tools to familiarize you with their existence and general utility. For extensive details on the application of observation tools we refer the reader to specific technical material (e.g., Bakeman & Dabbs, 1976; Gore, 1978; Hutt & Hutt, 1970; Sackett, 1978; Stephenson, Smith, & Roberts, 1975).

Audiotape recording on magnetic tape has been shown by numerous social scientists to be an excellent recording device in free field or interview studies. Verbal gestures, utterances, and specific sequential communication patterns can be identified through analyses of tapes. One advantage for using audiotaping during interview sessions is that the process of communication can remain relatively spontaneous when using tape recording technology coupled with sensitive periods of questions and answers. Further, audiotaping allows the researcher to hear responses, over and over again, during the data analysis segment of the study.

For example, in our own laboratories we had once used audiotaping to study the persuasion style of attractive versus unattractive college-age women (Adams & Read, 1983). In this persuasion study we had both attractive and unattractive women come to our laboratory to engage in a persuasion task. Each woman was asked to persuade another college student to eat as many M & M candies as possible during a three-minute period. Unbeknownst to each woman, the other student was a confederate who agreed to eat the first offer, but then pleasantly resisted all other persuasion attempts. Both the attractive and unattractive women were given an incentive to work hard in their persuasion attempts through instructions from the experimenter that he was willing to pay them 50¢ for each candy she could get the other student to eat in a three-minute period. For three minutes, all conversation was audiotaped. These tapes were then analyzed using a classification system of verbal influence styles by raters who were unaware of the actual physical appearance of the research subjects. Comparisons were then made of the ratings of the audiotapes between the attractive and unattractive groups. In general, the findings revealed that unattractive women were more likely to use deceptive and manipulative persuasion styles than were the attractive subjects.

In the past much observational research has been completed using simple checklist techniques. Typically the researcher watches for a specific period of time and then checks on a list the occurrence of such behavior for that period of time. For example, the observer may watch for 15 seconds and then record for 15 seconds. During the recording period the observer merely checks off the behaviors that occurred during the observational time period. This sequence is then repeated for another 15-second observation and 15-second record taking period. To use a computer analogy, this form of record taking is in a simple digital format indicating the presence (on) or absence (off) of a behavior during the observation time frame. Fortunately, with the advent of *event recorders*, such as an automated mechanical record taking device, more complex observational data can now be obtained. In many of the early commercially available event recorders (e.g., the Esterline–Angus Event Recorder, EMREC Event Recorder, etc.) the primary use of the device was to simply replace the checklist with a more mechanized technique of recording simple frequencies of behavior. (That is not to say these devices could not be used to measure types of data such as latency, duration, etc.) In its early form the event recorder was typically a drum with paper rolling over it and a series of small ink pens that made contact with the paper in systematic ways when triggered by the researcher to indicate the specific occurrence of an event. In the past several years, with the major advances in computer technology, more sophisticated event recorders have been developed. In particular, from the research laboratories of zoologists, animal psychologists, and ethologists, several highly sophisticated event recorders have been developed. Simpson (1979), for example, describes an event recorder system used at Cambridge University, England.

This system includes a 40-channel event-recorder that is operated by observers who press keys corresponding to specific channels. The keyboard is wired to a system that makes its electronic output computer-compatible. Thus, data are collected by pushing buttons to reflect the occurrence of specific behaviors. Electronic impulses are sent through the 40 channels into a computer stored program called DEC LINCTAPE. Upon request these data can then be analyzed by a PDP 12 computer. Data analyses can therefore be undertaken that not only recognize digital (on or off) recorded observations, but highly sophisticated analyses can be done on duration, latency, frequency, and sequencing of behavior. Indeed, Stephenson (1979) has described a highly complex computer-compatible grammar system called PLEXYN that can be used to study the subtle and sequentially complex nature of streams of social behavior.

Another tool of observational methodology is the *one-way mirror* room. This room consists of a mirror-like observational setting where the researcher can sit in a darker room adjacent to the research area and watch the behavior without being seen. Inside the lighted research room the participant sees only what appears to be a large mirror. Numerous laboratory observational studies are reported each year using this type of tool. The general sophistication of the populace, however, has resulted in the ability to identify such a room when entered. Hence, one must always question the "naturalness" of research conducted in one-way mirror research and note the possible limits to the generalization of the findings. But we have noted in our own research that young children are seldom inhibited by one-way mirrors even when they are fully aware that one can see through them. Also, we have noted that once the subject becomes engrossed in his or her own behavior little or no attention is given to the mirror.

Both *motion picture* and *audio-videotaping* have been extensively used by ethological researchers with animals and social psychologists studying interpersonal behavior. The advantage one gains in filming or taping behavior is the permanency of the record. Further, through miniviewers, editing machines, and still-frame mechanisms, frame-by-frame analyses of behavior can be completed. This close look at small units of behavior that are microseconds apart has allowed social scientists to study the world of "micro" level behavior. The effect is to put a "microscope" to work on the analysis of human interaction. Thus, filming and taping can be used to study behavior at very slow speeds and allows us to appreciate miniscule steps in social exchange. Some have argued that research using filming or taping offers a partial correction to the criticisms regarding the limitations of social survey research. Indeed, Schvaneveldt (1966), in a study of maternal overprotection, has shown how the two techniques when combined can be used to reliably and validly supplement each other. (See Tips for Consumers 11.2.)

Tips for Consumers 11.2

In field studies the two most common sampling strategies are time and event sampling. Time sampling involves recording behavior during specific time periods. Event sampling involves recording the frequency of behavior independent of time units. In assessing the appropriateness of one sampling technique over the other, the consumer of research should ask whether the researcher addresses the appropriateness of one technique over the other in the study of the topic under consideration. Is it possible that the researcher used the wrong sampling technique for the behavior under investigation? When "streams of behavior" are of particular interest the time sampling technique may be preferred. When mere frequency of occurrence, independent of precursors, is being studied the event sampling strategies may be most desirable.

OBSERVATION OF BEHAVIOR THROUGH THE UNOBTRUSIVE TECHNIQUE

Every form of methodology can be evaluated along a continuum of obtrusiveness to unobtrusiveness. *Obtrusiveness* has to do with the degree to which something is thrust on another without invitation. The more obtrusive the methodology the greater the chance of individuals behaving in atypical or guarded ways. This atypical behavior is the result of *reactivity* to observation. The more reactive the methodology the greater the limits to generalizability (external validity). Therefore, to cope with reactivity problems a number of so-called unobtrusive or nonreactive methodologies of observation have been utilized by social scientists (Brandt, 1972). In general, unobtrusive methods of study involve techniques in which individual (or group) behavior is studied, the cooperation of the subject is not required, and the methodology does not contaminate (confound) the subject's behavior.

Webb and his colleagues (Webb, Campbell, Schwartz, & Sechrest, 1981) have summarized numerous types of nonreactive (unobtrusive) measures of social behavior that can be used to supplement the observational strategies outlined earlier in this chapter.

Archival records may stand out as the most readily available, yet least utilized source of nonreactive measures of social behavior. Archive information is found in every library in North America. These materials are both inexpensive to obtain and readily available. Social behavior can be studied through available records, sales information, government reports, biographic, and other informal or personal written documents.

▶   For example, Simonton (1977) used archival information to study the influences of external forces on creativity. Upon identifying 10 classical composers, this researcher assessed for each 5-year period following the production of the composer's first work all recorded composition efforts. Further, during this period, through the use of various archival records, biographic stress factors (e.g., divorces, job changes, litigations, and lawsuits, etc.), physical illnesses, social reinforcements (e.g., awarded honorary doctorate, listing in *Who's Who*, etc.), number of contemporary competitors (gauged through the *Chronology of Composers* in a biographical dictionary), war intensity (tabulated through *The Encyclopedia of Military History*), and the degree of internal political disturbance (assessed through revolts, riots, etc.) were recorded for each 5-year period. The association between quantitative and qualitative compositions and their potential external influences were assessed using the various types of archival information. Some of the findings included the conclusions that (1) major themes by composers are more likely to emerge while the individual is young rather than old, (2) physical illness leads to a decrease in composition productivity, and (3) the more competition (currently active composers) the less likely the individual is to have his work recognized.

This investigation then serves as a good illustration of how nonreactive archival investigations might be utilized, in place of direct observation, as a means of studying certain types of social behavior. In particular, it seems well suited to the study of very special populations that contain rather rare individuals, such as outstanding composers, famous artists, or political leaders such as presidents.

Another form of nonreactive measure suggested by Webb et al. (1981) as an important research device is the study of social behavior through *physical traces*. Two specific measures of physical traces include the degree of erosion or accretion. *Erosion* measures, as the word implies, include the study of behavior through some degree of wear on a material substance. *Accretion* measures include the study of behavior through the deposit or collection of material substances. For example, one could study the impact and interest in particular kinds of reading material through the assessment of wear-and-tear on library books. Or one could study the desirability of certain picnic areas by family members through the assessment of garbage deposits in local picnic garbage receptacles.

▶   An illustration of the use of the physical traces through the process of accretion is found in a study by Rheingold and Cook (1975) on gender-related differences in the contents of six-year-old boys' and girls' bedrooms. These psychologists proposed that how parents furnish the rooms of their sons and daughters provides an index about appropriateness of behavior based on gender of the child. Bedrooms were canvased and objects in the rooms were counted that reflected the furnishings of the room. Comparisons were then made between boys' and girls' furnishings. Girls' rooms had more dolls, floral furnishings, and ruffly decorations. Boys' rooms had more animal toys, animal furnishings, sorting and shaping toys, and related materials. By the use of an accretion-based observational study, these researchers were able to document that parents create an environment that encourages differences through the construction of gender distinctive play environments.

Webb, Campbell, Schwartz, Sechrest and Grove (1981) have summarized numerous ◄ illustrations of the use of erosion measures in social science research. The erosion of tile around display areas in museums, wear of pages in library books, campsite erosion, or damage to vehicles are appropriate illustrations. While erosion measures are little used in observational study their potential is considerable and quite often informative.

In summary, nonreactive measures of social behavior are available, other than direct observational techniques, that can be used to study human behavior. A great deal of ingenuity is called for in this type of research, but the opportunities are almost endless. The nonreactive nature of such methodology makes them an important supplemental technique to observational methods.

Validity and Reliability Issues

All research methodologies have their place in the total scheme of science. One ultimate goal of science is to establish laws or at least principles of behavior that are valid across varying contexts. That is what is meant by *transcontextual validity*. As Weisz (1978) has aptly remarked: "To the extent that a...principle can be shown to hold good across physical and cultural setting, time, or cohort, it can be said to possess transcontextual validity" (p. 2). But how does observational methodology, in comparison to laboratory experimental designs, reach this goal? Weisz argues that laboratory experimental designs through the use of control groups and strong experimental designs help us to understand *what can happen* given certain specific independent variable influences. However, it is the observational field methods that tell us *what does happen* in the course of normal social living. That is, just because a particular variable can be influential upon a specific type of behavior, we have no assurance from laboratory research findings that in actuality it does have that influence in normal social environments, or how frequently it does influence behavior outside the laboratory setting. Hence, our goal of finding transcontextual validity in our theoretical principles requires both experimental laboratory and observational methodological studies to answer the "what can" and "what does happen" research questions.

In observational research, three basic dimensions underlie issues of internal validity (Tunnell, 1977). First, the researcher needs to specify a meaningful repertoire of *natural behaviors*. Second, the social scientist must specify the *natural setting*, physical or social context, to which a person is naturally exposed. Finally, the investigator must delineate a *natural treatment* or a discrete event that is temporally bound and would have occurred with or without the researcher's presence. The natural treatment within a given social context is therein predicted to elicit the specific natural behavior. Comparisons are made between differing social contexts to establish that the predicted context elicits the specified behavior. Such comparisons provide the essential test of internal validity. Generally, it is thought that natural treatments heighten the credibility of setting effects on human behavior. As Tunnell (1977) notes, "When research is made more credible to participants, one likely consequence is an increase in internal validity" (p. 433).

Issues of reliability in observation are generally resolved through documentation of two raters reaching agreement on what has been observed. Rate of agreement is frequently determined by the following simple formula:

$$\text{Reliability} = \frac{\text{Number of agreements}}{\text{Number of agreements plus disagreements}} \times 100$$

But to reach high agreement requires substantial observational skills. Some years ago Allport (1937) suggested several characteristics of good observers. It was thought that these characteristics were personal characteristics underlying good observational skills. Allport has suggested and Boice (1983) concurred that a good observer is likely to be a person with a rich store of social experience, has a similar background to the person being observed, is intelligent, insightful, and is detached from the observee.

Boice (1983) has also recommended that reliability in observation is enhanced by establishing clear discriminating criteria for recorded behaviors. Further, specific instructions on how to observe and record the behavior are essential. Knapp (1978) adds that a researcher can maximize observer reliability through (1) experience and training with subject–actors, (2) the use of discrete and familiar behaviors, while (3) providing sufficient time for observation and recording.

SUMMARY

Surveillance or observational techniques are utilized by social scientists in various ways. Four basic prototypes have been described in this chapter. While these four methodologies of observation have been described as four separate techniques it should be recognized that many researchers use a combination of two or more in their research endeavors. As we increase our consumption of scientific materials in professional activities, observational data increasingly become more in demand. As consumers of research, we should be vividly aware of the fact that observational data offer us much in understanding what *does* happen in individuals' normal social ecologies or environments. However, we should be cautious in our utilization of any particular unreplicated observation study given potential reactivity and confounding factors. Further, where possible, we should become aware of evidence related to our particular professional interests where investigations have been completed using nonreactive research methods. The latter techniques, when supplemented by observational data, offer a great deal to our understanding of social behavior.

To summarize, the following major points were presented in this chapter:

1. A classification of observational methods can be used to identify four prototypical techniques of observational research. Through the use of dimensions of environmental structure and formality of rating behavior, the following four methods can be identified:
   a. participant–observer studies that utilize informal rating strategies within an unstructured environment;
   b. nonstructured field observation studies that include formal rating techniques within an unstructured social ecology;
   c. structured field experiment studies that utilize informal ratings in a highly structured environment;
   d. laboratory observation studies that include both formal rating and highly structured environmental controls.
2. The technology of observation, which is in a continuing state of evolution, consists of using such equipment as tape recorders, event recorders, one-way mirror rooms, motion picture filming, and videotaping.

3. All forms of methodology can be evaluated on their degree of potential obstrusive-ness (i.e., uninvited intrusion). Such obtrusiveness can create a confounding factor called reactivity. Therefore, several types of nonreactive (low obstrusive) techniques are available to supplement observational techniques These so-called unobtrusive or nonreactive methods include, for example, the following:

   a. the use of archival records to study recorded behaviors of individuals;
   b. the use of physical traces, where individual erosion (wear) or accretion (deposits) are used as measures of behavior.

4. The ultimate strength of observational and nonreactive methods includes the primary capacity to specify what happens (behaviorally) in the normal social ecology of individual living.

PROBLEMS AND APPLICATIONS

1. As a classroom assignment, using the the four observational methodologies summarized in Figure 11.1, construct a study using each of the four methodological types to address the following research problems:

   a. the assumption that youths who go away versus those who remain at home while going to college have better or worse relations with their parents;
   b. the belief that drug usage is initiated through peer contacts;
   c. the hypothesis that mental adjustment is strained during the breakdown of a heterosexual romantic relationship.

2. Identify or formulate modifications to the four basic observational techniques that might be applied to observational research. What problems might be foreseen by such modifications? What additional strengths do such modifications provide?

3. What is meant by unobstrusive measurement? Can you think of examples appropriate for the study of (a) school achievement, (b) child abuse, (c) moral behavior, or (d) juvenile delinquency?

4. Identify three or more display areas on campus. As a class, decide what type or form of erosion *and* accretion measures might be used to assess the popularity of the three areas. Using the measures assess the three areas and as a class arrive at a consensus on which one of the three areas is the most popular or most utilized.

REFERENCES

Adams, G. R., & Read, D. (1983). Personality and social influence styles of attractive and unattractive college age women. *Journal of Psychology, 114*, 151–157.

Adams, G. R., & Hamm, N. (1973). A partial test of the "contiguity" and "generalized imitation" theories of the social modeling process. *Journal of Genetic Psychology, 123*, 145–154.

Allport G. (1937). *Personality.* New York: Holt.

Bakeman, R., & Dabbs, Jr., J. M. (1976). Social interaction observed: Some approaches to the analysis of behavior streams. *Personality and Social Psychology Bulletin, 2*, 335–345.

Barker, G. (1968). *Sociological psychology: Concepts and methods for studying the environment of human behavior.* Stanford, Calif.: Stanford University Press.

Benedict, R. (1946). *Patterns of culture.* New York: Penguin Books.

Berkowitz, L. (1975). *A survey of social psychology.* Hinsdale, Ill.: Dryden Press.

Bogdan, R. (1972). *Participant observation in organizational settings.* Syracuse, N.Y.: Syracuse University Press.

Boice, R. (1983). Observational skills. *Psychological Bulletin, 93,* 3–29.

Brandt, R. M. (1972). *Studying behavior in natural settings.* New York: Holt, Rinehart and Winston.

Cairns, R. B. (1979). *Social development: the origins and plasticity of interchanges.* New York: W. H. Freeman.

Denzin, N. K. (Ed.). (1970a). *Sociological methods: A sourcebook.* Chicago: Aldine.

Denzin, N. K. (1970b). *The research act: A theoretical introduction to sociological methods.* Chicago: Aldine.

Fielding, N. G., & Fielding, J. L. (1986). *Linking data.* Qualitative research methods series. Vol. 4. Beverly Hills: Sage Publications.

Fine, G. A., & Sandstrom, K. L. (1988). *Knowing children: Participant observation with minors.* Qualitative research methods series. Vol. 15. Beverly Hills: Sage Publications.

Gore, R. (1978). Eyes of science. *National Geographic, 153,* 360–388.

Humphreys, L. (1970). Tearoom trade: Impersonal sex in public places. *Transaction, 7,* 10–25.

Hutt, S. J., & Hutt, C. (1970). *Direct observation and measurement of behavior.* Springfield, Ill.: Charles C. Thomas.

Johnson, S. M., & Bolstad, O. D. (1973). Methodological issues in naturalistic observation: Some problems and solutions for field research. In Leo A. Hamerlynck, Lee C. Handy, & Eric J. Mash (Eds.), *Behavior change: Methodology, concepts and practice.* Champaign, Ill.: Research Press.

Junker, B. H. (1960). *Fieldwork: An introduction to the social sciences.* Chicago: University of Chicago Press.

Kessen, W. (1983). *Handbook of child psychology: Vol. 1: History, theory and methods.* (4th ed.). New York: Wiley & Sons.

Keniston, K. (1971). *Youth and dissent.* New York: Harcourt-Brace-Jovanovich.

Kirk, J., & Miller, M. L. (1986). *Reliability and validity in qualitative research.* Qualitative research methods series. Vol. 1. Beverly Hills, Sage Publications.

Knapp, M. L. (1978). *Nonverbal communication in human interaction.* New York: Holt, Rinehart and Winston.

Lamb, M. E., Suomi, S. J., & Stephenson, G. R. (1979). *Social interaction analysis: Methodological issues.* Madison, Wis.: University of Wisconsin Press.

Lewis, O. (1959). *Five families: Mexican case studies in the culture of poverty.* New York: Basic Books.

Liebow, E. (1967). *Tally's Corner: A study of Negro streetcorner men.* Boston: Little and Brown.

Malinowski, B. (1962). *Sex, culture and myth.* New York: Harcourt, Brace and World.

Marston, A. R., London, P., Cohen, N., & Cooper, L. M. (1977). *In vivo* observation of the eating behavior of obese and nonobese subjects. *Journal of Consulting and Clinical Psychology, 45,* 335–336.

Masters, W., & Johnson, V. (1966). *Human sexual response.* Boston: Little and Brown.

McCracken, G. (1988). *The long interview.* Qualitative research methods series. Vol. 13. Beverly Hills, Sage Publications.

Mead, M. (1922). *Coming of age in Samoa.* New York: Blue Ribbon Books.

Mead, M. (Ed.). (1937). *Cooperation and competition among primitive peoples.* New York: McGraw-Hill.

Montemayor, R., & Van Komen, R. (1980). Age segregation of adolescents in and out of school. *Journal of Youth and Adolescence, 9,* 371–381.

Olesen, V. L., & Whittaker, E. W. (1970). Role-making in participant observation: Processes in the researcher–actor relationship. In N. K. Denzin (Ed.), *Sociological methods: A sourcebook.* Chicago: Aldine.

Pearsall, M. (1965). Participant observation as role and method in behavioral research. *Nursing Research, 14,* 38.

Rheingold, H. L., & Cook, K. V. (1975). The contents of boys' and girls' rooms as an index of parents' behavior. *Child Development, 46,* 459–463.

Rosenthal, R. (1973). On the social psychology of the self-fulfilling prophecy: Further evidence for Pygmalion effects and their mediating mechanisms. In M. King (Ed.), *Reading and school achievement: Cognitive and affective influence.* New Brunswick, N.J.: Rutgers University Press.

Runkel, P. J., & McGrath, J. E. (1972). *Research on human behavior: A systematic guide to method.* New York: Holt, Rinehart and Winston.

Sackett, G. P. (1978). *Observing behavior* (vol. 2). Baltimore: University Park Press.

Schvaneveldt, J. D. (1968). The development of a film test for the measurement of perceptions toward maternal overprotection. *The Journal of Genetic Psychology, 112,* 255–266.

Sherif, M., Harvey, O. J., White, B. J., Hood, W. R., & Sherif, C. W. (1961). *Intergroup conflict and cooperation: The Robbers Cave experiment.* A publication of the Institute of Group Relations, Muzafer Sherif, Director, The University of Oklahoma, Norman, Okla.

Simonton, D. K. (1977). Creative productivity, age, and stress: A biographical time-series analysis of 10 classical composers. *Journal of Personality and Social Psychology, 35,* 791–804.

Simpson, M. J. A. (1979). Problems of recording behavioral data by keyboard. In M. Lamb, S. Suomi, & B. Stephenson (Eds.), *Social interaction analysis.* Madison, Wis.: University of Wisconsin Press.

Stephenson, G. (1979). *PLEXYN.* In M. Lamb, S. Suomi, & G. Stephenson (Eds.), *Social interaction analysis.* Madison, Wis.: University of Wisconsin Press.

Stephenson, G. R., Smith, D. P., & Roberts, T. W. (1975). The SSR System: An open format event recording system with computerized transcription. *Behavioral Research Methods and Instrumentation, 8,* 259–277.

Tunnell, G. B. (1977). Three dimensions of naturalness: An expanded definition of field research. *Psychological Bulletin, 84,* 426–437.

Webb, E. J., Campbell, D. T., Schwartz, R. D., & Sechrest, L. (1981). *Nonreactive measures in the social sciences.* Chicago: Rand McNally.

Weisz, J. R. (1978). Transcontextual validity in developmental research. *Child Development, 49,* 1–12.

Weller, S. C., & Romney, A. K. (1988). *Systematic data collection.* Qualitative research methods series. Vol. 10. Beverly Hills: Sage Publications.

Wright, H. (1960). Observational child study. In Paul H. Mussen (Ed.), *Handbook of research methods in child development.* New York: Wiley.

CHAPTER 12

Obtaining Data: In the Laboratory

OUTLINE

Introduction
Experimentation and the Laboratory Technique
Hiding the Independent and Dependent Variables
Deception Methodology
Role Enactment Methodology
Issues of Internal and External Validity
Ethical Issues in Deception
Debriefing
Summary
Problems and Applications
References

KEY TERMS

Deception methodology
Role enactment
Hypothetical role playing
Empirical role taking

Experimenter bias
Debriefing
Dehoaxing

STUDY GUIDE QUESTIONS

1. How does the researcher utilize the independent and dependent variable in experimental laboratory studies?

2. What is meant by deception methodology? Are there alternatives to such methodologies?
3. Can role enactment methodology play a substantial role in experimental laboratory research?
4. Are there limitations to internal and external validity in using role enactment techniques?
5. What are the central ethical issues in using deception in a laboratory study?
6. The concept of debriefing includes notions of dehoaxing and desensitizing. What does each of these notions mean?

Role of the Scientist

Experimental research focuses on the study of cause-and-effect relationships. The scientist is interested, in an experimental context, to study the effect of an independent variable (cause) on a dependent variable (or consequence). While the basic steps of experimentation are founded on the concept of the experimental design, the degree to which one must hide or not reveal the treatment (independent variable) varies with the research question asked. Scientists must decide whether deception is necessary or whether alternative experimental strategies can and should be used. As we discuss in this chapter, alternatives are available. However, in all forms of experimentation it is necessary to control for numerous "experimenter" effects to assure that the correct cause-and-effect relationship has been detected.

Role of the Consumer

All prevention and intervention programs are designed to initiate changes in attitudes, knowledge, feelings, or behaviors. Therefore, as a consumer of research one should learn to identify what factors when modified through a treatment effect can result in change. Research findings based on experimental techniques are likely to provide the strongest evidence for detecting factors that should be included in treatment programs designed to create behavioral change. However, consumers should be cautioned that unconfounded treatment effects can be observed in the laboratory that may not actually occur in the context of a more complex social living environment. Further, it is important to recognize that what is thought to be a true experimentally induced cause-and-effect can in actuality be a simple experimenter effect confound.

INTRODUCTION

Many of us had our first introduction to laboratory experimentation in high school chemistry. Beginning with a few beakers of chemicals, a lab book, and precautionary safety equipment, one learned from firsthand experience the steps of correct experimentation. Through experimental trial and error we tested the effects of combining varying chemicals and learned that certain combinations resulted in highly repeatable effects. Many of the same steps are undertaken in social science experimentation. In this chapter, we will review the essential ingredients to obtaining data in the laboratory. In an earlier chapter (see Chapter 7), we explored the basic designs involved in obtaining data within the available research designs. First, we shall begin with a brief discussion of the role of laboratory research, analyze how the independent and dependent variables are utilized, and examine two major strategies in laboratory methodology.

EXPERIMENTATION AND THE LABORATORY TECHNIQUE

The laboratory research technique is the major methodology employed during the experimental process. As outlined in Chapter 7, the experimental process involves comparisons of experimental and control groups under well-defined and structured conditions. To obtain such information, we typically utilize the highly structured confines of the research laboratory—although the experimental design can, in actuality, be applied in various contexts and settings.

The major contribution of the laboratory technique is its ability to control for confounding variable influences in identifying cause-and-effect relations between the independent and dependent variables. Within certain limits, laboratory research can be completed to study such broad social issues as aging, compliance to social pressure, effects of group membership, normative behavioral expectations, ecological influences, or institutional influences on human behavior. As noted in Chapter 7, one of the primary limitations of experimental laboratory research has to do with the possible artificiality of the laboratory setting. However, careful design of laboratory research experiences can minimize this problem.

HIDING THE INDEPENDENT AND DEPENDENT VARIABLES

North American social scientists are thoroughly ingrained with the notion that laboratory research variables need to be concealed to avoid the possibility of the research subject discovering the true purpose of the investigation. The general belief is that a subject would not behave in a natural manner if he or she were aware of the purpose or intent of the investigation. It is commonly maintained that the research subject, knowingly or unknowingly, would behave in ways that confirm the researcher's expectations and thus invalidate the results of the study.

But how do scientists keep the subject in the "dark" and still study the subject's behavior? Concealment of the purpose of a research project is established in two major ways. Either the independent variable is not disclosed, the dependent variable is hidden, or both (Kelman, 1976). In most research projects the subject is either *not informed* as to what independent or dependent variables are being manipulated, or *misinformed* as to the manipulation process. Therefore, the researcher maintains the subjects will act in a natural manner to the manipulation, given they are unaware of what is actually being manipulated. Just as frequently we are likely to hide the true intent of measurement. At the least deceptive level, we merely refrain from informing the subject what is actually being measured. At the most extreme we measure the opposite of what we say we are assessing. *Deception* methodologies are in reality the foundation of experimentation in social science.

Deception Methodology

Mixon (1977) has likened deception methodology to a "confidence game" where a con man deludes an individual to acquire their voluntary cooperation in a dishonest game of profits. Thus, deception research involves the use of false impressions for the sake of scientific gain. The scientific confidence game might be thought of as a sort of victimization of research subjects. Ethical issues abound when using such techniques. At the close of this chapter we shall return to these issues.

Milgram's (1963) study of obedience to authority stands out as a classic illustration of deception research. Under the pretense of a learning study, Professor Milgram had college students enter a research room accompanied by a research confederate who was disguised as a fellow student. The research subject was placed behind an apparatus that delivered shock to the student-confederate. Research subjects were instructed to administer shock to the student-confederate when he or she erred on a learning task. In reality the student-confederate only pretended to be shocked by the bogus apparatus, and the study was actually an investigation of obedience to authority (in this case obedience to the researcher). The major conclusion was that the majority (more than 60%) of the students were likely to follow the instructions of the researcher and administer the maximum amount of shock, which was clearly labeled on the apparatus as harmful. Hence, students thought they were engaging in a learning experience that was really a study of obedience, destructive obedience at that.

Both forms of deception are illustrated in this laboratory investigation. First, students were informed they were engaging in a learning study that was actually designed to study obedience. Second, they were led to believe that the administration of punishment for errors on learning tasks was a measure of learning efficiency. As we have noted, this measure was actually used to assess the degree of compliance to authority in the use of punishment instead of a learning measure. Hence, Milgram used deception in defining his independent variable (authority) and his dependent variable measure (administration of punishment).

Several social scientists have voiced their concern about identifying available research subjects for deception studies. The typical population sample for deception research comes from university and college enrollments (Higbee, Millard, & Folkman, 1982). All too frequently, social science research subjects come from introductory courses. The typical pattern is to post general descriptions announcements on appropriate bulletin boards where students can place their name as a volunteer subject for any one of a number of research projects. Usually this involvement is required in the name of science, or extra credit is given for each study in which the student completes participation. For the most part, students are not informed that deception may be part of the experimental laboratory experience (Campbell, 1969). However, arguments by Mixon (1977) assert that the reputation of science as an open, honest process is in question if the scientist fails to inform the subject that deception is required in a particular investigation. The ultimate question is whether we can afford to have a bank of social science facts built around false

---

Tips for Consumers 12.1

The use of deception methodology involves hiding the independent or dependent variable (or both). Unfortunately, when deception is used it becomes difficult to know whether the subject became aware or not of the intent of the study. Researchers can use various techniques to determine whether the subject was aware of the independent or dependent variable. To assess whether the deception was effective the consumer should look for evidence that the researcher can justify the variable was effective. The two most common techniques to look for in assessing the internal validity of the deception study include the following:

1. evidence from ratings after the study has been completed that the subject perceived certain characteristics of the experimental condition consistently with the actual event. For example, if research subjects experienced an interaction with a warm versus a cold confederate, did they rate the confederate as being more cold when in the cold condition? Or if the subjects interacted with a so-called physically attractive confederate did they rate this person as being significantly more attractive than a so-called unattractive confederate?

2. during the debriefing subjects are asked if they recognized what was actually being studied. For example, in conformity studies subjects are asked if they were aware of the actual experimental process and whether they behaved in a manner to fulfill the expectations of the researchers.

As a consumer making judgments about the internal validity of the deception study, it is most appropriate to expect the researcher to provide evidence that the deception condition created an effect and thus served as a true independent variable.

---

impressions, lies, and deceit. The counterpoint of course is, Can we afford to house a bank of social science facts that have been openly acquired, but lacking in validity? Fortunately, we have other data collection strategies that avoid this dilemma. (See Tips for Consumers 12.1.)

Role Enactment Methodology

As a substitute for laboratory deception, *role playing methodology* has been proposed as a viable alternative (e.g., Kelman, 1976; Miller, 1972). As Clyde Hendrick (1977a) notes:

> Role playing is a sociological construct . . . and is generally used to denote overt enactment of one's own role as appropriate to a given situation . . . the basic notion of role is often used to refer to reciprocal social positions (e.g., clerk–customer, husband–wife). (p. 468)

With each role in life there is a host of behaviors that are appropriate to the role. Thus, role playing is merely the enactment of social behaviors that are appropriate for a role in a given situational context. Indeed, Hendrick (1977a,b) explains that in all social science research, role enactment or deception methodologies included, it is assumed by the researcher that research subjects will behave in their typical manner according to their own self-role during any given experiment. In fact, an investigation is valid only to the extent to which people act according to their self-role. Therefore, when individuals are asked to respond how they should or would behave in particular situations according to their everyday self-role, their responses should be acceptable information for the scientific community.

In general, role enactment methodology requires the research participant to report what they would do in a particular social situation in which they are asked to pretend to be. Therefore, the subjects must make a cognitive decision about (1) how they would behave, (2) the social norms operating in the situation, and (3) the social desirability and consequences of their actions. Behavior is typically measured by the researcher using this methodology through verbal reports by the subject. More often than not, the research subjects are told to put themselves into a particular situation, are asked to read a script, and asked to report how they believe they would behave.

For example, Mixon (1977) was extremely successful in replicating the results ◀ reported by Milgram (1963) in his research on obedience through a role enactment study in which research participants responded to questions on behavior after hearing a script describing the behavior of the researcher and subject and examining a picture of the shock apparatus. More recent research by Geller (1978) in which degree of personal involvement was monitored throughout a role enactment replication of the Milgram study suggests that role playing strategies are most successful with subjects who can suspend the "as if" nature of such methodology and involve themselves in the role playing task as a realistic situation. In a summary paper, Alexander and Scriven (1977), in a symposium on role playing, state their position on the use of role enactment accordingly.

> It seems that when the focus is not on the methodology per se, role playing can be a legitimate technique for obtaining data. Apparently, role-playing procedures are acceptable when we study processes that involve conscious and purposive plans, negotiations, decision making strategies, and ordinary, everyday interactional patterns. (p. 456)

While role enactment methodology has its advocates, there are many who question its utility. Aronson and Carlsmith (1968) have questioned its lack of apparent realism. They argue that the lack of experimental realism, in which subjects are asked merely to respond passively to situations, provides little useful scientific information. However, Krupat (1977) maintains that the passivity criticism is easily handled by having subjects act rather than make judgments passively, thus eliminating the criticism of lack of spontaneity and realism. Cooper (1976) argues involved participation is better than role enactment because the first measures what people "would" do, while the latter primarily measures how people feel they "should" but not necessarily "would" behave. While several investigations comparing deception and role playing methodologies on experimental outcome (e.g., Holmes & Bennett, 1974) have failed to find equivalent results, other investigations, such as Mixon (1977) or Geller (1978), have shown that equivalent results can be obtained between deception and role enactment methodologies. The question as to whether role enactment is equivalent to deception methodology in its scientific usefulness is yet to be answered. However, its use in scientific journal reports is increasing, and there is little doubt in many scientists' minds that it is likely to gain in scientific credibility (see Hendrick, 1977a,b).

Given the experimental nature of role enactment methodology, Spencer (1978) offers a reasonable caution in the use of such methodology. Spencer reports there are two types of role playing methodologies currently in use. *Hypothetical role playing* consists of passive judgments to situational scripts in which the involvement of the role player is not monitored. Hence, we can never be sure how involved the subject actually is in the task. Therefore, it is argued we cannot be assured how reliable and valid the information is under hypothetical role playing. This argument is similar to that of Aronson and Carlsmith (1968), wherein they argue one cannot be assured that the subject has moved from the equivocal role of "as if" to an unequivocal role of "as is." *Empirical role taking,* on the other hand, involves experimental prescription of a role and reliable monitoring by the experimenter. Through *in vivo* observation of the subject during the role enactment task, the researcher documents whether or not the subject actually "gets into" the role assignment. This technique assures a certain degree of internal validity (measuring what you believe you are measuring) but does not assure external validity. In this case one cannot be assured without further comparative studies whether the results of empirical role playing research can be generalized to findings by deception studies.

In summary, deception research is very common in social science laboratory research. However, deception research appears to be increasingly less palatable to many young research scientists, due to the ethical issues related to deceit. Hence, role enactment methodologies that might be used to supplement deception methodology and decrease the conflict for the scientist associated with the ethics of deceit are evolving. There seems to be little disagreement that role playing is an acceptable methodology for the generation of hypotheses (Kelman, 1967; Miller, 1972); however, we have noted that scientists question whether it can become an equivocal replacement for deception research. Consumers of research might be cautious making professional generalizations based on role enactment theory, given its quasi-experimental nature, without identifying replication of the findings based on more traditional involved participation laboratory methodologies (such as deception).

Issues of Internal and External Validity

While the role of experimenter is an essential one in the scientific process, it also has the possible impact of a confounding variable. The effect of the experimenter on scientific results has been studied extensively in recent years (Rosenthal, 1964, 1966; Rosenthal & Rosnow, 1969). In particular, Rosenthal (1966) has identified five specific types of experimenter effects that can potentially influence a subject's behavior outside of the research treatment condition. While researchers do not consciously attempt to create intentional experimenter effects, numerous characteristics of the researcher can have serious confounding influences on subjects' behavioral responses in laboratory research. These effects, if present, confound the results of experimental and control group comparisons, leaving the scientists unsure as to whether the experimental treatment or the researcher created the specific change in behavior by the subjects. Thus, problems associated with internal validity become central to accepting cause-and-effect outcomes. Given most, if not all, data in laboratory settings are obtained during experimenter–subject interaction, it is important to delineate the five main types of factors that might be associated with *experimenter biasing effects* in laboratory research. Further, it would be wise for consumers of research to be on guard for such possible effects in research reports before building extensive intervention programs upon laboratory research that might be confounded by such biasing factors.

Biosocial attributes, such as the researcher's sex, age, or race, may influence the type, quantity, or completeness of information gained. A male subject may be inclined to behave in one way in front of a male researcher and another way in front of a female experimenter. A highly bigoted research subject may behave naturally with a white experimenter but not with a black experimenter. Youthful researchers may elicit different types of social behavior than elderly researchers, particularly given our cultural aging biases. Therefore, researchers may wish to control for such effects by comparing data gathered by males versus females, blacks versus whites, or young versus mature research scientists.

Psychosocial attributes are also possible confounding variables in laboratory research. Such personality characteristics as anxiety, need for approval, authoritarianism, or hostility of the experimenter can contribute to subjects' behavior. Likewise, such social psychological attributes as relative status or warmth of the experimenter can have a biasing effect such that high status versus low status, and warm versus cold experimenters, may elicit differential behavior in their subjects. As Rosenthal (1966) indicates, the primary manner of controlling for possible psychosocial experimenter bias effects is through either asking the experimenter about his or her own behavior or using standardized psychological tests that can identify and compare researchers with high, medium, and low psychosocial attributes. Therein, such attributes are studied to assess possible influences on subjects' behavior.

Situational factors, such as experimenter's acquaintanceship with the research subject, have likewise been found to be possible confounding influences in social science research. Pre-experimental acquaintanceships, for example, may influence the subject's behavior and be misinterpreted as an experimental effect. Or experimenters who are acquainted with certain subjects may share similar personality characteristics that lead to behavioral correlates independent of the treatment while appearing to be due to the experimental influence. This type of experimenter effect as it interacts with treatment influences in laboratory research creates a confounding situational effect that is almost impossible to interpret. To totally eliminate unexpected situational factors, such as the random chance of having an acquaintanceship with a subject, would require the elimination of contact between researchers and subjects. It is, in our minds, not in the best interest of science to eliminate researcher–subject interactions, given scientific discoveries require direct, firsthand experiences with the phenomenon under investigation—in this case human beings and their behavior. However, certain types of laboratory research do call for the control of such possible confounding influences.

Experimenter *modeling* can be an additional biasing factor in laboratory research. According to Rosenthal (1966), "When there is a significant relationship between the experimenter's own performance of the particular task he requires of his subjects and the performance he obtains from his subjects, we may speak of an experimenter's modeling effect" (p. 112). For example, Rosenthal notes that previous research has demonstrated that high authoritarian experimenters have been unable to convince research subjects of the value of nonauthoritarian educational methods. One way of controlling for such effects would be to utilize experimenters who are neutral or middle-of-the-road individuals who would not be modeling any type of extreme behavior.

A great deal of research now shows that *experimenter expectancy* also influences subjects' behavior. Thus, the expectancy of the researcher about how the subjects are anticipated to behave can lead to subjects' behaving in such a manner as to merely confirm the experimenter's expectations. From statements in Chapters 2 and 7 we know that the hypothesis consists of a proposed relation between an independent and dependent variable. The scientist thus expects a particular relation in the independent and dependent variables in scientific observation of behavior. Through subtle cues the scientist may, unintentionally, influence subjects to behave in manners consistent with this hypothesis. Perhaps one way of eliminating this possibility is to train research assistants who are naive or unaware of the scientists' hypothesis to collect laboratory data.

To summarize, several types of experimenter effects can lead to unexpected and undesirable confounding influences and limit internal validity in laboratory research. The experimenter, through his or her role and personal attributes, can influence the outcome of a study in such a way that one cannot be assured if it is experimenter effects or treatment effects that caused particular changes in human behavior. Most of these effects can be controlled through either added control group comparisons, statistical analyses, or pre-experimental precautions.

Experimental research has frequently been criticized due to its so-called failure to generalize to "real world" behavior because of sample bias or artificiality of settings (e.g., Babbie, 1975; Bannister, 1966). However, Mook (1983) has argued that much experimental research is not designed or intended to such generalization. Many times we are intending to ask less ambitious questions in our experimental laboratory research. We may simply be asking whether something can happen, rather than whether it usually or typically does happen. Other times we are merely making predictions that something should happen in a lab setting. Third, Mook (1983) suggests "we may demonstrate the power of a phenomenon by showing that it happens even under unnatural conditions that ought to preclude it" (p. 382).

It is our contention that most laboratory research is designed to establish controls over numerous confounding variables to assure high internal validity. Generalization from the experiment to the prediction of real-life behavior is frequently not a primary concern. Thus, much laboratory research is conducted in highly controlled environments to establish that a cause-and-effect relation can occur within a lab setting. Using such findings researchers may then enter the field and attempt to determine if the cause-and-effect relation does indeed occur when naturally occurring events manifest themselves and therein affect behavior. It is at this point that the researcher becomes concerned about external validity and attends to issues of sampling and the nature of the research setting.

▶ Mook (1983) uses the following example to make our last point clear. In a study of person perception reported by Argyle (1969), research subjects were asked to predict IQ differences between individuals wearing and not wearing eyeglasses after viewing them 15 seconds in a lab setting. The results indicated that the individuals wearing spectacles were predicted to have on the average 13 more IQ points. Thus laboratory experimentation revealed that in a brief laboratory encounter subjects will predict high intelligence toward persons wearing glasses. However, one might ask what external validity might there be for making judgments on a 15-second observation. Further, might not the exclusive focus on glasses exaggerate the independent variable's (wearing versus not wearing glasses) effect due to its isolation in the laboratory context? In addressing such validity issues, when the same phenomenon was studied in the context of a five-minute conversation (a real-life setting), wearing spectacles made no difference in predicting intelligence. This simple example illustrates that laboratory experimentation reveals what *can* happen under highly controlled conditions, but further research in settings with high external validity may reveal it is not likely to occur in natural environmental contexts. This does not make the laboratory findings useless, merely limited to certain confined conditions.

Ethical Issues in Deception

As we have indicated, experimental methods employing deception are definitely in vogue within certain realms of social science research. But what is actually meant by deception? And how often is this technique actually employed? Seeman (1969) presents evidence that between 1948 and 1963, for the *Journal of Personality* and the *Journal of Abnormal and Social Psychology,* the mean frequency of use per journal issue increased from 18.47% in 1948 to 38.17% in 1963. Further, Stricker (1967) reports that of the 457 articles that appeared in *Journal of Abnormal and Social Psychology, Journal of Personality, Journal of Social Psychology,* and *Sociometry* in 1964, 19.3%, or 88 articles, used some form of deception. More recently, Menges (1973) has shown that the use of deception techniques is no less infrequent in more contemporary scientific literature. No wonder Kelman (1976), some years ago, was compelled to comment, "I sometimes feel that we are training a generation of students who do not know that there is any other way of doing experiments in our field . . . too often deception is used not as a last resort, but as a matter of course" (p. 3). Can we say any less a decade or two later?

But the use of deception seems inherently alien to typical codes of research ethics. Most codes call for "openness" and "honesty" with the research participants. Are we not only developing increasing generations of researchers who rely on deception but also generations of subjects who expect scientists to deceive them? Perhaps Baumrind (1971) has encapsulated the issue of subject–scientist relations and the use of deception:

> The research psychologist [and social scientist] has many privileges not possessed by other people with whom the subject deals, and these privileges are granted to him on the assumption that he will be responsible, trustworthy, and altruistic in the conduct of his professional life. Fundamental moral principles of reciprocity and justice are violated when the research psychologist, using his position of trust, acts to deceive or degrade those whose extension of trust is granted on the basis of a contrary role expectation. . . . The harm is cumulative to the individual and society. (p. 890)

We, as social scientists, are unaware of the long-range implications. Let us all hope it does not undermine the real intent of an open and public science. We have, however, seen earlier in this chapter that new techniques (role playing methodologies) are being developed that can be used as an alternative to deception procedures.

Debriefing

The use of deception in social science research has created a need for an additional procedure, that of *debriefing* the subject. In many ways, debriefing is similar to a psychological "defense" mechanism of *undoing.* When we abuse, hurt, insult, or damage another, our internal feelings of guilt frequently lead us to make attempts at undoing or correcting the problem. The general mechanism is one of overreacting toward another in hopes that this positive behavior will cancel out prior negative feelings as if they had never developed or occurred. Experimental evidence suggests that debriefing procedures may, under certain conditions, actually be effective in correcting misconceptions or negative feelings (Berscheid, Baron, Dermer, & Libman, 1973). However, the outcome of the investigation when disclosed to the subject may actually have an increasingly negative effect if the subjects reacted in socially undesirable ways (e.g., Bickman & Zarantonello, 1978).

Holmes (1976a,b) has indicated that the importance of debriefing falls into two major categories. First, we debrief to "remove any misconceptions" that may have occurred during the experimental process. Second, we use debriefing as a means of removing any potential "undesirable consequences" for the research subject. Holmes (1976a) has further indicated that the debriefing process can be centered on two aspects of the experiment, the experimental *deception* or the research participant's *behavior*. The former technique is referred to by Holmes as *dehoaxing,* the latter as *desensitizing*.

But do we have evidence that suggests dehoaxing and desensitizing can actually "undo" undesirable consequences following a deception experiment? An extensive review of the experimental literature (Holmes, 1976a) indicates this technique when properly used can be reliable as a viable post-experimental technique for eliminating misconceptions and misinformation following participation in a deception investigation. But the responsibility for the success of such a procedure remains in the hands of the researcher, who must diligently maintain responsibility for assuring the effectiveness of the dehoaxing–debriefing process. A similar conclusion can be drawn on the utility of desensitization of the technique of insightful discussion about the nature of one's behavior (Holmes, 1976b). However, an added caution might be noted. In dehoaxing, the subject is deceived and is informed of such. His or her actual performance or behavior is ignored. The subject is left feeling justified for this action because of deception. Therefore, any remaining hostility about the experience is likely to be projected toward the "deceitful" experimenter, thus externalizing any residual anger.

In contrast, desensitizing the subject is typically used to help the person learn something about human behavior including his or her own self. No doubt if the subject's performance was admirable, the subject leaves the debriefing experience with a feeling of positive reinforcement, heightened self-esteem, and perhaps a sense of self-confidence. However, what of subjects who find they have performed questionably in socially desirable terms? As Holmes (1976b) himself indicates, there can be no refuting the fact that the subject actually behaved in the manner discussed. Further, subjects may readily see such behavior as deeply ingrained in their typical behavioral pattern. Typically, the researcher attempts to convince the subject that the behavior was situationally determined or that the behavior was not unusual or abnormal. If these techniques work as a debriefing procedure, which they appear to, we can be relieved of our ethical responsibility for the subject's well-being.

But what if we fail? It seems apparent that if desensitization following a deception experiment fails, the research participants are likely to be at further psychological risk, internalizing hostility and anger for their socially undesirable behavior. Further, one could speculate that failure may set into process the creation of an undesirable self-fulfilling prophecy.

Although a certain degree of deception experimentation may be justifiable on several ethical grounds, the responsibility of the researcher is expected to increase with the use of such a technique. Given the subject is put into an experience where there is potential psychological risk, postexperimental debriefing techniques become important and essential tools. (See Tips for Consumers 12.2.)

Tips for Consumers 12.2

Deception research requires adequate care be given to the debriefing process. In making a judgment about whether the researcher acted ethically, each deception study should be judged on its own worth. As a consumer of research, one must decide whether the deception was appropriate, acceptable, and ultimately beneficial. The choice of using deception research in program development hinges not only on the internal and external validity of the experimental technique, but the ethical foundation on which the study was completed. Before constructing intervention or prevention programs on a set of facts, the consumer should ask whether these two conditions have been met. It may be just as unethical to build an applied intervention program on unethically obtained facts as it was originally to acquire such facts through inappropriate scientific conduct. Therefore, each and every deception study should be scrutinized for the benefit(s) obtained, the possibility of alternatives, and the use of appropriate debriefing techniques at the closure of such studies. Ethical responsibility lies both with the researcher and the consumer.

SUMMARY

The collection of laboratory data is both an exciting and tedious process. It is a methodology of great precision and control. Many excellent studies in laboratory settings have provided humanity with an understanding of important cause-and-effect relationships between independent and dependent variables.

The major points we have made in this chapter about collecting data in laboratory settings include:

1. Most social scientists believe it is necessary to hide the independent and dependent variables in laboratory research. The assumption is that should the subject become aware of the intent and purpose of the investigation the study will be invalidated by the subject's awareness.

2. Two major types of laboratory methodologies stand out in research with human subjects.

   a. Deception research involves hiding the independent or dependent variables (or both) from the subject in an attempt to assure spontaneity and realism by the subject and his behavior.

   b. Role enactment methodology, on the other hand, relies upon the subject's ability to assume a role and report how he or she might respond in a specific situation. Two specific types of role enactment methodologies include

      (1) hypothetical role playing in which passive judgments are made on situational descriptions of human interactions

      (2) empirical role playing in which subjects are assigned specific roles and asked to engage in an experimental simulation while being monitored for degree of involvement

3. It is important to recognize that the experimenter can become a confounding variable in laboratory research through certain correlates of the role of researcher/experimenter. The experimenter's biosocial characteristics, psychosocial attributes, personal modeling, and expectancies, along with situational factors outside of the experiment,

can lead to unexpected and undesirable influences beyond the treatment condition on the research subject's behavior.

4. While deception research may, at times, be necessary, the ultimate impact on free scientific endeavor may be harmed.

5. When deception is used, two techniques are available for remediation of deceiving the subject
    a. dehoaxing, whereby the subject is informed of the experimental deception.
    b. desensitizing, whereby the subject is expected to learn something about his or her own behavior.

PROBLEMS AND APPLICATIONS

1. As a classroom assignment divide the class into four groups with each group responsible for finding a research study using deception in a sociological, home economics, psychological, education, or nursing project. Attempt to arrive at a nondeception alternative for each study. Have each group report to the class on their proposed alternatives.

2. There may be times when deception is so common in the form of everyday experiences that to experience an equivalence in a laboratory context may not be disturbing to a subject. Discuss what some of these contexts might be and create a deception laboratory study of similar nature.

3. Bring to class some naive subjects and have them role enact the Milgram obedience study. With half of the students use a dehoaxing technique and observe their reactions. For the remainder use a desensitization debriefing procedure and observe their reactions. Was one technique more useful than another? If so, why?

4. In class engage in a discussion as to whether you believe you can role play or role enact a life experience with the same realism as everyday life. Design a small experiment where you have individuals complete both a role enactment and a true experimental study, and compare the findings. Are they similar or different? Have the subjects discuss the distinctions they experienced between the two techniques.

REFERENCES

Alexander, C. N., Jr., & Scriven, G. D. (1977). Role playing: An essential component of experimentation. *Personality and Social Psychology Bulletin, 3*, 455–466.

Argyle, M. (1969). *Social interaction.* Chicago: Atherton Press.

Aronson, E., & Carlsmith, J. M. (1968). Experimentation in social psychology. In G. Lindzey & E. Aronson (Eds.), *The handbook of social psychology* (2nd ed., vol. 2). Reading, Mass.: Addison-Wesley.

Babbie, E. (1975). *The practice of social research.* Belmont, Calif.: Wadsworth.

Bannister, D. (1966). Psychology as an exercise in paradox. *Bulletin of the British Psychological Society, 19*, 21–26.

Baumrind, D. (1971). Principles of ethical conduct in the treatment of subjects: Reaction to the draft of the Committee on Ethical Standards in Psychological Research. *American Psychologist, 26*, 887–896.

Berscheid, E., Baron, R. S., Dermer, M., & Libman, M. (1973). Anticipating informed consent: An empirical approach. *American Psychologist, 28*, 913–925.

Bickman, L., & Zarantonello, M. (1978). The effects of deception and level of obedience on subject's ratings of the Milgram study. *Personality and Social Psychology Bulletin, 4,* 81–85.

Campbell, D. T. (1969). Prospective: Artifact and control. In R. Rosenthal & R. L. Rosnow (Eds.), *Artifact in behavioral research.* New York: Academic Press.

Cooper, J. (1976). Deception and role playing: On telling the good guys from the bad guys. *American Psychologist, 31,* 605–610.

Geller, D. M. (1978). Involvement in role-playing simulations: A demonstration with studies on obedience. *Journal of Personality and Social Psychology, 36,* 219–235.

Hendrick, C. (1977a). Role-taking, role-playing, and the laboratory experiment. *Personality and Social Psychology Bulletin, 3,* 467–478.

Hendrick, C. (1977b). Role-playing as a methodology for social research: A symposium. *Personality and Social Psychology Bulletin, 3,* 454.

Higbee, K. L., Millard, R. J., & Folkman, J. R. (1982). Social psychology research: Predominance of experimentation and college students. *Personality and Social Psychology Bulletin, 8,* 180–183.

Holmes, D. S. (1976a). Debriefing after psychological experiments: I. Effectiveness of post-deception dehoaxing. *American Psychologist, 31,* 858–867.

Holmes, D. S. (1976b). Debriefing after psychological experiments. II. Effectiveness of post-experimental desensitizing. *American Psychologist, 31,* 868–875.

Holmes, D. S., & Bennett, D. H. (1974). Experiments to answer questions raised by the use of deception in psychological research: I. Role playing as an alternative to deception; II. Effectiveness of debriefing after a deception; III. Effect of informed consent on deception. *Journal of Personality and Social Psychology, 29,* 358–367.

Kelman, H. C. (1976). Human use of human subjects: The problem of deception in social psychological experiments. *Psychological Bulletin, 67,* 1–11.

Krupat, E. (1977). A reassessment of role playing as a technique in social psychology. *Personality and Social Psychology Bulletin, 3,* 498–504.

Menges, R. J. (1973). Openness and honesty versus coercion and deception in psychological research. *American Psychologist, 28,* 1030–1034.

Milgram, S. (1963). Behavioral study of obedience. *Journal of Abnormal and Social Psychology, 67,* 371–378.

Miller, A. G. (1972). Role playing: An alternative to deception? *American Psychologist, 27,* 623–636.

Mixon, D. (1977). Why pretend to deceive? *Personality and Social Psychology Bulletin, 3,* 647–653.

Mook, D. (1983). In defense of external invalidity. *American Psychologist, 38,* 379–387.

Rosenthal, R. (1964). The effect of the experimenter on the results of psychological research. In B. Maher (Ed.), *Progress in experimental personality research* (Vol. 1). New York: Academic Press.

Rosenthal, R. (1966). *Experimenter effects in behavioral research.* New York: Appleton-Century-Crofts.

Rosenthal, R., & Rosnow, R. L. (Eds.). (1969). *Artifact in behavioral research.* New York: Academic Press.

Seeman, J. (1969). Deception in psychological research. *American Psychologist, 24,* 1025–1028.

Spencer, C. D. (1978). Two types of role playing: Threats to internal and external validity. *American Psychologist, 33,* 265–268.

Stricker, J. (1967). The true deceiver. *Psychological Bulletin, 68,* 13–20.

CHAPTER 13

Obtaining Data:
Projective and Indirect Methods

OUTLINE

A Historical View: The Sword as Stimulus
Defining Projective and Indirect Measures
> *A Profile of Selected Projective Techniques*
>> Sentence Completion Approaches
>> Word Association Measures
>> Double Entendre as Word Association
>> Story Completion Techniques
>> Association Techniques: The Rorschach
>> Thematic Apperception Test (TAT)
>> Children's Apperception Test (CAT)
>> Draw-A-Person Test
>> The Bender–Gestalt Test
>> Shopping List Method
>> "Spelunking" in Art: A Case of Psychodrama
> *Perspective-Taking about Projective and Indirect Methods for Obtaining Data*
Summary and Conclusions
Problems and Applications
References

KEY TERMS

Projective techniques
Indirect measures

Stimulus word
Double entendre words

Disguised measures

Projection

Covert feelings

Sentence completion

Sentence stub

Word association

Degree of structure

Self-revelation

Experimenter effects

Response latency

Story completion

The Rorschach

Free association

Inquiry time

Psychodrama

Sociodrama

STUDY GUIDE QUESTIONS

1. Do you believe that projective techniques have a vital role to play in social science research? Why?
2. What are the main characteristics of projective or indirect measures?
3. What are some of the main issues connected to the problem of validity in relation to the use of projective measures?
4. Are there particular strengths and weaknesses of projective techniques?
5. Why has the Rorschach test been so widely used by social scientists and interventionists?
6. In what type of research would one be most likely to use the Thematic Apperception Test?

Role of the Researcher

If researchers are to succeed in measuring the true attitudes, hopes, and behavior of people, it is clear that measures must be used that facilitate valid revelation of the self. Researchers are constantly faced with measurement situations in which respondents are either unwilling or unable to give the desired information. *Projective measures* were developed to be used in just such situations. Researchers use them to increase the ability and willingness of respondents to cooperate but at the same time not disclose the nature of the dependent variable under investigation.

Researchers should be aware of the types of projective measures, their strengths and limitations, and the conditions for using them. Reliability and validity problems pose major concerns for researchers who wish to use these techniques. One way of coping with this twin problem is to use projective techniques in conjunction with other measures. Some of the projective measures are quite structured and more objective, whereas others are very unstructured and require extensive training in order for an investigator to properly interpret the data.

Role of the Consumer

How objective are you as a consumer of research? Are you able to remove yourself from a situation or information and consider findings in a detached posture? Are you able to become involved in exercises where you are required to reveal your feelings, share your attitudes, and to "project" the real self? The broad area of projective techniques attempts to deal with our inner feelings so that we are both willing and able to share information with others without feeling threatened or inhibited.

Consumers of research need to know about these measures so as to carefully evaluate much of the research in the social sciences. Research in child study, therapy, counseling, and guidance, mental health, as well as consumer behavior, has used projective techniques extensively, and therefore, these areas are of particular interest to consumers of research.

A HISTORICAL VIEW: THE SWORD AS STIMULUS

If a respondent feels threatened, if the information sought after is sensitive or considered undesirable, and if the topic is value loaded, it may be very difficult or even impossible to obtain data through direct, conventional measures. If the person to be studied is "test wise" or if the information to be attained is readily apparent, it may be desirable to use an *indirect* or *disguised measure* to gather the data. Some subjects have the *ability*, but not the desire, to supply information, while others are *willing* but lack the ability to cooperate in the research process. *Projective* and *indirect* measures have been developed to address these two major problems.

One of the oldest and perhaps least recognized examples of using an indirect measure to assess human conflict was the case with Solomon and the two women who brought an infant before him to have him judge who was the true mother (1 Kings 3:16–28). As the situation is recorded, two harlots lived in a house and both gave birth to a child within a three-day period. During the night one of the mothers lay on her infant, and the baby died. The mother arose in the night and placed her now dead child at the bosom of the other woman and took this woman's baby to her own bosom. A conflict developed in the morning when the mother with the dead child attempted to feed it. She discovered that the dead child at her bosom was not her child. The women's inability to solve this argument of whose infant was still alive caused them to meet with King Solomon. After hearing their cases, he asked for a sword and directed that the living infant be cut into two equal parts and be given to the women. The true mother of the child pleaded with the king not to slay the infant, saying she would willingly let the other woman have the baby. The other woman would have allowed the infant to be slain and divided. King Solomon awarded the infant to the mother who pleaded for the baby's life to be spared, for he could accurately "read" the human emotions being displayed by these two mothers. The king's use of an *indirect* measure of truth telling created a situation in which the truth could emerge, whereas a direct confrontation had failed in arriving at a just decision. This example illustrates the problem of *willingness* of a person to disclose valid information.

Leaving King Solomon and tracing social behavior some 2,700 years to the present, it is apparent that people still have difficulties in both the willingness and the ability to disclose the appropriate information. This chapter seeks to cover the development, use, and types of indirect and projective measures that are available for research in social settings. This is a controversial area of methodology, with most investigators in agreement that reliability and validity are major problems in the use of most projective or indirect measures. The coverage here is intended to inform readers about this area of measurement and to review some of the strategies that have been developed to cope with projective and indirect measurement.

We are highly aware of the debates that surround the use of projective or indirect methods of measuring phenomena and realize that not all fields of research could or should make use of these measures. But since projective techniques have been used rather widely in the study of personality, deviancy, counseling, nursing, anthropology, and child development, we determined that it was important to at least cover the basic rudiments of their makeup and current utility in conducting research.

DEFINING PROJECTIVE AND INDIRECT MEASURES

Projective techniques are data collection devices using an unstructured stimuli or situation presented to a respondent. The respondent is expected to "project" the self into the situation of the stimuli in order to make sense and organize the stimuli. The assumption is made that a person will reveal important dimensions of self, personality, and experience while attempting to structure the stimuli. Frank (1965) discusses projective techniques as being very useful in tapping the private world of a person that otherwise could not or would not be revealed. The stimulus in a projective technique is purposefully ambiguous, thus allowing a person to reveal private fantasies and perceptions.

Murstein (1965) notes that the early view of projective techniques was that they would function as the equivalent of an X-ray to assess the covert world of a person. Furthermore, it was assumed that it was virtually impossible for a person to fake these tests. Neither of these claims has proven to be correct.

Gleser (1963) wrote a complete chapter on projective techniques for the *Annual Review of Psychology,* the first time that a chapter in this series had ever been devoted to this subject. Gleser viewed projective techniques as instruments that could measure a wide variety of complex responses presumably determined by the private feelings and attitudes of a person. Underlying psychodynamics are revealed through the use of such devices. The four most widely used projective techniques under this category are: Rorschach Test, the Machover Draw-A-Person Test, the Murray Thematic Apperception Test, and the Bender–Gestalt Visual Motor Test. The Goodenough Draw-a-Man Test was still widely used according to Gleser, but it had lost ground to the Machover version of this technique.

Subsequent chapters in the *Annual Review of Psychology* on projective techniques have been completed by Fisher (1967), Molish (1972), and Klopfer and Taulbee (1976). No new chapters in the *Annual Review of Psychology* have been published as of the late 1980s, but we predict that the next chapter on this topic will show high continued use. The use of such techniques has declined over time but is not dead, as indicated by the 500 journal articles pertaining to projective techniques for the review periods 1971–1974, which appeared in the 1976 volume. Klopfer and Taulbee (1976) conclude that the private and symbolic aspects of personality need evaluation since it is believed that most people in the long course of events are motivated by forces of which they are unaware. (See Tips for Consumers 13.1.) For example, Keen (1986) presents a fascinating book focusing on projective thinking in relationship to war and creating hostile images of the enemy. Using

---

Tips for Consumers 13.1

Please complete the ending to this situation. Be as detailed and honest as you can in the task: "At first, Mother told Melanie that she could not go to her swimming party unless she had her room clean. Melanie was upset, cried, moped around all day and refused to make her bed."

_____

_____

_____

_____

_____

Reflection points on your story completion

1. What is the main idea in your completion?
2. Did you find it hard or rewarding to complete the story? Why?
3. What do you believe would be the most common factor to be measured if you had 1,000 people complete the story and analyzed their responses?

---

these techniques, he shows that governments create a "phenomenology of the hostile imagination" (p. 13).

A Profile of Selected Projective Techniques

So-called projective techniques vary greatly in the degree to which they structure or leave the stimulus meaning open for a respondent. In fact, what we now call projective techniques were earlier referred to as projective _tests,_ but the idea of a test proved to be too demanding for the continual problems encountered in establishing reliability and validity for these techniques. Coverage of the techniques here is not meant to be a review of all measures available or potentially useful to the community of researchers and consumers of research in social science, but rather represents a profile of some of the better-known ones. Furthermore, we have selected examples to illustrate divergent strategies in this type of measurement and study. This section provides a brief coverage of some specific techniques that have been widely used in the study of social behavior and especially in clinical evaluation.

Sentence Completion Approaches.   The Sentence Completion Test is widely used as noted in the top ratings (Gleser, 1963; Klopfer & Taulbee, 1976) and would be classified as one of the more direct measures. In fact, Klopfer and Taulbee argue that this approach is no longer viewed as a projective test, "but is now widely regarded as a structured interview" (p. 562).

The Sentence Completion Test requests that a respondent complete a series of sentences. This technique is very adaptable and has proven to be useful in the assessment of personality. Sentence completion methods have been used with children, adults, the aged, and with both sexes. Furthermore, work has been done with pathological and nonpathological groups, clinical settings, institutions, anthropological study, marital satisfaction, classroom use, and management development (Daston, 1968).

It is, of course, assumed that a person is supplying important information about the self when he or she responds to a sentence stimuli. An example of sentence completion in action is reflected in the work of Stotsky and Weinberg (1956):

> When Dick failed in his new job, he....
> The men under me....
> Working for yourself....
> Dick worked best at....

The respondent is expected to complete the sentence for each of these stimuli as contained in these sentence stubs.

The Rotter Incomplete Sentence Test for College Screening (Rotter, Rafferty, & Schachtitz, 1965) is an interesting one for readers of this text as it was designed to assess adjustment of college men and women. The Rotter approach is illustrated in Table 13.1. It is possible to score such completion items using objective standardized manuals; thus, one has the advantage of an indirect measure coupled with a straightforward scoring system.

Daston (1968) observes that there is one basic style of sentence completion method, but there are literally scores of sentence completion tests. Most tests contain between 40 and 100 *stubs* and use the same type of format. The ease of administration is a factor in the popularity of this measure, as it can be administered in a group setting or singly. The wide use of these approaches in research indicates that investigators have confidence in the ability of this methodology to offer useful insights into people and their situations.

Sentence completion techniques on a continuum represent one of the more highly structured projective techniques used, and this greater objectivity allows the investigator to construct items for a specific purpose. This flexibility is one of the real advantages of this technique. As Daston (1968) observes, "What one gets out of a sentence completion test depends considerably on the test, the questions asked, and what one brings to it" (p. 280). Some investigators seek to understand formal content and evaluate sentence structure, spelling, and word usage. The majority of users seek to understand the meaning of content, and this emphasis can range from a rigorous evaluation to that of

TABLE 13.1. Incomplete Sentence Test for College Screening

Complete these sentences to express your real feeling. Try to do every one. Be sure to make a complete sentence.

1. I like....	20. I suffer....	36. I secretly....
2. The happiest time....	21. I failed....	37. I....
3. I want to know....	22. Reading....	38. Dancing....
4. Back home....	23. My mind....	39. My greatest worry is....
5. I regret....	24. The future....	40. Most girls....

Source: Adapted from J. B. Rotter, J. E. Rafferty, and E. Schachtitz, (1965). Validation of the Rotter Incomplete Sentence Test for college screening. From *The basic handbook of projective techniques*, edited by Bernard I. Murstein. Copyright © 1965 by Basic Books, Inc. Reprinted by permission of Basic Books, Inc., Publishers, New York.

assessing impressions or even intuitive feelings mentioned by respondents. Murstein (1965) summarizes general points for the entire range of projective techniques and concludes that the "most unexpected finding involving projective techniques over the past twenty years has been the strong showing made by the sentence completion method in a variety of studies" (p. xviii).

Word Association Measures.   The word association measures represent one of the oldest approaches. This approach is both simple in design and administration. Respondents are provided with a list of words and instructed to respond with the first word that comes to mind after having been exposed to each of the words on the list. Semeonoff (1976) notes that 1910 is the year generally accepted as the beginning of formalized use of the word association technique. The early interest stemmed primarily from a clinical point of view and then became of interest to researchers on specific topics.

Word association measures make the assumption that words brought forth as a result of stimulus words indicate inner feelings and attitudes of the person responding. Whether one "blocks" on certain words, the novelty of words used, or the actual response or association of words used, the assumption is that a respondent is revealing important data about the self. For example, when a person takes an objective instrument, there are few choices and very little opportunity for the person to reveal things about self, experiences, or inner feelings. Since the items are direct and objective, the responses should be open and objective and not subject to private interpretation. By contrast, in word association and other projective techniques, the structure is so minimal that the respondent is expected to provide the structure and meaning since it is not inherent in the question, words, or stimulus itself. For all practical purposes, the respondent is "forced" to project the self into the responses. A respondent is expected to manifest private interpretations from within the self, and these interpretations are then assumed to be accurate views of the way a respondent perceives his or her world and his or her particular role in that world.

Simplicity of construction and flexibility of use are two outstanding characteristics of word association measures. A pencil, some paper, a useful list of words, and a timing device constitute the necessary materials to use this procedure. Daston (1968) states that administration of word association measures should be individual and carried out in a setting free of noise or distractions so as to provide a conducive setting for the respondent to associate with the word list. The stimulus words are presented verbally from a list to the respondent. The respondent's obligations in the test are simple—merely write or say the first word that comes to mind when a stimulus word is spoken. The assumption is made that this type of word stimulus administered in this setting will enable the respondent to "project" information about personality, personal dynamics, fears, defenses, and other data about the "inner world."

We have included the entire Kent-Rosanoff Word Association List as presented in Daston's (1968) review of word association techniques. This list is more direct than some and contains fewer loaded or double meaning words (see Table 13.2).

▶   Use of word association techniques is decreasing in clinical settings, but the use of this approach in the area of verbal learning has increased (Daston, 1968). Anthropologists have also used word association tests for selected research. Word association techniques would be classified as *interpretive,* meaning that the respondent projects private meaning into a stimulus provided (Semeonoff, 1976).

TABLE 13.2. Kent-Rosanoff Word Association List

1. Table	26. Wish	51. Stem	76. Bitter
2. Dark	27. River	52. Lamb	77. Hammer
3. Music	28. White	53. Dream	78. Thirsty
4. Sickness	29. Beautiful	54. Yellow	79. City
5. Man	30. Window	55. Bread	80. Square
6. Deep	31. Rough	56. Justice	81. Butter
7. Soft	32. Citizen	57. Boy	82. Doctor
8. Eating	33. Foot	58. Light	83. Loud
9. Mountain	34. Spider	59. Health	84. Thief
10. House	35. Needle	60. Bible	85. Lion
11. Black	36. Red	61. Memory	86. Joy
12. Mutton	37. Sleep	62. Sheep	87. Bed
13. Comfort	38. Anger	63. Bath	88. Heavy
14. Hand	39. Carpet	64. Cottage	89. Tobacco
15. Short	40. Girl	65. Swift	90. Baby
16. Fruit	41. High	66. Blue	91. Moon
17. Butterfly	42. Working	67. Hungry	92. Scissors
18. Smooth	43. Sour	68. Priest	93. Quiet
19. Command	44. Earth	69. Ocean	94. Green
20. Chair	45. Trouble	70. Head	95. Salt
21. Sweet	46. Soldier	71. Stove	96. Street
22. Whistle	47. Cabbage	72. Long	97. King
23. Woman	48. Hard	73. Religion	98. Cheese
24. Cold	49. Eagle	74. Whiskey	99. Blossom
25. Slow	50. Stomach	75. Child	100. Afraid

Source: From A. J. Rosanoff (1927). *Manual of psychiatry* (6th ed., rev.). New York: Wiley, pp. 546–604. As contained in P. G. Daston, Word associations and sentence completion techniques, in A. I. Rabin (Ed.). (1968). *Projective techniques.* New York: Springer, pp. 264–289.

Double Entendre as Word Association. When one considers the area of sexuality, it is apparent that it may be difficult to obtain valid responses from direct, objective measures. It is unlikely that we could study the phenomenon directly, and when we ask people, they may report either an increase or decrease of the amount and types of experiences they have had. For example, men may emphatically deny homosexual experiences, and it is unlikely that many people would reveal incestuous relations. How might the characteristics of the researcher affect the responses given by a person? Abramson and Handschumacher (1978) investigated *experimenter effects* using a word association projective technique—*double entendre words.* A double entendre word is one with at least two meanings. For example, the word "prick" could refer to a small puncture received from a sharp pointed object, or it could refer to a man's sex organ.

Abramson and Handschumacher hypothesized that when respondents in their study ◀ heard the double entendre words, the sex of the experimenter would influence whether they gave a sexual response to the words. Forty male undergraduates and 40 female undergraduates were tested individually on their responses to 30 sexual words, which were interspersed with 20 nonsexual words. Examples of sexual words included "snatch," "rubber," "bust," "nuts," "park," "prick," "make," and so on. The nonsexual words lacked any sexual connotation and included "light," "chair," "tobacco," "table," "health," and so on.

The experimenters were either male or female and ranged in status from a college sophomore to a professor. The experimenter was randomly assigned to each respondent, and administered the words one at a time. The respondent gave word associations to the sexual and the nonsexual words, and the experimenter recorded them. At the same time, the *response latency,* or how long the respondent took to reply, was recorded. It was assumed that when someone was given a double entendre word, he or she would think of both meanings and then take time to decide which response to give. In other words, there should be a longer response latency to a double entendre word than there would be to a regular word.

These authors (Abramson & Handschumacher, 1978) found that men gave many more sexual responses to the double entendre words than women, and males with a male experimenter gave more sexual responses than males with a female experimenter. There were also longer response latencies with the double entendre words with a female experimenter, though not with a male experimenter. These results could be interpreted in several ways, including the notion that respondents could take longer to reply to the female experimenter because they are not sure she knew the words had sexual connotations. Second, respondents may have a longer latency because they tried to judge her reactions and possibly decide which meaning to give; or third, they may have been so surprised to hear a woman using sexual slang that they thought about that rather than answering immediately.

In any research of this nature there is a dilemma; it is important to keep the measure of the dependent variable as uncontaminated as possible by human factors such as lying and social desirability, but there is also an ethical responsibility to the individuals under study. In order to fulfill this ethical obligation, many researchers have their participants sign agreements that their part will be anonymous. Following the study, all participants should be fully informed about the nature of the study and how they contributed. All questions should be answered. Abramson and Handschumacher engaged in a debriefing session following their study, telling the respondents that a disguised technique (projective) was used. (See Chapter 12 for more detail on the importance and method for debriefing.)

Story Completion Techniques.   Story completion techniques are in the same family as word association and essentially tap inner feelings of the respondent in a similar way. The idea is simple: A respondent is provided with a story stimulus, which may be the beginning of a story or even a plot outline, and then instructed to complete the story (Lansky, 1968).

▶ To understand the development of moral judgments in children, Piaget (1932) asked children to complete the endings to various stories. Hartshorne and May (1928) likewise used this approach in attempting to understand the nature of moral development as related to character and deceit. The following example from the work of Piaget illustrates the basic strategy:

> One Thursday afternoon, a mother asked her little girl and boy to help her around the house, because she was tired. The girl was to dry the plates and the boy was to fetch in some wood. But the little boy (or girl) went and played in the street. So the mother asked the other one to do all the work. What did he (or she) say? (Piaget, 1932, p. 276)

The story is very open and the child is completely free to finish the story as he or she sees fit. The instructions to the storyteller can range from very open, as in this illustration, to instructions where the respondent is directed to finish the story in some context or even to tell "what really happened."

Lansky (1968) notes that the story completion approach to measurement can be very useful, particularly when used and integrated within a theoretical framework. More recent research tends to emphasize greater structure, use of control variables in order to test hypotheses, and emphasis on specific subject matter.

Association Techniques: The Rorschach.   The Rorschach, as a projective technique, is in the same category as sentence and story completion approaches: A stimulus is given and the respondent is then invited to associate, interpret, or complete something. The Rorschach test is named after the late Hermann Rorschach, a man trained in medicine and an active psychiatrist. The test consists of 10 standard inkblots and is no doubt the best known of all the projective techniques. The 10 inkblots are composed of 5 black inkblots, 2 black and red, and 3 multicolored. The instructions are simple, as the investigator directs the respondent to tell what he or she sees on the card while looking at each inkblot. The respondent is free to project onto each stimulus for as long as needed and in any way desired. The investigator plays a passive role during the administration of the cards so that *free association* can occur, with this phase followed up by an inquiry time in which the investigator assesses the nature of each answer with the respondent.

This test has been widely used in clinical evaluation, personality assessment, and correlated with many other variables in an attempt to develop patterns and useful interpretations to such patterns.It is assumed that a respondent brings feelings, attitudes, hostilities, memories, and frustrations to the test situation, and these in part are projected into each of the 10 inkblots. Research indicates that what we actually project can also be influenced by the personality of the examiner (Sanders & Cleveland, 1965). Gleser (1963) found that the Rorschach was consistently the most heavily used projective technique.

Parker (1983), in an extensive meta-analysis of the reliability and validity of the Rorschach test, concluded that typical reliabilities were in the order of .83 and validity coefficients ranged from .45 to .50 and higher.

Thematic Apperception Test (TAT).   The TAT would certainly rank near the top in terms of use, perceived utility, and importance as a projective measure. It is a structured variation of story completion, since a respondent is shown a series of interpretive pictures and then invited to tell stories as a function of the picture stimulus. The respondent has to study or project heavily into some very abstract pictures, whereas other pictures in the test are more direct to interpretation by the "projecting person." The TAT came into being in 1935 with a publication by Morgan and Murray. These authors stated that the TAT is built on the premise that when a respondent reacts to an ambiguous social situation, he or she is also likely to expose his or her personality. Murray's work and the interpretation of this test are heavily embedded in psychoanalytical theory. The test is sufficiently flexible that heavy use has occurred in the clinical setting as well as in research activities.

In fact, it was Murray (Murray, Barrett, & Homburger, 1938) who first introduced and coined the idea of projective tests or techniques. Murray saw projective measures as procedures to assess the inhibited and repressed facets of normal persons, and the stimuli were seen as ways to stimulate people to release their expressions in either word or action. The TAT is known as a *construction technique,* as the respondent is expected to construct a story after having been stimulated by one of the pictures.

Rosenwald (1968) asserts that the TAT has been the most widely used projective technique to study motivation and that clinicians continue to make heavy use of it in their diagnostic work. He claims this high use and visibility are due to two factors: (1) TAT is relatively easy to use in comparison to other projective measures, and (2) TAT has an "academic-humanistic origin" (p. 172). Additionally, Murray's view of personality has made the TAT popular as a research tool to many students of personality.

The TAT is composed of 20 cards, varying from Card 1 (a young boy contemplating a violin), Card 4 (a woman clutching a man who is straining away, with a second woman shown in the background), and Card 20 (a shadowy figure standing under a lamp post, the background is very dark). The TAT is typically given verbally to a respondent and all 20 cards are to be used, although Murray believed it was appropriate to use less than the total in a given situation. The test was designed to be given to children as young as 4 years of age. The TAT can also be administered to a respondent as a written test in which he or she writes responses to each of the cards.

▶ *Children's Apperception Test (CAT).*   The CAT is to be used as a "game" with children and uses animal figures in lieu of human figures in the picture material. The test has proven to be useful because children do identify more readily with animals than with humans. The test, designed for children aged 3 to 10, consists of 10 cards showing animals in a variety of themes, such as a monkey being attacked by a tiger (Card 7), a white rabbit sitting up in bed in a darkened room with the door wide open (Card 9), and three chicks with spoons seated at a table containing a large bowl of food (Card 1). A shadowy figure of a big chicken is shown in the background of the card (Semeonoff, 1976).

▶ *Draw-A-Person Test.*   Goodenough's Draw-A-Man test, published in 1926 and heavily used for many years, only recently has been surpassed in usage by the Machover Draw-A-Person Test (1949). Much of the earlier work interpreted the Goodenough test as an intelligence test, but this practice officially was abandoned in the 1960s (Semeonoff, 1976). The basic assumption underlying this type of projective technique is that when a person engages in the task of drawing a picture of a person, he or she in fact draws a picture of the self. As stated by Machover,

> the human figure drawn by an individual who is directed to "draw a person" relates intimately to the impulses, anxieties, conflicts and compensations characteristic of that individual. In some sense, the figure drawn is the person, and the paper corresponds to the environment. This may be a crude formulation, but serves well as a working hypothesis. (1949, p. 35)

Swensen (1965) concludes that there is little evidence to support the broad and inclusive hypothesis concerning the Draw-A-Person test as asserted by Machover. He does recognize that many clinicians regularly use this test; he believes it offers useful data and also agrees in some cases that it does offer some insight as to a client's stresses. Also,

---

Tips for Consumers 13.2

Validity and reliability are major concerns to the research community as well as consumers of research in relationship to the use of projective techniques. These are valid concerns and one should be on guard as to claim of outcome versus evidence given for reliability and validity. It may be useful to apply the following questions when evaluating the overall utility of projective techniques:

1. Would I be willing to have this projective technique used on me if a major decision were to be made using the results of the test?
2. Would you in general feel good about a school district using projective methods for routinely assessing adjustment of children? Your own child?
3. What has been your exposure to and reaction of projective measures in your life to this point in time? Why?

---

some evidence argues for the use of the Draw-A-Person Test as a rough assessment tool that may indicate level of adjustment. (See Tips for Consumers 13.2.)

A recent experiment on human figure drawing tests (Feher, Vandecreek, & Teglasi, 1983) illustrated that such tests do have limited validity, but the debate on their validity and utility will continue and should.

The Bender–Gestalt Test.   The Bender–Gestalt Test is composed of nine geometric figures, and each of the figures is presented on an index-size card. One set of cards developed by Bender and the other set by Hutt are most commonly used. Hutt (1968) notes that the ease of administration, the simplicity of the test, and utility for both clinical and research work have made the test very popular over the years since it was first developed in 1938.

Hutt indicates that the test has been most widely used (1) to assess disturbance in the context of perceptual-motoric realms of behavior and (2) as a projective measure to determine various aspects of personality. It is a nonverbal test, and this has merit for a number of respondents and evaluation situations. The range of applicability is wide— from childhood through the adult state and across social class, ethnic, and language groupings.

The Bender–Gestalt Test, composed of the nine geometric designs, contains dots, lines, angles, and curves combined to form a variety of relationships. Individuals see the designs and then are invited to reproduce what they have seen. Billingslea (1965) notes that this test remains in high use by clinicians and that it is often used in conjunction with other tests to help determine the presence of organic brain pathology. Additionally, the test is capable of discriminating the psychotic person from the nonpsychotic.

Figure 13.1, which consists of a circle and square placed closely together, is typically presented first in the test. Hutt (1968) notes that a child needs to be about 7 years of age before the figure is perceived and reproduced with accuracy.

Shopping List Method.   A very straightforward and interesting construction of a projective technique applied to consumer behavior occurred in the work of Haire (1950). Haire reasoned that when consumers are approached directly with questions about likes and dislikes regarding certain products, they often give false and misleading answers to

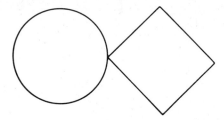

Figure 13.1. Circle and Square from Bender–Gestalt Projective Test. (*Source:* M. L. Hutt. The projective use of Bender–Gestalt Test. In A. I. Rabin [Ed.] [1968], *Projective techniques.* New York: Springer, p. 401.)

questions. For example, Haire notes that for the question, "Do you use instant coffee?", if people say "no" they explain that the flavor is not desirable.

To understand the process of likes and perceptions, Haire had 58 female shoppers respond to two shopping lists as shown in Table 13.3. Half of the 58 women reacted to List I and the other half to List II. The women were directed to read the shopping list and then describe the shopper in terms of personality and other characteristics. The only difference between List I and II is the coffee entry, but this was sufficient to cause about half of the women to describe the instant coffee shopper (List I) as sloppy, lazy, a poor planner, single, or an office girl. In contrast, the Maxwell House Coffee shopper (List II) was seen by the same women as being frugal, interested in her family, sensible, and thrifty.

Follow-up with these women to determine what coffee they had at home illustrated that women who had instant coffee had given more favorable reactions to the instant coffee shopping list than women who had regular grind coffee. Haire concludes that the decision to buy instant coffee is influenced by perceptions of what constitutes a good wife and homemaker, not just dislikes about flavor.

This assumption was proven to be correct when one new fictitious item, "Blueberry Fill pie mix," was added to both lists and given to women shoppers. Descriptions of these new lists were almost identical, thus verifying the notion that shoppers were projecting their own beliefs and values in regard to certain products. Haire (1950) concludes that "motives exist which are below the level of verbalization because they are socially unacceptable, difficult to verbalize cogently, or unrecognized" (p. 656).

TABLE 13.3. The Shopping List Approach

List I	List II
1¹/₂ pounds of hamburger	1¹/₂ pounds of hamburger
2 loaves of Wonder bread	2 loaves of Wonder bread
Bunch of carrots	Bunch of carrots
1 can Rumford's baking powder	1 can Rumford's baking powder
Nescafé Instant coffee	1 lb. Maxwell House coffee (drip grind)
2 cans Del Monte peaches	2 cans Del Monte peaches
5 lbs. potatoes	5 lbs. potatoes

Source: From M. Haire (1950). Projective techniques in marketing research. *Journal of Marketing, 14, 644–656.* Reprinted by permission of The American Marketing Association.

The Shopping List Method is particularly useful because we are able to provide a 28-year update in the work of Holbrook and Hughes (1978). They, like Haire (1950), reasoned that consumer behavior may at times be the result of subconscious reaction, cultural values, or feelings that stem from perceived social unacceptability. If these factors are in effect, consumer choices are very difficult to directly assess because respondents are either unable or unwilling to report true feelings. To test this notion, Holbrook and Hughes used the Shopping List Method with 100 housewives in suburban areas of New York City and Washington, D.C. Four different lists were used as shown in Table 13.4.

The shoppers were also asked to read the lists and project themselves into the situation as far as possible until they were able to describe the characteristics of the women who used the list to buy groceries. Holbrook and Hughes used a 33-item bipolar adjectival list of descripters instead of open-ended descriptions used by Haire and others using the Shopper's Checklist.

The findings indicate that the convenience foods shopper is still perceived as somewhat of a spendthrift, but she was no longer viewed as lazy, sloppy, a poor planner, disinterested in homemaking, or as a bad wife. The fascinating change in perception was that the convenience foods user was described as an employed single girl, busy, timesaving, quick, fast working, outgoing, friendly, on the move, imaginative, urban, lively, and adventurous. Holbrook and Hughes (1978) conclude that

> among the Eastern housewives...little trace remains of the negative stereotype once attached to convenience foods in general and to instant coffee in particular. Rather, for these shoppers, the use of convenience foods now appears to be associated favorably with the pursuit of a career and an active, exciting social life. What was once a social stigma has now become the norm. (p. 328)

TABLE 13.4. Changing Set Roles and the Shopper's Checklist

Natural Maxwell House List	Natural Nescafé List
1½ pounds of hamburger 2 loaves of white bread Bunch of carrots One can Davis baking powder 1 lb. Maxwell House coffee (drip grind) 2 cans Del Monte peaches 5 lbs. of potatoes	List was the same as Natural Maxwell House except that Nescafé was the coffee entry.

Convenience Maxwell House List	Convenience Nescafé List
1½ pounds of hamburger Taystee Brown 'n' Serve rolls Birds Eye peas & carrots, butter sauce One can Davis baking powder 1 lb. Maxwell House coffee (drip grind) 2 cans Del Monte peaches Stouffer's potatoes au gratin	List was the same as Convenience Maxwell House except that Nescafé Instant coffee was the entry.

Source: From M B. Holbrook and N. G. Hughes (1978). Product images: How structured rating scales facilitate using a projective technique in hypotheses testing. *Journal of Psychology, 100,* 323–328.

▶   One other feature of the Holbrook and Hughes (1978) study has to do with using a scaling technique combined with projective measurement style. A number of researchers using projective techniques have suggested this as a useful strategy in coping with reliability and validity. Schvaneveldt (1968) likewise used a 105-item, Likert-type rating scale in conjunction with 10 filmed episodes to measure perceptions toward maternal overprotection. Respondents viewed each film episode and the projector was stopped while they rated the items for that specific episode and so on through all 10 patterns. Scoring in such a technique is very straightforward, respondents are highly motivated because of the film stimuli, and reliability and validity proved to be quite satisfactory.

▶   *"Spelunking" in Art: A Case of Psychodrama.*   A somewhat different and novel use of projective techniques has been demonstrated by Rush (1978) in using a new graphic technique—"spelunking"—as part of the experience in art therapy. In the art therapy program, patients were invited to take a metaphorical journey to the inside of a cave and while there draw their images. Rush analyzed the drawings from a Jungian perspective, which assumed that the drawings were reflective of where the patients are and how far they have to go. Rush also assumed that the cave was a rich symbol for such an exercise since it contains images of the earth, mother, the life cycle from womb to tomb, and rebirth.

Results of the analysis showed that some patients only drew the cave entrance, some the short entry into the cave, others showed passing into the depths of the cave, and others the complete traversing of the cave. Rush concluded that patients who entered deeply into the cave or took a complete journey from the entrance to the exit were less emotionally disturbed and exhibited a better prognosis than patients who only had entrance contact or minor entry into the cave.

From a projective technique point of view, the assumption is that the patients projected their inner feelings, conflicts, security, and self-orientation into the art–cave experience and the outcome captures their feelings of emotional health. This example would fall into the category of psychodrama via the art experience.

In *psychodrama,* respondents are invited to act out a variety of roles and the investigator is cast into the role of observer. Psychodrama can reveal various clues that can be used to assess behavior. A variation of this approach is called *sociodrama,* with the respondent taking on or acting the role of someone else, and the investigator again playing the role of observer. It is assumed that the respondent places the real self into the drama and thus reveals thoughts and feelings, in short, communicates with the self, another, or with a group. One of the specific advantages of psychodrama and sociodrama is that investigators can observe respondents acting out specified roles in a defined situation. If normative roles are to be played, it is possible to observe the degree of accuracy or distortion carried out in the drama act. Since we typically know what is "normally" contained in role behavior, we can assess the self projected into the situations by determining what parts have been added or deleted.

Perspective-Taking about Projective and Indirect Methods for Obtaining Data

It seems clear that projective and other indirect methods for obtaining insight into people and social conditions will be with us in some form for a long time. The major utility of such measures has to do with the need to obtain data from people when they are unable or unwilling to tell about themselves or situations. As noted, projective measures generally have lower levels of validity and reliability than do other types of instruments a scientist can use, but their use remains rather high in spite of these limitations. It may become more and more useful to use projective measures in conjunction with other data collective strategies in order to exploit the utility of such devices on sensitive topics but at the same time use other devices to better cope with reliability and validity. In short, projective measures are very specialized questionnaires, interviews, or multi-faceted data gathering activities.

In a text dedicated to the goal of making research methodology understandable to a variety of research aspirants and a broad range of consumers of research, we believe that projective techniques are important tools. The great diversity and utility of projective techniques can be further shown in the work of Lefcourt and Martin (1986) who document the role of humor in everyday life stress. A sense of humor is a good coping technique, very similar to the role of a projective technique in research. Both humor and projective technique facilitate getting through some ordeal that otherwise may not be possible. Their continued use in personality study, criminal behavior, counseling, nursing, and careers is certain. Both the researcher and consumer of research should be informed as to these techniques' mission, utility, and the problems associated with their use.

SUMMARY AND CONCLUSIONS

The fact that the majority of projective techniques, disguised measures, and less-structured measures have failed to demonstrate either high or consistent validity and reliability has deterred neither the development nor the use of these techniques. This broad area of measures generally referred to as projective techniques seeks to measure attitudes and perceptions in situations where it is believed that respondents will be either unable or unwilling to disclose their true feelings. Because of personal threat, feelings of inadequacy, privacy, deviancy, or role expectation, respondents sometimes have difficulty revealing themselves.

1. Projective techniques reach people indirectly or sometimes as a disguised measure, hence the belief that people will "project" themselves into a situation and reveal the sought-for information.
   a. The stimulus or test situation in a projective technique is not directly clear or understandable; thus, one must work or "project" the self to make sense of it.
   b. To complete the picture and bring meaning and a sense of understanding, one becomes immersed in the situation and reveals his or her self.
   c. Since the investigator knows what was in the original technique stimulus, it is believed that we can identify the parts that were added, and in this way, obtain useful information. Furthermore, a projective technique is supposed to be able to "extract" the covert information painlessly and leave the respondent feeling good because awareness of self relevation was not self-evident.
2. Most of the projective measures were developed for use in clinical practice, and their heaviest use has been in that setting, but many of them have been used quite widely in research, especially in conjunction with other instruments.
   a. Some of the techniques are quite highly structured, such as the sentence

completion, word association, or the Bender–Gestalt, and can be scored more objectively.

b.   Other measures, such as the Rorschach, Thematic Apperception Test, and the Draw-A-Person Test, are very unstructured, and their response latitude as well as variance of interpretation are very broad.

c.   There is a subjective and "artful" nature needed in the interpretation of many of the techniques, especially ones like the Rorschach. Just as the stimulus is not directly clear to the respondent, it appears that the answers are not always clear, or at least objectively clear, to investigators.

3.   Sentence completion, word association, the double entendre, and the story completion would be classified as completion methods, since these tests share the common feature that a respondent is expected to complete the stimulus, but within the boundaries of that suggested by the stimulus. These techniques are more restrictive than the Rorschach.

4.   These respective projective techniques have been used most heavily by practitioners, and the use continues today because it is believed that such techniques provide valuable insight and information concerning people. Researchers also continue to make use of these measures, especially in conjunction with other instruments.

5.   The most recent development of the so-called Shopping List Method is an interesting example of applying the projective technique to the world of the consumer in the marketplace, and the results are quite astounding. It would appear that variation of this type would be a useful application of projective techniques. This approach also illustrates how the changing norms of a society influence the type of material that respondents project into a situation stimulus, once again illustrating the dynamic nature of human and social behavior.

PROBLEMS AND APPLICATIONS

1.   Go to the counseling and testing office on your campus and take a projective test such as the Rorschach, Draw-A-Person Test, or the Minnesota Mulitphasic Personality Inventory (MMPI). Discuss with other class members the testing experience and try to determine if the test results accurately reflect the way you see yourself.

2.   To what degree does your own major area of study or discipline make use of projective or indirect methods? Why? Do you feel your discipline should use these types of instruments more often?

3.   Locate a recent study in your discipline or closely related discipline that used a projective or indirect method for collecting data. Evaluate the study and determine the degree to which the study was strengthened or weakened as a result of the data collection method.

4.   Are there any conditions in which subjects should be told that a projective method is being used to obtain data that would be hard to obtain in a more direct measure? Should subjects ever be told that the projective test measures a particular trait or attribute?

5.   Form a discussion session with other students and outline ways that consumers of research can be made more knowledgeable about the advantages and disadvantages of projective tests and indirect methods of measurement.

REFERENCES

Abramson, P. R., & Handschumacher, I. W. (1978). Experimenter effects on responses to double entendre words. *Journal of Personality Assessment, 42,* 592–596.

Billingslea, F. Y. (1965). The Bender–Gestalt: A review and a perspective. In B. I. Murstein (Ed.), *Handbook of projective techniques.* New York: Basic Books.

Daston, P. G. (1968). Word associations and sentence completion techniques. In A. I. Rabin (Ed.), *Projective techniques.* New York: Springer.

Feher, E., Vandecreek, L., & Teglasi, H. (1983). The problem of art quality in the use of human figure drawing tests. *Journal of Clinical Psychology, 39,* 268–275.

Fisher, S. (1967). Projective methodologies. In P. R. Farnsworth, O. McNemar, & Q. McNemar (Eds.), *Annual Review of Psychology, 18,* 165–190. ·

Frank, L. K. (1965). Projection methods for the study of personality. In B. I. Murstein (Ed.), *Handbook of projective techniques.* New York: Basic Books.

Gleser, G. C. (1963). Projective methodologies. In P. R. Farnsworth, O. McNemar, & Q. McNemer (Eds.), *Annual Review of Psychology, 14,* 391–422.

Goodenough, F. L. (1926). *Measurement of intelligence by drawings.* Yonkers-on-Hudson: World Book.

Haire, M. (1950). Projective techniques in marketing research. *Journal of Marketing, 14,* 649–656.

Hartshorne, H., & May, M. A. (1928). *Studies in the nature of character. Volume 1: Studies in deceit.* New York: Macmillan.

Holbrook, M. B., & Hughes, N. C. (1978). Product images: How structured rating scales facilitate using a projective technique in hypotheses testing. *Journal of Psychology, 100,* 323–328.

Hutt, M. L. (1968). The projective use of the Bender–Gestalt Test. In A. I. Rabin (Ed)., *Projective techniques.* New York: Springer.

Keen, S. (1986). *Faces of the enemy.* San Francisco: Harper & Row.

Klopfer, W. G., & Taulbee, E. S. (1976). Projective tests. In M. R. Rosenzweig & L. W. Porter (Eds.), *Annual Review of Psychology, 27,* 543–567.

Lansky, L. M. (1968). Story completion methods. In A. I. Rabin (Ed.), *Projective techniques.* New York: Springer.

Lefcourt, H. M., & Martin, R. A. (1986). *Humor and life stress.* New York: Springer-Verlag.

Machover, K. (1949). *Personality projection in the drawing of the human figure.* Springfield, Ill.: Charles C. Thomas.

Molish, H. B. (1972). Projective methodologies. In P. H. Mussen & M. R. Rosenzweig (Eds.), *Annual Review of Psychology, 23,* 577–614.

Morgan, C. D., & Murray, H. A. (1935). A method for investigating fantasies: The Thematic Apperception Test. *Archives of Neurology and Psychiatry, 34,* 289–306.

Murray, H. A., Barrett, W. G., & Homburger, E. (1938). *Explorations in personality.* New York: Oxford University Press.

Murstein, B. I. (Ed.). (1965). *Handbook of projective techniques.* New York: Basic Books.

Parker, K. (1983). A meta-analysis of the reliability and validity of the Rorschach. *Journal of Personality Assessment, 47,* 227–231.

Piaget, J. (1932). *The moral judgment of the child.* New York: Harcourt, Brace.

Rosenwald, G. C. (1968). The Thematic Apperception Test. In A. I. Rabin (Ed.), *Projective techniques.* New York: Springer.

Rotter, J. B., Rafferty, J. E., & Schachtitz, E. (1965). Validation of the Rotter Incomplete Sentence

Test for college screening. In B. I. Murstein (Ed.), *Handbook of projective techniques*. New York: Basic Books.

Rush, K. (1978). The metaphorical journey: Art therapy in symbolic exploration. *Art Psychotherapy, 5*, 149–155.

Sanders, R., & Cleveland, S. E. (1965). The relationship between certain examiner personality variables and subjects' Rorschach scores. In B. I. Murstein (Ed.), *Handbook of projective techniques*. New York: Basic Books.

Schvaneveldt, J. D. (1968). The development of a film test for the measurement of perception toward maternal overprotection. *Journal of Genetic Psychology, 112*, 255–266.

Semeonoff, B. (1976). *Projective techniques*. New York: Wiley.

Stotsky, B. A., & Weinberg, H. (1956). The prediction of the psychiatric patient's work adjustment. *Journal of Counseling Psychology, 3*, 3–7.

Swensen, C. H., Jr. (1965). Empirical evaluations of human figure drawings. In B. I. Murstein (Ed.), *Handbook of projective techniques*. New York: Basic Books.

CHAPTER 14

Obtaining Data: Documents of the Past

OUTLINE

A Historical Perspective
Advantages to Using Documents
Types and Sources of Historical Data
Salem Parish Records: A Primary Source
Documents: Unobtrusive Data
Letters, Diaries, and Private Papers
Archives
Mission and Church Records
Physical Trace Measures
Data Banks
Proving the Validity of Documents and Other Historical Evidence
The Case of the Cardiff Giant
Content Analysis
Turning Content into Scientific Data
Content Analysis as "Observation"
Replacement—No; Alternative—Yes
Perspective-Taking about Documents as a Method for Obtaining Data
Issues in Validity and Reliability
Summary
Problems and Applications
References

KEY TERMS

Historical sources
Documents
Historical perspective
Primary sources
Secondary sources
Historical artifacts
Content analysis
Unobtrusive measures
Obtrusive measures
Corroboration

External criticism
Internal criticism
Archives
Erosion measures
Accretion measures
Data bank
Date of origin
Testing for truth
Heisenberg factor
Reactive effects

STUDY GUIDE QUESTIONS

1. As applied to research, what is a research document?
2. What are some of the main advantages to using documents in conducting research in the social sciences?
3. It is asserted that documents generate unobtrusive data. What does this mean and do you agree?
4. How does one go about establishing whether certain documents or evidence in behalf of documents are actually valid?
5. What are the main elements of content analysis?
6. What are physical trace measures? Identify a problem where data could be collected using this type of measure.

Role of the Researcher

It is important that social science in general develop a perspective leading to a greater use of records of the past. Historical records of a great variety are readily available, but they have received relatively little attention from contemporary researchers. These are important records for doing sensitive contemporary studies, for obtaining samples and using measures which are unobtrusive, and for overcoming the limitations of generational-bound data. What we believe as scientists, how we conduct research, and what we tend to investigate have in part been determined by history. It is asserted that every social scientist must be a historian to effectively carry out successful research. Using documents, understanding the historical method, and knowing how to use content analysis are important factors for the researcher in understanding and using records of the past. The availability and capability of computers create the conditions whereby researchers can be most creative in the use of secondary, historical, and documentary type data.

Role of the Consumer

Historical research with documents involves three primary activities: (1) searching for and sifting the asserted facts, (2) interpretation, and (3) the written word or narration. The consumer of research is typically only aware of the third step—the written word. It is essential that a consumer of research know about the sources and the methods of arriving at conclusions based on using documents of the past. How does one tell an authentic document from a false one? How much evidence is necessary to prove something in a historical context?

History did occur, activities in everyday life have roots going back through many generations, and a more correct understanding is obtainable by linking multiple time perspectives. Documents do not supply the final truth, for history and social science are always in the process of being rewritten. The consumer of historical and documentary research plays a vital role in seeing that the research is challenged and eventually written again. In fact, consumers can be more sensitive to their own documents that they create such as letters, video tapes, audio tapes, pictures, scrap books, and a variety of other personal, family, and related activities.

A HISTORICAL PERSPECTIVE

Carl Sandburg's (1954) moving biography of Lincoln is successful in allowing the reader to know Mr. Lincoln in a personal and intimate manner. Throughout the work, Sandburg introduces hundreds of people, tells in detail their roles, discusses the stress that goes through Lincoln's mind, and invites the reader into placing piles of flowers on his grave after the long and exhausting journey to Springfield. As we place each delicate fragrant flower and long-stemmed rose on the grave we know that the prairie and the war years are over, the President is dead. This powerful historical and biographical work of Lincoln was written drawing on documents, records, letters, reports, some interviews, and thousands of notes which Sandburg labored over in his pursuit of Lincoln. Most historians believe he was largely successful in finding Lincoln and making him an intimate man to those who read these fact-filled pages.

Sandburg's Lincoln is a classic example of using historical sources to tell a story, depict an era, or uncover unknown data about a person or situation. Social scientists are intellectually aware of the great abundance of records, documents, diaries, letters, newspapers, genealogical records, magazines, and other personal documents that are available, but for the most part these types of data have only been used by a small audience. Social science research, like all other sciences, has fads and popular activities, and the use of documents for research has not been popular in the past fifty years, although it was perhaps the dominant mode of research in the nineteenth century (Pitt, 1972). Pitt asserts that historical-document-based research is becoming increasingly more important. Certainly several publications would indicate that documents as a rich source of data have been rediscovered (Webb, Campbell, Schwartz, & Sechrest, 1966; Hareven, 1978; Aries, 1962; Laslett, 1965; Jackson & Winchester, 1979).

We can define documentary research as activity in which evidence is extracted from sources such as population censuses, school records, vital statistics, cemetery records, diaries, autobiographies, personal letters, economic records, books, magazines, speeches, court records, congressional records, laws and regulations, and a host of other materials or sources stored away by various sectors of societies and individuals. Any record (written or oral) that contains information about human behavior, social conditions, and social processes can be subsumed under the broad area of *documents*. Iredale

(1973) asserts that more people examine and use registers of baptisms, marriages, and burials than any other types of document available for various types of research. History is obviously included in this concept since it is the one record that is a conscious effort to portray mankind's achievements. What we believe as researchers, how we do our activities, and what we tend to research are in part determined by history. As noted by several great thinkers, "if you don't know history, you don't know anything." And as Senn (1971) notes, "Every social scientist, therefore, must be a historian of sorts" (p. 72). We devote a full chapter to this area as an important data gathering device. That which follows will attempt to further define this approach to research, various types of records, and methodologies for using document-based data.

ADVANTAGES TO USING DOCUMENTS

Nevins (1938) notes that history allows people to sense their relationship with the past, understand their present moment, and to a degree chart their course in the near future. Contemporary beliefs, truths, biases, and aspirations are more fully understood by looking back, back to earlier generations and the events creating the forces that social scientists tend to focus on in their generation of research activity. The events, beliefs, habits, attitudes, dreams, and despair are typically not novel to a time or place, but have been swept and swirled for generations of mankind. It is no wonder that many of our attempts to link observed consequences with alleged causes turn out to be frustratingly impotent, for we are attempting to isolate both consequence and cause out of immediacy. Only by understanding historical processes and deeply involved chains of events can we begin to know how the social order works.

▶ Another advantage of using the resources of the past to understand human-social behavior is that errors in interpretation can be avoided if we check current observations or reports with historical records. Pitt (1972) notes the case of Lloyd Warner's work with Yankee City in which he misinterpreted certain aspects of the city by trusting contemporary reports. This error could have been avoided by taking advantage of a number of records.

The authors were startled and amused a number of times in the late 1960s and early 1970s with a number of publications that had "discovered" communes, utopian communities, and the "city of God" as brand new events and failed to note that this seemingly "new birth" was merely a light murmur in comparison to the avalanche that occurred in nineteenth-century America.

▶ A third advantage in using documents for research is that of having comparative bases (i.e., a now and then). *Middletown,* by Helen and Robert Lynd (1929), would be a clear example of this perspective. The Lynds first visited and reported about Muncie, Indiana, in 1929, and did a follow-up in 1937. Caplow and Bahr (1979) completed another study of Middletown in the late 1970s, and Bahr and Chadwick (1985) studied religion and the family in Middletown in the mid-1980s. This process is essential if one is to understand change, growth, stress, and many of the other dynamic concepts making social science research somewhat unique. It is of course true that we can make some comparisons on a limited basis with panel and longitudinal studies (see Chapter 5), but time and expense greatly limit many of these comparisons.

A fourth advantage (Pitt, 1972) is that one can accomplish with already existing records what is impossible to do with gathered primary data. The reason for this is that groups, societies, tribes, and movements die, stop, or become "swallowed up by modernization," and when this has occurred, the only recourse to data is the written record or other types of artifacts that are available to help answer questions (p. 5). Furthermore, it is not practical time-wise to go out into the "field" and gather primary data on a variety of problems for research when perhaps equally good data are already available and can be analyzed much more rapidly than primary data.

Another related advantage has to do with access to data in the living world—sometimes political or social conditions do not permit investigators to obtain complete information that could be supplemented through documents. Pitt (1972) refers to this as the ancillary function of secondary records. Documents of a great variety offer the researcher additional insights, and reliability checks vital in coping with problems in measurement or sampling error. Pitt notes that primary fieldwork is not allowed in the communist world, but document-historical work is permitted with a rich supply of untapped records.

Another reason for the study of history and documental evidence in the social sciences is that we learn from it. History is truly similar to contemporary social-behavioral science. History focuses on mankind, and methodologically there is much interchange. If there is a difference, it lies in the time perspective: history as a discipline is unique in focusing on the past (Senn, 1971).

Historical perspectives in research help the investigator to use the best time period for the understanding of some event or process. This time perspective is critical for assessing the linkages of events that lead to an important issue or if one desires to understand the consequences of an event. For example, questions about Bible reading in public school are not new to the United States as is often assumed, but were a volatile question in the 1840s which led to rioting in the streets and the death of several dozen soldiers and civilians. Lannie and Diethorn (1968) report that this bitter confrontation over Bible reading was due to a combination of Catholic versus Protestant and foreign versus native-born conflicts that resulted in open warfare in the streets. What is old and what is new are often only the difference between what one generation has seen or remembers versus the sequence of events that history records over a long period of time.

TYPES AND SOURCES OF HISTORICAL DATA

Documents and other types of historical data can be classified into two main divisions, *primary* and *secondary* sources. As noted earlier in Chapter 3, *primary* sources of data are firsthand or eyewitnesses of some event, happening, or social engagement. Examples of eyewitnesses categorized as primary sources would be those who viewed the eruption of Mt. St. Helens in 1980, the shooting of President Reagan in March of 1981, individuals riding on the bus in Montgomery, Alabama, on December 1, 1955, when Rosa Parks, a black woman (Coombs, 1972), confronted the racial status quo, and those luminaries who were inner circle witnesses of the marriage of Prince Charles and the "shy" Diana in the summer of 1981. Primary accounts are classified as such because one who recorded the event was either a witness (firsthand) or a participant in the event.

In contrast, *secondary sources* are reports concerning some event by someone who was there neither as a witness nor participant, but rather received information about the event from a witness or participant, read about the event, or is someone who has made a special effort to understand the event. Secondary sources may be used and are sometimes useful in historical research, but researchers tend to avoid using them unless primary data sources are not available.

Many types of records are developed and maintained for the express purpose of functioning as a primary record for future needs. Documents of this type classified as primary sources include diaries, letters, chapters, constitutions, laws, court decisions, official minutes or records, autobiographies, genealogies, contracts, deeds, wills, licenses, affidavits, declarations, certificates, receipts, advertisements, maps, films, pictures, paintings, inscriptions, recordings, magazine accounts, and research reports. The following example vividly illustrates the nature of documentary research, how certain records are obtained and used, and the flexibility that is possible in such research.

Salem Parish Records: A Primary Source

▶ The 1973 study by Farber provides an interesting illustration of using historical records and content analysis in understanding the relationship between tuberculosis (consumption) in nineteenth-century Salem, Massachusetts, and sex, marriage, childbearing, and death. Both external and internal criticism are evident as one reviews his procedures for arriving at the stated conclusions.

Farber used statistics from lists of deaths in the Salem East Church Parish records from 1785 to 1819. These death lists included not just members of the church but others in the general area. These records were particularly detailed, for they contained information on age, cause of death, and in a large number of entries, data on family history, the number of children in the household, identity of the parents of the deceased, occupation, and marital status. Farber verified these records against entries recorded in William Bentley's diary (1905–1914) and other Salem Vital Records (1916–1925). Farber notes that

> perhaps the most extensive source of data was a set of files I developed from numerous entries in the Essex Institute Historical Collections on roughly 235 families and several hundred of their relatives by blood and marriage. These entries were of the kind ordinarily used in historical research—diaries, letters, newspapers, notes on lodge members, and their families, official documents, genealogies, wills, and property transfers. (p. 38)

The main goal in Farber's use of these documents was to understand the meaning of consumption and to relate this meaning to labeling and symbolic factors that might be attributed to consumption. The germ theory of disease was not accepted as being valid in Salem in 1800. Also, he was interested in understanding the circumstances associated with consumption as a cause of death. An example of a typical entry in the records was:

> March 17, 1812. Mary, Widow of Benjamin Babidge. Consumption, 41 years. Lost their property with Col.S. Archer in the speculation of that debtor....Distress of mind ended in consumption. (p. 39)

Farber reports that in the age range of 25–44, 52 women died with consumption as the cause of death, while 67 died of other causes, usually "fever." Additional findings illustrate the utility of documents to perform rather detailed analysis of data in regard to a problem like consumption in nineteenth-century Salem. Analyzing the data by place of birth, he found women were more likely than men to stay in Salem or the immediate area. In regard to age at first marriage, consumption had a specific impact, as women with this disease married at a later age on the average than women dying of other causes.

Assessing the records in terms of marital status, Farber found for the general population in Salem that about 75% were married by the middle-age period. With consumptive women, slightly under 50% were married. Each of the unmarried categories (separated, widowed, single) showed twice the percentage of consumptives as compared with other populations in the records. Only about 15% of women dying of other causes were separated or widowed, while 29% of consumptive-death women were in these categories. Furthermore, the records show that single, never-married females in the middle-age category died of consumption, whereas less than 10% of women classified into other causes of death had never been married.

Farber (1973) thus concludes that consumptive women had a high rate of nonmarriage, they married at a later age, and since they married later had to take less desirable men for their husbands. Additionally, a strong relationship exists between consumption and failure in the performance of wife and mother roles.

Consumptive women had an average of 2.75 children living at the time of their death compared to an average of 3.07 for women dying of other causes. Farber concludes that these differences are not due to differences in fecundity, but rather reflect differences in child death rate and a shorter marital duration for the consumptive women. A longer state of nonmarriage is thus a better predictor of population growth with these women than was the high prevalence of illness itself.

Finally, content analysis of several statements in the records indicates a special meaning about women with consumption and values the disease held for the community. These women took on a label suggesting they were special, worthy, and noble individuals. "The East Church Parish death records frequently contain reference to the worthiness, the good nature, the excellent character, the exemplary life, and the delicate nature of young women who died of consumption—much more than in the case for other diseases" (p. 45). Farber concludes that dying of consumption in Salem was viewed as a special way of death, a purification in one context. One's hell and doom in life due to consumption could be used as a special request for salvation in death. In fact, salvation had been almost attained. In sum, Farber clearly shows that one must use documents if perspective of the past is to be blended with views of the present. Illness, status of women, reactions to death, and mobility are all measurable within the context of such work.

Other types of evidence anthropologists and archeologists deal with on a systematic basis would include artifacts such as fossils, skeletons, tools, food, clothing, buildings, furnishings, coins, implements of war, art objects, and jewelry. Individuals or cultures did not purposely build and leave these types of evidence for the purpose of preserving, nor were they intended to be used in transmitting information about peoples at a later time. It is clear that such relics do serve a useful purpose and are examples of primary sources for research focused on looking back, of reconstructing what used to be, and understanding certain questions posed in this regard.

Another primary source that is available in each generation for an unspecified length of time is referred to as oral testimonies or accounts. People who participated in or

---

Tips For Consumers 14.1

When Mrs. Truman died in October of 1982, the *New York Times* obituary eulogized her as a very quiet, unassuming woman who continually fought efforts by the press to pry into her life or to modify the stance she had chosen—to be in her husband's shadow. She was once asked what qualities she judged most necessary for a president's wife. She answered, "Good health and a sense of humor."

The obituary ended with a story about President Truman finding his wife burning some of his love letters to her. Why was she burning them? "Why not," she said, "I've read them several times." "But think of history," he admonished. "I have," she replied (Hofstadter, 1983).

As you reflect on documents that might be useful for research or consumer education, what have been your experiences? Have you ever burned that which researchers might find useful? What documents are held by your family or other groups to which you might belong that would be valued for research purposes?

We request that you assess personal records or selective documents and use them for your own research or consumership. You may also wish to make a copy available for others who might be doing related research on a topic where they would be valuable.

---

witnessed events do not live forever, and if one is to be successful in obtaining oral accounts, one has to talk to such people in a specified time period or be forced to work from secondhand sources (Willey & Schvaneveldt, 1983). (See Tips for Consumers 14.1.)

The further removed the secondary source is from the eyewitness or participation level of involvement, the more suspect it becomes as a useful point of information for research. Old stories passed on down through family generations, folklore, history textbooks, and even encyclopedias would all be in the secondary source category. Furthermore, one would want to be very careful in relying on any one of these as being valid without first verifying the information reported. It is, of course, recognized that professional reputation and judgment are at stake in history books and encyclopedias, and skilled scholars have prepared these secondary works from primary sources.

DOCUMENTS: UNOBTRUSIVE DATA

We have already noted that documents may be primary or secondary, old or new, and organized specifically for research purposes or unwieldy to use because they were maintained for purposes other than research. In this section we will define and illustrate some of the main types of documents most likely to be used in research projects in social science.

Letters, Diaries, and Private Papers

▶ The research by Thomas and Znaniecki (1918) is one of the best known studies completed using letters written by Polish immigrants in the United States and their remaining relatives still in Poland. Thomas and Znaniecki were able to classify the letters by category, and the two-volume set contains these letters by Polish family members separated by an ocean and culture. *The Polish Peasant in Europe and America* stands as a classic in the use of personal letters. Analysis of these letters indicates varied themes, individual stress, family disorganization, and crisis overtures on the theme of what it personally means to be away from home and experiencing the hazing of acculturation.

Biographers draw heavily on letters, diaries, and private papers for their research, and the extensive work on Jefferson by Brodie (1974) would be a well-known example from history. The presidential papers of each executive contain these types of documents and are housed in a library to facilitate the work of many scholars doing work on a specified president. To illustrate volume, it took over 20 semi-trucks to carry the personal papers of Jimmy Carter from Washington, D.C., to Plains, Georgia. Keep in mind that this reflected just one, four-year term.

Many private individuals save letters, personal papers, and especially diaries which have been used extensively. Much of the work on colonial life in New England, stress of the Civil War in Southern States, and community life on the frontier is known to us because of the rich letters, personal papers, and diaries left behind. Libraries at the city, county, school, and university level are excellent places to find or receive help in locating such documents. The United States Library of Congress maintains an exceptionally large collection of personal materials, many of which are available on microfilm. The greater the future in history the more readily personal records will be available. Research focusing on local community people or events will require extensive networks of communication to locate and obtain permission to use private records. These personal sources are often very rewarding for research because in addition to letters, personal papers, and diaries, one may also have access to photograph albums, souvenirs, momentos, and other items saved by persons.

Archives

Until governments at various levels started to accumulate and catalog extensive documents and then later made these available to scholars, researchers had to rely on private papers or other published books to obtain material. Nevins (1938) notes that it was not until the latter part of the eighteenth century that public archives became available for research. An *archive* literally refers to a place where public records are maintained—the public records and documents that are generated for and in behalf of the people. The United States built its first official building and appointed the Office of Archivist in 1936. The completed building provided 5½ million cubic feet and protected valuable papers from fire, burglary, dust, and so on.

Most university libraries house a "special collections" area and a director of the area who functions as the archivist and maintains the collection in a usable order for various investigators. Such collections may also exist at the city or county level, and of course, each state has extensive materials in the state archives. The world's largest collection of genealogy records is stored in vaults deep inside the Wasatch mountains in Utah. These records are available for a variety of family- and history-related studies (Wright, 1981).

Archives have extensive materials on almost every phase of development—including demographics, economics, political change, history, photographs, speeches, and diplomatic materials. Perhaps the best-known and most-used source in archives would be the United States census. A census represents a gigantic cross-section of every household in the nation, and this material was collected during a specified period for all households.

When census data are published, they are usually grouped, but researchers have made extensive use of census tracks or specific areas within a defined location. The census has been completed each decade going back to 1790, thus providing a useful historical scope for many research problems.

▶ Many of the official documents are eventually published and can be checked out from libraries. As an example, Beaglehole (1955) published the journals and related papers of Captain Cook's travels to the South Pacific. Other publications concerning these travels had occurred, but the Beaglehole publication reflects Cook's travels and observations in their original form. A recent example of archival materials would be the Mayhew and Myers (1980) publication, *A Documentary History of American Interiors from the Colonial Era to 1915.* This volume is an excellent collection of pictures, drawings, and other descriptions showing how people lived, their furnishings and the personal tastes in decoration over two centuries.

Mission and Church Records

▶ Pitt (1972) asserts that mission and church records are very important for a variety of scholarly pursuits, but especially valuable to the anthropologist. Missionaries were often the first to enter a particular area, and their diaries, records, and business notes contain firsthand accounts of the people, their practices, and the land. Pitt notes that letters written home are very useful, as they reflect the observations of missionaries over a time dimension and in a comparative mode. Some mission records are restricted in usage, and it is well to point out that a very particular point of view might prevail in some of the materials, since missionaries went to "save" people.

Church and parish records, archives, and other documents represent some of the best and oldest records available for research. It was the church who was not only the keeper of records but also keeper of the community, as noted in our example of Farber's (1973) detailed work on consumptive women of Salem. It was in the church and parish setting that education, facilities, and motivation existed for record keeping. In addition to the rather well-known data concerning birth, confirmation, marriage, and death, church records often have very valuable data on school tuition, church dues, building projects, and other information about the people and events in the community (Pitt, 1972).

Physical Trace Measures

▶ Some very novel and unobtrusive methods of assessing behavior in everyday life fall into the categories of *erosion,* or selective wear and tear observation, and *accretion,* measures that reflect buildup or deposits (Webb et al., 1966). Webb and his associates refer to observations in the Chicago Museum of History indicating that floor tiles around certain exhibits wear out much more rapidly than others (those around hatching chicks had to be replaced as often as every six weeks), while others reflected little wear. It seems clear that study of tile wear and tear along with replacement would provide useful data concerning the popularity of various exhibits.

Other examples of erosion measure would include traffic patterns on lawns, frequency of checkout of books from a library, and the dirt, finger marks, and bent pages on books. Use of a car can be assessed by wear and tear on front seats, rear seats, trunk, and perhaps slick rear tires may indicate the presence of a dragster in the household.

In contrast to erosion measures, *accretion* focuses on buildup of some type; the ◄
fingerprint in criminal investigation is perhaps the best-known example. Also, soil from
shoes, thread from garments, a hair from the head, or the cast-off cigarette butt are all
examples of accretion seen in police investigations, but certainly are available to the
social scientist. We noted in Chapter 1 that Jack Anderson regularly rummaged through
the garbage of the late J. Edgar Hoover to find out information about his personal habits
and life-style. Webb et al. (1966) made reference to an automobile dealer in Chicago who
had his mechanics check the position of the radio dial of all cars brought in for service.
This provided a sample of about 50,000 per year, and the data from these checks were
then used to determine which stations the car dealers used for advertisement purposes.

Kinsey, Pomeroy, Martin, and Gebhard (1953) make reference to differences ◄
between the amount and types of graffiti found in men's and women's public restrooms.
Randall (1979), in a delightful account of life and habits of the truly rich inhabiting the
mansions of the Gold Coast on Long Island, notes that it was a common practice for
significant ladies of the evening to fling off their undergarments as their great cars carried
them home after a joyous party. It would only seem proper that an enterprising social
scientist in the early twentieth century might have made significant observations on who
gave parties, attendees at parties, and how frequently this practice occurred!

In sum, erosion and accretion data may be very helpful in obtaining unobtrusive and
readily available measures on a variety of problems. Webb et al. (1966) also note that
these modes of data collection are most useful when one is attempting to study incidence,
attendance, frequency, and consumer habits. The unique point about such measures has to
do with the fact that the data are produced by people who never suspect that investigators
may use it for research.

Data Banks

The final type of source for documents we will cover is the *data bank*. These banks
contain specific data sets, films, samples, and other materials which may be borrowed or
copies purchased for research purposes. The Human Relations Area Files (HRAF) with
its home base at Yale and branch locations in many universities is a well-known bank used
primarily by anthropologists and sociologists. Pitt (1972) notes that historians, political
scientists, and other social science researchers are making increased use of data bank
sources. Hofferbert and Clubb (1977), for example, provide a detailed overview of social
science archive data and suggestions for using these types of data.

PROVING THE VALIDITY OF DOCUMENTS
AND OTHER HISTORICAL EVIDENCE

If 17 separately and independently maintained diaries survived an eighteenth-century
community in America and all of these various accounts are in agreement with one
another in describing weather conditions, settlement patterns, medical care, religious
participation, and entertainment over a 40-year period, one could place considerable faith
in the validity of the events reported. This process of establishing counterevidence is
known as *corroboration* and refers to verification. In our example, it is important to be
able to determine that the diaries are independent accounts, that is, that each person

wrote and maintained a diary independent of, and separate from, the diaries of the others. It may be that the diary keepers were merely repeating each other and do not constitute 17 separate accounts at all; hence no multiple verification (corroboration) exists. Corroboration refers to the process of confirming, verifying, proving, and establishing support for some claim—it is matching up claims with evidence or matching up various reports in regard to some alleged outcome. When all witnesses are in agreement, we say that corroborative evidence is very high and we can place considerable confidence in the report.

Ideally, it would be the ultimate goal of science for the investigator to collect everything of importance on a research problem; since this is rarely possible or practical, most investigators attempt to collect everything available that appears to be of importance to the problem (Senn, 1971). This strategy permits the investigator to work on a problem, but the availability, accessibility, and quality of materials available may actually result in a redefinition of the problem. Often the project will have to be stopped or even abandoned if certain records or needed evidence are not available for whatever reason to the researcher.

The Case of the Cardiff Giant

▶ Regardless of whether one is successful in obtaining all the resources and records wanted for a project or whether the ideal number and type have been modified, the scientist must verify the authenticity of the documents to be used to complete the research. Failure to verify or corroborate can lead to disaster and at best extreme embarrassment and ruination of professional credibility. A classic example of distortion and eventual verification is found in the Cardiff Giant episode reported by Hynd (1955). This story is of George Hull, who lived in Binghamton, New York, in the 1860s and his contact with a Methodist evangelist named Turk, who "inspired" Hull to "believe" a passage in Genesis 6:4 making reference to giants having lived and walked on the earth.

The Cardiff Giant was 10 feet 4½ inches tall, weighed in at 3,000 pounds, and was found in 1869, buried about three feet deep in a farmer's field near Cardiff, New York. The discovery created a tremendous amount of interest sufficiently great that two scientists from Yale University examined it in detail and verified it as a fossilized human figure. This same opinion of authenticity was reached by archeologists from the New York State Museum. Men of such high eminence as Ralph Waldo Emerson and Dr. Oliver Wendell Holmes made statements declaring that the find was both bona fide and of very ancient origin. Hynd notes that several dozen clergymen went to see the giant and declared that it was authentic and constituted direct evidence of the truthfulness of the story as contained in the book of Genesis.

Even P. T. Barnum became interested in the giant, tried to buy it, and when this proved impossible, had an exact duplicate made and placed it in a museum in New York City. A law suit developed in regard to the duplicate, a judge alleged that the original was a fake, and this series of events prompted a newspaper reporter to engage in a detailed investigation. He was able to trace the delivery of a large box to Chicago labeled as machinery. This shipment was made about a year before the discovery of the Cardiff Giant. His detailed investigation revealed that Hull had shipped a block of gypsum from Iowa to the area and that it weighed the same as the box marked machinery. With additional evidence gathered from a hotel, the railroad, and drayage company records, the reporter discovered that the box had been delivered to the 900 block of North Clark Street in Chicago where the owner of the building finally confessed to the role he played in the story, which implicated Hull and an artist who had created the giant figure in Chicago.

The giant was buried in the earth in New York after it had been treated with sulfuric acid to "age" it and then later it was "accidentally" discovered by some well diggers. It is an interesting case because Hull never made claims about the find, he just remained quiet and let a score of other people make a variety of claims concerning the authenticity and the antiquity of the giant figure. It was only after the careful and methodological research of the reporter that the hoax was discovered and the real story behind the Cardiff Giant became known. The activity of the reporter would be referred to as *external criticism,* for he followed some hunches and rumors, traced certain records, checked out shipments and weights, and eventually revealed the facts behind the reports that had apparently fooled several prominent "experts" who had examined the Cardiff Giant. Few, if any, of us will ever be confronted with a "Cardiff Giant" requiring verification, but on a smaller scale we will be professionally committed to check out, verify, and authenticate the claims of the various documents or artifacts with which we may work.

As noted in the above example, one of the very important methods to verify a document or object is to determine *the date of origin.* Such dating evidence can lead to the rejection of a document or object as being a hoax or at least not what you thought it was, or it can prove it to be the thing which was claimed. Key elements in dating include scrutiny to assess language, writing style, use of certain words, and other examples of style or form that might indicate a difference between alleged claims and that which might be discovered. Accurate age of an artifact can now be determined by radio carbon-14 analysis.

One of the most interesting and notorious examples of attempting to validate documents was the case of Mark Hoffman (Sillitoe and Roberts, 1988). Several thousand documents were scrutinized in detail because of criminal activity associated with Hoffman. Documents that were allegedly written between 1792 and 1929 were subjected to ultra-violet examination, microscopic analysis (stain, solubility, printing flaws), and Scanning Auger Microscopy Dating (SAMD). The final outcome indicated that many of the documents "discovered" by Hoffman were, in fact, clever forgeries.

If the painting is not a true Rembrandt, Picasso, or Renoir then who painted it? Is it a fake? These are old questions in art and other areas of creative renditions, and while not so common in social science research it is important to note that fakeries, forgeries, and a host of other distortions have been passed off as real throughout history (Klein, 1955). Experienced researchers and writers get to know writing style, word use, sentence length, and content treatment of various writers and can do much to determine the authenticity of an alleged author. *Time Magazine* (1983, Magnuson) carried a most informative account of the techniques employed to prove that the recent Hitler diaries were fakes.

If one wants to know if an author of some work is credible, if there are sound credentials, and if the person has done previous work on a problem, then it is possible to check these types of questions. Reference sources such as *American Men of Science,* professional directories, and other reference works can often provide specific useful information. If the author has appropriate credentials, belongs to legitimate societies, and the publication is in a solid journal, it can be routinely concluded that the work is authentic and that the research claims are legitimate. Editors of journals and those who are responsible for programs have already done much screening and weighing of these very questions before the article or presentation was ever accepted.

▶   In April of 1981, the *Washington Post* was awarded the very prestigious Pulitzer Prize for the work of one of its reporters, Janet Cooke, who wrote "Jimmy," the story of an 8-year-old heroin addict. Cooke, the alleged author, later confessed that she made up the report—the boy did not exist. The story was fabrication. The award was withdrawn from the *Post* and given to Teresa Carpenter of the *Village Voice*. The *Post* apologized through an editorial, "This newspaper...was itself the victim of a hoax—which we then passed along in a prominent page-one story.... How could this have happened?" (McGrath, 1981).

In case one concludes that fraud only occurs in journalism or in the nineteenth century, Broad's (1981) writing in *Science* provides a historical perspective on the problem and how Congress and the agencies responsible for monitoring research funds are taking a new look at shady practices. Science is said to be self-correcting and its own watchdog, subjecting scientific inquiry to rigorous policing.

A third test in verification is called *testing for truth* (Senn, 1971). This process involves three basic questions: (1) Did the author know the truth and was the author able to tell the truth? (2) Did the author accurately report the truth? (3) Were there or are there independent witnesses to the alleged truth contained in the report or document? Senn (1971) notes that, in general, "a person is able to tell the truth to the extent that they were close to the event in time and space, able to understand what he was reporting, and interested in and attending to the event in question" (p. 82). This is another argument for using primary sources in document-based research, for the closer one is to the real event in terms of time, participation, or a firsthand witness status, the greater the probability and capability of the person to be truthful.

Senn (1971) notes that even if one is close to the event and knows the truth he or she may not be willing to disclose the truth. Factors such as secrecy, propaganda, classified information status, or a variety of personality factors may function to prevent one from obtaining the truth. If one can determine that the author was capable and willing of telling the truth, then the main question for the researcher to decide is if the events were correctly reported.

An additional question dealing with truth telling refers to independent witnesses or the ability of somebody else to authenticate the claim of the author. All things considered equal, the more testaments that are given, the more confidence a community of researchers is likely to place in a claim.

We referred earlier in the chapter to the process of verification known as *external criticism,* and this process has been covered in part. External criticism includes all of those steps as reflected in questions like: "Is this document or artifact what it propounds to be?" The major question of "when" it was written—the dating concern is a major part of external criticism. "Where" it was written or "where" the specimen originated is likewise important in verification. The motive or the "why" along with "who" wrote it or created it constitutes the major step in the elaborate process of external criticism. These questions focus primarily on the question of validity—truth telling.

Another important dimension in working with historical documents or records has to do with *internal criticism,* that is, what does the record or document mean? "Does the record tell us anything besides what it seems to say?" (Senn, 1971, p. 84). External criticism as reviewed has been primarily developed by historians but is now widely used by all science. Internal criticism had been more developed and used by other forms of social science to deal with feelings being portrayed by the author that go beyond the factual part of the report. What kind of a personality does the author have as based on writing style, content, and productivity? In short, internal criticism is the attempt to understand the total content of what an author has potentially written. The language in the social sciences, the less precise meaning of many concepts, and the multiple interpretations of many relationships create conditions in which the use of internal criticism is more common than in the physical or biological sciences. In sum, since social science is more often written in the common language of the people, it is subject to more private meanings and multiple interpretations than the "private" language used by other branches of science. Now that we have covered many of the types of documents, the reliability and validity issues important in using such sources, and hopefully developed a strong rationale for the importance of research using documents of the past, we now move to a major research procedure for historical-documentary research. This procedure is known as content analysis and in this section the major features of this methodology are presented.

CONTENT ANALYSIS

Content analysis is a research tool for the scientific study of speeches, records, and other written communications to determine key ideas, themes, words, or other messages contained in the record. It is important because counting is usually involved, and thus it is a quantifiable research tool for the study of documents that have traditionally posed difficult problems. It is important to note that content analysis can be either quantitative or qualitative in nature. In the first type, the goal is to determine frequency or duration of events, while in the latter the goal is to understand subjective content such as attitudes or values. Holsti (1969) has defined content analysis as a procedure for applying the scientific method to documentary evidence. Since content analysis is carried out on the basis of specific rules, each step is defined for the reader, an important step in science so that replication can follow.

While content analysis is relatively new as a methodological tool for wider use in the social sciences, it has a long history. Rosengren (1981) notes that in Scandinavia during the eighteenth century, content analysis was extensively used to assess words in religious hymns and sermons. Words were counted by various groups in Sweden to make claim for their particular arguments in proving or disproving heresy. A sentence of death or imprisonment could result, so it is clear that content analysis was carried out with deadly intent and rigor.

In another recent work on content analysis, Krippendorff (1980) asserts that "content analysis is one of the most important research techniques in the social sciences; it seeks to understand data not as a collection of physical events but as symbolic phenomena and to approach their analysis unobtrusively" (p. 7). The notion of obtrusiveness is important and should be dealt with at this point. In numerous chapters, we have mentioned that respondents might distort, openly lie, or "color" their responses in peculiar ways. The facts that we are interviewing, that subjects have received a questionnaire, and that human subjects are cloistered, if in a laboratory experiment, make it certain that the measurement process is having some impact on the attitudes, behaviors, and meanings they are likely to share with us. This influence in the measurement process is referred to as reactive effects. Most of our direct measures have a high potential for creating reactive effects because they are obtrusive; that is, they directly enter into a person's life and influence that situation. It is commonly recognized that the measurement tool itself may affect the outcome. We laughingly joke about being nothing but a "number in the system" or a "guinea pig" in the big lab, but we are actually referring to the process of manipulation and testing.

Webb et al. (1966) note several ways in which respondents can react to research, including awareness that they are being observed or tested. In fact, measurement itself can have effects on subjects. Stereotyped responses and interaction can take place between the investigator and the respondent which communicate the feeling of being measured. This obtrusiveness or test-research influence has been referred to as the Heisenberg (1930) factor, since this phenomenon was clarified by him.

If a measure is unobtrusive, it does not cause the problems just examined. Unobtrusive measures do not create reactive effects or the "guinea pig syndrome." It is obvious as to why documents, artifacts, and other records do not create these types of measurement effects. These research materials are similar to the properties of physical sciences in that they are static, not dynamic, in nature.

Turning Content into Scientific Data

As noted, content analysis refers to the process of assessing contents of documents by using *objective, systematic,* and *typically quantitative* criteria. These features make it reliable and valid; thus, one should be able to consistently come up with the same results and the results should accurately reflect the data from a document. It is in this context of analysis that Dibble (1963) asserts that historians make efforts to infer events from the large number of documents routinely used. The historian and others who draw on documents to a large degree study events not directly accessible to observation; hence, these events are studied inferentially (Winks, 1968).

In addition to the observation that content analysis is objective as well as unobtrusive, a second characteristic is that it accepts or readily deals with *unstructured material* (Krippendorff, 1980). Researchers prefer to have their materials structured, as they are easier to code, analyze, and understand. If one is to use a variety of potentially useful documents for research, it is not always possible to have structured data. Diaries, biographies, and other forms of written material were not prepared with science or analysis in mind and hence require a methodology quite different from the routine ones employed by most researchers. These unstructured materials can be meaningfully and successfully analyzed using content analysis.

A third feature of content analysis involves *sensitivity* to *context* and *symbolic forms* in communications (Krippendorff, 1980). In typical empirical research one tends to separate symbolic meanings from the categorical nature of the data. Krippendorff asserts that in some research it may be desirable to "analyze verbal data as symbolic phenomena" (1980, p. 31). Thus, situational, semantic, and even political consequences can be researched. It is also possible to analyze data from a document in a context quite different from the one being used in the source; thus, the symbolic qualities derived may be only known to the researcher.

A fourth characteristic of content analysis is that it can handle or cope with *large volumes* of data (Krippendorff, 1980). If the amount of data is very large, it will no doubt be necessary to use multiple researchers with the necessary training to maintain necessary reliability. In this scope of the project, one would undoubtedly employ machines, including computers, and a carefully defined set of procedures to successfully complete the project.

Content Analysis as "Observation"

The reader will recall that in structured observation one observes and records within the boundaries of certain categories, rules, or guides—this same procedure is followed in content analysis. Instead of observing interaction in process, one reads or analyzes content within the context of rules established for the work. The purpose of the study, the nature of the material, and desired analyses determine the number and type of categories that will be used in content analysis. Once these categories are established, *content analysis is a systematic process of locating words, phrases, ideas, or meanings that fit into the codes*. This is nominal measurement, as we are just counting labels or words according to categories, but the categories should be mutually exclusive and exhaustive. This means that each idea or word should be classified into only one category and the procedure for the analysis must be capable of handling all content in the document under study.

Content analysis is thus a valuable research tool, a data gathering device that involves coding, tabulating, and analyzing existing data located in many sources. As noted previously, the outcome of this procedure can be quantitative or qualitative or a combination of the two. The method to be used in a particular study should be explicit so that research colleagues or other researchers at a later time might use the same procedures. In this context, content analysis calls for a very explicit, carefully defined set of procedures. The strength and attractiveness of content analysis is that it enables researchers to work on storehouses of data that otherwise would not be used because the scientific method would be virtually impossible to apply.

In a content analysis study to determine if changes have occurred in kinship ◄ affiliation, Schvaneveldt (1966) studied 131 autobiographies. Observation of dedications in numerous books caused several questions to emerge concerning the significance of the dedication in relation to family structure: *What are the social correlates associated with an author who dedicates a book to the extended family in preference to a spouse or children?*

In terms of documental research, the study sought to determine the utility of examining the structure of the family in the United States as reflected in the dedication of autobiographies. It was hypothesized that American authors born during the latter part of the nineteenth century, who today are publishing their autobiographies, would dedicate more of their works to the nuclear family, whereas authors born about the middle of the nineteenth century, who published their works about 1900, will have dedicated more of them to the extended family. Autobiographies were selected for the project because this form of writing has a very high rate of being dedicated to someone, a necessity for this type of project.

Through the process of content analysis, information was obtained on the author's date of birth, date of publication, marital status, nationality, and to whom the book was dedicated. A dedication such as "To the memory of my younger brother" was considered to be reflective of the family of orientation. In contrast, a book dedicated "To my beloved wife, Helen" was considered to be reflective of the family of procreation. A dedication to the family of orientation was analyzed as being in the typology of the extended family; whereas a dedication to the family of procreation was considered to be in the typology of the nuclear-oriented family.

The results indicate that an author is much more likely to dedicate a book to a member of the family of procreation than to the family of orientation. Table 14.1 provides a view of the data for the basic question and also indicates authors who dedicated their autobiography to a nonfamily person.

The question of kinship affiliation and preference is an important one and has been studied widely, especially in anthropology and sociology. The present example illustrates one novel approach to this question by using records of the past, records that are assumed to reflect a preferred orientation to kinship.

▶ In a contemporary study, Sullivan and O'Connor (1988) used content analysis to study the portrayal of women's roles in American society. Data were gathered from 364 advertisements appearing in eight magazines published in 1983. The researchers compared their findings with those of similar studies done in 1958 and 1970. They found that fewer women are portrayed in a family setting, more women are shown in professional working roles, and more ads portrayed women with an image of independence when compared to earlier ads. However, although American society supports egalitarian ideals, women are still being portrayed in decorative roles. Overall, contemporary ads frequently depict men and women as equals. Compared to the ads published in the earlier time periods, today's ads reflect more precisely the variety of women's roles.

▶ Taylor (1988) provides a rich and detailed account of station life in Australia. The monograph is remarkable in providing extensive documentation, illustration, and richness to a neglected contribution made by these pioneers and pastoralists. He uses early photos, period illustrations, and colorful detail to show life in the eighteenth and nineteenth centuries in the back land of Australia.

We have attempted to document that many rich sources of data exist other than newly generated samples. As noted by Nevins (1938), "The newspaper, the weekly magazine, the monthly review, are indeed full of hints which ought to send alert men delving

TABLE 14.1. Autobiographical Dedications According to Extended, Nuclear, and Nonfamily Orientations between 1880 and 1930

Date of Birth	Extended		Nuclear		Nonfamily	
	Number	Percentage	Number	Percentage	Number	Percentage
1830–1880	10	7	23	18	35	27
1880–1930	15	11	31	24	17	13

Source: From J. D. Schvaneveldt (1966). The nuclear and extended family as reflected in autobiographical dedication: A comparative study. *Journal of Marriage and the Family, 28* (4), 495–497. Copyright 1966 by the National Council on Family Relations, 3989 Central Ave. N.E., Suite #550, Minneapolis, MN 55421. Reprinted by permission.

Tips for Consumers 14.2

As a consumer of all kinds of research, it is important that you reflect on some of the real advantages of using documents in completing many types of research. Some of the major advantages include these:

1. Documents do not react. One can safely assume that the research itself does not substantially change the record. A researcher may be selectively biased, but that is a different issue.
2. A major problem in longitudinal research has to do with cost, retention and cooperation of respondents, and related attrition problems. Where documents are available covering a long period of time, one has access to longitudinal data largely free of the problems usually associated with longitudinal study.
3. Many topics of supreme importance to society are possible to study only by means of document sources.
4. Documents such as diaries are very potent sources for finding out how people really felt about certain issues. Because they recorded feelings, knowing the document would not be read while they were still living, they were much more likely to be candid in stating their true feelings.

---

occasionally into the past" (p. 369). A knowledge of the past, of history, is needed to cast the present into perspective. Using documents enables researchers to lengthen their focus, and Nevins asserts that we must refocus from generation to generation. "What seemed wisdom to our fathers is often folly to us; what is intensely dramatic to our age may seem naive and banal to the next" (1938, p. 21). (See Tips for Consumers 14.2.)

REPLACEMENT—NO; ALTERNATIVE—YES

By now it should be apparent that many researchers often use only their semicaptive student audiences for their samples. Since such samples are available, inexpensive, and tolerably willing, this use is understandable for very selective projects, but what are the alternatives? Broschart (1978) wanted to know more about the lives of female Ph.Ds., and obviously one does not sample undergraduates to understand this problem! Broschart selected women doctorates at random from pages of *Who's Who of American Women,* thus making use of a prepared document available and waiting on the library reference shelf. She selected a sample of 415 women who had supplied biographical information and then examined the content of these materials to determine if a relationship existed between family situation and professional status, professional recognition, and professional productivity.

She predicted that single women would have higher professional status, recognition, and productivity than married women, and expected married women without children to rank higher on all three measures than married women with children. What she found was that marital status is related to professional status, that single women hold higher professional positions than married women, and married women with children hold the lowest positions of all. However, professional recognition and productivity were unrelated to the family status of the women doctorates. Married women with children were found to have more publications in scholarly journals than women who were childless.

Broschart attributed these results to career interruptions. She hypothesized that married women would be subjected to more moving and changing jobs in order to accommodate husbands as well as their own well-being. The interruptions of child-bearing would further decrease the professional status of the women with children, but productivity and recognition would be unaffected by either moving or breaks to bear children. Broschart claims a woman's status is a result of her "pattern of labor market participation" (p. 76) rather than her professional productivity or recognition.

While the results from this study are interesting, we are primarily concerned with the methodology employed in this use of a document source. Broschart abstracted biographical data on these women doctorates, 1,000 women in all, from *Who's Who of American Women* (8th ed., 1974–1975). Content analysis was carried out on a subsample of the total group of 415 professional women who held a Ph.D.

The criterion used by this publication for selecting individuals in *Who's Who of American Women* is the reference value of the biographies, which are composed of two parts: (1) the position of responsibility held by the person, and (2) the level of achievement attained by the person. The information contained in the volume is supplied by the women and edited by the publishing staff. The edited version is subsequently returned for biographical verification. It is reasonable to conclude that women who are both motivated and willing to submit personal information about themselves might differ in a number of respects from women who are not willing to share the same information about themselves. While we overcome *reactive effects* of measurement with this type of sample, we cannot make specific statements about the representativeness of the *sample*.

PERSPECTIVE-TAKING ABOUT DOCUMENTS AS A METHOD FOR OBTAINING DATA

The major advantages of using documents in social science research include accessibility of data, nonreactive effects, historical perspective, and the great number of research areas that can be studied by no other approach. Subject cooperation problems are, for the most part, eliminated, but finding sources and obtaining access to sources can pose special problems in document research. A researcher has more freedom to work with documents in terms of time and location and can probe within the limits of the source, clearly issues that are more difficult in conducting research with people in a live sample. Document-based research has limitations in regard to obtaining understanding of contemporary questions, and it does not generally lend itself to assessment of specific social problems. Documentary research as a data source is an area that more social scientists need to work in and know how to use.

Issues in Validity and Reliability

It is important to remember that no matter how reliable you are in using documents of the past or how reliable the maker of the document was, they are primarily useful because we expect that they are also valid sources. Documents are especially useful from a reliability and validity standpoint because they are nonreactive, they do not change, they were prepared in many cases for research purposes, they typically do not stagnate, and researchers can use them in very creative ways. Many problems can only be studied by using documents and perhaps this is a major advantage, especially in terms of validity. One does not have to depend on or expect recall, cooperation, or willingness. If one can reasonably assure that documents were carefully prepared, truthfully recorded, and relevant for research, then one can be assured of highly useful sources of data for a diverse program of research.

SUMMARY

It is impossible to understand the present unless one knows the past, for the present is embedded in the past. To focus only on data from new samples is to ignore the rich storehouses of data which have been accumulated over the many centuries of behavior in social networks. Documents of a broad variety, such as censuses, school records, vital statistics, cemetery records, diaries, biographies, personal letters, books, magazines, speeches, court records, congressional records, laws and regulations, and artifacts, comprise some of the main sources available to investigators.

1. This chapter cataloged documents under five broad types:
    a. letters, diaries, and privates papers,
    b. archives,
    c. mission and church records,
    d. physical trace measures, and
    e. data banks.

    These categories are available to almost all investigators in social science at the community, county, university, state, and national levels.

2. The several advantages of using historical sources in social science research may be summarized as perspective taking, cross-validation, comparison, research on extinct groups, accessibility, and a sense of historical understanding.

3. Samples for significant research can be readily obtained from documents at a fraction of the cost when compared to newly generated samples.
    a. Furthermore, research through the five main types of documents discussed would be classified as unobtrusive.
    b. Since such measures are unobtrusive, one almost eliminates the major problem of reactive effects with samples, or what has been referred to as the Heisenberg factor.

4. Documents may be primary or secondary in nature, and the best research is done with primary sources since they originated via eyewitnesses or participants in the situation. The further removed a documentary source is from the eyewitness or participant level, the more suspect it becomes as useful information for research.

5. Researchers have an obligation to verify or "prove" the validity of the sources used in documentary research.
    a. One of the main ways for establishing validity is known as corroboration, that is, establishing counterevidence for a particular claim.
    b. Expert testimony is often useful in validating the authenticity of certain documents.
    c. Determining date or origin, authorship, and significance of the data is important in verification.

    d. Truth telling along with external and internal criticism was reviewed as procedure for "proving" the usefulness of documents in historical research.

6. Documentary research has taken on an increased importance in recent years because of methodological refinements in content analysis. Content analysis was defined as a research tool for the scientific study of documents to determine trends, frequency, existence, and key themes either in a quantitative or qualitative mode.

    a. Content analysis is important as a research tool because the procedure can be sufficiently articulated that replication can occur—a very important step in science.

    b. Content analysis as a procedure involves the development of categories, coding, tabulating, and analyzing data extant in the written word.

7. Using historical documents as data and content analysis as a research tool will not solve all research problems, nor will they replace original samples and other heavily used procedures for analyzing data. They are, however, important alternatives and supplements to be used in a variety of projects.It is a challenge and professional need for a new generation of researchers and consumers of research to develop an awareness of the richness and utility of documentary research.

8. Finally, we noted that all social scientists should be functional historians. And as Nevins (1938) so pointedly states, "The history written of and by Americans in the last generation not only illuminates our past, but suffuses a glow which more than anything else—more than the work of sociologists, economists, or political experts—lights up our immediate future. The American who ignores it has neglected the most vital part of his education" (p. 21).

PROBLEMS AND APPLICATIONS

1. Outline the advantages and disadvantages of primary versus secondary documents and identify the conditions for using one or the other or both.

2. What types of historically related research have been done in your own discipline of academic study and to what degree have they been used? Why? Do you believe that your discipline would benefit from more historically related research?

3. What kinds of documents or historical research could or should be done that would be most beneficial to consumers of research?

4. Complete a critique of a recent example of historical research in your area of major discipline. In what ways did the author(s) make novel use of documents of the past?

5. Discuss with other students the statement, "It is impossible to understand the present unless one knows the past, for the present is embedded in the past." In what ways do you agree and why?

6. Visit an archive center and obtain firsthand information as to its function and how you as a researcher or consumer of research can utilize services of the center.

7. Develop and complete a small data gathering program in which you gather your information from a diary, oral history, or other document form.

REFERENCES

Aries, P. (1962). *Centuries of childhood: A social history of family.* New York: Vintage Press.

Bahr, H. M., & Chadwick, B. A. (1985). Religion and family in Middletown USA. *Journal of Marriage and the Family, 47,* 407–414.

Beaglehole, J. C. (1955). *The Journals of Captain James Cook.* London: Cambridge University Press.

Broad, W. J. (1981). Fraud and the structure of science. *Science, 212* (4491), 137–141.

Brodie, F. M. (1974). *Thomas Jefferson: An intimate history.* New York: Norton.

Broschart, K. R. (1978). Family status and professional achievement: A study of women doctorates. *Journal of Marriage and the Family, 40,* 71–76.

Caplow T., & Bahr, H. M. (1979). Half a century of change in adolescent attitudes: Replication of a Middletown survey by the Lynds. *Public Opinion Quarterly, 43,* 1–17.

Coombs, N. (1972). *The black experience in America.* Boston: Twayne.

Dibble, V. K. (1963). Four types of inferences from documents to events. History and Theory, 3(2), 203–221.

Farber, B. (1973). Women, marriage and illness: Consumptives in Salem, Massachusetts, 1785–1819. *Journal of Comparative Family Studies, 4,* 36–48.

Hareven, T. K. (Ed.). (1978). *Transitions: The family and life course in historical perspective.* New York: Academic Press.

Heisenberg, W. (1930). *The physical principles of the Quantum Theory.* Chicago: University of Chicago Press.

Hofferbert, R. I., & Clubb, J. M. (Eds.). (1977). *Social science data archives: Applications and potential.* Beverly Hills, Calif.: Sage.

Holsti, O. R. (1969). *Content analysis for the social sciences and humanities.* Reading, Mass.: Addison-Wesley.

Hynd, A. (1955). The real story of the Cardiff Giant. In A. Klein (Ed.), *Grand deception.* New York: J. B. Lippincott.

Iredale, D. (1973). *Enjoying archives.* Newton Abbott, England: David & Charles.

Jackson, E., & Winchester, I. (1979). *Records of the past.* Toronto: The Ontario Institute for Studies in Education.

Kinsey, A. C., Pomeroy, W. B., Martin, C. E., & Gebhard, P. H. (1953). *Sexual behavior in the human female.* Philadelphia: W. B. Saunders.

Klein, A. (Ed.). (1955). *Grand deception.* New York: J. B. Lippincott.

Krippendorff, K. (1980). *Content analysis.* Beverly Hills, Calif.: Sage.

Lannie, V. I., & Diethorn, B. C. (1968). For the honor and glory of God: The Philadelphia Bible Riots of 1840. *History of Education Quarterly, 8*(1), 44–106.

Laslett, P. (1965). *The world we have lost.* New York: Scribner's.

Lynd, R. S., & Lynd, H. M. (1929). *Middletown.* New York: Harcourt Brace.

Lynd, R. S., & Lynd, H. M. (1937). *Middletown in transition.* New York: Harcourt Brace.

McGrath, E. (1981, April 27). Fraud in the Pulitzers. *Time, 117,* pp. 52–53.

Magnuson, E. (1983, May 16). Hitler's forged diaries. *Time, 121,* p. 36.

Mayhew, E. N., & Myers, M. (1980). *A documentary history of American interiors from the colonial era to 1915.* New York: Scribner's.

Nevins, A. (1938). *The gateway to history.* New York: Appleton-Century.

Pitt, D. C. (1972). *Using historical sources in anthropology and sociology.* New York: Holt, Rinehart and Winston.

Randall, M. (1979). *The mansions of Long Island's Gold Coast.* New York: Hastings House.

Rosengren, K. E. (1981). *Advances in content analyses.* Beverly Hills, Calif.: Sage.

Sandburg, C. (1954). *Abraham Lincoln: The prairie years and the war years.* New York: Harcourt Brace.

Schvaneveldt, J. D. (1966). The nuclear and extended family as reflected in autobiographical dedications: A comparative study. *Journal of Marriage and the Family, 28*(4), 495–497.

Senn, P. R. (1971). *Social science and its methods.* Boston: Holbrook Press.

Sillitoe, L., & Roberts, A. D. (1988). *Salamander.* Salt Lake City: Signature Books.

Sullivan, G. L., & O'Connor, P. J. (1988). Women's role portrayals in magazine advertising: 1958-1983. *Sex Roles, 18* (3/4), 181–188.

Taylor, P. (1988). *Station life in Australia.* Sydney: Allen & Unwin.

Thomas, W. I., & Znaniecki, F. (1918). *The Polish peasant in Europe and America* (Vols. I and II). Boston: Badger.

Webb, E. J., Campbell, D. T., Schwartz, R. D., & Sechrest, L. (1966). *Unobtrusive measures.* Chicago: Rand McNally.

Willey, G. Y., & Schvaneveldt, J. D. (1983, October). *Childhood experiences in Mormon polygamous families at the turn of the century.* Paper presented at the National Council of Family Relations, St. Paul, Minn.

Winks, R. W. (1968). Historian as detective. *Texas Quarterly, 11,* 44–51.

Wright, N. E. (1981). *Preserving your American heritage.* Provo, Utah: Brigham Young University Press.

CHAPTER 15

Obtaining Data: Evaluation Research

OUTLINE

Introduction
Politics of Evaluation
Misconceptions of Evaluation Research
Major Types of Evaluation Practices
    Needs Assessment
    Program Management
    Outcome Assessment
    Efficiency Analysis
The Methodology of Evaluation
    Nonexperimental and Experimental Methods
    Survey Method
    Benefit–Cost and Cost-Effectiveness Analysis
    Management Methods
Measurement: Issues of Reliability and Validity
    Respondent Predisposition
    Evaluator Predisposition
    Evaluation Procedures
An Illustration
Summary
Problems and Applications
References

KEY TERMS

Evaluation methodology
Benefit–cost analysis
Evaluation practices
Misconceptions
Needs assessment

Program management
Outcome assessment
Efficiency analysis
Formative vs. summative evaluation

STUDY GUIDE QUESTIONS

1. What role do politics play in evaluation research?
2. Are there common misconceptions of evaluation research?
3. Are there major types or categories of evaluation research? Do each of these techniques have their own special type of methodology?
4. Can experimental or survey methods be applied in evaluation research contexts?
5. Does evaluation research provide particular problems associated with reliability and validity issues?
6. Can evaluation methodologies be equated to the general notion of problem solving? How?

Role of the Scientist

The application of scientific methodology to program management can be undertaken through evaluation research. The ultimate utility of such research is improved program management, cost effectiveness, and improved intervention strategies. Through evaluation research a social scientist can offer suggestions for important changes in intervention and application. Likewise, through appropriate evaluation research a scientist can justify the need for social intervention through verification of program effects.

Role of the Consumer

Understanding the various dimensions of evaluation research and how it can be used to improve and maintain program effectiveness is an important responsibility of any interventionist. Evaluation research should be seen as applied program research in social service settings. Its utility in broadening program effectiveness makes evaluation a necessary tool for interventionists who are interested in assuring positive outcomes from their efforts.

INTRODUCTION

Society has come to call for accountability in programs supported by taxes and contributions. The call for such accountability has been accelerated by recent economic conditions. We believe this is, in reality, a healthy outcome from a somewhat less healthy economic condition (Pierson, Bronson, Dromey, Swartz, Tivnam, & Walker, 1983). For example, educators are being called on to verify schooling outcomes. Social workers are having to document family service effects (Affholter, Connell, & Nauta, 1983). Law enforcement agents are being asked to show their ability to reduce crime rates or driving while intoxicated (Grube & Kearney, 1983). Thus, a potentially healthy form of accountability in social intervention is emerging in the United States. Rossi (1972) refers to this national trend as "testing for success and failure in social action" (p. 11). As our society continues to engage in social policy and welfare program experimentation, through large scale intervention programs like Head Start, Job Corps, Community Action Program, or the National Institute of Law Enforcement and Criminal Justice, rational decisions are called for concerning a cost–benefit ratio. With multiple social welfare programs competing for limited financial resources and taxpayers showing signs of reaching upper taxation limits, cost–benefit analyses are becoming important tools in determining program support. Programs that are more costly than beneficial must be eliminated, while beneficial programs need to be supported. Perhaps more than one intervention program offers strong promised effects while producing questionable outcomes.

To accomplish the important task of identifying effective programs, evaluation research is undertaken. *Evaluation research assesses program effectiveness* (i.e., delineates the degree to which program goals and intervention promises are achieved by such groups as the social welfare program staff and administration).

In the conduct of evaluation research, almost every research methodology summarized in this text can be utilized. However, the distinctive features of evaluation research differ from basic social science research. Foremost, as an applied endeavor evaluation research is undertaken to influence the policymaking process of social intervention (Worthen & White, 1987). Second, as Rossi and Wright (1977) have indicated, the precise definition and operationalization of the program, its goals, and proposed impact are not provided by the researcher but by the policymakers. That is, the evaluation researcher must have clear and unambiguous statements by the social interventionist to assess program effects. Hence, the researcher must turn to the policymaker to supply important program information. Third, another important distinct feature of evaluation research is that it is limited to the research setting of the intervention program. As such, Rossi and Wright (1977) argue the intervention setting can create certain specific limits to the evaluation study. As these evaluation specialists remark:

> Requirements of the research setting often pose a unique problem: the research setting may preclude the use of the soundest possible research methods. Political and moral considerations, for example, may rule out randomized field experiments or even prevent the use of an adequate control group. (p. 8)

Thus, evaluation research is undertaken for policymaking, requires the interventionist to define the program goals and intervention process, and utilizes the normal methodologies of basic science, but such uses may be limited in their utility by the research setting.

POLITICS OF EVALUATION

Evaluation research is not free of political issues. Social welfare programs are political creations emerging from "the rough-and-tumble of political support, opposition, and bargaining" (Weiss, 1975a, p. 14). Governmental agencies and their bureaucracies are continually competing for increasing influence and budgetary support. Many social program administrators may be more concerned with the development of long-range support, public image, and expansion than with the documentation of achieving program goals.

The general receptivity to program evaluation is likely to vary from one agency to another. Should program administrators believe that their program would be compared to another in competition for political and financial support, they may not readily accept evaluation research. Even more threatening would be the prospect of being compared to another program that was loosely evaluated and appears to be successful in its achievement of program goals, but due to weak methodology, questionable measurements, or faulty assumptions the evaluations are misleading. Fortunately, social programs with long-range support and strong political backing are more likely to have administrators who are receptive to evaluation.

Therefore, evaluation researchers, in comparison to basic social science investigators, must be cognizant of the political conditions in which they complete their evaluation study. Only through sensitivity to the political setting in which evaluation research is completed can social scientists gain increasing acceptability by program administrators. As federal, state, and local agency programs call for program impact and outcome evaluation (as part of the program process in the growing trend toward accountability), social scientists will find an important role in applied intervention programs.

MISCONCEPTIONS OF EVALUATION RESEARCH

Given evaluation research is a relatively new professional role for social scientists, it should come as no surprise that several misconceptions are found among scientists and policymakers alike (Edwards, Guttentag, & Snapper, 1975). First, there is a commonly held misconception that social programs are fixed and unchanging entities. For example, one Job Corps program is thought to be the equivalent of any other. While local programs may be financed through the same agency, there is a great deal of difference between programs with the same goals. Hence, one program may be effective while another may not. Yet, both may be financed from the same administrative structure or agency.

A second misconception is that only experimental designs are useful in coming to understand program effectiveness. Thus, many professionals force evaluation research into pseudoexperimental designs resulting in the use of questionable group comparisons. While control group comparisons are usually desirable, they are only truly beneficial when subjects can be randomly placed into experimental and control group treatments. In most social programs randomization is impossible. Therefore pretest–posttest comparisons, with baseline information on the participants prior to the program experience, must be used as the control group comparison in certain evaluation studies.

MAJOR TYPES OF EVALUATION PRACTICES

Worthen and Sanders (1987) have offered a useful conceptualization of evaluation practices. In their broadest purpose evaluation practices are designed to (a) provide a for decision making and policy formulation, (b) to assess and evaluate progress, (c) to monitor and manage, while (d) being utilized to improve programs and materials. Further, Worthen and Sanders make a distinction between formative versus summative evaluation. *Formative* evaluation focuses on improving the program by providing useful information to the staff and administration. It is generally undertaken by someone inside the program and is commonly an ongoing or frequent process. The basic questions focus on: What is working? What needs improvement? How can the program be improved? In contrast, *summative* evaluation is undertaken to certify program utility. It is undertaken to assure potential consumers and/or funding agencies of program effectiveness or usefulness. Usually an external evaluator is contracted for this task. The most common questions addressed in summative evaluation include: Is the program effective? Is there a reasonable cost–benefit ratio? What clients are best served by this program? Are there specific conditions which make the program most effective?

While formative evaluation usually includes an internal reviewer, and summative evaluation an external reviewer, Worthen and Sanders suggest that both forms of evaluation can include an internal or an external reviewer component. However, in the case of summative evaluation, we believe external review teams, with no invested interest in program management, are seen by consumers and funding agencies as providing the most objective and least biased evaluation.

Worthen and Sanders indicate that evaluation can be objective-oriented, management-oriented, consumer-oriented, expertise-oriented, and adversary-oriented in its basic approach. Objective-oriented evaluation focuses on assessing specific established goals or objectives that are delineated by the program providers. Management-oriented evaluation focuses more on decision making and policy formulation. Consumer-oriented approaches focus on the evaluation of products and materials. Expertise-oriented evaluation primarily utilizes professional expertise to judge program effectiveness. Adversary-oriented approaches attempt to raise questions and engage in evaluation practices that address questions by those in favor of and those opposing the program goals, directions, and activities. While the varying approaches suggested by these two evaluation experts are useful and important to recognize, the actual methodology of evaluation can be categorized under the headings of needs assessment, program management, outcome assessment, and efficiency analysis (Touliatos & Compton, 1988).

Needs Assessment

Needs assessment focuses on the identification of basic problems, including documentation of size or frequency of a problem, the population in need, and the nature and scope of issues surrounding the problem. In needs assessment, evaluators look at census data, existing descriptive data, local community, state, regional, and national data regarding the problem, and related information. Frequently, local hearings with public testimony are held. Further, special or targeted surveys are completed to gather perceptions about the problem and to document perceived needs.

One illustration of needs assessment evaluation involves an undertaking to identify the most pertinent emerging concerns about families (Jenson & Daly, 1988). Through the use of an "environmental scan," issues regarding family well-being were addressed. Using information obtained from congressional committees, federal research and demonstration grants, governmental organizations, polling reports, cooperative extension specialists, and consulting experts, a rank ordering of the 20 most pressing needs was developed. Concerns about aging, teenage parenting, child abuse and neglect, work and childrearing, health care, AIDS, single parenting, drug abuse, stress, youth suicide, and stepparenting were recognized as the most perceived needs that should be addressed by national initiatives.

Program Management

As we noted earlier, continuous and ongoing evaluation related to program management (e.g., diagnosis, planning, work/time analysis, etc.) should in our judgment, always be an integral part of social program administration. Both outcome and impact indexes of program success should ideally be included in the evaluation process. Impact refers to the scope or breadth of program influence, and outcome refers to success—usually interpreted in terms of changing individuals' behavior or life-style for the better. Only through continuous assessment of program impact and outcomes can we be fully assured of the effectiveness of a program in achieving its goals.

▶   For example, in 1983 the California legislature mandated a statewide youth suicide prevention program. In one evaluation of this program, Nelson (1987) administered a curriculum and instrument survey to students, school staff, and parents. Attitudinal and cognitive variables were measured in an 18-item questionnaire. Feedback has been obtained on what is most liked and least liked about the curriculum and suggestions solicited regarding ways to improve the program. This management evaluation resulted in finding out that students liked to learn how to handle their own feelings and occasional depression. Some found the program too repetitive, while others indicated that more coverage was needed and that they would like to hear from individuals who had considered committing suicide. Further, over 96% of the respondents indicated that the program was helpful to them in one or more ways.

Outcome Assessment

In summative evaluation, assessment is undertaken regarding outcome. Many times this form of evaluation utilizes a pretest-posttest experimental and control group design. The primary interest here is in providing evidence of cause and effect.

▶   For example, Mills (1987) completed a study on the intervention effectiveness of training of personal and interpersonal functioning for behavioral problem youths. Students were trained in listening skills, respecting others' opinions, and awareness of emotions. Relaxation, art, and decision-making skills training were provided. Analyses of program effectiveness were completed by comparing groups at the completion of the program. Students not only showed enhanced skills, but there was evidence that they were less disruptive in class, had improved class participation, and displayed a more positive attitude about school.

Efficiency Analysis

Efficiency analysis focuses on cost–benefit assessment. That is, can the cost be justified by the benefits received. The process typically includes a monetary framework where the ratio between cost and productivity is assessed against some comparable standard. As Touliatos and Compton (1988) note, many times a dollar value cannot be readily placed on a given outcome. Therefore, a cost-effectiveness analysis is used as an alternative.

To illustrate this approach, we can readily draw on our administrative experiences at our university. On several occasions we have had to look at programs to determine whether they are being managed efficiently. One way of assessing the productivity of a faculty in the form of classroom activities is to generate a faculty-to-student ratio. If in comparing two programs regarding their effectiveness, we find one program has a ratio of 1:12 and another 1:30, we ask whether the lower ratio program is using its faculty in an effective way or not. Likewise, if the faculty salaries for the 1:12 ratio program are averaging $32,000 while those for the 1:30 group are only $26,000, we question whether the cost–benefit ratio is acceptable to the institution.

THE METHODOLOGY OF EVALUATION

As is true in social science in general, there are important preconditions to the evaluation assessment process. Three specific preconditions for testing or evaluating program effectiveness must be met (Rutman, 1977). First, there needs to be a clearly articulated program structure and operation. Hence there must be a coherent and accurate definition of the program service. Common sense tells us we cannot evaluate what we cannot define. Second, evaluators must be informed as to the specific goals and proposed effects of the intervention program. Planners, managers, and administrators must provide clearly stated short- and long-range goals and objectives void of political rhetoric and ambiguity. And third, the program rationale must provide a clear statement linking program structure and operation to proposed goals and effects. Such justification is a necessary ingredient to determine if the state program is actually associated with the desired program outcomes. Without a rationale for the proposed connection between program function and program effects (outcome), it is impossible to make any meaningful cause-and-effect evaluation.

Once the above three preconditions are met, the social scientist can use a variety of methodological strategies to evaluate social action programs (Cain & Hollister, 1972). To a large extent, the methodologies of evaluation are identical to those reviewed and summarized in the earlier chapters of this text. Therefore, we shall only briefly review the most common types of evaluation methodologies. Table 15.1 summarizes the principal types of evaluation methodology (Perkins, 1977).

Nonexperimental and Experimental Methods

Laboratory experimentation, field experiments, and observational study can be used in evaluation research. Pretest–posttest control group designs are appropriate when subjects can be randomly assigned to experimental treatment groups. Full control of subject placement is a requirement and thus makes the use of experimental design uncommon in evaluation research. Field experimentation is used when pretest and posttest scores can be obtained around a program experience when no control group is used. Rather, a time series strategy is utilized in which baseline scores are gathered on subjects' behavior, a program is introduced, and posttreatment measurements are obtained. Intervention effects are determined by a change in the measurement pattern (i.e., posttreatment scores rise or fall below those of pretreatment measures). In naturalistic observation or the case

TABLE 15.1. Summary of Principal Evaluation Methods

Methodological Type	Equivalent Term	Characteristics
Experimental design	Laboratory study	Full control over scheduling of experimental stimuli
Quasi-experimental design	Field experiment	Partial control over experimental stimuli
Nonexperimental design	Naturalistic observation case study	Relatively little control over rival explanations of hypothesized treatment effect
Survey research	Sample survey	Static correlation studies typically employing multivariate techniques to analyze data collected from large samples
Benefit–cost analysis	System analysis	Evaluation of the relative effectiveness of alternative programs judged in relation to economic costs
Cost-effectiveness analysis	System analysis: Cost–outcome analysis	Comparison of alternate programs on the basis of program costs and results measured in equivalent units
Administrative audit		Evaluation of program policies and practices in terms of compliance with internal and external standards
Operations research	System analysis: Management science	Application of scientific quantitative methods to develop optimal solutions to the problems of program operations

Source: Adapted with permission from Dennis N. T. Perkins (1977), Evaluating social interventions: A conceptual schema. *Evaluation Quarterly, 1,* 639–656.

study method, individuals are observed without control over treatment. Hence, inferences are based on expectations assumed to be related to intervention effects.

▶ The evaluation of preschool effects on the mitigation of negative consequences of divorce provides an example of experimental methods in evaluation. In one evaluation study, children from both divorced and intact families were placed in a preschool program designed to enhance cognitive development and social competence. Children were given pretest measures before the educational experiences and posttest measures at the end of the program. Further, a control group of children, who remained at home, were given pretest and posttest measures as a comparison group. Comparisons of pretest scores determine equivalence of samples. Contrasts between children on posttest assessments determine program effects. Comparisons between pretest and posttest scores through difference scores (pretest minus posttest) provide evidence of change. If difference scores are larger for the children in the preschool program than for the children from the intact homes who are either in the experimental or control groups, one can conclude program effectiveness (e.g., see Crossman & Adams, 1980).

Survey Method

Through sampling strategies and questionnaires, programs can be evaluated on a one-shot survey basis. Correlation analyses allow the evaluator to draw inferences between program variables and indexes of intervention outcome. For example, the length of time spent in group therapy could be correlated with measures of interpersonal adjustment. While larger samples can be obtained that increase external validity, and reliable and valid measurements can be developed, only treatment inferences can be made since survey methodology is nonexperimental.

A recent illustration of the use of survey methods in evaluation research is found in a study of the effects of 4-H programs on social development of adolescents. In 10 counties, 4-H-involved and noninvolved youths were identified from school rolls. A random sample was drawn and a questionnaire mailed for response by both parents and adolescents. Questionnaire responses by youths and parents were compared according to whether the adolescents were involved or not involved in 4-H to determine if there is any evidence to suggest 4-H-programs may encourage positive social developments as proposed in program objectives. This evaluation study indicated that 4-H programs influence, at least, the development of social cohesion skills (Young & Adams, 1984).

For example, Table 15.2 from this investigation contrasts the average differences between the two groups on interpersonal and social skill levels. While the statistics (Wilks Lambda) indicated the two groups differed in interpersonal skills, the size of the difference (55.15 versus 55.72) is trivial and meaningless. However, differences between 4-H-involved and noninvolved groups suggest a meaningful and significant difference in social cohesion skills.

Benefit–Cost and Cost-Effectiveness Analysis

Two similar, yet distinct, evaluation methodologies are associated with what is called systems analysis. Both methods include a cost assessment dimension. However, in benefit–cost evaluation, monetary budgets are compared between alternate programs of equally perceived impact. In comparison, cost-effectiveness analysis compares alternate program costs and intervention impact and outcome using equivalent measures for both programs. In both assessment methodologies, financial budgets are important, and accountability is viewed in monetary terms (although Nagel, 1983, argues nonmonetary variables should be recognized in benefit–cost evaluations).

TABLE 15.2. **Differences between 4-H-Involved and Noninvolved Youths on Interpersonal and Social Skills**

Social Skills	Participation in 4-H		Wilks Lambda	P
	Noninvolved	Involved		
Interpersonal	55.15	55.72	.97	.05
Social	44.30	46.71	.99	.05

Source: Modified and adapted from R. L. Young and G. Adams (1984). Youth group effects: 4-H program objectives and psychological development during early adolescence. *Journal of Primary Prevention, 4,* 225–239.

▶   For example, two teenage pregnancy programs might be compared on effectiveness in reducing risk for the infant. A medical-oriented program providing physician care only might be compared with a more social program focusing on parent education. The two programs could be compared on health of the infant. Then programs can be compared on costs. If both programs are equally beneficial for the infant, but one is less expensive, that program would be preferred on a benefit–cost comparison.

Management Methods

Two management evaluation strategies are frequently used. In the administrative audit, evaluations are completed on compliance with policy standards. At universities, for example, Affirmative Action offices are continually checking to determine if academic departments are complying with the standards of equal employment opportunities. Operation research uses statistical quantitative methods to assist in management practices. Through the application of scientific quantitative methods based on sampling probabilities, the evaluator tries to identify optimal program functions and operations.

MEASUREMENT: ISSUES OF RELIABILITY AND VALIDITY

Evaluation research, since it is tied to the specific goals and objectives of individual social action programs, has special problems related to measurement. While it is ideal to use standardized, proven measurements that have weathered the test of time and have verified evidence of validity and reliability, standardized assessment devices frequently are not available to evaluate the specific goals of a given intervention program. Hence, evaluation researchers are, perhaps more often than not, called on to develop measurements that can be utilized in assessing program effects (Popham, 1974).

In the development of evaluation measures, all of the earlier discussed issues related to reliability and validity apply equally here (Nunnally & Durham, 1975). However, several specific problems can emerge in the methodology of evaluation that might limit these important elements of measurement. The most common types of evaluation methodologies include interviewing, mailed questionnaires or telephone surveys, and to a much lesser degree, observation (Weiss, 1975b). While evaluation data can be reliable without necessarily being valid, the goal of good social science is to build its conclusions on both reliable and valid measurements.

Perhaps it is validity issues that create the greatest problem in evaluation research. The evaluation researcher must assure that he or she is measuring the concepts that are purported to be measured. However, numerous sources of error can create factors that allow inaccuracy to emerge in the data collection and measurement process. Three types of sources that may lead to invalid measurement are summarized by Weiss (1975b) and center around the respondent, interviewer or evaluator, and the study procedures.

Respondent Predisposition

During evaluation the respondent may either intentionally or unintentionally contribute to inaccuracy in the evaluation process, thus limiting the reliability and validity of the evaluation conclusions. For example, the motivations behind the evaluation may not be understood by the respondents. This may in turn lead to suspicion and hostility by the respondents and inaccurate or incomplete information. Such indifference or hostility leading to poor cooperation can, however, be overcome through proper communication concerning the goals of evaluation. Another limiting factor centers around the available information to the respondents. Care must be taken in evaluation research to assess respondents who have accessibility to the information, goals, or impact of the program. Further, it is possible that respondents may lack the insight or cognitive skills necessary to offer accurate information. The evaluators must build rapport, trust, and reassurance with their respondents. Should this fail, there are statistical means to extract from respondents' responses some error resulting from a desire to be seen as socially acceptable.

Evaluator Predisposition

The evaluator can likewise bring potential sources of error that limit reliability and validity. For example, the evaluator could (1) be uncomfortable with the respondents, (2) appear uneasy in the research situation, (3) fail to establish interpersonal rapport, or (4) bring to the evaluation process attitudes, expectations, or prejudices that could bias the respondents' responses. However, these factors can be controlled by the evaluator through training, supervision, or selection of evaluation personnel with specific skills or traits.

Evaluation Procedures

One of the greatest threats to reliability and validity centers around weaknesses in methodological procedures. All of the methodological suggestions and guidelines reviewed in previous chapters apply here, but several procedural issues stand out as important considerations in evaluation research. For example, to assure respondents' cooperation, the study must be introduced and accurately explained to the participants to assure them of the confidentiality of the evaluation and implications of the study outcome. Also, sponsorship or agency support should be clarified to the respondents in the discussion of study outcome implications. Further, complicated, lengthy, or poorly worded intervention evaluation measures are likely to minimize respondents' cooperation. Finally, controversial or extremely sensitive topics can create an added source of error. Evaluation on sensitive topics (e.g., family violence, child abuse, sexual aberrations, addiction, etc.) can create guarded and defensive responses that lead to misrepresentation and error. (See Tips for Consumers 15.1.)

AN ILLUSTRATION

Ross (1976) has presented a summary of evaluation research directed at understanding an important legal issue. The basic premise was that sharp increases in legal penalties for illegal actions (e.g., traffic violations) are offset by those who administer the law (e.g., judges). In investigating this assumption, Campbell and Ross (1968) studied the effects of Connecticut Governor Ribicoff's passage of a bill in 1955 requiring judges to punish speeding violators with 30-day license suspensions, with the judges under threat of not being reappointed should they fail to comply with the law. However, an examination of police and court records revealed the number of arrests in the six months prior to the passage of the law totaled 4,377, while six months after the bill passed, the total number of arrests included only 2,735 violations. These data suggest law officers, due to the harsh

---

Tips for Consumers 15.1

With the growing interest nationally in primary prevention, an increasing number of state- and federal-sponsored programs are being developed to decrease the likelihood of undesirable consequences occurring for high-risk populations. To study primary prevention from an evaluation perspective the prestest–posttest experimental control group design would be advantageous. However, good evaluation research includes the use of multiple methodologies. In reading primary prevention research, and judging its evaluative worth, a consumer should ask:

1. If an experimental evaluation design was used was the researcher able to draw a random sample for both the experimental and control groups?
2. In using a survey instrument were the researchers able to devise an assessment having some degree of reliability and validity?
3. In benefit–cost analysis did the researchers provide a clear-cut statement on the rationale for determining what is cost-efficient?
4. In management assessments were the policy and procedures carefully delineated? Failure to provide details on program functions and operations make the utilization of the management evaluation questionable.

A consumer or evaluation researcher should ask questions such as these to assess the applicability and utility of evaluation research studies.

---

penalty, may have reduced their arrests in marginal cases. But what about judges—were they equally affected by the new legal restrictions? Campbell and Ross compared the number of accused drivers not found guilty of speeding during the five years (1951–1955) prior to the passage of the new legal consequences with those accused of the same violation during the following four years (1956–1959). In support of their original assumption that those applying the law are likely to diminish extreme punitive (legal) consequences, these evaluation researchers found that there was a sharp increase in the percentage of speeding violators found *not* guilty after the passage of the law in 1955. Hence, evidence was presented by Campbell and Ross demonstrating that excessively harsh penalties are likely to be diminished by law enforcement agents rather than function as an immediate deterrent of such violations. The most obvious conclusion one could draw from this evaluation study, in terms of program management, is that as legislative bodies pass increases in penalties for specific violations, they must also limit the discretionary actions of those who enforce the law, but who are equally likely to resist the initial harshness through subtle changes in their professional (legal) actions. Such unsuspected outcomes can only be detected when social or legal programs are accompanied by systematic evaluation efforts comparing program effects with baseline trends existing prior to the program initiation. (For a second illustration on the relation between mandatory jail sentences for drinking and driving, see Grube & Kearney, 1983.)

SUMMARY

Evaluation research, as an emerging professional area for social scientists, utilizes all of the varying types of methodologies common to general social science research. However, the goals of evaluation are specifically applied in nature.

Evaluation research plays an important role in helping us, as consumers of research, improve our program intervention and identifying effective program procedures.

In this chapter the major points related to evaluation research were these:

1. Evaluation research is undertaken to
   a. influence policymaking and
   b. assist in program management while determining program effectiveness.
2. Evaluation research is often completed within the setting of political conditions that require a sensitivity to the political process surrounding program intervention.
3. Several misconceptions exist about social programs and evaluation. These misconceptions include the belief or assumption that
   a. intervention programs are fixed and stable entities;
   b. experimental designs are the only useful technique in evaluation study.
4. Evaluation research can be formative or summative.
   a. Formative research focuses on internal program evaluation for the sake of effective management.
   b. Summative research focuses on external-based program evaluation for the sake of assuring effectiveness.
5. Actual program evaluation practices can focus on assessment of objectives, management, consumer outcome, expertise, or adversary approaches.
6. Actual evaluation methodology draws on needs assessment, program management, outcome assessment, and efficiency analysis. Commonly program evaluation will include some or all of these methodological frameworks.
7. Limits to reliability and validity in evaluation measurement can be introduced through
   a. respondent characteristics and predispositions related to motivation, accessibility of information, cognitive skills, and social desirability traits;
   b. evaluator predispositions associated with attributes of the researcher;
   c. confounding factors associated with evaluation procedures.

PROBLEMS AND APPLICATIONS

1. How might psychologists, social workers, educators, sociologists, or professionals in your discipline differ in their emphases in applied evaluation research? On what independent and dependent variables are each of these professionals most likely to focus?
2. As a classroom discussion activity assume you are the staff of a state-funded program assigned to provide foster care for youths who are wards of the juvenile court. The state legislature has charged you with the responsibility of proving your effectiveness in child care. Likewise, you perceive additional program and budgetary needs. Outline the steps you would take in completing the evaluation project. Specify the key measures of program effectiveness.
3. How would evaluation projects differ for the assessment of prevention- versus intervention-oriented social service programs?
4. Identify how evaluation efforts could be used to improve the educational program at your college.
5. Obtain a copy of the following article:

   Steven Ungerleider and Steven A. Block. (1988). Perceived effectiveness of drinking-driving countermeasures: An evaluation of MADD. *Journal of Studies on Alcohol, 49,* 191–195.

Analyze how one can evaluate program directions from the policy perspective delineated from survey findings from 212 chapters of Mothers Against Drunk Driving.

REFERENCES

Affholter, D. P., Connell, D., & Nauta, M. (1983). Evaluation of the child and family resource program: Early evidence of parent–child interaction effects. *Evaluation Review, 7,* 65–79.

Cain, G. G., & Hollister, R. G. (1972). The methodology of evaluating social action programs. In P. H. Rossi & W. Williams (Eds.), *Evaluating social programs: Theory, practice and politics.* New York: Seminar Press.

Campbell, D. T., & Ross, H. L. (1968). The Connecticut crackdown on speeding: Time-series data in quasi-experimental analysis. *Law and Society Review, 3,* 33.

Crossman, S. M., & Adams, G. R. (1980). Divorce, single parenting, and child development. *Journal of Psychology, 106,* 205–217.

Edwards, W., Guttentag, M., & Snapper, K. (1975). A decision-theoretic approach to evaluation research. In E. L. Struening & M. Guttentag (Eds.), *Handbook of evaluation research* (Vol. 1). Beverly Hills, Calif.: Sage.

Grube, J, & Kearney, K. (1983). A "mandatory" jail sentence for drinking and driving. *Evaluation Review, 7,* 235–246.

Jenson, G. O., & Daly, R. T. (1988). Family and economic well-being: Environmental scan, executive summary. U.S. Government Printing (#201-087-807191ES).

Mills, M. C. (1987). An intervention program for adolescents with behavior problems. *Adolescence, 22,* 91–96.

Nagel, S. (1983). Nonmonetary variables in benefit–cost evaluation. *Evaluation Review, 7,* 37–64.

Nelson, F. L. (1987). Evaluation of a youth suicide prevention school program. *Adolescence, 22,* 813–825.

Nunnally, J. C., & Durham, R. L. (1975). Validity, reliability, and special problems of measurement in evaluation research. In E. L. Struening & M. Guttentag (Eds.), *Handbook of evaluation research* (Vol. 1). Beverly Hills, Calif.: Sage.

Perkins, D. N. T. (1977). Evaluating social interventions: A conceptual schema. *Evaluation Quarterly, 1,* 639–656.

Pierson, D., Bronson, M., Dromey, E., Swartz, J., Tivnam, T., & Walker, D. (1983). The impact of early education: Measured by classroom observations and teacher ratings of children in kindergarten. *Evaluation Review, 7,* 191–216.

Popham, W. J. (1974). *Evaluation in education: Current applications.* Berkeley, Calif.: McCutchan Publishing.

Ross, H. L. (1976). The neutralization of severe penalties: Some traffic law studies. *Law and Society Review, 10,* 403–413.

Rossi, P. H. (1972). Testing for success and failure in social action. In P. H. Rossi & W. Williams (Eds.), *Evaluating social programs: Theory, practice and politics.* New York: Seminar Press.

Rossi, P. H., & Wright, S. R. (1977). Evaluation research: An assessment of theory practice and politics. *Evaluation Quarterly, 1,* 5–52.

Rutman, L. (Ed.). (1977). *Evaluation research methods: A basic guide.* Beverly Hills, Calif.: Sage.

Touliatos, J., & Compton, N. H. (1988). *Research methods in human ecology/home economics.* Ames, Iowa: Iowa State University Press.

Weiss, C. H. (1975a). Evaluation research in the political context. In Elmer L. Struening & Marcia Guttentag (Eds.), *Handbook of evaluation research* (Vol. 1). Beverly Hills, Calif.: Sage.

Weiss, C. H. (1975b). Interviewing in evaluation research. In E. L. Struening & M. Guttentag (Eds.), *Handbook of evaluation research* (Vol. 1). Beverly Hills, Calif.: Sage.

Worthen, B. R., & Sanders, J. R. (1987). *Educational evaluation: alternative approaches and practical guidelines*. New York: Longman.

Worthen, B. R., & White, K. R. (1987). *Evaluating educational and social programs*. Boston: Kluwer-Nijhoff Publishing.

Young, R. L., & Adams, G. (1984). Youth group effects: 4-H program objectives and psychosocial development during early adolescence. *Journal of Primary Prevention, 4,* 225–239.

SECTION V

Data Analysis and Report Writing

In previous sections of this text we have introduced the use of theory in hypothesis testing, fundamentals of measurement and sampling, essential components of research design, and the most common data collection techniques in social research. In this section, we will introduce the fundamental steps in data analysis, the underlying meaning of statistical decision making, the common myths associated with data analysis, some fundamentals of computing elementary statistics, and the process of data presentation. Further, as part of understanding the research process, we provide the opportunity of becoming acquainted with the essential components of the formal research report. Understanding how the research report provides information on each of the major elements of social science research should enhance your ability to use research in your future educational and career experiences. Finally, as an epilogue we will briefly engage in summarizing some reflections on the content of this text.

CHAPTER 16

Conceptualizing the Process of Data Analysis

OUTLINE

Introduction
A Decision-making Process
Fitting the Statistic to the Question
Two Major Roles of Statistics
    Descriptive Statistics
    Inferential Statistics
        Measuring Association
        Measuring Differences
Types of Errors in Statistical Decision Making
Common Myths about Statistical Significance
    Odds-against-Chance Myth
    Replication or Reliability Myth
    Valid Research Hypothesis Myth
Summary
Problems and Applications
References

KEY TERMS

Question of association
Question of difference
Descriptive statistics
Inferential statistics
Null hypothesis

p value
Type I error
Type II error
Myths about significance

327

STUDY GUIDE QUESTIONS

1. What are the two major roles of statistics? What is meant by the terms *descriptive* and *inferential statistics?*
2. How does a researcher deal with the concept of error in statistical decision making? Is there more than one type of error?
3. Are there common myths about what statistical analyses can and cannot do for the researcher? What are they?

Role of the Scientist

Statistical decision making is an integral part of social science research. It allows a scientist to use precise rules in decision making. Likewise, statistical tools allow the researcher to (1) evaluate the association between two or more variables, or (2) test the difference between two or more research groups. This chapter introduces some of the general conceptualizations behind statistical analyses and reviews the various tabular and graphic displays of data. This chapter provides the conceptual foundation for the use of statistics in decision making.

Role of the Consumer

In reading and using social science research, statistical decision making allows a consumer to make judgments about the proposed relation between independent and dependent variables. Understanding the rules behind these decision-making activities assists the consumer of research in understanding when errors in decision may have occurred. Likewise, this chapter debunks some of the common myths surrounding statistical decision making.

INTRODUCTION

Decision making is an integral part of everyday living. It is common for us to ask ourselves is this thing larger than that thing? Does this item cost more or less than that item? Are two things commonly observed or found together? To answer such questions we apply certain rules of logic and typically some form of numerical system to make appropriate comparisons. In the same manner that we engage in decision making in everyday life, scientific decision making draws on rules of logic. However, the rules are more closely associated formal statistical conventions. In this chapter we shall briefly review the general or most typical decision making process that is foundational to statistical conventions.

A DECISION-MAKING PROCESS

We believe most social scientists follow the general steps outlined in Figure 16.1. To begin, a scientist typically has some form of a conceptualization or theory about the phenomenon under investigation. From this theory the scientist generates testable hypotheses. To test these hypotheses all essential variables must be carefully defined and operationalized into measurable units. Using sound research designs, data are collected. From this point on, the scientist must begin to make sound decisions, based on rules of logic, regarding the accuracy of the predictions within the hypothesis and the nature of support the evidence provides for the theory. Hence, the major decision-making activities center around hypothesis testing.

FITTING THE STATISTIC TO THE QUESTION

The importance of the question in scientific research can never be overemphasized. Only when the scientist asks good questions can scientifically useful answers be found. While there is no simple form of question that is best suited for the scientific process, there are two specific types of questions that emerge regularly in the research process. These questions evolve out of the scientist's use of inductive and deductive reasoning. In many cases, the scientist wishes to pursue the possible understanding of a phenomenon by asking whether there is some possible relationship between a host of variables. That is, the researcher may wish to ask if social class, a family history variable, health factors, or personal adjustment have any relation with each other. In essence, the question is one of *degree of association.* Is there a relationship between two or more variables and to what extent are they associated? In other problems, the scientist wishes to answer whether different levels of a factor predict differences in behavior. This type of a question then is *one of difference.* The researcher may ask if a particular variable is more influential than another in causing a change in a dependent variable measure, or might ask if there is a significant difference between two or more groups on the same behavior.

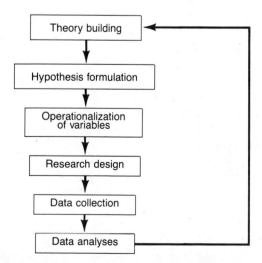

Figure 16.1. Decision-making Process

The question of association requires the use of correlational statistical techniques, while the question of differences requires the use of tests of significance. Statistical techniques, as one of the researcher's tools, can help the investigator make defendable conclusions about the degree of association or differences between groups. However, we must always remember it is the quality of the question and the manner in which appropriate methodology is used to find the answer that determine whether the statistical decision can provide a useful conclusion. Thus, the statistical exercise is primarily a tool to help make objective and decisive decisions.

TWO MAJOR ROLES OF STATISTICS

Descriptive Statistics

Two primary types of statistics are available to help us to make scientific decisions. Typically they are called descriptive and inferential statistics. *Descriptive statistics* help us describe certain characteristics of the research sample. Two basic types of measures are used in this descriptive process. A measure of *central tendency* offers us the opportunity to identify the most common score or feature. Central tendency measures include the mean, median, and mode. The *mean* is a simple arithmetic average that most of us have been calculating since we learned how to divide. The *median* is that score which is equivalent to the 50th percentile. Put another way, when all scores are ranked from lowest to highest, the median is that score which is exactly in the middle, with half of the remaining scores falling below and the other half falling above the median score. The *mode,* in comparison, is simply the most frequently observed measure. Each of these central tendency measures offers us the ability to identify the most common characteristic of a sample or group of people. But to have a full descriptive picture we must also generate an understanding of *variability (dispersion).*

While measures of central tendency tell us about the most common feature, measures of variability tell us to what degree the scores in the sample fall away from this central tendency. For example, we might find that the average adult male is six feet tall, but the variability around that score may be as much as one to two feet. Variability is measured in three primary ways. The *total range,* which is the easiest and quickest to ascertain, is merely the range between the lowest and highest scores. In comparison, a *quartile range* can be calculated that identifies the distribution of scores into four equal distances from the central tendency (usually the median in this case). Hence, one can show what the scores were for the bottom 0–25%, 26–50%, 51–75%, and 76–100% of the range. The most widely used measure of dispersion is the *standard deviation.* In general terms, the standard deviation is a kind of average of all the deviations about the mean of the sample. Measures of variability give us an indication of the breadth of responses around the central tendency and can be useful in understanding to what degree individuals vary in their behavior.

Put to use, measures of central tendency and variability give us a portrait of the sample through identifying the most common score or feature of a group (sample) and give us information on how the individual scores from the sample vary around this central point. In many research endeavors this is the sole type of statistical information that is needed to describe the sampled population under consideration. Many times researchers merely wish to identify the central attitude, position, or opinion of a specific group of people, and to note the degree of variability within the group toward this attitude. However, more often than not, the researcher is likely to have asked a question that moves beyond mere description into inference.

Inferential Statistics

Inferential statistics are important aids in helping to make decisions about testable hypotheses. As Kerlinger (1973) notes:

> An *inference* is a proposition or generalization derived by reasoning from other propositions, or from evidence. Generally speaking, an inference is a conclusion arrived at through reasoning. In statistics, a number of inferences may be drawn from tests of statistical hypotheses. We conclude that methods A and B really differ. We conclude from evidence, say $r = .67$, that two variables are related. (p. 186)

Hence, inferences are drawn when we use statistics to help us make decisions about possible associations, or differences, between two or more things.

Measuring Association.   Perhaps the most common inference statistic to test the degree of association is the Pearson's Product–Moment Coefficient of Correlation (r). When computed, r gives us information about the extent to which two things are related (i.e., the extent to which variation in one variable is associated with variation in another). As we noted in the earlier chapter on reliability and validity, the correlation coefficient value can range from a $+1.00$ (perfect positive correlation), through zero (no correlation), to -1.00 (perfect negative correlation). In Figure 16.2 we have graphed the three types of relationships to help clarify what is meant by the r value.

Let us assume a study was done by a student to examine the possible relationship ◀ between children's age and their ability to perform on a simple learning task. If the

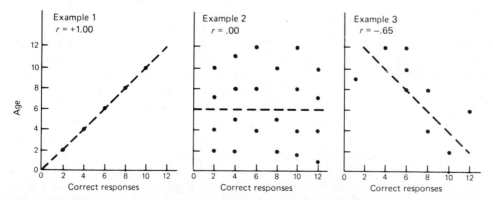

Figure 16.2. The Three Basic Types of Associations in Correlational Analyses

student were to find a perfect relationship between age of the child and ability to perform, Example 1 of Figure 16.2 would approximate such a relationship. As the graph depicts, with each new increment in age there is a parallel increment in the ability to do the task. Should the researcher student, however, find no association between age and learning, Example 2 of Figure 16.2 might depict such a relationship. In this case, age is unrelated to the ability to learn the task. It is possible, however, that older children could perform the task less well than younger children, in which case a negative correlation would be found similar to that illustrated in Example 3 (Figure 16.2). It can be seen that the older children perform less efficiently than the younger children; hence, a negative correlation implies that as the values of one variable increase, the variations in the other variable decrease. While correlations are useful to assess the type of association between two variables, it should be kept in mind that they do not prove causation. Merely because two variables are associated with each other does not mean they cause each other's variation.

Measuring Differences.   To assess for differences between treatment groups, tests of significance are employed. One very common technique is the statistic called the *t*-test. The *t*-test and all other tests of significant differences (e.g., Chi square) are statistical tools to help us decide if we can or cannot accept a "straw dog" assumption called the *null hypothesis*. The null hypothesis is the basic criterion against which all tests of significance are judged.

Specifically, the null hypothesis states that the experimental and control groups are not different from each other on the average score (central tendency) and that any difference observed between the two groups is due to mere sampling fluctuation (random error). Random error implies that the reason two groups differ is that during the sampling they were drawn in such a manner that differences between them were established due to chance factors. Therefore, the test of significance (such as the *t*-test, which tests for mean group differences) is utilized to help estimate if the observed differences between two groups can be considered as being beyond chance due to mere sampling fluctuation. Through the use of mathematical probabilities, the researcher attempts to determine how often a difference as large as the one observed between the two groups (experimental and control) can be expected to be found as a result of chance or sampling. If chance is determined to be very rare, the null hypothesis is rejected. That is, sampling and chance are disregarded as an alternative for the observed difference. The level of sampling error (chance differences) is determined through the *p* value, which gives us information about the proportion of time we can expect to find mean differences from our sampled population under the null hypothesis. The general convention is that a .05 level or better must be observed before we reject the null hypothesis. (Better in this case means the smaller the *p* value, the less likely chance factors under the null hypothesis are operating.)

▶ Suppose we have 20 students in each of two groups and the experimental group has a mean IQ of 100 and the control group a mean IQ of 90. In this comparison of samples, the difference between the two groups is 10 ($100 - 90 = 10$). Let us assume we have computed a *t* test on these data and found that the reported difference was significant ($p < .05$). A *p* value of .05 in this hypothetical example would be interpreted to mean that one would expect to find chance or sampling differences as large as 10 IQ points in 5 pairs of samples should 100 samples be drawn from the same population. Hence, the researcher must make a calculated decision. Knowing that, 5% of the time, differences as large as 10 points can be observed by chance alone, the researcher must make a decision as to whether to reject or accept the null hypothesis. The researcher can actually make a decision to reject the null hypothesis when in actuality the differences are due to chance. Therefore, many researchers hope to obtain p values much less than .05 and are, for example, only likely to report their data as rejecting the null hypothesis when the p value is very low (e.g., $p < .01$ which means a 1% chance factor). As Carver (1978) states, "Statistical significance simply means statistical rareness" (p. 383). Results are considered significant from a statistical perspective because they are expected to occur only rarely under the random sampling assumptions of the null hypothesis.

Since we are dealing with rarity and probability, there are problems with making wrong decisions, or errors, in statistical decision making as well. The advantage, however, is that we can place probability statements on the likelihood of making such errors when using statistics, while we are not able to do so when making nonmathematical statements of reason. With this in mind, let us turn to a brief description of the type of possible errors in statistical decision making.

TYPES OF ERRORS IN STATISTICAL DECISION MAKING

There are four basic types of decisions related to the acceptance or rejection of the null hypothesis. Table 16.1 conceptualizes these decisions. There are two major dimensions to statistical decision making related to the null hypothesis. First, the null hypothesis has the possibility of being true or false. If it is true, you will recall this means the differences between the experimental and control group are actually due to chance. If it is false, the differences are real (the treatment effect made a difference). Second, the researcher must make a decision to accept or reject the null hypothesis based on the available data.

There are two correct decisions that are the goal of the scientist. First, the researcher can accept the null hypothesis when in reality it is correct. This means the researcher says there are no significant statistical differences between the two groups when there are no differences other than those due to chance variation. Second, the researcher can reject (not accept) the null hypothesis when it is false. That is, the researcher can indicate there are significant statistical differences between the two treatment groups when in reality these differences are not due to chance variability. In the former case, the researcher says he has faith there are no differences between the two experimental groups, and he is correct in his decision. In the latter, she says there are differences, and she is likewise correct.

However, there is also room for making an error in statistical decision making. Hence, two error factors must be recognized. The first and least frequently recognized

TABLE 16.1 Decision Errors Related to Acceptance or Rejection of the Null Hypothesis

| | When null hypothesis is | |
	True or	False
Accept	Correct decision	Type II error
or		
Reject	Type I error	Correct decision

error is commonly called the *Type II error*. It is possible for the researcher to accept the null hypothesis that no differences other than chance exist between the two experimental groups, when the variation is actually due to true and reliable variation. Therefore, to accept the null hypothesis when it is false misleads the researcher into believing there are no real differences between the experimental and control groups when there really are true variations. This error can be a very costly one when dealing with the treatment of important problems (e.g., health, social, or welfare problems).

▶   For example, we know that teenage pregnancy has harsh consequences on teenagers' long-range welfare. Hence, a comparison of two types of prevention programs may lead the researcher to suspect one experimental program is better than another, yet due to a Type II error to accept the null hypothesis when real (and hopefully meaningful) differences exist between the programs. Therefore, the researcher may discard the "stronger" program in favor of the " weaker" one because it is more costly and therein lose the differential and more effective impact of the discarded program. To decrease this error, researchers dealing with extremely important social and health problems frequently reduce the p value in helping to make decisions related to rejecting or accepting the null hypothesis. The advantage this offers is that they are less likely to accept a false null hypothesis. Further testing of the program will then be completed to determine if the experimental program is actually better than the other program in preventing teenage pregnancy.

The second type of error, and the one most frequently attended to, is called a *Type I error*. This error involves rejecting a true null hypothesis. In this case, the researcher decides there are real differences between the two experimental groups when these differences are actually due to chance variation. This error is guarded against by keeping the p value small. When convention allows researchers to talk about statistical significance when the value reaches $p < .05$, many researchers are skeptical unless the p value is much smaller (e.g., $p < .01$ or smaller). Hence, when the probability level is set at .01, the researcher is making only a 1% chance of a Type I error.

One of the dilemmas in dealing with Types I and II errors is a reciprocal relation between the two errors (Friedman, 1972). By attempting to reduce Type I errors through increasing the stringency of the p value the prospects of making a Type II error are greatly enhanced. However, Friedman (1972) has shown that by increasing the sample size of the experimental groups there is an improvement in the probability of finding significant statistical differences between treatment conditions, while keeping the possibility of making Types I or II errors at an acceptable level. Therefore, the best safeguard against incorrect statistical decision making is through efficient random sampling with large numbers of observations and appropriate experimental and control group designs to eliminate chance factors (confounds) in the data.

COMMON MYTHS
ABOUT STATISTICAL SIGNIFICANCE

Carver (1978) believes that most scientists view statistical significance testing as a substitute for replication. Should the scientist demonstrate that chance factors (null hypothesis) can be eliminated, then the reported differences between the two experimental groups should be replicable. Yet, Carver argues, to eliminate chance does not provide evidence for replicability. The only truly justifiable way to test for replicated results is through repeated replication studies. As Stevens (1971) has stated:

> In the long run scientists tend to believe only those results that they can reproduce. There appears to be no better option than to await the outcome of replications. It is probably fair to say that statistical tests of significance . . . have never convinced a scientist of anything. (p. 440)

Hence, Carver argues that statistical significance testing is a trivial exercise which flourishes primarily because we view it (incorrectly) as a substitute for replication. Nevertheless, it does flourish, and we doubt whether it will ever be discarded as an important decision-making tool in accepting or rejecting the null hypothesis. However, we do agree with Carver that it is important to be conscious of several common myths or "fantasies" (to use Carver's term) about what so-called significance testing does for the statistical decision-making process. Therefore, we shall briefly review common myths about what many view as the function of significance testing in the hopes that this introduction will lead beginning students to be cautious in their interpretation of statistical evidence.

Odds-against-Chance Myth

This myth is assumed when the researcher reports that the p value is an indication of the degree to which the research results were *caused by chance*. The p value has nothing to do with reporting what the odds are that the results can be attributed to chance. Rather, the p value merely gives us an indication of *expected* sampling error (chance differences) as large as those observed between the two groups.

Replication or Reliability Myth

As we mentioned earlier, Carver has argued that some researchers incorrectly interpret statistical significance as the probability of obtaining the same results when a given experiment is put under replication. Hence, researchers will report the term "reliable differences." However, statistical significance testing has nothing to do with replication or reliability. It is the methodological ability of the researcher to control and manipulate the independent variables under the exact same conditions that determine the probabilities of finding the same results.

Valid Research Hypothesis Myth

Researchers, likewise, may interpret the size of the p as an index of the degree to which their hypothesis is valid. While many scientists will draw a connection between the p level and the "valid" hypothesis, there is no justifiable reason to make such an inference. Even though one can reject a null hypothesis in favor of experimental group differences, this does not eliminate all other rival hypotheses. Validity of a research hypothesis hinges on repeated confirmation, not statistical significance testing.

SUMMARY

Statistical decision making is an important part of the scientific process. It helps the researcher to make objective decisions based on probability levels. However, statistical manipulations can never become a replacement for effective methodology. Methodological considerations must always precede, in importance, statistical decision making. Poorly gathered, highly confounded data can never be made more or less useful by statistical finesse when the data are unreliable and of questionable validity. Further, science moves ahead by asking good critical questions and not by forcing the questions to fit the statistic.

Nonetheless, statistical analyses serve multiple and useful functions for the scientist and consumer alike. In particular, they offer important information on the probability of chance having influenced the final research decision. Further, descriptive statistics offer additional advantages. Through central tendency and variability measures (1) a careful and complete picture can be drawn about behavior, (2) large amounts of data can be drawn on to understand "typical" or "average" behavior, and (3) an individual's behavior can be understood in perspective to others. In addition, inferential statistics can help one to (1) make decisions about differences between treatment groups in an objective manner and (2) make inferences about a larger population based on a drawn sample. Science requires the use of statistical decision making in that scientific decisions must be made through public means and in a manner that can be repeated by others.

In summary, the major points reviewed in this chapter include:

1. The two major roles of statistics include
   a. a description of the characteristics of the research sample through measures of central tendency and dispersion;
   b. the establishment of inferences related to hypotheses based on evidence about the degree of association or differences.
2. The straw dog role of the null hypothesis is to help the researcher make decisions related to possible sampling fluctuations and chance factors.
3. Statistical decision-making errors related to the null hypothesis include the following:
   a. Type I error: Rejecting the null hypothesis, when in fact it is true.
   b. Type II error: Accepting the null hypothesis, when in fact it is false.
4. A number of common myths prevail about significance testing. These myths incorrectly assume that the p value implies
   a. the degree to which chance caused a research result;
   b. the reliability or replicability of a finding; or
   c. the validity of a research hypothesis.

PROBLEMS AND APPLICATIONS

1. Go to the library and look up one of the following research articles (or one assigned by your professor):

   John M. Gottman and Lynn F. Katz. (1989). Effects of marital discord on young children's peer interaction and health. *Developmental Psychology, 25,* 373–381.

David Buss. (1989). Conflict between the sexes: Strategic interference and the evocation of anger and upset. *Journal of Personality and Social Psychology, 56,* 735–747.

Martin Reite, Kristine Kaemingk, and Maria L. Boccia. (1989). Maternal separation in Bonnet Monkey infants: Altered attachment and social support. *Child Development, 60,* 473–480.

After reading the article carefully determine what the research hypotheses were, whether they used tests of association or tests of differences to examine their hypotheses, and what kinds of graphic displays of data they presented. Did the data support their hypothesis?

2. If you were testing the utility of a new drug to cure cancer how would you deal with Types I and II statistical errors? In comparison, if you were doing a series of laboratory experiments on the effects of certain reinforcements to pigeon pecking behavior how would you deal with Types I and II statistical errors? What differs between these two studies that makes you behave differently (or similarly) between types of research?

3. Drawing from your classwork in your major, identify a theory, and develop a testable hypothesis. Describe the methodology of the study and the type of statistical decision making you would engage in (i.e., tests of association or differences). What kind of descriptive statistics would you use to describe your research sample? How would you prepare a graphical or figural display of your data?

REFERENCES

Carver, R. (1978). The case against statistical significance testing. *Harvard Educational Review, 48,* 378–399.

Friedman, H. (1972). *Introduction to statistics.* New York: Random House.

Kerlinger, F. N. (1973). *Foundations of behavioral research* (2nd ed.). New York: Holt, Rinehart and Winston.

Stevens, S. S. (1971). Issues in psychophysical measurement. *Psychological Review, 78,* 426–450.

CHAPTER 17

Understanding Research Results

OUTLINE

Introduction
Measurement Levels and Parametric versus Nonparametric Statistics
Descriptive Statistics
 Raw Frequencies and Percentages
 Measures of Central Tendency
 Measures of Dispersion
 A Research Illustration: Descriptive Statistics
Measures of Association
 The Phi Coefficient
 The Pearson Product-Moment Correlation Coefficient
 Summary
Tests of Significant Differences
 The Chi Square
 The t-Test
 One-Way Analysis of Variance
 Summary
Summary
Problems and Applications
References

KEY TERMS

Frequencies

Frequency distribution

Percentages

Skewness

Mean	Pearson *r* test
Median	*t*-test
Mode	Chi square
Range	One-way analysis of variance
Standard Deviation	Nonparametric
Sign test	Parametric
Phi coefficient	

STUDY GUIDE QUESTIONS

1. How does level of measurement influence decisions regarding the use of statistics?
2. What statistics are used to provide a basic descriptive of a data set?
3. How do social scientists measure the degree of association between behaviors, attitudes, or opinions?
4. How can we test for possible significant differences between groups regarding their behaviors?

Role of the Scientist

Statistical decision making is an important undertaking. It is the final process undertaken with the data to test the null hypothesis. Typically, the scientific process includes learning how to (1) prepare the data for statistical analysis, (2) present data in statistical descriptive terms, and (3) utilize statistics to test a null hypothesis. This chapter, as the second in a two-part sequence, provides an introduction to each of these steps with examples on how statistical analyses can be applied to real research problems. The fundamentals of statistical decision making of the methodological process are summarized here as part of the research act.

Role of the Consumer

This chapter provides a fundamental introduction on how researchers use statistics to make decisions regarding their data. To read and understand research reports requires at least an elementary understanding of how social scientists draw on and compute simple descriptive and inferential statistics. In this chapter, you will be introduced to the basic fundamentals of statistics and how they can be applied to numerous research contexts. Illustrations of basic computations will be provided to establish an initial understanding of how simple statistical decision making is undertaken by social scientists and how final decisions are derived.

INTRODUCTION

In the previous chapter we explored the use of statistics in scientific decision making. Our fundamental argument is that once data are obtained using a sound conceptual or theoretical framework, an appropriate hypothesis, and appropriate methodology, statistical analyses can be used to assist the researcher in drawing correct decisions about the findings. In Chapter 16, we reviewed the conceptual underpinnings of statistical decision making, reviewed various ways in which data can be presented, and provided the general foundation for this chapter.

In this chapter we will review the process of statistical analyses beginning with the general assumption that you are aware that data analysis is preceded by the construction of a hypothesis, the specification of a sound research design, and the implementation of a methodology of data collection. The remaining steps of the research process (outside of writing the report) will be reviewed in this chapter.

We shall begin with a discussion of selecting statistical strategies based on the level of the scale used to measure the dependent variable(s). Next we shall discuss the nature and types of statistics used to describe the data set. Then we shall summarize the utility of measures of association and tests of significant differences. This chapter is provided as a basic foundation to statistical analyses. A comprehensive statistical text should be utilized for complete coverage on statistical techniques, procedures, and analyses.

MEASUREMENT LEVELS AND PARAMETRIC VERSUS NONPARAMETRIC STATISTICS

Many different types of statistics have been developed for making decisions and drawing conclusions from a data set. The appropriateness of a given statistical technique, in part, is determined by the level of measurement used. In Chapter 8 we discussed the four basic levels of measurement: nominal, ordinal, interval, and ratio. As you will recall, nominal data are at a categorical level. Ordinal data are at a rank order level, while interval and ratio levels have a zero point and standard units of distance between each point of measurement. In selecting statistical analyses for the nominal and ordinal levels researchers use nonparametric statistical techniques, whereas interval and ratio scales can be assessed using parametric strategies.

Parametric statistics require meeting several important assumptions before they can be used, while nonparametric techniques do not. To use a parametric statistic the following conditions should be met. First, it is assumed that the data have been drawn from a population that is normally distributed: that is, it is assumed that a sample from a larger population has been drawn and that the scores are equally spread between the high and low ends (range) of possible scores. Second, it is assumed that variances between any groups constituting the sample (e.g., males and females, whites and blacks) are approximately equal—that is, it should be established that any given group or subgroup within the sample doesn't have small or extremely large ranges in their scores. Finally, all measures must be based on equal interval scales—interval and ratio. This requirement is needed for appropriate applications of addition, subtraction, multiplication, and division as specified in parametric tests.

Gross departures from the three assumptions underlying parametric tests can result in distorted (and sometimes blatant misrepresentation) of findings. Fortunately, there are nonparametric techniques that can be applied to data sets which require no more than categorical or ordinal data. Likewise, these techniques can be applied to interval and ratio data when they fail to meet the three basic assumptions of parametric tests.

DESCRIPTIVE STATISTICS

As you will recall from the previous chapter, statistical decision making draws on two major types of statistics: descriptive and inferential statistics. Descriptive statistics provide a general portrait of what is being studied. Inferential statistics are used to assess differences between groups and the association between two or more variables. In the remainder of this chapter, we shall examine some of the fundamental statistical analyses that are undertaken by social scientists in making decisions about what their data are telling them. We will begin with an overview of descriptive statistics and their computations and summarize with a research example.

Raw Frequencies and Percentages

The most basic form of statistic is the *frequency*. A frequency is simply the number of events or objects in a category. Frequency *distributions* can be presented either as a simple frequency distribution or in the form of grouped data. You have probably seen both types of frequency distributions in the course of your education where teachers have presented the results of a classroom test. An illustration of the two techniques is summarized in Tables 17.1 and 17.2. As you can see the simple frequency distribution gives the exact number of persons receiving a specific score. In contrast the grouped

TABLE 17.1. Raw Scores and Their Frequencies on a Course Exam

Score	Frequency	Score	Frequency
97	1	84	3
96	1	83	6
95	2	82	3
94	1	81	3
93	1	80	2
92	2	79	1
91	1	78	1
90	3	77	2
89	2	76	1
88	3	75	1
87	1	74	2
86	4	73	1
85	5	72	1

TABLE 17.2. Frequencies for Aggregated Intervals from Exam Scores in Table 17.1

Interval	Frequency
95–100	4
90–94	8
85–89	15
80–84	17
75–79	6
70–74	4

technique is presented in the form of frequencies for specified intervals. The interval method is less precise but still provides a general summary of the data.

The typical pictorial representation of a frequency distribution assumes the form of a frequency *polygon*. A frequency polygon is a line graph such as that illustrated in Figure 17.1. The advantage of presenting one's raw or interval frequencies is to assess the degree to which the data approximate a normal bell-shaped curve. A normal curve of distribution and variations of the data is depicted in Figure 17.2. (The normal curve assumes conceptual and theoretical importance to understanding a statistical concept called dispersion or variance.) We shall return to the importance of the normal curve later. Variation from the typical approximation of a normal distribution is called *skewness*. As Figure 17.2 depicts two general types of skewness are possible. In what is called a *negatively skewed* distribution the scores are heavily concentrated toward the upper end of the frequency distribution. In such a distribution, the typical person scores high on the variable. When scores in a frequency distribution are predominantly at the lower end of the distribution the curve is *positively skewed*. In this type of distribution, the variable is infrequently observed or a relatively rare occurrence. The general assumption in statistical parlance is that random sampling of a large population should result in a frequency distribution that approximates the theoretical normal curve. Thus, most scores emerge toward the middle with few scores occurring as one moves to the extremes.

At times it is useful to represent one's data as a *percentage* of the total frequency of scores. This is particularly true when comparisons are being made between two or more groups with different sample sizes.

For example, in a study of children's test scores on an arithmetic task it was found that of the 70 boys taking the test 30 solved the task correctly. In comparison, of the 82 girls taking the task 34 were able to solve the problem. To compare the two groups it is useful to convert the number of correct scores into a percentage for both boys and girls. To do so, one follows the simple formula:

$$\text{Percentage} = \frac{\text{Number correct}}{\text{Total number possible}} \times 100$$

In our simple illustration this converts to 42.9% correct for boys and 41.5% for girls. Therefore, while there were actually more total girls able to solve the problem, when the

Figure 17.1. A Frequency Polygon of Exam Scores

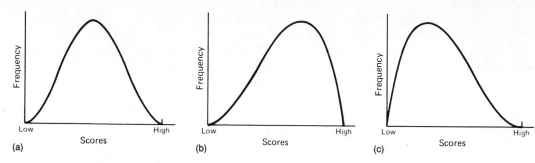

Figure 17.2. Three Examples of Curves: (a) Normal Curve; (b) Curve Negatively Skewed to the Left; (c) Curve Positively Skewed to the Right

frequency of correct responses is compared to the total number possible, the actual percentage is just a little smaller than that for boys.

In summary, raw frequencies and percentages can be used to provide a simple description of the cases represented by each score. Further, these descriptive statistics can be converted into a frequency distribution. This distribution can be compared to the theoretical normal curve to estimate the degree to which the data approximate such a normal distribution. If data load heavily to the high end of the distribution, the curve is said to be negatively skewed. If the scores load to the low end of the curve, it is said to be positively skewed.

Measures of Central Tendency

To describe the frequency distribution, measures of central tendency are used to depict the most typical (or average) score within the distribution. The three most popular measures of central tendency include the *mode*, arithmetic *mean*, and the *median*. Each provides a somewhat different measure of the most central score.

As Bartz (1971) has written: "The French expression 'a la mode' literally means the vogue, or in style" (p. 28). Thus, the *mode* as a measure of a central tendency is simply the most frequently observed score. The mode is obtained by a simple visual inspection of the frequency distribution. For example, in Table 17.1 the most frequent score is 83 with 6 subjects. In Table 17.2 when grouped data are presented the modal interval would be 80–84. While the mode is readily obtained, it is a very crude measure of the central tendency. As such it is the least useful.

The most used measure of central tendency is the *arithmetic mean*. The mean is simply the average score. To compute the mean one uses the simple formula of:

$$\text{Mean} = \frac{\text{Sum of the scores}}{\text{Total number of cases}}$$

Thus the arithmetic mean involves summing all of the scores and dividing that figure by the total number of cases.

Returning to Table 17.1, for example, we find that the sum of all of the scores equals 4,567. The total number of cases equals 54. Dividing 4,567 by 54, one obtains an arithmetic mean of 84.6. Therefore, the average person in this classroom example had a score of 84.6 correct. This mean score can be used to show how individuals compare to the average performance for the group as a whole.

Another commonly used measure of central tendency is the *median*. The median is a measure that represents the point that exactly separates the upper half from the lower half of the scores on the frequency distribution. The median is calculated using the following formula:

$$\text{Median} = \frac{\text{Number of cases plus 1}}{2}$$

That is, the median is calculated by summing the number of cases and adding 1, while dividing that sum by 2. Once again, in the case of Table 17.1, the number of cases equals 54. Adding 54 plus 1 and dividing by 2 results in a median score of 27.5. That is, counting from the bottom up, the median is that score which is halfway between the 27th and 28th raw score on the frequency distribution. In this case the median is halfway between a score of 84 and 85 which is naturally 84.5. As with the arithmetic mean, the median does not have to be an actual score in the frequency distribution. However, like the mean the median represents a central point in the distribution of scores.

We can see that in computing the mode, mean, or median from the simple frequency distribution in Table 17.1, the results are very similar. This is generally the case when the frequency distribution approximates a normal curve. However, when data are either negatively or positively skewed the mean and median can be greatly divergent. At that time the researcher must either (1) choose which central tendency measure to use or (2) report both.

▶   An illustration of how easily a misleading picture can emerge from using the wrong measure of central tendency can be seen in the analyses of data summarized in Table 17.3. In a local grade school the school board was interested in the so-called "average" salary of teachers. Therefore, in response to the request, a principal listed the salaries of all personnel at the school and computed the mean and median scores. As you can see, the distribution of salaries was positively skewed to the right because of the principal's and school psychologist's larger than average salaries.

TABLE 17.3. A Distribution of School Personnel Salaries

Nine-Month Salary	Personnel
$9,000	Teacher A
$9,000	Teacher B
$9,500	Teacher C
$9,800	Teacher D
$10,000	Teacher E
$10,000	Teacher F
$10,500	Teacher G
$14,200	Teacher H
$18,000	Counselor
$22,000	School psychologist
$25,000	Principal

In Table 17.3 the lowest salary was $9,000 and the highest salary was $25,000. The average salary of the frequency distribution of salaries reflected by the mean is $13,363. However, the arithmetic mean is greatly influenced by extreme scores. Therefore, in skewed distributions the mean can be misleading. This becomes very evident when one calculates the median income for this distribution. The median is only $10,000. Thus, the extreme incomes in the $22–25,000 range pulled the central tendency from $10,000 to $13,363. The difference of over $3,000 can be very misleading and represents a substantial sum of money. If the data are skewed, it is generally more accurate to show the median as opposed to the mean. Therefore, it is important to know if the data are skewed or approximate a theoretical normal curve. If data approximate the normal bell-shaped curve the mean is generally the most appropriate measure of central tendency. The general principal used by researchers to acquire data that approximate a normal bell-shaped curve is to utilize large samples. Our own research experience has revealed that when samples approximate or exceed 200 subjects, in most cases, a normal distribution is highly probable.

Measures of Dispersion

As was just reviewed, the various measures of central tendency provide a statistical description of the "average" or "most typical" score in a frequency distribution. With the mean or median, we can speak to the most central score. But another descriptive tool focuses on the degree of variability around the central score. It is equally important to know to what degree other scores vary from the central point. This variability is assessed by a *measure of dispersion*. The simplest measure of dispersion is the *range*. The range is the distance between the two extreme scores.

For example, in Table 17.3 the lowest salary was $9,000 and the highest was $25,000. Therefore, the range is $25,000–$9,000 = $16,000. The range tells us in simple descriptive terms the degree of dispersion that exists in our frequency distribution. One important limitation to the use of the range as a measure of dispersion is that it is easily altered by one or two extreme scores. For example, if the school psychologist's and principal's salaries were removed from the frequency distribution the range would be reduced to $9,000 (a reduction of $7,000). Yet another limitation of the range is that it is based exclusively on only two scores—the highest and lowest values. Therefore, it tells us very little about the pattern of variability throughout the frequency distribution.

The most frequently used and most efficient measure of dispersion is the *standard deviation*. In simple terms the standard deviation is the average variability around the mean. As Guilford (1965) has stated: "The standard deviation is a kind of average of all the deviations about the mean of the sample" (p. 72). That is, in any frequency distribution there are scores that fall above and below the mean. The average of these deviations from the mean provides the fundamental basis for calculating and interpreting the standard deviation.

The formula for calculating the standard deviation is a little more complex than previous calculations. One standard formula that represents the standard deviation (sometimes represented by S.D.) is:

$$S.D. = \sqrt{\frac{\Sigma x^2}{N}}$$

In this formula S.D. stands for standard deviation. The $\Sigma\ x^2$ refers to the sum of all squared deviations from the mean. And N is the number of scores in the frequency distribution.

▶   Let us turn to a simple illustration to demonstrate how the standard deviation is calculated. Recently Nancy worked part-time for a local grocery store. At the end of the summer she was interested in determining what her average weekly salary was and to what degree on the average her salary varied from week to week. To discover the answers to her question she prepared the following frequency distribution (Table 17.4) and computed a mean and standard deviation.

As summarized in Table 17.4 the calculation of the mean and standard deviation is relatively straightforward. The mean is calculated by summing the salaries for each week and dividing by the 8-week period. The standard deviation is calculated by subtracting from each weekly salary the mean score of $40 to arrive at a deviation score. This score is then squared to eliminate all negative signs. Next, the squared deviations are summed and divided by the total number of weeks. Finally, this value is modified through a square root. Thus, Nancy made an average of $40 per week over an 8-week period with a standard deviation in salary from this mean figure of approximately $11.73.

The most frequent use of the standard deviation is to provide an estimate of the percentage of cases that fall within the range of one standard deviation to the next. In a normally curved distribution most scores will typically fall between + or − 1 S.D. The percentage of cases within each standard deviation is depicted in Figure 17.3.

Returning to the data summarized in Table 17.4 this means that approximately 67 percent of the weekly salaries over the 8 weeks will range between approximately $28 − $52 (+ or − 1 S.D.), while the remaining approximately 33 percent will be less than $28 and greater than $52 during the 8-week period. (See Tips for Consumers 17.1.)

TABLE 17.4. A Frequency Distribution on Weekly Salaries and the Calculation of a Mean Salary and Its Corresponding Standard Deviation

	Salary	x	x²	
Week 1	$45.00	+5.00	25.00	$M = \dfrac{320}{8} = \$40$
Week 2	$30.00	−10.00	100.00	
Week 3	$40.00	0.00	0.00	
Week 4	$60.00	+20.00	400.00	
Week 5	$25.00	−15.00	225.00	
Week 6	$30.00	−10.00	100.00	$\text{S.D.} = \sqrt{\dfrac{\Sigma x^2}{N}}$
Week 7	$55.00	+15.00	225.00	
Week 8	$35.00	−5.00	25.00	
			$\Sigma x^2 = 1100$	$= \sqrt{\dfrac{1100}{8}}$

$$= \sqrt{137.5}$$

$$= \$11.73$$

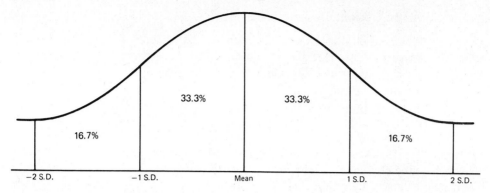

Figure 17.3. Normal Distribution and Percentage of Scores between Each Area of the Curve

---

Tips for Consumers 17.1

In reading and using descriptive statistics some basic factors might be kept in mind:
1. *In regards to measures of central tendency:*
   a. While descriptive, the mode is least useful, and can be deceiving about the frequency distribution.
   b. When evidence of the frequency distribution is presented indicating it approximate the normal curve, the mean is the best choice.
   c. When the distribution is skewed, the median should be used to avoid distortion of the central tendency due to extreme scores.

2. *In regards to measures of dispersion:*
   a. The range should be reported and used when it is appropriate to provide information about the extremes of scores.
   b. While the standard deviation should always be reported when mean statistics are used, the standard deviation provides important information about variability or dispersion of scores around the mean.

As a consumer of research it should always be remembered that it is relatively easy to be deceived by the choice of descriptive statistics reported. Look for evidence, in reading a research report, of information on both central tendency and dispersion. Also, determine if evidence is reported of possible skewness in the frequency distribution and critically examine whether the mean or median is the most trustful measure of central tendency. Knowing and using these guides permit one to be a more informed, competent, and successful evaluator of research results.

A Research Illustration: Descriptive Statistics

▶ In May of 1980, a major disaster occurred in and around Othello, Washington. The Mt. Saint Helens volcano erupted sending ash down wind and covering all of Adams County. The consequences of the ashfall were unknown. The town of Othello was paralyzed. The real and perceived threat was great.

While this unfortunate event created tremendous havoc in this community, it did offer one benefit. Social scientists were able to use this naturally occurring event to study the effects of a catastrophe on stress reactions. In one such study (Adams & Adams, 1984), a comparison was made of more than 25 stress reaction behaviors between a pre-disaster baseline of 7 months and a post-disaster 7-month period. The general notion is that if a disaster actually creates a stress reaction the post-disaster baseline should show an average increase from the pre-disaster period. One way to compare the two baseline periods is to prepare a pre- and post-disaster baseline graph such as that depicted in Figure 17.4. A visual inspection of the three illustrative graphs shows a general increase from June through December of 1980 which followed the disaster in May, when contrasted to a seasonally adjusted comparison of June through December of 1979. Another way to compare the baselines is to examine the central tendencies and measures of dispersion. We have for illustrative purposes calculated the mean and median, range and standard deviation for each of the pre- and post-disaster frequency distributions for three stress reaction measures. These measures include the number of clients served at the local mental health agency, the number of forms filed by police on domestic violence, and the number of total forms filed for arrests in general.

Visual inspection of the pre-disaster to post-disaster baseline frequencies reveals that there is an increase in occurrence of behavior for two to three months following the disaster with a decline thereafter toward the pre-disaster baselines. The comparison of means between the pre- and post-disaster baselines shows an average increase in the occurrence of all three measured behaviors. The median scores, which are generally lower than the means due to the skewness of the data, show an identical trend. In all cases the ranges between pre- and post-disaster baselines are overlapping and the standard deviations are somewhat similar. However, on the post-disaster baseline behaviors of domestic violence and general arrests, there is greater variability. A visual inspection of the line graphs for the post-disaster baselines will visually illustrate the greater number of peaks and valleys from one month to the next. These "peaks and valleys" are reflected in a larger standard deviation—showing greater variability around the mean.

Data such as those summarized in Figure 17.4 can be presented to argue that natural disasters create a stress reaction in a community and increase domestic violence, general unrest, and mental health needs. Comparisons of the frequency distributions, means, medians, ranges, and standard deviations provide descriptive information about the "average" monthly response rate and the "variability" between months from that average. In this illustration, we can, descriptively speaking, conclude that the community of Othello, Washington, was indeed affected by a stress reaction to the catastrophic events surrounding the eruption of Mt. Saint Helens. However, the conclusion based on descriptive data is based only on a visual inspection of the facts and can be subject to error. One must ask, "How large of a mean or median difference is necessary to be sure we are not making an error in judgment?" "Is it possible that the differences between the pre- and post-disaster means are too small to be truly different?" We shall return to the

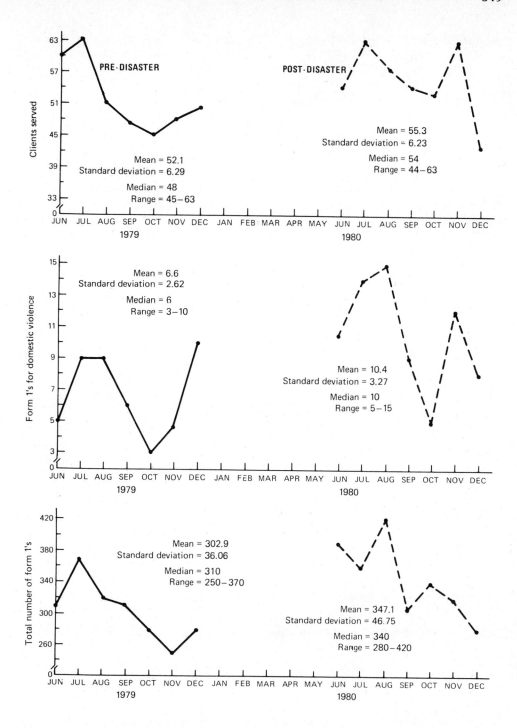

Figure 17.4. Pre- and Post-test Baseline Comparisons Surrounding the Mt. Saint Helens Catastrophe. (*Source*: Copyright 1984 by the American Psychological Association. Adapted by permission.)

question of tests of difference later. Let us first examine how social scientists look at issues of association.

MEASURES OF ASSOCIATION

Commonly, researchers are interested in whether two or more research variables hold a significant association. In this research question one is asking, "What is the relationship between two distributions of scores?" This research question is best addressed by correlational analyses. As we reviewed in the previous chapter, a correlation is a statistic that tells one to what extent two things are related or to what extent the variation in one variable is associated with variability in another. You will likewise recall that this variability can be positive, negative, or of no relation. One illustrative way to see these relationships from a simple frequency distribution comparison of two variables is found in Table 17.5.

In the two distributions for variables A_1 and B_1, on two measures where a score from 1–5 can be obtained, it can be seen that each subject gets an identical score on both variables. Further, as subjects score high on one variable, they likewise score high on another. This is illustrative of a perfect positive correlation that would be represented by $r = +1.00$. In the second set of variables A_2 and B_2, as subjects score high on one variable, they score low on the other. This represents a perfect negative correlation ($r = -1.00$). The third set of frequency distributions reflect a series of scores on variables A_3 and B_3 where the variability between the two scores is unsystematic and approximates a zero-order correlation. Let us turn now to the computation of two frequently used correlational statistics, remembering correlations can range from -1.00 to $+1.00$, with a midpoint of .00. The first technique, the *phi* coefficient, is a nonparametric strategy that can be used on nominal data. The second technique, Pearson product-moment correlation, is a parametric technique that can be used with interval and ratio data.

The *Phi* Coefficient

One correlational technique that can be readily used with dichotomous (categorical) data is the *phi* coefficient. The computation of this statistic is designed around a 2×2 table. (See Table 17.6.)

For example, let us assume that you have a job of working as a consumer specialist. Further, that you have the data on repair histories for two types of televisions. A local

TABLE 17.5. A Simple Frequency Distribution for Five Subjects Used to Illustrate Three Correlational Associations

Subject	Variables A_1	B_1	Variables A_2	B_2	Variables A_3	B_3
Tom	1	1	1	5	1	3
Mary	2	2	2	4	2	1
Henry	3	3	3	3	3	5
Jerry	4	4	4	2	4	2
Jean	5	5	5	1	5	4

TABLE 17.6. Correlation Table

	Television	
	Less expensive	**More expensive**
No repairs	40 *a*	10 *b*
Repairs of $50.00 or more	*c* 10	*d* 40

group of citizens is interested in getting information on the best available television for the price. You know that one television is less expensive to purchase than the other, but you are unsure about the cost of maintenance. To provide consumers with some information about the relationship of cost of purchase and maintenance you take your available data and develop a simple 2 × 2 contingency table.

You have records on 100 total televisions—50 records for each type. What correlation is there between purchase price and maintenance? To estimate the association between these two dichotomous variables a *phi* coefficient can be computed using the following formula:

$$Phi = \frac{ad - bc}{\sqrt{(a + b)(a + c)(b + d)(c + d)}}$$

Looking back to our table we can now plug in the appropriate numbers and compute the *phi* coefficient.

$$Phi = \frac{(40 \times 40) - (10 \times 10)}{\sqrt{(40 + 10)(40 + 10)(10 + 40)(10 + 40)}}$$

$$= \frac{1600 - 100}{\sqrt{(50)(50)(50)(50)}}$$

$$= \frac{1500}{\sqrt{6250000}}$$

$$= \frac{1500}{2500}$$

$$= .60$$

The *phi* coefficient indicates a correlation between the initial cost of a television and repairs of *phi* = .60. That means that according to the correlation, more expensive televisions actually require more repairs. Returning to the 2 × 2 table you can see that 40 out of 50 expensive televisions required repairs of $50 or more, while only 10 out of 50 less expensive televisions required similar maintenance. As a consumer specialist you might, based on this correlation, educate your constituents in looking at the relation between initial costs and projected likelihood of repair bills. In our simple hypothetical example, it would appear more economical (assuming similar picture quality) to purchase the less expensive television. Not only would you make a less costly purchase but you are less likely to have to pay for expensive repair bills.

The Pearson Product-Moment Coefficient

Perhaps the most widely used method of correlational analyses, the Pearson r is a common technique to be employed when data are from interval scales. You will recall from the scaling and measurement chapter (see Chapter 8) that interval scales have a hypothetical zero point and equal distance from one score to the next (i.e., the distance between 1 and 2 is the same as between 2 and 3, etc.). The computation of the Pearson r is slightly more complex than *phi* and is based on the following formula:

$$r = \frac{\dfrac{\Sigma XY}{N} - M_x M_y}{\text{S.D.}_x \ \text{S.D.}_y}$$

In this formula, r refers to the correlation, N is the number of pairs of scores, and ΣXY is the sum of the products of each multiplied paired scores. M_x and M_y are the means of the X and Y frequency distributions. And S.D._x and S.D._y are their standard deviations.

▶   A simple illustration of the use of the Pearson r is found in the frequency distribution shown in Table 17.7. In this example, a local homemaker came to the county extension agent and asked for some assistance in understanding how to manage her finances. Her husband had died recently and for years he kept track of the income and paid the bills. Now that she was living on a more fixed income she wanted to know how to reduce some heating costs and plan her budget. She had chosen to stay in her home but the home provided more space than she used. Because of heating costs, she closed off approximately one-third of her home. She needed, however, for budgeting purposes an estimate of the cost to heat her home and needed to know if proportionately for each of the months

TABLE 17.7. Past and Projected Yearly Heating Costs

Month	Heating Costs	
	Past	Projected
January	$150	$100
February	$162	$106
March	$130	$98
April	$105	$80
May	$40	$20
June	$20	$10
July	$5	$5
August	$4	$4
September	$15	$5
October	$48	$24
November	$105	$60
December	$148	$75

whether she needed to budget for different amounts of money as past billing years had required. Using a formula for the proportion of space now heated and past monthly costs the home-agent estimated the new projected monthly costs. Then she computed a correlation to determine if the projections paralleled a reduced but proportionately similar variation in monthly costs. The figures for the real and estimated costs are seen in Table 17.7.

A simple visual inspection of the data indicates that there was, as expected, decreased cost of heating. A computation of a Pearson r correlation will give a general indication as to how the reduced figures parallel the monthly variations of the former real costs: that is, we would expect that higher monthly costs prior to modifications would be associated with reduced but equally higher proportionate costs for colder months. The series of figures in Table 17.8 and below shows how the formula can be used to arrive at a Pearson r coefficient.

TABLE 17.8. Finding a Pearson r Coefficient

Pre-costs			Post-costs	
X	X²	Y	Y²	XY
150	22,500	100	10,000	15,000
162	26,244	106	11,236	17,172
130	16,900	98	9,604	12,740
105	11,025	80	6,400	8,400
40	1,600	20	400	800
20	400	10	100	200
5	25	5	25	25
4	16	4	16	16
15	225	5	25	75
48	2,304	24	576	1,152
105	11,025	60	3,600	6,300
148	21,904	75	5,625	11,100
932	114,168	587	47,607	72,980

$$M_x = \frac{932}{12} = 77.67 \qquad\qquad M_y = \frac{587}{12} = 48.92$$

$$\text{S.D.}_x = \sqrt{\frac{\Sigma x^2}{N} - M^2} \qquad\qquad \text{S.D.}_y = \sqrt{\frac{\Sigma y^2}{N} - M^2}$$

$$= \sqrt{\frac{114168}{12} - (77.7)^2} \qquad\qquad = \sqrt{\frac{47607}{12} - (48.9)^2}$$

$$= \sqrt{9514 - 6037.3} \qquad\qquad = \sqrt{3967.3 - 2391.2}$$

$$= \sqrt{3476.7} \qquad\qquad = \sqrt{1576.1}$$

$$= 58.96 \qquad\qquad = 39.70$$

Substituting the values into the formula, we get the following:

$$r = \frac{\frac{\Sigma XY}{N} - M_x M_y}{S.D._x \ S.D._y}$$

$$= \frac{\frac{72980}{12} - (77.7 \times 48.9)}{(58.96 \times 39.70)}$$

$$= \frac{6081.7 - 3799.5}{2340.7}$$

$$= \frac{2282.2}{2340.7}$$

$$= .98$$

The means between the real and projected savings due to closing portions of the home down and keeping it unheated show a monthly average savings of $(77.67 - 48.92)$ $28.75. Further, the correlation coefficient of $r = .98$ indicates that projected reductions per month correctly reflect that more proportionate monthly budget dollars will still be needed to heat the home during the colder and higher natural fuel energy consumption months.

Summary

The correlation is a useful statistic for assessing whether the variation in one frequency distribution is shared with the variation in another. The *phi* and Pearson *r* are two commonly used correlational techniques. The statistics can be used to assess whether a zero order relation, positive, or negative association exists between two variables.

TESTS OF SIGNIFICANT DIFFERENCES

In addition to asking questions of association, social scientists frequently ask questions of differences. For example, in laboratory research we ask if the experimental group manifests greater performance than that of the control group. Or we might ask, once random assignment is completed, if on the pretest measures the experimental and control group differ. In essence, this question is asking if two samples drawn from the same population when placed randomly into two separate groups show evidence of responding differently on pretesting. If randomization has worked they should not.

As we reviewed in the previous chapter, inferential statistics are used to test research hypotheses that assume significant differences between groups. We do so by testing the null hypothesis that assumes no differences exist between the measures of central tendency for the two groups. Hence, inferential statistics have been developed to assess whether two sample means or medians differ enough to go beyond standard error or chance alone. Simply stated, the question one addresses with inferential statistics is whether the two sample means are disparate enough to be beyond chance.

In making tests of difference the experimenter usually specifies the risk he or she is willing to take in making an error. This error is commonly called the Type I error. Type I error involves the possibility of predicting differences when, in reality, no difference truly exists. The most common convention is to set the Type I error at a probability of .05. In other words, by setting the probability of .05 the researcher is willing to risk that if the same test were completed 100 times, five of those tests could result in an incorrect conclusion. In extreme cases researchers set their probability levels at .01 to avoid a Type I error in their decision making. However, it should be made clear that this is an extremely rigorous test for differences.

Further, a researcher can select from a one-tail or a two-tail probability. If the researcher has reason to predict a specific positive or negative direction to the anticipated results, a one-tail test can be used. If, however, one cannot be sure if the results will be either positively or negatively directed, then a two-tail test should be used. The advantage of the one-tail test is that it is (1) based on a strong logical notion of directionality, usually through a strong theory or prior evidence, and (2) mathematically it allows for a greater chance of finding the difference when in actuality it exists.

To understand the basis of this notion, consider the fact that if you set the probability of error at .05 you have designated the total error you are willing to tolerate. If you use a two-tail test then .025 of potential error in judgment is in one direction, and the remaining in the other. However, if you designate a two-tail test then all your judgment and its corresponding probability (probability = .05) is based in a single direction. For excellent reading on this issue we suggest turning to a classic text by Allen Edwards (1967).

In simple terms, when we compute a test of significance, we ask if the central tendencies of two groups are large enough to warrant our concluding they are reflecting differences big enough to warrant a conclusion of significant differences between groups. To avoid a major Type I statistical error, we typically set our probability of making an error at .05 (or smaller, .01 or .001). We then compute a selected test of difference and determine if that computed value suggests a conclusion of a significant difference. In making this decision we test the null hypothesis that no differences exist between the two groups regarding their measures of central tendency and dispersion. We can use a one-tail test when direction is either predicted or when only one direction is of interest to us and enhance our likelihood of finding the predicted difference in the statistical test. When a direction cannot be predicted then we must use a more conservative one-tail test.

Next, we shall briefly illustrate how a chi square, *t*-test, and one-way analysis of variance can be computed to test for differences. The chi square test is an example of a simple nonparametric technique. The *t*-test and the one-way analysis of variance require meeting the assumptions of parametric tests discussed earlier.

The Chi Square

This test of significance is commonly and correctly used in tests of significant differences when discrete or dichotomous data are used. It can be used where the researcher has yes or no answers, right or wrong, male or female, Democratic versus Republican choices, and other dichotomous responses. Likewise, it can be extended to include three or more response categories when needed.

Let us illustrate the use of chi square with a simple illustration.

To begin, the basic formula for computing a chi square reads as follows:

$$\chi^2 = \sum \frac{(f_o - f_e)^2}{f_e}$$

▶ Let us use a simple example where 30 men and 30 women in an introductory class in college are asked if abortion legislation should be approved to make such activities illegal. The research question is as follows: Do college students hold opinions that abortion activities should be illegal? Responses to the question are answered by indicating "Yes," "No," or "Undecided."

Given the importance of this issue for women, data such as these are commonly analyzed so as to detect possible sex differences. There are three ways in which opinions of the two sexes could be compared. We could find three chi square values—one test of significance for each of the three types of responses, comparing male versus female reactions. Other options could be to calculate each separately and then sum the chi squares and compare men versus women. Another technique could be to ignore gender differences and use the combined male and female frequencies. For purposes of illustration we shall test the hypothesis that no sex differences (null hypothesis) exist for all the frequencies taken together.

Frequencies and actual computations are reported here in Table 17.9. The first step is to record the frequencies for males and females regarding their Yes, No, or Undecided responses. We then sum the number of responses to each of the possible categories. For example, for Yes we had 9 males and 15 females, with a total of 24 individuals. Given we are testing a null hypothesis of no gender differences and we have 24 responses, a $50/50$ split would result in an expected frequency of 12 responses by each gender. Therefore, in a $50/50$, or null hypothesis, expectation the expected frequency would be computed accordingly: 24 individuals divided by 2 gender categories which equals 12 per group. By repeating this process for the No and Undecided categories we arrive at expected frequencies of 7 and 11 respectively. We can check our calculations by adding down the expected frequency column and our answer should be 30 for the males and 30 for the females.

Next we find the deviations (observed frequency minus expected frequency). Each of these columns when summated should add to zero. In the next computation we square the values to eliminate the signs. Finally, we divide the squared discrepancies by their own expected frequency, and then sum the pairs of ratios for each row and arrive at a chi square for each response category. These chi square values are listed in the final column of the computations. The sum of the three is 9.36, which is the chi square for all six frequencies combined. This value indicates the total discrepancy that exists between those that were observed and what one would expect by chance under a null hypothesis.

To determine whether this value is large enough to suggest a discrepancy exists that is bigger than expected by chance from the null hypothesis one must be guided by two final computational processes. First, we must calculate what is known as degrees of freedom. This process involves adding the number of response categories and subtracting a value of 1. Given we have three categories, when we subtract 1 we arrive at 2 degrees of freedom. Turning to a table of chi square values (see Table A in Appendix) we look down

TABLE 17.9. Chi-Square Example

Response	Frequency Observed f_o			Frequency Expected f_e		$f_o - f_e$		$(f_o - f_e)^2$		$(f_o - f_e)^2/f_e$ χ^2		
	Men	Women	Both	Men	Women	Men	Women	Men	Women	Men	Women	Both
Yes	9	15	24	12	12	−3	+3	9	9	0.75	0.75	1.50
No	12	2	14	7	7	+5	−5	25	25	3.57	3.57	7.14
Undecided	9	13	22	11	11	−2	+2	4	4	0.36	0.36	0.72
Sums	30	30	60	30	30	0	0			4.68	4.68	9.36

357

the column headed *df* and look for 2 degrees of freedom. Then we read across the row to the level of probability that we are most comfortable with. As you will recall the standard probability used is typically .05. We find that a probability of .05 requires a chi square equaling or greater than 5.99. Given our calculated chi square is 9.36 we find we can reject the null hypothesis and conclude that gender differences do exist in the subjects' responses.

Likewise, we can look back at our data to find out if the differences that exist are at the response level of Yes, No, or Undecided. Looking at the chi square values for each of the rows we can once again use our table to determine where gender differences exist. Given we have one response type and two genders, our degree of freedom equals 1. In looking at the table of chi square probabilities, we find at the probability level of .05 we need to have a value equal to or greater than 3.84. In that the chi square value of 7.14 is the only one to exceed 3.84, we can conclude that our gender difference is mostly accounted for by males responding significantly more with a response of No than females.

The *t*-Test

One of the most widely used tests for differences between means is the Fisher *t*-test. The basic formula for this test is:

$$t = \frac{M_1 - M_2}{\sqrt{\dfrac{\Sigma x_1^2 + \Sigma x_2^2}{N_i \ (N_i - 1)}}}$$

In this formula M_1 and M_2 are the means for the two samples. Σx_1^2 and Σx_2^2 are the squared deviations from the means (sum of squares) for the two samples. And N_i is the size of the sample for either of the two equal sized frequency distributions.

▶   Let us return for a moment to Figure 17.4. In addition to examining the descriptive statistics, let us assume we also wish to ask whether the mean differences between the pre- and post-disaster frequencies in domestic violence are beyond chance (significantly different). To test this assumption we could use the Fisher *t*-test formula and arrive at the following statistical computations:

$$t = \frac{6.6 - 10.4}{\sqrt{\dfrac{48 + 75}{7 \ (7 - 1)}}}$$

$$= \frac{-3.8}{\sqrt{\dfrac{123}{42}}}$$

$$= \frac{-3.8}{\sqrt{2.93}}$$

$$= \frac{-3.8}{1.71}$$

$$= -2.22$$

To determine if the t value of 2.22 is large enough to justify refuting the null hypothesis (or assume there are true sample mean differences), one must compute the *degrees of freedom* for the test. Degrees of freedom refer to the number of measures that are free to vary and, therefore, that convey information. In the present case, one mean statistic is drawn from the first distribution of scores and another mean from the second distribution and, therefore, not allowed to vary; thus, the degrees of freedom are $N_1 + N_2 - 2$ or $7 + 7 - 2 = 12$. Using the degrees of freedom a critical value is obtained that must be equaled or exceeded to be considered statistically significant ($p < .05$). This value, obtained from Table B in the Appendix is 1.78. Given the t value is 2.22, we are able to reject the null hypothesis and assume that the mean differences between the pre- and post-disaster baselines are significantly different.

Let us further illustrate the use of the t-test in testing for significance. In recent years in our own research program at Utah State University, we have attempted to study the implications of social competency for social relations. We are concerned about the notion that certain young children, due to their limited social skills, establish an unpopular relationship with their peers. In turn, the unpopular relationship over an extended period of time may heighten the potential for mental health problems. In an early unpublished pilot study, we focused on the potential relation between peer popularity and overt physical aggressiveness among boys. In a study of 10 children, 5 of whom were identified by sociometric techniques as highly popular and 5 of whom were perceived as highly unpopular, we observed free play social behavior in a preschool playground setting. Over a two-week period we observed and recorded the frequency of physical aggressive behavior and established a total two-week aggressive score for every child. Using these data we could ask two pertinent research questions: (1) are there significant differences between popular and unpopular boys in their aggressive behavior? and (2) to what degree does peer popularity correlate with aggressive conduct? The actual ratings of peer popularity and the frequency of aggressive behavior along with several computations are shown in Table 17.10.

To address the first question a t-test can be used to assess whether the high versus the low popularity group differs significantly in their aggressive tendencies. An inspection of the frequency distributions indicates that the children ranged from a low of 7 total aggressive acts to a high of 36. Further, the 5 popular children (A–E) ranged from 8–10 on a 10-point popularity scale while the 5 unpopular children ranged from 1–3 (F–J). Treating the two extremes in popularity as separate groups, it was possible to test the null hypothesis that no significant differences in frequency distributions on aggressive behavior were evident between the popular and unpopular groups. The Fisher t value after substitution reached 4.08. With 8 degrees of freedom, the critical value needed to reject a null hypothesis is 3.36 for $p < .01$. Given the calculated value exceeds 3.36, we must reject the null hypothesis and assume that the frequency distribution for aggressive behavior for the unpopular children is beyond standard error for that of the popular children. Thus, we conclude that on the average the unpopular children were, in our study, more frequently aggressive than popular children.

One-way Analysis of Variance

The t-test is a widely used test of significance when interval data and two comparison groups are used. Frequently, research includes more than two sets of measures on the

TABLE 17.10. Peer Popularity versus Frequency of Aggression

	Child	Popularity Rating		Total Frequency of Aggression		
				X	x	x^2
	A	10		7	−2.6	6.76
	B	9		6	−3.6	12.96
Popular group	C	9	$M_1 = 9.6$	10	.4	.16
	D	8		12	2.4	5.76
	E	8		13	3.4	11.56
						$\Sigma\, 37.2$
	F	3		16	−8.2	67.24
	G	3		21	−3.2	10.24
Unpopular group	H	2	$M_2 = 24.2$	23	−1.2	1.44
	I	2		25	.8	.64
	J	1		36	11.8	139.24
						$\Sigma\, 218.8$

Substitution in formula:

$$t = \frac{M_1 - M_2}{\sqrt{\dfrac{\Sigma x_1^2 + \Sigma x_2^2}{N_i\,(N_i - 1)}}}$$

$$t = \frac{9.6 - 24.2}{\sqrt{\dfrac{37.2 + 218.8}{5\,(5 - 1)}}}$$

$$= \frac{-14.6}{\sqrt{\dfrac{256}{20}}}$$

$$= \frac{-14.6}{3.58}$$

$$= 4.08$$

same dependent variable. When two or more groups are being compared we commonly then use a one-way analysis of variance.

The one-way analysis of variance is based on what is commonly called the *F* test. The *F* test is a ratio of treatment variance to error variance. If the ratio is 1 or less than the treatment, differences are equal to random error. However, as the ratio expands beyond 1 the probability of a significant treatment effect increases.

The general formula for testing differences between groups is as follows:

$$F = \frac{\text{MS (Treatment)}}{\text{MS (Error)}}$$

► Let us illustrate the utility of the *F* test through a brief illustration. For simplicity assume that we have three treatment groups designated as k. The following display gives the values of the dependent variable X for each subject in each treatment group. We let X identify any given measurement point with the first subscript k designating the treatment group and second subscript n the subject within the group. In our illustration, k can take values of 1, 2, or 3 in that we have three treatment groups. Because we have 5 subjects in each group, n can take a value of 1, 2, 3, 4, or 5. To compute an F test (one-way analysis of variance) we must go through the following computations.

Treatment 1 $(k1)$		Treatment 2 $(k2)$		Treatment 3 $(k3)$	
X	X^2	X	X^2	X	X^2
$X_{11} = 10$	100	$X_{21} = 10$	100	$X_{31} = 2$	4
$X_{12} = 13$	169	$X_{22} = 8$	64	$X_{32} = 3$	9
$X_{13} = 14$	196	$X_{23} = 7$	49	$X_{33} = 7$	49
$X_{14} = 13$	169	$X_{24} = 5$	25	$X_{34} = 2$	4
$X_{15} = 15$	225	$X_{25} = 10$	100	$X_{35} = 6$	36
$\Sigma X_1 = 65$	$\Sigma X_1^2 = 859$	$\Sigma X_2 = 40$	$\Sigma X_2^2 = 338$	$\Sigma X_3 = 20$	$\Sigma X_3^2 = 102$
$\overline{X}_1 = 13.0$		$\overline{X}_2 = 8.0$		$\overline{X}_3 = 4.0$	

We let ΣX be the sum of $X_{11} \ldots X_{15}$, and so on. Then $\overline{X}$ is the mean of all kn measures. Similarly, we let ΣX_k be the sum for k-th treatment and $\overline{X}_k$ be the mean for the k-th treatment. We then compute the following computations that provide the total *sum of squares* (X^2), the *within treatment* sum of squares (error term), and the *treatment* sum of squares. Collectively, these three values fulfill the following terms:

$$\text{Total} = \text{Within} + \text{Treatment}$$

In the case of the total sums of square, the following computation is completed.

$$\sum_1^{kn} X_{kn}{}^2 - \frac{(\Sigma X_{...})^2}{kn} = 1299 - \frac{(125)^2}{15} = 257.33$$

For the within treatment sum of squares we compute three separate values for each k treatment group using the following formula:

$$\sum_1^n (X_{1n} - \overline{X}_1)^2$$

For K treatment groups (1, 2, and 3, respectively) we have

$$\sum_1^n (X_{1n} - \overline{X}_1)^2 = 859 - \frac{(65)^2}{5} = 14$$

$$\sum_1^n (X_{2n} - \overline{X}_2)^2 = 338 - \frac{(40)^2}{5} = 18$$

$$\sum_1^n (X_{3n} - \overline{X}_3)^2 = 102 - \frac{(20)^2}{5} = 22$$

Summing these values we arrive at the within treatment sum of squares.

$$\text{Treatment}_{\text{within}} = 14 + 18 + 22 = 54.0$$

For the between treatment sum of squares we use the following formula

$$n\sum_{1}^{k} (\bar{X}_k - \bar{X})^2 = \sum_{1}^{k} \frac{(\Sigma X_k)^2}{n} - \frac{(\Sigma X...)^2}{kn}$$

Using our data set we arrive at

$$\text{Treatments}_{\text{between}} = \frac{(65)^2}{5} + \frac{(40)^2}{5} + \frac{(20)^2}{5} - \frac{(125)^2}{15} = 203.33$$

Each of the three sums of squares is associated with different degrees of freedom. Each is expressed as follows:

Total Sum of Squares $= kn - 1 = 3 \times 5 - 1 = 14$
Within Treatment Sum of Squares $= k(n-1) = 3 \times 5 - 1 = 12$
Between Treatment Sum of Squares $= k - 1 = 3 - 1 = 2$

To compute our final ratio we must finish our analysis by calculating the *mean square* for our *treatment* and error (within) terms. These formula and their actual computation are as follows:

$$MS_{\text{within}} = \frac{\Sigma x_1^2 + \Sigma x_2^2 + \Sigma x_3^2}{k(n-1)}$$

$$= \frac{14 + 18 + 22}{3(5-1)}$$

$$= 4.5$$

$$MS_{\text{treatment}} = \frac{nn\sum_{1}^{k} (\bar{X}_k - \bar{X}..)^2}{k-1}$$

$$= \frac{203.33}{3-1} = 101.67$$

The results of such calculations are commonly summarized as follows:

Source of Variation	Sum of Squares	df	Mean Square	F Value
Treatments	203.33	2	101.66	22.59
Within Treatments	54.00	12	4.50	
Total	257.33	14		

Once again, to determine if the test of significance exceeds the probability level of .05 we must turn to an F distribution table (see Table C in the Appendix). In that our *df* are $^2/_{12}$ we look for *df* for numerator of 2 and *df* for denominator of 12. We set our type I error at .05 and compute $1 - \alpha = .95$. We then look across the row of the table to find the value for $^2/_{12}$ at .95 to equal 4.75. In that our F value was 22.59 we reject the null hypothesis and conclude there was a substantial treatment effect in our study.

Summary

Tests of significance can be used to make decisions regarding accepting or rejecting the null hypothesis. Such tests are available for use with either nominal or ordinal data and are commonly called nonparametric tests, or with interval and ratio data and are referred to as parametric tests. Three of the most common forms of tests of significance include the chi square, *t*-test, and one-way analysis of variance. Many more complicated tests of significance can be identified and utilized. These three merely reflect an introduction to statistical tests that are used in social science research.

SUMMARY

In this chapter we have extended our conceptual framework from Chapter 16 to illustrate several uses of statistics in social science. For both consumers and researchers alike, a basic understanding of statistical computations allows the user of science to access statistical decision-making practices. In this chapter our major points were the following:

1. Level of measurement must be assessed in determining the appropriate statistic for a data set. Nonparametric tests are used with nominal and ordinal data. Parametric tests can be used with interval or ratio data if they meet the assumptions of normality, homogeneity of variance, and equal appearing intervals between data points.
2. Descriptive statistics primarily consist of raw frequencies (or percentages), measures of central tendency, and measures of dispersion. The most commonly used include
    a. raw frequency distributions presented in simple or interval categories
    b. measures of central tendency including means, medians, and modes
    c. measures of dispersion including ranges and standard deviations
3. Measures of association are used to judge the degree to which two or more variables covary. Commonly used techniques include the *phi* coefficient and Pearson *r* correlation.
4. Tests of significance can be computed to test the null hypothesis. Three common techniques include the chi square, *t*-test, and one-way analysis of variance.
5. Throughout this chapter you have been introduced to several basic elementary statistics. While these basics provide some of the fundamentals of statistical decision-making, more extended training in a formal statistical course is necessary to expand your skills and knowledge.

PROBLEMS AND APPLICATIONS

1. Assume you have recently been hired by your local job service agency and have been asked to present to the local community college a statement of present salaries for various types of employment opportunities. Using the following salary figures prepare a statement that uses what you believe are the most appropriate descriptive statistics. Calculate those statistics and be prepared to justify why you used them.

Teacher	$9,500	Grocery clerk	$8,200
Carpenter	$11,000	Computer Analyst	$18,400
Clerical work	$8,200	Electrician	$14,200
Painter	$9,300	Barber	$5,800
Shoe salesman	$7,600	Laborer	$9,400
Street cleaner	$9,100	Plumber	$13,400
Child care worker	$6,600	Accountant	$15,900
Computer sales	$12,700	Truck driver	$9,900
Management assistant	$14,500	Personnel manager	$13,400
Janitor	$6,600	Administrative assistant	$10,800

2. Assume you have just completed a study of political voting preferences and income levels. You are an assistant to a local mayor who is running again for office. Using both descriptive and inferential statistics compute various types of statistics that might be useful to the mayor in preparing for his reelection campaign. The simple frequency distribution from your interview study is as follows:

Interview Subject	Voting Preference	Income Level
A	R	$22,250
B	R	$18,400
C	D	$33,400
D	R	$44,000
E	D	$16,400
F	D	$9,600
G	R	$24,900
H	D	$15,000
I	R	$13,300
J	D	$11,800
K	R	$27,700
L	D	$17,400
M	R	$19,900
N	D	$6,600
O	R	$48,600
P	D	$31,300

NOTE: R = Republican voting preference; D = Democratic voting preference.

3. Returning to the chapter on reliability, use your new skills in computing correlations by generating a split-half reliability coefficient for the scores from one of your examinations from this class. What is the appropriate correlation? Was the test a reliable one?

4. In class, discuss how correlational statistical analysis provides different decision-making information from that of tests of significance. How could they be used to arrive at similar conclusions?

REFERENCES

Adams, P., & Adams, G. (1984). Mount Saint Helens' ashfall: Evidence for a disaster stress-reaction. *American Psychologist, 39*, 252–260.

Bartz, A. E. (1971). *Basic descriptive statistics for education and the behavioral sciences.* Minneapolis, Minn.: Burgess Publishing.

Edwards, A. (1967). *Statistical methods.* New York: Holt, Rinehart and Winston.

Guilford, J. P. (1965). *Fundamental statistics in psychology and education* (4th ed.). New York: McGraw-Hill.

Winer, B. J. (1962). *Statistical principles in experimental design.* New York: McGraw-Hill.

CHAPTER 18

The Research Proposal
and Scientific Report

OUTLINE
Introduction
Understanding the Research Proposal
    Research Problem
    Review of Literature
    Objectives and/or Hypotheses
    Procedures
    Summary
Understanding Research Reports
    Writing Style
    Format
        Title
        Abstract
        Introduction
        Method
        Results
        Discussion
        Summary
A Brief Research Report Illustration
Criteria for Evaluating Reports
    Practices to Avoid
    Scientific Substantive Issues
    Stylistic Issues
    Originality
    Trivia

Scientific Advancement
Conclusion
Summary
Problems and Applications
References

KEY TERMS

Research proposal
Research problem
Review of literature
Objectives and hypotheses
Procedures
Research Report
Title

Abstract
Introduction
Method
Results
Discussion
References
Evaluative criteria

STUDY GUIDE QUESTIONS

1. What function does a research report or research proposal serve?
2. What major components of a research proposal are found in most proposal formats?
3. What is the general protocol of the formal research report?
4. What types of information are included in the introduction, methods, results, and discussion sections of a research report?
5. How does one evaluate the quality of a research report? Are there general criteria for making an evaluation?
6. Are there practices to avoid in preparing a good research report? What might they be?
7. What role does style, originality, or content play in preparing a high quality report or proposal?

Role of the Scientist

Science is a public endeavor. It requires publicly seeking funding for experimentation and the dissemination of findings through report preparation. Through precise, concise, and clear writing a scientist can help others comprehend what is to be done or what has been found. The primary tools of writing are the grant proposal and research report. In this chapter we review the essential ingredients of each. Since science is a public endeavor it requires writing skills. The major functions of these roles are described in this chapter.

Role of the Consumer

To read a grant proposal or to understand the findings of a research report requires a basic knowledge of the proposal and report protocol. Knowing the basic elements common to both the proposal and report enhances one's skills at reading and evaluating the content. Therefore, understanding the typical protocol of the proposal and report allows the consumer to identify the specific elements of each and enhances one's ability to evaluate and judge the worth of such written documents.

INTRODUCTION

The two most common documents in science include the grant proposal and the research report. To acquire funding the scientist must enter into a competitive funding process to secure resources to complete scientific investigations. This process requires the completion of a grant proposal. While each agency has its own protocol and format for submitting a grant proposal, all forms require similar attention to several basic factors. In this chapter we shall briefly summarize several of the most common elements that are included in a proposal. Once funding has been obtained and the project is completed, the scientist is expected to publish the findings for public scrutiny and utilization. To do so, the investigators must prepare a formal document that is presented to editors of scientific journals who complete a peer review process to determine if the study is of high enough quality and technical correctness to warrant publication. In both cases, the proposal and research report are reviewed for quality and completeness and are submitted through a peer review process. Therefore, the quality of content, style of presentation, conciseness, and coverage must be carefully attended to by investigators.

UNDERSTANDING THE RESEARCH PROPOSAL

A research proposal is written to provide a document for evaluation by a funding agency. A proposal should be prepared in a logical manner and should summarize the objectives of the study, the methodology to be employed, and the proposed analyses of facts obtained from the study. Typically, a research proposal includes a section on the research problem, a critique or review of basic published literature, a statement on objectives or hypotheses, and a summary of procedures to be used.

Research Problem

The statement of the problem provides the logical foundation upon which the proposal is built and places the specific focus of the project into context. Frequently, a problem statement begins with a statement of need. Commonly the need is for either a full understanding or an adequate knowledge base, the desire for necessary information for public policy, or the call for adequate facts about cause-and-effect treatment or prevention information.

Review of Literature

Typically, the review of literature is a state-of-the-art analysis of what we currently know or don't know about the problem under investigation. This review is presented in a way not only to analyze current knowledge but also to highlight the importance of the problem. As part of the review of literature the investigator typically indicates the need for new or extended direction of research on the topic, calls for replications, or identifies shortcomings and necessary new directions or redirections. Further, where controversial evidence is found, or competing theoretical or methodological issues are notable, a strong review of literature recognizes these problems and suggests solutions. Reviews of literature in grant proposals are never exhaustive and are typically based on very careful selection of the most pertinent information.

Objectives and/or Hypotheses

In most proposals a formal objective or aims statement is required. Indeed, we believe a statement of objective is absolutely necessary. Often this section begins with a short paragraph on the general purpose of the proposed study. It is then followed by one or more clearly stated objectives: For example, to determine if television viewing predicts aggressive behaviors among detention center youths who are incarcerated for a 48-hour period. Ideally, the objectives are followed by a specific statement regarding the predicted association between the research variables under consideration. Either directional or null hypotheses can be used. However, if there is either a strong theoretical framework or clear and consistent past research which suggests a direction to findings, we maintain a directional hypothesis is preferred.

Procedures

The procedure or methodology section of the study commonly includes several components. In the proposal the investigators describe the population under consideration and the sampling procedures to be used to find a group that represents the larger population. In some cases a full population can be used. However, more commonly a smaller but representative sample is utilized. Following a description of the sample, the investigator generally describes the research design to be used in collecting the data. This section describes the nature of the correlational, descriptive, experimental, analytic, or observational design to be used to gather facts. In yet another component of the procedure section the investigators summarize their instrumentation and discuss the reliability and validity of their measurement strategies. The type and nature of the data are summarized and delineated. The final component includes a summary of the procedures for analyzing the data. Generally, these procedures are discussed separately for each hypothesis in the proposal.

Summary

The basic sections of a grant proposal provide important information about the proposed project. The statement of the problem focuses the reader on the general area and its importance. The review of literature builds an empirical or theoretical framework for further work. The objectives and hypotheses identify the basic questions to be addressed—preferably through the use of directional hypotheses. Finally, the procedures section provides information on sampling, research design, measurement, and data analysis. As you will find, these basic components of the proposal are also found, in slightly different forms, in the research report too.

UNDERSTANDING RESEARCH REPORTS

Writing Style

Scientific, technical, or formal report writing convention calls for a writing style that is precise, concise, and economical. The author of a scientific report must attempt to avoid ambiguity by vague references to general terms with no concrete meaning. Above all else, the manuscript must have an orderly flow of ideas with meaningful transitions between subsections of the manuscript. Many times, headings and subheadings will serve the important role of assisting meaningful transitions. There should always be proper consideration of the reader's time and thus an emphasis on economy of expression. Hence, consideration for others through precision, conciseness, and economy of words should be kept in mind.

Format

Social science reports draw on a common format for two important reasons. Foremost, a common format assures equivalent types of information across reports. Certain essential elements of the scientific process are necessary ingredients to understanding any research report. Therefore, a common format helps to ensure that essential elements will be available in every report. Also, a common format assists the reader in ease of reading scientific research. If specific research information is available under common headings across reports, the consumer of research finds it easy to locate particular types of report information.

A number of common headings identifying parts to a manuscript are used in formal research reports. Several excellent sources are available for in-depth study of the major parts of a formal report. In particular, social science students should be familiar with the *Publication Manual of the American Psychological Association* (1983, 3rd ed.). As a guide to effective reading (or writing) of formal research reports, we shall briefly summarize the major elements of such reports and provide an example of a short research report as an illustration.

Title.   The title serves two important functions. First, it offers the reader some initial information about the content of the article. As such it is advisable that the title of a research report include some information about (1) the independent and dependent variables used in the study, or (2) the major finding or relationship disclosed by the investigation. Second, the title is drawn on by abstracting or by computer retrieval systems as the major indexing information source. Misleading or poorly titled studies may thus be lost to mainstream scientific audiences.

Abstract.   The abstract is a brief summary of the major elements of the research project. It offers a mechanism whereby the reader can quickly preview the contents of the article. The abstract should include a statement on the major hypothesis, information on how the hypothesis was tested, primary results, and theoretical or practical conclusions or implications. Where possible, information about sampling and population parameters should be included. Usually this is done within a 125- to 175-word limit. Thus, economy of words is essential. Like the title, the abstract should be written with care. In reviewing research literature in which an extensive number of investigations have been completed, researchers are likely to draw heavily on the abstract in determining whether to read the study in full.

Introduction.   The introduction serves two major roles. First, it outlines the theoretical rationale for the study and reviews previous research pertinent to the current study. Second, through a review of selected research, or inductive reasoning, hypotheses or research questions are derived and formally stated.

Given limited journal page space, the researcher is usually urged to limit the literature review and description of theoretical propositions to the most pertinent and relevant information. Where possible, the author refers the reader to reviews or surveys previously published on the research topic. While brevity is essential, it should never be used at the expense of clear understanding or precise detail. In general, the author of a research report prepared for journal publication must assume the reader will be aware of the research topic area and thus does not need an extensive review of all the previous research on the topic. Rather, the initial goal of an effective introduction is to provide a clear overview of the theoretical or conceptual rationale of the study and to provide a statement on the major findings and conclusions of previously relevant research.

Once the theoretical or conceptual foundation in the form of a review is complete, research questions or hypotheses are formally stated. The goal of this section of the report is to provide a clear sense of what has been addressed by the scientist. Hence, a logical linkage between the research problem, any theoretical or conceptual propositions, and hypotheses or research questions should be apparent.

A consumer of research can pose several questions that should be answered through a careful reading of a well-prepared introduction section. The reader of a research report, for example, should ask some of the following questions to maximize understanding of the introduction. What is proposed to be manipulated and measured in the study? What is the logical or theoretical rationale behind each hypothesis? What specific results are expected?

Method.   The method section offers an important description of the sample, research apparatus or materials, and experimental procedure. This section of the report must be written in enough detail to allow other investigators an opportunity to replicate the study. The method section, therefore, provides information about how the study was conducted and enables an assessment of the methodological appropriateness of the research design to test the stated hypothesis.

Information about the sample, usually labeled the *subjects* section describes the background of the research participants. Major demographic characteristics that are outlined usually include information about sex, age, race, social class status, and education. In certain types of reports geographic location and institutional background of the population under study are specified. The *apparatus* or *research materials* subsection briefly describes the testing materials or equipment utilized in the investigation. Enough information must be given to assure future possibilities of replication by other scientists. The *procedure* of the study outlines the step-by-step conduct of the investigation. When very specific instructions are given to the research participants, the author reports them in detail. If experimental manipulations are used, the details of the design are carefully outlined. When standard testing procedures are used, the author typically does not describe the procedures in great detail. Rather, the test is referred to with references for further reading.

Results.   The results section summarizes the research data. If the data are extensive, they are usually presented in tabular or graphic form. Briefer reports may be written in such a way that research results may be presented economically within the text itself. The data must be presented in sufficient detail to enable the reader to draw a conclusion regarding support of the hypothesis.

Discussion.   The discussion typically begins with a statement about the tested hypothesis. A clear statement should be made about the degree to which the data support the hypothesis. Results are interpreted in regard to theoretical and practical implications and are qualified where necessary. In certain instances suggestions for improvement in future research may be appropriate. Authors are expected to be straightforward, brief, and to the point. When the discussion is very brief, researchers may combine the results and discussion into one section.

Summary.   Six basic sections of a research report are commonly found in professional journals. The title gives the initial information about manuscript content. The abstract offers a condensed summary. The introduction provides a brief literature review, offers information on purpose and problem, and usually includes a subsection on hypotheses. The methods section summarizes research procedures and techniques. And the results section summarizes the data, while the discussion usually wraps up the study with theoretical and practical implications. (See Tips for Consumers 18.1.)

A BRIEF RESEARCH REPORT ILLUSTRATION

To assist the reader in further understanding the conventions of report writing, we have included in this section an example of a brief research report from our own laboratory. This report reflects the type of research investigation that many college students are likely to have participated in as subjects. At the margin of each section of the report "highlight" comments reflect the major components provided by the authors. The highlight comments should be viewed as brief summaries of the essential ingredients of formal report writing.

Tips for Consumers 18.1

The format of most research reports is very similar. In reading the report look for the following headings or sections. Each element of the report provides important information.

1. The *title* should provide information about the topic of study, the primary variables, and hint to the major finding.
2. The *abstract* should provide a condensed summary of the study and the major findings.
3. The *introduction* should provide the rationale for the study, identify the key variables, and delineate the objectives or hypotheses.
4. The *method* section should describe the sample, procedures, and measurements.
5. The *results* section summarizes the types of statistical analyses undertaken and the findings. The findings should be pertinent to the hypotheses.
6. The *discussion* should review the findings, summarize the findings in regard to past research, and provide direction for future investigations.

In reading research reports a consumer can accelerate the amount of time needed to study a given research report by being aware of where one can find particular types of information in a report. Any report that fails to provide these six fundamental components has limited utility for the consumer.

This report is a condensation of an article published in the *Journal of Divorce* (Crossman, Shea, & Adams, 1980).

Title offers information about the independent and dependent variables.

EFFECTS OF DIVORCE ON EGO DEVELOPMENT AND IDENTITY FORMATION OF COLLEGE STUDENTS

The authors are listed in their order of responsibility for the project, and the location of the research center is provided.

Sharyn M. Crossman, Judy A. Shea, and Gerald R. Adams
Utah State University

The abstract includes information about:
(1) Dependent variable measures
(2) Independent variables
(3) Sample size
(4) Findings and conclusion

ABSTRACT

Level of ego development, locus of control, and identity achievement were assessed in 294 college students who came from intact, divorced, and divorced-remarried family backgrounds. Contrary to popular assumptions, divorce backgrounds were not predictive of lower scores on the three measures. In fact, males from divorced families held higher ego-identity achievement scores than males from intact or remarried families. Further, no evidence was found for the argument that remarriage (stepfathering) may attenuate negative consequences of divorce on college students' development.

The introduction includes information about:
(1) Previous research conclusions
(2) Two formal research hypotheses

INTRODUCTION

Numerous investigations have attempted to delineate the negative consequences of father-absence on children's cognitive, social, and personality development (e.g., Chapman, 1977; Mitchell & Wilson, 1967; Santrock, 1970). Some investigations report negative consequences for adolescents from father-absent families while others do not. However, recently Chapman (1977) compared college students from father-absent, stepfather, and intact families on cognitive measures of field independence and scholastic aptitude. While males from father-absent families held lower scores than males from intact homes, the students from the stepfather family backgrounds fell in between the two former groups. For females there was no theoretically consistent relation between cognitive performance and family history.

Although Chapman argues that the presence of a stepfather may be associated with attenuation of father-absence effect on a child's development, his evidence is not absolutely consistent with such a statement. While having a stepfather was associated with improvement in scholastic aptitude, it was not predictive of a higher field independence score. Therefore, the attenuation effects of divorce–remarriage on college students' development is still questionable.

Hetherington, Cox, and Cox (1975) have presented evidence indicating that while divorce may have disorganizing effects on a child's behavior, the typical father-absent family regains stability and equilibrium in the months that follow, with little or no permanent negative effects on the child's development. Research by Gurin and Epps (1975) on college students from black American colleges would support this contention. Father-absence was found to be unrelated to college students' grades, entrance test scores, achievement, aspirations, commitments, self-confidence, or values.

Given the equivocal research findings of father-absence effect on individual development, two hypotheses were tested. First, it was hypothesized that college students from divorced families would not differ from students from intact family backgrounds, particularly given that Hetherington et al. have presented evidence with younger children suggesting only a temporary effect on children's behavior due to divorce. Although Chapman's (1977) data tentatively suggest an attenuating effect due to stepparenting, it was also hypothesized that no such effect would emerge in this investigation.

*The method section includes informa-
tion about:*
(1) Sample characteristics
(2) Random sample selection process
(3) Assessment research materials (tests)

METHOD

Participants included 294 Caucasian college students from the College Environment and Ego Development Research Project (a longitudinal study) at Utah State University. Students from eight academic departments in five colleges were randomly drawn for participation. Individual subjects were contacted by phone but interviewed in person. Of those contacted 90% agreed to participate. During the interview participants reported their parental family history in regard to divorce, separation, and remarriage. Thirty-three subjects had experienced a divorce, of which twenty-four had a history of divorce and remarriage, while eight had a divorce background without remarriage of the custodial parent.

Three measures were gathered representing assessments of ego functions (e.g., Maddi, 1968) thought to be core elements of personality styles by personologists such as Erikson, Rotter, and Sullivan. The Marcia (1966) Ego-Identity Incomplete Sentence Blank (EI-ISB), which assesses ego-identity achievement, was completed by participants. Levenson's (1974) Locus of Control Scale was completed to measure the degree to which the subject viewed himself as a personal determinant of social reinforcement. Finally, the Loevinger, Wessler, and Redmore (1970) Incomplete Sentence Blank was administered to assess the general level of ego functioning. In this study, the Item Sum Score (Redmore & Waldman, 1975) was utilized to give a general level of functioning in a relative sense between those students who had a history of divorce versus those who did not. In the latter measure a lower level of ego development functioning implies the use of impulsive and self-protective mechanisms in defining the world of experience, while upper levels are thought to indicate autonomous, self-critical thought, with tolerance for ambiguity and configural complexity.

*The combined results and discussion
include information about:*
(1) Reliability information
(2) Results with a brief qualification
(3) Conclusions

RESULTS AND DISCUSSION

To assure that the EI-ISB was reliably scored, two raters independently scored the responses. Interrater reliability was $r = .92$, $p < .001$. Further, the Loevinger et al. (1970) measures of ego development was scored by two independent raters using the Item Sum Score defined by Redmore and Waldman (1975). Interrater reliability was $r = .86$, $p < .001$.

Does an early divorce have an enduring effect on students' ego development? To address this question, a series of analysis of variance computations were completed on the three ego development measures using a Sex × Family History (Divorce versus Intact Family Background) factorial. The only measure to approach significance was ego-identity development. Contrary to popular assumptions, F (1,289) = 3.34, $p < .06$, individuals having experienced divorce held higher ego-identity scores on the EI-ISB than persons from intact family backgrounds. However, a significant Sex × Family Background interaction, F (1,289) = 4.97, $p < .03$, revealed males from divorced backgrounds were more likely to have higher ego-identity levels than males from intact families or females from divorced or intact family histories. The latter three groups did not differ significantly on this measure.

Contrary to previous research on father-absence, which reports negative consequences for children experiencing divorce, the present data suggest either no significant effect or positive consequence on ego functions when comparing students from divorced and intact family backgrounds. Consistent with Chapman's findings, our data suggest effects of father-absence may be primarily influential on males' development. However, contrary to his evidence that father-absence has negative effects on males' cognitive performance and ability, the present findings suggest it may have positive effects on identity formation. Perhaps the absence of a father stimulates mothers and teachers to prompt male children into an early crisis and search for self-identity. Failure to find inter-individual differences and self-perceptions of control suggests that the effects of father-absence may have little bearing on the level of ego-functioning children from divorced family backgrounds obtained when they are of college age. Since 92 percent of the sample indicated divorce in their family occurred their third through seventh year of life, these data suggest that while previous research indicates certain negative consequences for social and personality development during childhood, these effects may not be evident by young adulthood.

Although there were few differences between students from intact and divorced families in this study, it has been argued that remarriage is likely to remediate divorce effects. However, a series of t-test comparisons between the divorce and remarriage groups on the three ego development measures failed to reach significance ($p > .05$), leaving Chapman's (1977) argument for attenuation effects by step-parenting on college students' development in question.

The reference section includes information about:
(1) Location of previous published research on the problem
(2) Location of published measurements

REFERENCES

Chapman, M. (1977). Father absence, stepfathers, and the cognitive performance of college students. *Child Development, 48*, 1155–1158.

Gurin, P., & Epps, E. G. (1975). *Black consciousness, identity, and achievement.* New York: Wiley.

Hetherington, E. M., Cox, M.C., & Cox, R. (1975, April). *Beyond father absence: Conceptualization of effects of divorce.* Paper presented at the meetings of the Society for Research in Child Development, Denver, Colo.

Levenson, H. (1974). Activism and powerful others: Distinctions within the concept of internal external control. *Journal of Personality Assessment, 28*, 377–382.

Loevinger, J., Wessler, R., & Redmore, C. (1970). *Measuring ego-development 2. Scoring manual for women and girls.* San Francisco: Jossey-Bass.

Maddi, S.R. (1968). *Personality theories: A comparative analysis.* Homewood, Ill.: Dorsey Press.

Marcia, J.E. (1966). Development and validation of ego-identity status. *Journal of Personality and Social Psychology, 3*, 551–558.

Mitchell, D., & Wilson, W. (1967). Relationship of father absence to masculinity and popularity of delinquent boys. *Psychological Report, 20*, 1173–1174.

Santrock, J.W. (1970). Influence of onset and type of parental absence on the first four Eriksonian development crises. *Developmental Psychology, 3*, 273–274.

Redmore, C., & Waldman, E. (1975). Reliability of a sentence completion measure of ego development. *Journal of Personality Assessment, 39*, 236–243.

As an illustration of the major elements of a research report, it should be noted that the fundamental components outlined by the example are found in most published research. Further, this example can be used to make comparisons against more extended published articles or apply the material on the evaluation of formal research reports.

CRITERIA FOR EVALUATING REPORTS

In recent years scientists have attempted to identify what is considered by their colleagues as desirable research article characteristics. That is, what should and should not be included in a good research report. Through an extensive survey study of some 300 consulting editors of nine professional journals, Gottfredson (1978) has identified a variety of components that are used by fellow scientists in evaluating the worth of a given research report. Six of his identified components seem particularly noteworthy in understanding important dimensions of a "good" research report.

Practices to Avoid

This list consists of the "don'ts" of research report writing. Consulting editors strongly agree that misrepresentation of any kind is unacceptable to the scientific community. To misrepresent the intent of the research design, the findings, the primary issues, and the like, is unacceptable. Further, the use of lofty jargon when plain English will suffice and the mere publication for the sake of personal aggrandizement are negatively evaluated as professional behavior.

Scientific Substantive Issues

This evaluative dimension deals with one of two important "dos" in research report writing. In certain ways this dimension deals with the impact of the report. Good reports are thought to be innovative, comprehensive, and unifying. They are to deal with an important topic, demonstrate a new theoretical perspective, or summarize the research field. Therefore, in the research report process the article itself is expected to have substantive impact on its readers.

Stylistic Issues

The writing of the report is equally important. It is expected to be well written. The report should include an abstract, key references, tables, figures, and be clearly presented in an organized and logical manner. The report should convince a reader that the study was competently done and that the findings are relevant to other work.

Originality

A key factor in the evaluation of a research report centers around originality and heuristic procedure. The more the report offers in the way of something new, be it theoretical, conceptual, or methodological, the more likely it will be viewed in favorable terms.

Trivia

The more a given research report creates a feeling of "who cares?" or "so what?" the less favorably it is likely to be viewed. If the manuscript is seen as offering little or nothing to the field and is viewed as dull or mediocre it will likely receive negative evaluation from consulting editors. Hence, researchers need to demonstrate the importance of their project or topic if it is not in the mainstream of scientific inquiry.

Scientific Advancement

If the research report is viewed as speaking to a key problem in social science, or provokes controversial dialogue or implications for future research, it is viewed as having a potential impact on scientific advancement. Such manuscripts are viewed in very favorable terms.

Conclusion

There are specific "do's" and "don'ts" in writing research reports. Misrepresentation is viewed as the most distasteful factor that can lead to poor evaluation. This seems extremely important given that science is built on honesty and truthfulness. The more substantive impact the article can have through its topical content or originality, the more favorably it is viewed by the scientific reading audience. While scientific advancement is influential in article evaluation, good writing style appears a must. Finally, trivial research questions or problems are not viewed with favor, nor are mediocre research reports given much credence.

SUMMARY

Proposal preparation and report writing are ever continuous activities in professional careers. While the best way to become familiar with the content of proposals and research reports is through writing and reading them, this chapter offers the foundation necessary to identify the major elements of each.

The major points in this chapter include these:

1. The research proposal is a written document for seeking funding through an agency and is evaluated by a peer review committee for worthiness of support. The proposal typically includes information on
    a. the research problem and its contemporary importance;
    b. past research, current theory, needed directions, and research focus as part of the review of the literature;
    c. objectives and hypotheses;
    d. procedures to be used, including a description of sampling, design, measurements, and proposed data analyses.
2. The research report generally includes the following sections:
    a. the *title* of the manuscript;
    b. the *abstract*, which briefly summarizes the content;
    c. the *introduction*, which provides the theoretical review, pertinent previous research summary, and hypotheses;
    d. the *method section*, which describes the subjects, research apparatus, and experimental procedures;
    e. the *results*, which summarize the findings;
    f. the *discussion*, which summarizes the conclusions;
    g. the *reference list*, which provides the bibliography of citations found in the article.

3. Six criteria for evaluating the "goodness" of a research report include:
    a. the "don'ts" of research report writing;
    b. the importance of scientific substance;
    c. obvious stylistic or expression factors;
    d. issues related to originality;
    e. negative consequences of trivial research questions;
    f. the impact of scientific advancement.

PROBLEMS AND APPLICATIONS

1. In class, analyze the example of a research report in this chapter and critique it on the six criteria for evaluating a report. How could this brief report be improved?
2. Identify a research report on a similar topic in the fields of psychology, sociology, family studies, and home economics. Then analyze the report formats for similarities and differences.
3. As a class prepare a small research proposal of 4–5 pages. Identify the topic and problem. Then in groups of 3–4 students write a small proposal that includes a section on problem, a brief literature review, an objective and hypothesis, and a procedures section. Have each group provide a copy of their proposal for critique by all other groups. This experience will heighten the awareness of the difficulty of preparing a quality report for peer evaluation.
4. Read the *Publication Manual of the American Psychological Association* (3rd Edition) and in class discuss the major facets of writing format for proposal or report preparation.

REFERENCES

American Psychological Association. (1983). *Publication Manual of American Psychological Association* (3rd ed.). Washington, D.C.: Author.

Crossman, S. M., Shea, J. A., & Adams, G. R. (1980). Effects of parental divorce during early childhood on ego development and identity formation of college students. *Journal of Divorce, 3,* 263–272.

Gottfredson, S. D. (1978). Evaluating psychological research reports: Dimensions, reliability, and correlates of quality judgments. *American Psychologist, 33,* 920–934.

Epilogue

OUTLINE

Reflections on Understanding Research Methods
The Need for Reasoned Argument
Speaking to Each Other
Learning by Doing
Clarifying Contradictions
Using the Lumber in the Attic
Optimism or Pessimism?
Easy Facts and Sensitive Opinions
It Pays to Be Smart
The Researcher–Consumer
References

KEY TERMS

Cultural lag
Reasoned argument
Research optimism

Research pessimism
Sensitive opinions
Researcher–consumer

REFLECTIONS ON UNDERSTANDING
RESEARCH METHODS

The twentieth century is particularly outstanding in that it has produced individuals, families, and other significant groups that are heavily impacted by society at large. The enormous changes in technology, social upheaval, and the electronic revolution remind us once again of the useful notion of *cultural lag* as proposed by Ogburn (1964). Ogburn observed that technology changes more rapidly than does the ability of society to cope, adapt, and adjust to sudden change.

George Orwell's anti-utopian *Nineteen Eighty-Four* (1949) is appropriate to reflect on this time. He proposed many revolutionary ideas and predicted multiple changes that would impact mankind and general society. People would need special skills, coping mechanisms, and a general research orientation previously unrecognized. Have we reached that point in society today? Have science, technology, and day-to-day living become too frantic or too static?

Many sincerely believe that we have made outstanding changes in our ability to generate, store, and process information, but the quality and usefulness of the information stored may have changed little. We have information but do not know how to use it effectively. Decision making, judgment, competence, and a scientific foundation are vitally needed to better equip students of today for the world of tomorrow.

We believe that an understanding of research methodology, an appreciation for empirical assessment, and the facility for conducting research are urgently needed by citizens of the world. While many of us need to know how to conduct quality research and much of this research is needed, we have argued throughout the text that all citizens need to know how to evaluate, appreciate, criticize, and competently consume research. There is no choice on the matter if one is to thrive or even survive in a world of electronics, microchips, and space travel.

THE NEED FOR REASONED ARGUMENT

We believe there is a vital need for *reasoned argument* in conducting and consuming research. In fact, this idea was highlighted in the 1962 message by John F. Kennedy in which he presented four basic and essential rights of consumers in a society such as the United States. In his message to Congress he identified the following rights:

1. the right to *safety*—to be protected against the marketing of goods and services which are dangerous to your health, life, or limb;
2. the right to be *informed*—to know enough to guard yourself against fraudulent advertising, inaccurate labeling, unfair and deceptive practices, and to have facts which enable you to get full value for your dollar;
3. the right to *choose*—to have, as far as possible, access to a variety of products at reasonable prices;
4. the right to be *heard*—to obtain legal redress of complaints and grievances when the marketplace fails.

Indeed, "one of the basic challenges facing the consumer movement in the 1980s is to re-emphasize these original goals and to make clear that its [government] aim is to disperse power and information to you, the individual, not consolidate it within a bureaucracy" (Porter, 1979, p. 1195). One might further assert that the only real protection for the consumer is to be informed and to be on guard. It is in this context that we have invited the readers of *Understanding Research Methods* to learn about research procedures, principles of scientific thinking, sampling, and decision making—to mention just a few of the major principles that were treated in this text. This has not been a consumer advocacy text nor is it an exclusively focused text on decision making. It is a research methods text in which we invited would-be researchers and consumers of research (and the comfortable blend of these two groups) to learn about how research data are generated and interpreted so as to increase one's competence *as a researcher and as a consumer* of research.

SPEAKING TO EACH OTHER

We challenge consumers of research to provide the needed stimulus for researchers, especially those in the wide array of social science, to provide more direct guidelines and articulate research needs. Quality research needs good consumers of research—it is a hard-surfaced, two-way street. For too long science has not adequately listened to the voice of the consumer and for an equally long time, the consumer of research has not voiced personal needs to those in a strategic position of rendering assistance. These two forces should and must be better friends, and work together to solve the problems of a complex society.

Researchers have to speak to an audience wider than their peers, and consumers must voice their needs to those who do more than merely consume. We have suggested multiple avenues for such dialogue throughout the text. There is no particular magic or specified steps for accomplishing this goal; rather it is a process, that hopefully can become a life-style for many. In short, we are suggesting that informed consumers of science will be instrumental in making more competent researchers in the community of social science.

LEARNING BY DOING

Cleaveland (1941) noted that

> the art of horse-sitting is acquired rapidly if one keeps at it from daylight 'til dark, day after day, so we quickly learned to ride by the simple process of riding. Mounted on a horse, we were useful in direct proportion to our powers of observation and our ability to interpret what we saw, faculties, of course, which are sharpened by interest. Our interest was boundless. (pp. 103–104)

We fully agree with Cleaveland that nothing substitutes for learning about some concern more than merely doing it. We have presented a broad based text on how to do research, many rules, numerous suggestions, and multiple examples of how to do it. Our advice now is do it! You will find that the rules really do help. Like Cleaveland's advice on horse riding, you will be successful in research in direct proportion to your ability to use your powers of observation and the related task of interpreting what is observed. Some researchers are very adept at observation, others keen with interpretation, but we challenge all readers to blend these two vital parts of the research art. Furthermore, we invite consumers of research to also sharpen their skills with observation and interpretation by this same art—the art of doing (consuming research) over and over.

CLARIFYING CONTRADICTIONS

Both researchers and consumers of research need to stay active in their respective spheres. Change will come, must come, and will probably be welcomed as it comes. An elderly woman in Huston's (1979) book on women in Third World nations noted that great changes came into her life, especially, following World War II. She noted

> things were quite different from what they are now. We got these clothes only recently. We used to wear something from banana fibers just to cover our lower parts. It was scratchy, but we were used to it. I think all the changes came when the church came. We got our clothing, and then we said we should cover our bodies and go to school—maybe go to church. (p. 20)

This old woman in Kenya went on to relate how the old days were better. She noted that people in the old days lived to be very old and when one died everyone would go to the funeral because it was a rarity to participate in a funeral. She noted that more people die now than in previous times. As the conversation continued she stated that "now children don't die as much any more because we have doctors and hospitals nearby" (p. 31). As is obvious, the statements about "more people dying today" and "children don't die as much," are somewhat contradictory statements.

We can interpret and clarify these apparent contradictions by assessing the impact of health care on the family, longevity, and the community at large in Kenya. In reality, infant mortality used to be extremely high and those who reached old age were rare members of the social system. The old woman was correct in asserting that there were fewer adult deaths due to the simple fact there were relatively few adults to die in old age. There are more funerals to go to now, because people survive into adulthood, old age, and then die.

USING THE LUMBER IN THE ATTIC

Many of our day-to-day questions, contradictions, or distortions can be clarified through checking, evaluating, and engagement in objective assessment. Whether it be an anthropologist in Kenya, a social worker in New York City, a sociologist in rural

Pennsylvania, a home economist in Texas, or a nurse in San Francisco—the need is basically the same. It is a need to have clear thinking, to articulate important questions, and to make needed observations and calculated useful conclusions. These are the essential parts of science and they are clearly the core elements in consuming science in most spheres of life. As researchers and consumers of research we need to be able to use what William Faulkner (Cullen, 1975) referred to as the "lumber in the attic." Faulkner was referring to the ability to observe and correctly interpret one's environment.

OPTIMISM OR PESSIMISM?

As we think of research, research tools, and the application of research one school of thought tends to be optimistic. This school believes that science and the computer will bring greater freedom, more individuality, and a more personal, even humane society. It is believed that a higher standard of living will come, that human drudgery will be reduced, and a shorter work week will emerge. Furthermore, the avalanche of home-based computers will bring great help to the family and small businesses, and will provide stimulation, recreation, and analytic thinking activities for all who use them. With research technology, especially the computer, it is conceivable that the average person will have a greater say in decision making, more polls will be conducted, and a more democratic society will emerge.

In contrast to the optimistic projection, the more pessimistic school argues that research and computers will not produce greater levels of freedom or personal well-being. Further, the argument is made that individual freedom and general humanity will be lowered. Computers will dominate the individual, not vice versa. Members of society will increasingly have less freedom and be subjected to more depersonalization. The art of life, the human elements, will be pushed aside in favor of more efficiency brought on by the capabilities of mass society, a postindustrial mentality, and the blandness of a computer world.

For example, research has already been carried out to assess the utility and feasibility of using voice-print analyzers in computerized teaching systems of the future. Such hardware would give teachers the capability of determining the student's identity, mental stability, and even current emotional state. Does this sound like an Orwellian prophecy that has come true in your life? Do you welcome such computer hardware? Would you feel comfortable living and learning in an environment where computer-assisted hardware can determine whether you are happy, sad, calm, or upset? What is the balance between privacy and progress?

EASY FACTS AND SENSITIVE OPINIONS

Facts are easy to come by—just ask any person on the street—but *sensitive opinions,* refined thoughts, or far-reaching provocative questions are more difficult to create. It is an art to have sensitive opinions. Much of the muscle of social science research has been oriented to assessing opinions, describing behavior, and making projections for the future. Competent assessment of opinion is a polished art and we owe apologies to no one. The fool can readily predict the future; the scientist is more often content in describing the present or past and making tentative comments about the future. We should not be overly conscious of who we are or where we have been in our social science research. True, we need to reflect, to assess, and to criticize, but we need to do it with purpose, not with pessimism. The observations of Pasternak (1958) in *Doctor Zhivago* are important for us to consider in regard to introspection and the future:

> But what is consciousness? Let's see. A conscious attempt to fall asleep is sure to produce insomnia, to try to be conscious of one's own digestion is a sure way to upset the stomach. Consciousness is a poison when we apply it to ourselves. Consciousness is a light directed outward, it lights up the way ahead of us so that we don't stumble. It's like the headlights on a locomotive—turn them inward and you'd have a crash. (p. 60)

We are relatively optimistic about the future for students, for their teachers, and for the general population. It is a good time to be alive, to study, to work, and to help do the necessary research and teaching leading to a more enlightened world. Life depends in part on your occupation, income and how you spend it, how you use your time, and your personal environment. One thing remains certain for both the researcher and consumer of research—as the world becomes more complicated, more people must specialize. We will need experts to help us out in the consumer decision-making problems of a modern technological society. It is our hope that most of you will become either the experts to conduct the needed research in this process or the experts to guide and direct the millions of consumers in need of the advice and direction that you can offer them.

IT PAYS TO BE SMART

We believe that if the law in the United States discriminates, it is probably more on the basis of knowledge distribution than anything else. The simple and piercing truth is that smart people know enough either to benefit themselves or hire an expert, for example, the lawyer. It is a truism that the smarter you are about taxes, the less you usually have to pay to the government. In short, the more knowledgeable you are, the better will be your chances for coping with an increasingly complex economic system and social world.

As you reflect on research designs, modes of data collection, issues of reliability, validity, type of sample, and analysis of data, it is important to be aware of where you have come from and where you are going. Did you know that 10% of the families in the United States with the highest incomes earned more total income than did the entire 50% of the families with the lowest income? Furthermore, the wealthiest 5% of families have more than 40% of all the wealth! Just these findings alone show where a lot of research can be conducted and where many consumer research-based decisions are needed (Katona, Mandell, & Schmeideskamp, 1970).

We suspect that most Americans seek justice in the law and some even find it. The shining luster of the legal process does indeed radiate the promise of justice. Historically, people have been persuaded that the law will protect their rights, preserve their liberty, and secure their property. We are arguing that the law can be substantially augmented by using science in everyday life. This can be done by learning how to ask the right research questions, knowing how to carry out useful research, and then developing a consumer-research orientation that enables one to evaluate, plan, and apply from a new perspective.

THE RESEARCHER–CONSUMER

There are no substitutes for good ideas. With good ideas, a large array of research tools can be put into force to research these good ideas. With research skills, a scientist has a vital role to play with the informed consumer to neutralize in part the thesis of George Orwell, who, as noted, predicted that our nation was headed for a world of scarcity, wanton cruelty, facism, and perhaps constant warfare. On this Orwell theme, Theobald (1982) argued that *Nineteen Eighty-four* can be avoided if the human race will grow up. It must grow up or be blown up.

It has been observed by many that the 1980s were a consumer-oriented decade. One of the tenets of the consumer movement is that the consumer has the right to be informed. The quality of your life and the state of your emotional well-being depend on this type of information. As we move to a new decade of the 1990s, it appears that consumer and research issues will focus more on the quality of the natural environments, needs of the homeless, and demograpic shifts based on race, ethnicity, and age.

We conclude by hoping that the turn of the century will be a happy relationship of the researcher and the consumer working as a dynamic team. This combination can and should work well together. We have attempted to show that the processes of conducting and consuming research are not totally different. Neither can function adequately without the other. We sincerely invite you to continue in your work as a researcher and consumer of research, to ask the right questions, carry out quality research, and make competent consumer decisions that will lead to a more rational life for all.

REFERENCES

Cleaveland, A. M. (1941). *No life for a lady*. Boston: Houghton Mifflin.

Cullen, J. B. (1975). *Old times in the Faulkner country*. Baton Rouge: Louisiana State University Press.

Huston, P. (1979). *Third World women speak out*. New York: Praeger.

Katona, G., Mandell, L., & Schmeideskamp, J. (1970). *1970 survey of consumer finances*. Ann Arbor: Institute for Social Research.

Ogburn, W. F. (1964). *On culture and social change*. Chicago: University of Chicago Press.

Orwell, G. (1949). *Nineteen Eighty-four*. New York: Harcourt, Brace and World.

Pasternak, B. (1958). *Doctor Zhivago*. New York: New American Library.

Porter, S. F. (1979). *Sylvia Porter's new money book for the 80s*. Garden City, N.Y.: Doubleday.

Theobald, R. (1982). *Avoiding 1984*. Chicago: Swallow Press.

Appendix

TABLE A. Table of Chi Square

df	P = .99	.98	.95	.90	.80	.70	.50	.30	.20	.10	.05	.02	.01	.001
1	.000157	.000628	.00393	.0158	.0642	.148	.455	1.074	1.642	2.706	3.841	5.412	6.635	10.827
2	.0201	.0404	.103	.211	.446	.713	1.386	2.408	3.219	4.605	5.991	7.824	9.210	13.815
3	.115	.185	.352	.584	1.005	1.424	2.366	3.665	4.642	6.251	7.815	9.837	11.341	16.268
4	.297	.429	.711	1.064	1.649	2.195	3.357	4.878	5.989	7.779	9.488	11.668	13.277	18.465
5	.554	.752	1.145	1.610	2.343	3.000	4.351	6.064	7.289	9.236	11.070	13.388	15.086	20.517
6	.872	1.134	1.635	2.204	3.070	3.828	5.348	7.231	8.558	10.6645	12.592	15.033	16.812	22.457
7	1.239	1.564	2.167	2.833	3.822	4.671	6.346	8.383	9.803	12.017	14.067	16.622	18.475	24.322
8	1.645	2.032	2.733	3.490	4.594	5.527	7.344	9.524	11.030	13.362	15.507	18.168	20.090	26.125
9	2.088	2.532	3.325	4.168	5.380	6.393	8.343	10.656	12.242	14.684	16.919	19.679	21.666	27.877
10	2.558	3.059	3.940	4.865	6.179	7.267	9.342	11.781	13.442	15.987	18.307	21.161	23.209	29.588
11	3.053	3.609	4.575	5.578	6.989	8.148	10.341	12.899	14.631	17.275	19.675	22.618	24.725	31.264
12	3.571	4.178	5.226	6.304	7.807	9.034	11.340	14.011	15.812	18.549	21.026	24.054	26.217	32.909
13	4.107	4.765	5.892	7.042	8.634	9.926	12.340	15.119	16.985	19.812	22.362	25.472	27.688	34.528
14	4.660	5.368	6.571	7.790	9.467	10.821	13.339	16.222	18.151	21.064	23.685	26.873	29.141	36.123
15	5.229	5.985	7.261	8.547	10.307	11.721	14.339	17.322	19.311	22.307	24.996	28.259	30.578	37.697
16	5.812	6.614	7.962	9.312	11.152	12.624	15.338	18.418	20.465	23.542	26.296	29.633	32.000	39.252
17	6.408	7.255	8.672	10.085	12.002	13.531	16.338	19.511	21.615	24.769	27.587	30.995	33.409	40.790
18	7.015	7.906	9.390	10.865	12.857	14.440	17.338	20.601	22.760	25.089	28.869	32.346	34.805	42.312
19	7.633	8.567	10.117	11.651	13.716	15.352	18.338	21.689	23.900	27.204	30.144	33.687	36.191	43.820
20	8.260	9.237	10.851	12.443	14.578	16.266	19.337	22.775	25.038	28.412	31.410	35.020	37.566	45.315
21	8.897	9.915	11.591	13.210	15.445	17.182	20.337	23.858	26.171	29.615	32.671	36.343	38.932	46.797
22	9.542	10.600	12.338	14.041	16.314	18.101	21.337	24.939	27.301	30.813	33.924	37.659	40.289	48.268
23	10.196	11.293	13.001	14.848	17.187	19.021	22.337	26.018	28.429	32.007	35.172	38.968	41.638	49.728
24	10.856	11.992	13.848	15.659	18.062	19.943	23.337	27.096	29.553	33.196	36.415	40.270	42.980	51.179
25	11.524	12.697	14.611	16.473	18.940	20.867	24.337	28.172	30.675	34.382	37.652	41.566	44.314	52.620
26	12.198	13.409	15.379	17.292	19.820	21.792	25.336	29.246	31.795	35.563	38.885	42.856	45.642	54.052
27	12.879	14.125	16.151	18.114	20.703	22.719	26.336	30.319	32.912	36.741	40.113	44.140	46.963	55.476
28	13.565	14.847	16.928	18.939	21.588	23.647	27.336	31.391	34.027	37.916	41.337	45.419	48.278	56.893
29	14.256	15.574	17.708	19.768	22.475	24.577	28.336	32.461	35.139	39.087	42.557	46.693	49.588	58.302
30	14.953	16.306	18.493	20.599	23.364	25.508	29.336	33.530	36.250	40.256	43.773	47.962	50.892	59.703

Source: From J. P. Guilford. [1965]. *Fundamental Statistics in Psychology and Education. 4th Ed.* McGraw-Hill. Reprinted from Table III of Fisher's *Statistical Methods for Research Workers,* Oliver & Boyd, Edinburgh and London, 1932; by kind permission of the author and publishers. For *df* larger than 30, the value from the expression $\sqrt{2\chi^2} - \sqrt{2df - 1}$ may be interpreted as a *t* ratio.

TABLE B. Student's *t* Distribution

df	Percentile Point						
	70	80	90	95	97.5	99	99.5
1	.73	1.38	3.08	6.31	12.71	31.82	63.66
2	.62	1.06	1.89	2.92	4.30	6.96	9.92
3	.58	.98	1.64	2.35	3.18	4.54	5.84
4	.57	.94	1.53	2.13	2.78	3.75	4.60
5	.56	.92	1.48	2.01	2.57	3.36	4.03
6	.55	.91	1.44	1.94	2.45	3.14	3.71
7	.55	.90	1.42	1.90	2.36	3.00	3.50
8	.55	.89	1.40	1.86	2.31	2.90	3.36
9	.54	.88	1.38	1.83	2.26	2.82	3.25
10	.54	.88	1.37	1.81	2.23	2.76	3.17
11	.54	.88	1.36	1.80	2.20	2.72	3.11
12	.54	.87	1.36	1.78	2.18	2.68	3.06
13	.54	.87	1.35	1.77	2.16	2.65	3.01
14	.54	.87	1.34	1.76	2.14	2.62	2.98
15	.54	.87	1.34	1.75	2.13	2.60	2.95
16	.54	.86	1.34	1.75	2.12	2.58	2.92
17	.53	.86	1.33	1.74	2.11	2.57	2.90
18	.53	.86	1.33	1.73	2.10	2.55	2.88
19	.53	.86	1.33	1.73	2.09	2.54	2.86
20	.53	.86	1.32	1.72	2.09	2.53	2.84
21	.53	.86	1.32	1.72	2.08	2.52	2.83
22	.53	.86	1.32	1.72	2.07	2.51	2.82
23	.53	.86	1.32	1.71	2.07	2.50	2.81
24	.53	.86	1.32	1.71	2.06	2.49	2.80
25	.53	.86	1.32	1.71	2.06	2.48	2.79
26	.53	.86	1.32	1.71	2.06	2.48	2.78
27	.53	.86	1.31	1.70	2.05	2.47	2.77
28	.53	.86	1.31	1.70	2.05	2.47	2.76
29	.53	.85	1.31	1.70	2.04	2.46	2.76
30	.53	.85	1.31	1.70	2.04	2.46	2.75
40	.53	.85	1.30	1.68	2.02	2.42	2.70
50	.53	.85	1.30	1.67	2.01	2.40	2.68
60	.53	.85	1.30	1.67	2.00	2.39	2.66
80	.53	.85	1.29	1.66	1.99	2.37	2.64
100	.53	.84	1.29	1.66	1.98	2.36	2.63
200	.52	.84	1.29	1.65	1.97	2.34	2.60
500	.52	.84	1.28	1.65	1.96	2.33	2.59
∞	.52	.84	1.28	1.64	1.96	2.33	2.58

Source: From B. J. Winer. [1962]. *Statistical Principles in Experimental Design*. Reproduced with permission of McGraw-Hill.

TABLE C. *F* **Distribution**

df for denom.	$1 - \alpha$	\multicolumn{12}{c}{*df* for numerator}
		1	2	3	4	5	6	7	8	9	10	11	12
1	.75	5.83	7.50	8.20	8.58	8.82	8.98	9.10	9.19	9.26	9.32	9.36	9.41
	.90	39.9	49.5	53.6	55.8	57.2	58.2	58.9	59.4	59.9	60.2	60.5	60.7
	.95	161	200	216	225	230	234	237	239	241	242	243	244
2	.75	2.57	3.00	3.15	3.23	3.28	3.31	3.34	3.35	3.37	3.38	3.39	3.39
	.90	8.53	9.00	9.16	9.24	9.29	9.33	9.35	9.37	9.38	9.39	9.40	9.41
	.95	18.5	19.0	19.2	19.2	19.3	19.3	19.4	19.4	19.4	19.4	19.4	19.4
	.99	98.5	99.0	99.2	99.2	99.3	99.3	99.4	99.4	99.4	99.4	99.4	99.4
3	.75	2.02	2.28	2.36	2.39	2.41	2.42	2.43	2.44	2.44	2.44	2.45	2.45
	.90	5.54	5.46	5.39	5.34	5.31	5.28	5.27	5.25	5.24	5.23	5.22	5.22
	.95	10.1	9.55	9.28	9.12	9.10	8.94	8.89	8.85	8.81	8.79	8.76	8.74
	.99	34.1	30.8	29.5	28.7	28.2	27.9	27.7	27.5	27.3	27.2	27.1	27.1
4	.75	1.81	2.00	2.05	2.06	2.07	2.08	2.08	2.08	2.08	2.08	2.08	2.08
	.90	4.54	4.32	4.19	4.11	4.05	4.01	3.98	3.95	3.94	3.92	3.91	3.90
	.95	7.71	6.94	6.59	6.39	6.26	6.16	6.09	6.04	6.00	5.96	5.94	5.91
	.99	21.2	18.0	16.7	16.0	15.5	15.2	15.0	14.8	14.7	14.5	14.4	14.4
5	.75	1.69	1.85	1.88	1.89	1.89	1.89	1.89	1.89	1.89	1.89	1.89	1.89
	.90	4.06	3.78	3.62	3.52	3.45	3.40	3.37	3.34	3.32	3.30	3.28	3.27
	.95	6.61	5.79	5.41	5.19	5.05	4.95	4.88	4.82	4.77	4.74	4.71	4.68
	.99	16.3	13.3	12.1	11.4	11.0	10.7	10.5	10.3	10.2	10.1	9.96	9.89
6	.75	1.62	1.76	1.78	1.79	1.79	1.78	1.78	1.77	1.77	1.77	1.77	1.77
	.90	3.78	3.46	3.29	3.18	3.11	3.05	3.01	2.98	2.96	2.94	2.92	2.90
	.95	5.99	5.14	4.76	4.53	4.39	4.28	4.21	4.15	4.10	4.06	4.03	4.00
	.99	13.7	10.9	9.78	9.15	8.75	8.47	8.26	8.10	7.98	7.87	7.79	7.72
7	.75	1.57	1.70	1.72	1.72	1.71	1.71	1.70	1.70	1.69	1.69	1.69	1.68
	.90	3.59	3.26	3.07	2.96	2.88	2.83	2.78	2.75	2.72	2.70	2.68	2.67
	.95	5.59	4.74	4.35	4.12	3.97	3.87	3.79	3.73	3.68	3.64	3.60	3.57
	.99	12.2	9.55	8.45	7.85	7.46	7.19	6.99	6.84	6.72	6.62	6.54	6.47
8	.75	1.54	1.66	1.67	1.66	1.66	1.65	1.64	1.64	1.64	1.63	1.63	1.62
	.90	3.46	3.11	2.92	2.81	2.73	2.67	2.62	2.59	2.56	2.54	2.52	2.50
	.95	5.32	4.46	4.07	3.84	3.69	3.58	3.50	3.44	3.39	3.35	3.31	3.28
	.99	11.3	8.65	7.59	7.01	6.63	6.37	6.18	6.03	5.91	5.81	5.73	5.67
9	.75	1.51	1.62	1.63	1.63	1.62	1.61	1.60	1.60	1.59	1.59	1.58	1.58
	.90	3.36	3.01	2.81	2.69	2.61	2.55	2.51	2.47	2.44	2.42	2.40	2.38
	.95	5.12	4.26	3.86	3.63	3.48	3.37	3.29	3.23	3.18	3.14	3.10	3.07
	.99	10.6	8.02	6.99	6.42	6.06	5.80	5.61	5.47	5.35	5.26	5.18	5.11
10	.75	1.49	1.60	1.60	1.59	1.59	1.58	1.57	1.56	1.56	1.55	1.55	1.54
	.90	3.28	2.92	2.73	2.61	2.52	2.46	2.41	2.38	2.35	2.32	2.30	2.28
	.95	4.96	4.10	3.71	3.48	3.33	3.22	3.14	3.07	3.02	2.98	2.94	2.91
	.99	10.0	7.56	6.55	5.99	5.64	5.39	5.20	5.06	4.94	4.85	4.77	4.71
11	.75	1.47	1.58	1.58	1.57	1.56	1.55	1.54	1.53	1.53	1.52	1.52	1.51
	.90	3.23	2.86	2.66	2.54	2.45	2.39	2.34	2.30	2.27	2.25	2.23	2.21
	.95	4.84	3.98	3.59	3.36	3.20	3.09	3.01	2.95	2.90	2.85	2.82	2.79
	.99	9.65	7.21	6.22	5.67	5.32	5.07	4.89	4.74	4.63	4.54	4.46	4.40
12	.75	1.46	1.56	1.56	1.55	1.54	1.53	1.52	1.51	1.51	1.50	1.50	1.49
	.90	3.18	2.81	2.61	2.48	2.39	2.33	2.28	2.24	2.21	2.19	2.17	2.15
	.95	4.75	3.89	3.49	3.26	3.11	3.00	2.91	2.85	2.80	2.75	2.72	2.69
	.99	9.33	6.93	5.95	5.41	5.06	4.82	4.64	4.50	4.39	4.30	4.22	4.16

Source: From B. J. Winer. [1962]. *Statistical Principles in Experimental Design.* Reproduced with permission of McGraw-Hill.

TABLE C (continued)

df for numerator												1 − α	df for denom.
15	20	24	30	40	50	60	100	120	200	500	∞		
9.49	9.58	9.63	9.67	9.71	9.74	9.76	9.78	9.80	9.82	9.84	9.85	.75	
61.2	61.7	62.0	62.3	62.5	62.7	62.8	63.0	63.1	63.2	63.3	63.3	.90	1
246	248	249	250	251	252	252	253	253	254	254	254	.95	
3.41	3.43	3.43	3.44	3.45	3.45	3.46	3.47	3.47	3.48	3.48	3.48	.75	
9.42	9.44	9.45	9.46	9.47	9.47	9.47	9.48	9.48	9.49	9.49	9.49	.90	2
19.4	19.4	19.5	19.5	19.5	19.5	19.5	19.5	19.5	19.5	19.5	19.5	.95	
99.4	99.4	99.5	99.5	99.5	99.5	99.5	99.5	99.5	99.5	99.5	99.5	.99	
2.46	2.46	2.46	2.47	2.47	2.47	2.47	2.47	2.47	2.47	2.47	2.47	.75	
5.20	5.18	5.18	5.17	5.16	5.15	5.15	5.14	5.14	5.14	5.14	5.13	.90	3
8.70	8.66	8.64	8.62	8.59	8.58	8.57	8.55	8.55	8.54	8.53	8.53	.95	
26.9	26.7	26.6	26.5	26.4	26.4	26.3	26.2	26.2	26.2	26.1	26.1	.99	
2.08	2.08	2.08	2.08	2.08	2.08	2.08	2.08	2.08	2.08	2.08	2.08	.75	
3.87	3.84	3.83	3.82	3.80	3.80	3.79	3.78	3.78	3.77	3.76	3.76	.90	
5.86	5.80	5.77	5.75	5.72	5.70	5.69	5.66	5.66	5.65	5.64	5.63	.95	4
14.2	14.0	13.9	13.8	13.7	13.7	13.7	13.6	13.6	13.5	13.5	13.5	.99	
1.89	1.88	1.88	1.88	1.88	1.88	1.87	1.87	1.87	1.87	1.87	1.87	.75	
3.24	3.21	3.19	3.17	3.16	3.15	3.14	3.13	3.12	3.12	3.11	3.10	.90	5
4.62	4.56	4.53	4.50	4.46	4.44	4.43	4.41	4.40	4.39	4.37	4.36	.95	
9.72	9.55	9.47	9.38	9.29	9.24	9.20	9.13	9.11	9.08	9.04	9.02	.99	
1.76	1.76	1.75	1.75	1.75	1.75	1.74	1.74	1.74	1.74	1.74	1.74	.75	
2.87	2.84	2.82	2.80	2.78	2.77	2.76	2.75	2.74	2.73	2.73	2.72	.90	6
3.94	3.87	3.84	3.81	3.77	3.75	3.74	3.71	3.70	3.69	3.68	3.67	.95	
7.56	7.40	7.31	7.23	7.14	7.09	7.06	6.99	6.97	6.93	6.90	6.88	.99	
1.68	1.67	1.67	1.66	1.66	1.66	1.65	1.65	1.65	1.65	1.65	1.65	.75	
2.63	2.59	2.58	2.56	2.54	2.52	2.51	2.50	2.49	2.48	2.48	2.47	.90	7
3.51	3.44	3.41	3.38	3.34	3.32	3.30	3.27	3.27	3.25	3.24	3.23	.95	
6.31	6.16	6.07	5.99	5.91	5.86	5.82	5.75	5.74	5.70	5.67	5.65	.99	
1.62	1.61	1.60	1.60	1.59	1.59	1.59	1.58	1.58	1.58	1.58	1.58	.75	
2.46	2.42	2.40	2.38	2.36	2.35	2.34	2.32	2.32	2.31	2.30	2.29	.90	8
3.22	3.15	3.12	3.08	3.04	3.02	3.01	2.97	2.97	2.95	2.94	2.93	.95	
5.52	5.36	5.28	5.20	5.12	5.07	5.03	4.96	4.95	4.91	4.88	4.86	.99	
1.57	1.56	1.56	1.55	1.55	1.54	1.54	1.53	1.53	1.53	1.53	1.53	.75	
2.34	2.30	2.28	2.25	2.23	2.22	2.21	2.19	2.18	2.17	2.17	2.16	.90	9
3.01	2.94	2.90	2.86	2.83	2.80	2.79	2.76	2.75	2.73	2.72	2.71	.95	
4.96	4.81	4.73	4.65	4.57	4.52	4.48	4.42	4.40	4.36	4.33	4.31	.99	
1.53	1.52	1.52	1.51	1.51	1.50	1.50	1.49	1.49	1.49	1.48	1.48	.75	
2.24	2.20	2.18	2.16	2.13	2.12	2.11	2.09	2.08	2.07	2.06	2.06	.90	10
2.85	2.77	2.74	2.70	2.66	2.64	2.62	2.59	2.58	2.56	2.55	2.54	.95	
4.56	4.41	4.33	4.25	4.17	4.12	4.08	4.01	4.00	3.96	3.93	3.91	.99	
1.50	1.49	1.49	1.48	1.47	1.47	1.47	1.46	1.46	1.46	1.45	1.45	.75	
2.17	2.12	2.10	2.08	2.05	2.04	2.03	2.00	2.00	1.99	1.98	1.97	.90	11
2.72	2.65	2.61	2.57	2.53	2.51	2.49	2.46	2.45	2.43	2.42	2.40	.95	
4.25	4.10	4.02	3.94	3.86	3.81	3.78	3.71	3.69	3.66	3.62	3.60	.99	
1.48	1.47	1.46	1.45	1.45	1.44	1.44	1.43	1.43	1.43	1.42	1.42	.75	
2.10	2.06	2.04	2.01	1.99	1.97	1.96	1.94	1.93	1.92	1.91	1.90	.90	12
2.62	2.54	2.51	2.47	2.43	2.40	2.38	2.35	2.34	2.32	2.31	2.30	.95	
4.01	3.86	3.78	3.70	3.62	3.57	3.54	3.47	3.45	3.41	3.38	3.36	.99	

Index

Abstracts, 54, 57–64
  on computer-assisted retrieval systems, 60–62, 68–69
  list of, 58–64
  in written reports, 371, 373
Abstracts in Anthropology, 58
Absracts of Health Care Management Studies, 58
Abstracts on Criminology and Penology, 58
Accretion measures, 247, 294, 295
Administrative audit, 318
American Doctoral Dissertations, 64
American Psychological Association, writing syle, 56, 370
Analysis. *See* Data analyses
Anthropology
  abstracts, 58
  descriptive research in, 107–108
Archives, 246–247, 293–294
Arts and Humanities Citation Index, 64
Association measures. *See* Measures of assocation
Attributes, 153
  biosocial, 259
  psychosocial, 259

Belief system. *See* Frames of reference
Bender-Gestalt Test, 277

Between-subjects design, 142–144
Bibliography, 56, 57, 377. *See also* Reference sources
Biological Abstracts, 58
Biosocial attributes, 259
Bipolar adjective ratings, 163–165

Cafeteria-style questions, 209–210
Camera filming, 246
Card catalogs, 52–54
Carry-over effects, 143
Case study research
  described, 114
  selectivity in, 108–111
Causation, 36
  experimental–control group designs and, 137–141
  theory formation and, 41–43
Child Development Abstracts and Bibliography, 58
Children, research guidelines for, 33
Children's Apperception Test (CAT), 276
Chi square, 355–358
Church records, 294
Clinical interviews, 217
Closed-ended questions, 201–202
Cluster probability sample, 180
Coefficient of equivalence, 88–89

Coefficient of internal consistency, 88–89
Coefficient of reproducibility, 163
Coefficient of stability, 87, 89
Computers
    in content analysis, 301
    future impact of, 387–388
    retrieval systems based on, 52–54
        abstracts in, 61–62, 68–69
        indexes in, 68–69
Concurrent validity, 83
Confidentiality, as ethical consideration, 28–33
Confounding factors, 136. *See also* Extraneous
        variables
Construction technique, 275–276
Construct validity, 51, 84–86
Consumers of research
    knowledge of research methodology by,
        10–12
    rights of, 10, 384–385
Content analysis
    of films, 184–186
    of historic documents, 290–292, 299–302
        characteristics, 301–302
        example of, 290–292
        observation, 301–302
Content validity, 83–84
Control group, 137. *See also* Experimental
        laboratory method
Convenience sample, 180–181
Convergent–discriminant validation, 86
Cooperation rate, 212
Correlation coefficient, 85, 87, 88, 89,
        334–335, 350–354
Corroboration, 296
Cost-benefit analysis
    as ethical consideration, 27–33
    of evaluation research, 317–318
Cost-effectiveness analysis, of evaluation
        research, 317–318
Counting, empirical approach and, 19–20
Covert feelings, 269
Crime and Delinquency Abstracts, 59
Criminal Justice Abstracts, 58
Criterion-related validity, 81–83
    concurrent, 82–83
    predictive, 81–83
Cross-sectional research, 109, 114, 115
Cultural lag, 384
Cumulative Book Index, 64
*Cumulative Index to Nursing and Allied Health
        Literature*, 64

Cumulative scales, 162–163
Current Contents, 64–65
Current Index to Journals in Education, 65
*Current Population Survey in the United
        States*, 191

Data
    analysis of. *See* Data analyses
    collection of. *See* Data collection
    defined, 13
    empirical, 19–20
    frame of reference and. *See* Frames of
        reference
    methodology, theory and, 13–14
Data analyses, 328–363
    decision errors in, 333–334
    example of, 334
    in field research, 124
    myths about statistical significance and,
        334–335
    question formulation and, 329–330
        descriptive, 330–331, 343–347
        inferential, 331–333, 354–363
Data banks, 295
Data collection, 114–116
    case study approach to, 108–111, 114
    cross-sectional approach to, 109, 114, 115
    for descriptive research, 113–116
    through evaluation research. *See* Evaluation
        research
    in exploratory research, 113–116
    in field research. *See* Field research
    through historical documents. *See*
        Documents
    through interviews. *See* Interviews
    in laboratory experiments, 253–265
        basic technique of, 254
        hiding independent and dependent
            variables, 254–263
    through literature reviews. *See* Literature
        reviews
    longitudinal design approach to, 109–111,
        116
    method of, and sample size, 183–184
    observational techniques for. *See*
        Observation
    projective and indirect methods, 267–281
        perspective on, 280
        selected types of, 270–280
    through questionnaires. *See* Questionnaires
    survey approach to, 114, 317

Date of origin, 297
Debriefing, 261–263
Deception methodology, 255–256
  debriefing in, 262–263
  ethical consideration in, 261–262
  role playing as alternative to, 256–258
Decision making. *See* Data analyses
Degree of precision, 183
Degree of structure, 272
Degrees of freedom, 356–363
Dehoaxing, 262
Demographic information, 211–212
Dependent variables, 41. *See also* Extraneous
    variable
  defined, 137
  in field experiments, 128–132
  hiding of, in experimental laboratory
    method, 254–263
Deployability, theory of, 41
Descriptive research, 106–113
  anthropological, 108–109
  data collection methods for, 113–116
  defined, 106–107
  focus of, 107
  functions of description and, 107
  questions in, 111–112
  richness of words in, 113
  selectivity in, 108–111
Descriptive research designs, 106–113
Descriptive statistics, 330–331, 341–347
  example of use of, 348, 350
  measures of central tendencies, 330–331,
    343–345
  measures of dispersion, 330–331, 345–347
  raw frequencies and percentages, 341–343
Desensitizing, 262–263
Detroit Area Study, 191
Developmental Disabilities Abstracts, 59
Diaries, 292–293
Differential subject selection, 91
Directional hypothesis, 42–43
Discussion, report, 372, 375–377
Disguised measures, 268. *See also* Projective
    techniques
Dissertation Abstracts International, 59–60,
    64
Documents, 286–306
  advantages of using, 288–289, 303
  as alternative to other sources, 303–304
  content analysis of, 290–292, 299–302
  perspective on, 287–288, 304

  as primary and secondary sources,
    289–292, 298
  types of, 292–295
  validity and reliability of, 295–299
Double-barreled questions, 205
Double entendre word assocations, 273–274
Draw-A-Person Test, 276–277
Duration measures, 236
Dynamic phenomena, 158

Ecological validity, 94, 144, 263
Education Index, 65
Education Resources Information Center
    (ERIC), 62, 65
Efficiency analysis, 314
Efficient causation, 36
Element, 178
Empirical approach, 19–20
  hypothesis testing in, 41–43
  theory development in, 40–41
Empirical role taking, 258
Environmental Abstracts, 60
Equivalent-forms method, 88
Erosion measures, 247, 294–295
Ethics, 27–35, 43–44
  of deception methodology, 261–262
  financial incentives and, 34
  in research with special populations, 33–35
  responsibilities of researchers and, 28–33
Evaluation research, 310–320
  example of, 319–320
  issues of reliability and validity, 318–320
  measurement in, 318–319
  methodology of, 315–318
    benefit-cost and cost-effectiveness
      analysis, 317–318
    management, 318
    nonexperimental and experimental
      methods, 315–316
    survey, 317
  misconceptions of, 312
  politics of evaluation and, 311–312
  purpose of, 310–311
  types of, 312–314
    efficiency analysis, 314
    needs assessment, 313
    outcome assessment, 314
    program management, 314
Event recorders, 244–245
Event sampling, 237–240
Exceptional Child Education Abstracts, 60

Exchange theory, 39
Expectancy, experimenter, 260
Experimental control, 137–142
Experimental group, 137. *See also*
    Experimental laboratory method
Experimental laboratory method, 136. *See also*
    Field research, field experiments
  data collection in, 253–265
    basics of, 254
    hiding independent and dependent
      variables, 254–263
  for evaluation research, 315–316
  experimental-control group design in,
    137–142, 258–260
    posttest-only, 140–141
    pretest-posttest, 138–149
    Solomon four-group, 139–141
  for field experiments, 241–243
  social behavior perspective and, 39
  strengths and weaknesses of, 144, 254
Experimental mortality, 92–93
Experimental risk, as ethical consideration,
    27–33
Experimenter effects, 123, 241, 259–260,
    273–274
Experimenter modeling, 259–260
Exploratory research, 103–106
  data collection methods for, 113–116
  flexibility of, 103–104
  functions of exploration and, 107
  process and activity in, 104–105
  serendipity and, 104
Exploratory research designs, 103–106
External criticism, 297–299
External validity
  defined, 89–90
  in experimental laboratory method, 260–261
  factors limiting, 93–94
  obtrusiveness of observation technique and,
    246–247
Extraneous variables, 90–95
  defined, 90
  differential subject selection, 91
  ecological validity, 94, 144, 263
  in evaluation research, 318–319
  in experimental-control group design,
    137–142, 259–260
  experimental mortality, 92
  experimenter effects as, 123, 241, 259–260,
    273–274

historical events, 90–91
instrumentation, 92
interaction between selection bias and
    experimental/independent variable, 94
in longitudinal research, 116
maturation of subjects, 90, 93
in observation techniques, 241
pretesting, 91–92
reactive effects, 93, 142–143, 241, 246
selection-maturation effects, 93
statistical regression, 92–93

Face validity, 78, 81–82
Field entry, 122–123
Field notation, 123–124, 233–235
Field research, 120–134
  described, 121, 122
  descriptive approach to, 111–112
  field experiments, 127–132
    defined, 128
    for evaluation research, 315–316
    examples of, 128–132
    observational techniques in, 238–243
  field studies, 121–127
    examples of, 121, 125–127
    observational techniques in, 231–238
    perspectives on, 121–122
    procedures for, 122–125
Films
  catalogs of, 52–53
  content analysis of, 184–185
  recording on, 246
Filter questions, 206
Financial incentives, 34
Focused interview, 214–215
Food Science and Technology Abstracts, 60
Formal rating techniques, 231, 235–238,
    240–243
Formative evaluation, 313
Frames of reference, 35–40, 44–45
  described, 17, 36–37
  in psychology, 37–38
  in sociology, 38–40
  in theory and hypothesis testing, 41–43
Free association, 275
Frequency, 341–343
Frequency distributions, 342–343
  measures of cental tendency of, 330–331,
    343–345, 347
  measures of dispersion of, 330–331

Frequency measures, 236
Frequency polygons, 349
Functional relationship, 315–316
Funneling, 209

Gallup Opinion Index, The, 65
Gallup Poll, The, 191
Gerontological Abstracts, 60
Graphs, frequency polygons, 349
Guttman-type scales, 162–164

Hardware, computer, 387–388
Heisenberg factor, 300. *See also* Extraneous
    variables
Heterogeneous population, 182–184
Historical Abstracts, 60
Historical artifacts, 291
Historical documents. *See* Documents
Historicity effect, 91
History, as extraneous variable, 90–91
Home Economics Research Abstracts, 60
Homogeneous sample, 183
Hospital Abstracts, 61
Humanities Index, 66
Human Relations Area Files (HRAF), 295
Human Resources Abstracts, 61
Hypotheses, 41–43
    defined, 41
    null, 42–43, 331–333
    role of literature review in building, 51–52,
        70–71
    statement of, 42–43
    testing of, 41–42
    types of, 42
Hypothetical proposition, 41
Hypothetical role playing, 258

Idiographic hypothesis, 42
Independent variable, 41. *See also* Extraneous
    variables
    defined, 137
    in field experiments, 128–132
    hiding of, in experimental laboratory
        method, 254–263
Indexes, 54
    on computer-assisted retrieval systems,
        68–69
    list of, 64–68
    purposes of, 56–57, 64
Index Medicus, 66

Index of Economic Articles, 66
Index to Literature on the American Indian, 66
*Index to Periodical Articles by and about
    Blacks*, 66
Index to Religious Periodical Literature, 66–67
Indirect measures, 269–270. *See also*
    Projective techniques
Inference, 152
Inferential statistics, 331–333, 354–363
    example of, 356–358, 359, 361–363
    measurements of association, 331–332,
        350–354
    Pearson's *r*, 352–355
    phi coefficient, 350–352
    tests of significant differences, 331–332
        chi square, 355–358
        one-way analysis of variance, 359–363
        t-test, 358–359
Informal rating techniques, 231, 234–235,
    238–240
Informed consent
    forms for, 31–32
    special populations and, 33–34
Inquiry time, 275
Instrumentation, 151, 152. *See also* Scales
    as extraneous variable, 92
    for observation, 243–246
Interactionalism, 37–38
Internal criticism, 299
Internal validity
    defined, 89–90
    in experimental laboratory method,
        258–260
    factors limiting, 90–93
    observational technology and, 248
Interrater reliability, 241
Interval measurement, 155, 157
Interviews, 14, 212–223
    advantages of, 212–213
    characteristics of, 216–220
    of colleagues in literature review process, 52
    nature and type of, 216–220
        clinical, 217
        focused, 214–215
        nondirective, 216–217
        questionnaires, 218. (*see also*
            Questionnaires)
        telephone, 217–218
    note-taking in, 213, 222–223
    presence of third parties in, 202–203

Interviews (*continued*)
   social fact perspective and, 38–39
   techniques for conducting, 219–222
      aiming for quality, 220–221
      door approach, 219–220
      presentation of self, 219
      probes, 221–222, 223
      rapport and morale level, 212–213, 221
   validity and reliability of, 224
Introduction, report, 371, 374
Item analysis, 160–161

Known criterion groups, 82–83

Laboratory method. *See* Experimental
      laboratory method
Latency measures, 236, 273–274
Legal considerations, 31–32
Legitimacy of field researchers, 122–123
Letters, 292–293
Levels of measurement, 155–158
   interval, 155, 157
   nominal, 155–157
   ordinal, 155, 156–157
   ratio, 155, 157–159
Librarians, 52, 69
Library
   archives in, 246–247, 293–294
   importance of knowledge of, 52, 54
   locating historical documents through, 293
Likert-type scales, 160–162, 209–212, 280
Literature reviews, 49–74
   examples of, 69–72
   goals of, 50–52, 53, 72
   procedures for, 52–57
      library materials in, 52–53, 54
      steps in, 54–57
      writing in, 53, 56–58
   sources in, 57–69
      abstracts, 54, 57–64, 68–69
      card catalogs, 52–53, 54
      computer retrieval systems, 52–53, 54, 60,
         61–62, 68–69
      indexes, 54, 57, 64–68
Logistics, 125
Longitudinal research, 108
   described, 116
   selectivity in, 109–111

Mailed questionnaires, 204–205

Material causation, 36
Maturation, as extraneous variable, 90, 93
Mean, 330–331, 343–344
Measurement, 79–89, 150–170. *See also*
      Reliability; Validity
   concept of, 151
   cultural origins of, 153–155
   data collection for. *See* Data collection
   elements of, 152
   in evaluation research, 318–319
   functions of, 154–155
   levels or types of, 155–158
      interval, 155, 157
      nominal, 155–156
      ordinal, 155, 156–157
      ratio, 155, 157–158
   scales in. (*see* Scales)
Measures of association, 331–332, 350–354
   correlation coefficient, 85, 87, 88, 89,
      331–333, 350–354
   Pearson *r* coefficient, 352–354
   Phi coefficient, 350–352
Measures of central tendency, 330–331,
      343–345
Measures of dispersion (variability), 330–331,
      345–346
Mechanistic frame of reference, 37
Median, 330–331, 360
Meta-analysis, 71
Method, report, 371–372, 375
Mission records, 294
Mode, 330–331, 343
Modeling, experimenter, 259–260
Motherhood and Mourning: Perinatal Death
      (Peppers and Knapp), 188–189
Motion pictures, 246
Motivation
   of interview respondents, 212–213, 218, 221
   of questionnaire respondents, 202–203

National Opinion Research Center (NORC),
      191
National probability sample, 190
Natural situation, 122–123, 235–238, 248. *See
      also* Ecological validity
Needs assessment, 313
Nominal measurement, 155–156
Nomothetic hypothesis, 42
Nondirective interviews, 216–217
Nonexperimental methods, 315–316

Nonprobability samples, 180–181
Nonstructured field observational methodology, 235–238
Note taking
  in field research, 123–124, 234–235
  for interviews, 213, 222–223
  in literature reviews, 54–56
  in participant-observer methodology, 234–235
Null hypothesis, 42–43, 333–334
  decision errors related to, 333–334
  myths about statistical significance and, 334–335
Numerical descriptions, 107
Nurse and the Mental Patient, The (Schwartz and Shockley), 125–126
Nutrition Abstracts and Reviews, 61

Objectivity, 17. *See also* Frames of reference
  empirical approach and, 19–20, 40–43
  information based on, 211–212
Observation, 229–251
  in evaluation research, 315–316
  in field research, 123, 231–243
    field experiments, 238–243
    field studies, 230–238
  high environmental structure, in 238–243
  low environmental structure in, 232–238
  social definition perspective and, 39
  technology, 243–248
Observer bias, 241
Obtrusive measures, 300. *See also* Extraneous variables
  external validity and, 246–247
One-way analysis of variance, 359–363
One-way mirrors, 245–246
Open-ended questions, 200–201
Operationalization, 40
Operation research, 318
Oral history, 291–292
Order-of-merit method, 211
Ordinal measurement, 155, 156–157
Organismic frame of reference, 37
Outcome assessment, 314

Participant-observer methodology, 232–235
Participation rate, 202–205, 212
Patterns, 17
  in hypothesis formation, 41–42
  as requirement of theory, 41

Pearson *r* coefficient, 352–354
Percentages, 342
Periodicals, 57
Phi coefficient, 350–352
Photocopies, 55
Physical trace measures, 247, 294–295
Policy. *See also* Evaluation research
  literature reviews and, 71
  research as basis for, 15–16
  special populations and, 34
Politics, evaluation research and, 311–312
Population, 177
  special, 33–35
Posttesting
  defined, 90
  in posttest-only control group design, 140–141
  in pretest-posttest control group design, 138–142, 315–316
Practice effects, 143
Practice of research, 12–13
Precision, theory, 41
Predictability
  in hypothesis formation, 41–42
  as requirement of theory, 41
Predictive validity, 81–82
Pretesting
  defined, 90
  as extraneous variable, 91–92
  in pretest-posttest control group method, 138–142, 315–316
Primary sources
  defined, 53
  historic documents as, 289–292, 298
Prison populations, 34–35
Privacy, 235
  as ethical consideration, 28–33 (*see also* Ethics)
Private papers, 292–293
Probability, 154
Probability samples, 179–180
  sample size and, 182–183
Probes, in interviewing, 221–222, 223
Projective techniques, 270–281
  defined, 269–270
  perspective on, 280
  types of, 270–281
Program management, 314
Propositions, 51
Psychodrama, 280

Psychological Abstracts, 61–62
Psychology
    abstracts in, 61–62
    frames of reference in, 37–38
Psychosocial attributes, 259
Public Affairs Information Services (PAIS), 67
*Publication Manual of the American
        Psychological Association*, 56, 370
Purposeful sample, 181–182
P value, 332–333

Quartile range, 330
Questionnaires, 200–212
    administration of, through interviews, 218,
        221
    arrangement and layout of, 208–209
    characteristics of, 200
    construction of questions for, 205–208
    defined, 200
    question order on, 208–209
    response rate and, 204–205
    sensitive questions on
        obtaining answers to, 208
        response rate and, 202–203
    social fact perspective and, 38–39
    types of questions in, 200–202
        closed-ended, 201–202
        open-ended, 200–201
        style and, 209–212
    validity and reliability of, 224
Questions. *See also* Interviews; Questionnaires
    as basis for research topics, 14–15, 19
    in descriptive research, 111–112
    in exploratory research, 104–105
    formulation of, 330–333
Quota sample, 182

Random error, 332–333. *See also* Sampling
        error
Randomization
    as advantage of laboratory
        experimentation, 143
    in posttest-only control group design,
        140–141
    in pretest-posttest control group design,
        138–142
    in probability samples, 179–180, 182–183
Range, 330–331, 345
Ranking exercises, 210–211

Rapport
    in field research, 123
    in interviews, 212–213, 221
Rating techniques
    formal, 231
        in laboratory observation studies,
            241–243
        in nonstructured field observational
            methodology, 235–238
    informal, 231
        in participant-observer methodology,
            234–235
        in structured field experiments, 238–240
    reliability in, 241–248
Ratio measurement, 155, 157–158
Reactive effects, 93, 241, 246, 300. *See also*
        Extraneous variables
Readers' Guide to Periodical Literature, 67
Reading, report. *See* Research reports
Reasoned argument, 384–385
Recording strategies interview, 222–223.
        See also Note taking
Reference cards
    preparation of, 55
    reviewing and organizing, 56
Reference sources
    abstracts, 54, 57–64, 68–70
    card catalogs, 52–53, 55
    computer-assisted retrieval, 52–53, 54,
        61–62, 68–69
    indexes, 54, 57, 64–69
Regularity, 17
Reinforcement contingencies, 39
Reliability, 86–89. *See also* Replication
    defined, 77
    equivalent-forms method of determining, 88
    of evaluation research, 318–319
    of interviews, 224
    observational techniques and, 241, 248
    of projective techniques, 280–281
    of questionnaires, 224
    of research report conclusions, 94–95
    split-half method of determining, 88
    test-retest method of determining, 87
Reliability coefficient, 87–89
Replication
    as basis for reliable research, 94–95
    empirical approach and, 19–20
    literature reviews and, 51
    statistical significance testing as substitute
        for, 334–335. (*see also* Reliability)

Research codes of ethics, 28–33
Research design
    between-subjects versus within-subject,
        142–144
    data collection and. *See* Data collection
    defined, 103
    descriptive, 106–113
    experimental-control group, 137–143,
        258–260
    exploratory, 103–106, 113–116
    field experiments in, 127–132, 238–243
    field studies in, 121–127, 230–238
    strengths and weaknesses of laboratory
        experimentation, 144
Researcher-consumer, 389
Research methodology
    basic steps in, 17–18
    data, theory and, 13–14
    data analysis in (*see* Data analysis)
    data collection in (*see* Data collection)
    defined, 13, 16
    design in (*see* Research design)
    empirical approach in, 19–20, 40–43
    frames of reference in (*see* Frames of
        reference)
    importance of knowledge of, 8, 10–12
    importance of training in, 16–17
    practice of research and, 12–13
    research reports in (*see* Research reports)
    scientific method in, 20–22
    social science, 18–19, 21–22
    terminology of, 20
Research proposal, 368–380
    criteria for evaluating, 378–379
    example of, 372–377
    format, 370–372
    literature reviews as, 53, 56–57
    objective/hypotheses, 369
    reliability of conclusion of, 94–95
    review of literature, 369
    statement of problem, 368–369
    validity of conclusions of, 89–94
    writing style, 370
Research Relating to Children, 62
Response latency, 273
Response rate, questionnaire, 204–205
Response set, 206
Response style, 206
Results, report, 372, 375–377
Review articles, 54
Risk, experimental, 27–33

Role enactment methodology, 256–258
Rorschach, 275

Sage Family Studies Abstracts, 62
Sage Race Relations Abstracts, 62
Sage Urban Studies Abstracts, 62
Sample, 178
Sample size, 182–183
Sampling, 172–184
    advantages of, 178–179
    in cross-sectional research, 115–116
    in documentary research, 303–304
    event, 237–238
    examples of, 184–191
    helps in, 191
    importance of, in descriptive research, 114
    in longitudinal research, 116
    size of samples in, 182–183
    in survey research, 114–115
    terminology of, 177–178
    types of, 174–177, 179–182
    nonprobability, 180–182
    probability, 179–180
    uses of, 173–174
Sampling error, 174–175
    sample size and, 182–183
Sampling frame, 178
Sampling units, 178
Scales, 158–167. (*see also* Measurement)
    cumulative or unidimensional, 162–163
    levels of measurement and, 155–158
    properties of, 158–159
    semantic differential, 163–165, 212
    sociometric, 165–167
    style and types of questions for, 209–212
    summated, 159–162
Schools of thought. *See* Frames of reference
Science Citation Index, 67
Scientific method, 20–22
Scope, theory, 41
Secondary sources
    defined, 53
    historic documents as, 289–290, 292
Selection of subjects, 91, 93, 94
Selectivity, in descriptive research, 108–111
Self-revelation, 272–273
Semantic differential scales, 163–165, 210
Sensitive questions, 388. *See also* Privacy;
        Projective techniques
    in interviews, 214–215
    on questionnaires, 202–203, 208

Sensitization effects, 144
Sentence completion approaches, 270
Sentence stubs, 27
Serendipity pattern, 104
Shopping List Method, 277–280
Simple random sample, 179
Simulation studies, 34–35
Single-subject methodology, 315–316
Skewness, 342
Snowball sample, 181 ·
Social Science and Humanities Index, 66
Social Science Index, 67
Social sciences
   research methodology in, 18–19
   scientific methods in, 21–22
Social Sciences and Humanities Index, 67
Social Sciences Citation Index, 68
Social Work Research and Abstracts, 58
Sociodrama, 280
Sociological Abstracts, 62–63
Sociological Imagination, The (Mills), 111
Sociology, frames of reference, 38–40
Sociometric measurement, 165–167
Solomon four-group design, 139–140
Special populations, 33–35
Split-half method, 88
Standard deviation, 330, 345–347
Standards, 153
Standards for Education and Psychological Tests, 77–78
Static phenomena, 158
Statistical analysis. *See* Descriptive statistics; Inference statistics
Statistical regression, 93
Stimulus word, 272
Story completion techniques, 274–275
Stratified random sample, 180
Structural functionalism, 39
Structured field experiments, 238–240
Structuring of environment, 231–243
   high level of, 238–243
   low level of, 232–238
   significance of, 231–232
Subjects
   bias of, 241
   maturation of, 90, 93
   selection of, 91, 93, 94
Subpoenas of information, 28–29, 31–32
Summated scales, 159–162

Survey research
   described, 114
   in evaluation research, 317–318
Symbolic interactionism, 39
Systematic random sample, 179–180

Tape recorders, 222–223, 247
Taxonomies, 124
Telephone interviews, 217–218
Testing for truth, 298
Test-retest method, 87
Tests of significance, 354–363
Thematic Apperception Test (TAT), 275–276
Theory, 40–43
   defined, 13, 40
   essential ingredients for, 40
   evaluating quality of, 41
   frame of reference in. *See* Frames of reference
   hypotheses in, 41–43, 51–52, 70–71, 331–333
   literature review in development of, 51–52, 71
   methodology, data and, 13–14
Time sampling, 237
Title, report, 370–371, 373
Topics
   ideas for, 14–15
   selection and refinement of, 54
Total range, 330–331
Trait rating, 238
Transcontextual validity, 247–248
Trust, field research, 123
T test, 332–333
Type I error, 333–334
Type II error, 333–334

United States Political Science Documents (USPSD), 68
University Microfilms International, 60
Unobtrusive measures
   documents as, 292–295
   external validity and, 246–247

Validity, 78–86
   construct, 51, 84–86
   content, 83–84

criterion-related, 82–83
  concurrent, 83
  predictive, 82–83
defined, 77
in descriptive research,107
ecological, 94, 144, 263
of evaluation research, 318–319
in experimental laboratory method, 258–261
external (*see* External validity)
face, 78, 81–82
of historical evidence, 295–299, 304–305
internal (*see* Internal validity)
of interviews, 224
observational techniques and, 246–248
of projective techniques, 280–281
of questionnaires, 224
of research report conclusions, 89–94

  external, 89, 93–94
  internal, 89, 90–93
sample size and, 182–183
Variables, 40, 41. *See also* Dependent variable;
  Independent variable
correlation of, 85
Verbal descriptions, 108

Within-subject design, 142–143
Women Studies Abstracts, 63
Word association measures, 272
*World Agriculture Economics and Rural
  Sociology Abstracts*, 63
World Textile Abstracts, 63–64
Writing. *See also* Research reports
  instruction in, 370–372
  of literature reviews, 53, 56–57